Wen xuan, or SELECTIONS OF REFINED LITERATURE

PRINCETON LIBRARY OF ASIAN TRANSLATIONS

Wen xuan

OR SELECTIONS OF REFINED LITERATURE

VOLUME TWO: Rhapsodies on Sacrifices, Hunting, Travel, Sightseeing, Palaces and Halls, Rivers and Seas

XIAO TONG (501–531)

Translated, with Annotations by

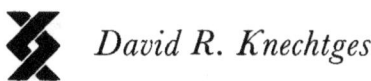 *David R. Knechtges*

PRINCETON UNIVERSITY PRESS

Library of Congress Cataloging in Publication Data will be found
on the last printed page of this book

ISBN 0-691-06701-5

This book has been composed in Monophoto Baskerville by Asco Trade
Typesetting Ltd., Hong Kong

Clothbound editions of Princeton University Press books are printed
on acid-free paper, and binding materials are chosen for strength
and durability. Paperbacks, although satisfactory for personal collections,
are not usually suitable for library rebinding

Printed in the United States of America by
Princeton University Press, Princeton, New Jersey

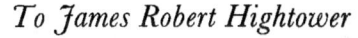

To James Robert Hightower

Contents

CONTENTS

Maps

Acknowledgments

The preparation of this volume has taken much time and labor. I have received assistance from many persons, and I cannot mention all of their names here. As with volume one, the person who has assisted me the most is Chang Taiping, who has helped with annotating the text, writing characters, and interpreting difficult passages. I have also received excellent help from three research assistants, Stephen Allee, Alan Berkowitz, and Stuart Aque. I am particularly indebted to Mr. Aque for drawing the maps. Others who have assisted me in various ways are my colleagues William G. Boltz, Roy Andrew Miller, and Jerry Norman. I want to thank Andrew Plaks for his numerous suggestions for improving the translation. In the preface to volume one, I neglected to give credit to Kang-i Sun Chang and Min-chih Chou for locating the 1529 edition of the *Wen xuan*, the preface to which graces the dust jacket. I also am grateful to Miriam Brokaw, recently retired from Princeton University Press, who ably oversaw the publication of volume one.

I owe special thanks to the National Endowment for the Humanities, the Graduate School Research Fund and the China Program of the University of Washington for providing financial support for the *Wen xuan* translation project.

Introduction

This volume continues the translation of the rhapsodies (*fu*) in the *Wen xuan*. The pieces in chapters 7 through 12 include some of the most famous *fu* poems in the Chinese literary tradition. The best known of these are "Rhapsody of Sir Vacuous" and "Rhapsody on the Imperial Park" by Sima Xiangru, who is the acknowledged creator of the epideictic *fu*, with its ornate displays of verbal virtuosity. The *fu* of Sima Xiangru are notorious for their long catalogues of animal, plant, fish, and mineral names, many of which are often only vaguely identified even by the most learned commentaries. Sima Xiangru's language is particularly rich, especially his alliterative and rhyming descriptives.

Rivalling Sima Xiangru in the power of his language is Yang Xiong, two of whose rhapsodies, "Plume Hunt" and "Tall Poplars Palace," also are on hunts. Yang's most distinguished work is "Sweet Springs Palace Rhapsody," which relates an imperial procession to a Han touring palace where sacrifices to the supreme Han deity, the Grand Unity, were performed. Although Yang's rhapsodies show great verbal skill, he was even more concerned with the content of his poems, and he was particularly concerned with using the *fu* to convey a moral message. Thus, in each of the introductions attached to his *fu* Yang explains that the primary purpose of the piece was "to sway" opinion. In Yang Xiong's case, the mind he sought to sway was the emperor, whose extravagance and ostentation Yang deemed unworthy of a "ruler of men."

The influence of Sima Xiangru and Yang Xiong is apparent in many of the other *fu* writers included in this volume. The same epideictic style can be seen in such rhapsodies as Wang Yanshou's "Hall of Numinous Brilliance in Lu" and He Yan's "Hall of Great Blessings," both of which are noted for their great care in describing architectural details. Among the most linguistically taxing of all *fu* are the Mu Hua's "Rhapsody on the Sea" and Guo Pu's "Rhapsody on the Yangzi River." The latter poem by the most learned glossographer in Chinese history is replete with numerous strange and rare words.

In the Later Han dynasty, some *fu* poets began to compose, not for emperors, but for themselves, and they wrote in a much simpler style. One important subgenre was the travel *fu*, three of which are contained in the *Wen xuan*. The first of these is Ban Biao's "Rhapsody on a Northward Journey," which describes the poet's travels from Chang'an into the northwest frontier area near the Great Wall. Following Ban Biao's piece is a "Rhapsody on an Eastward Journey" by his daughter Ban Zhao (Cao Dagu). This *fu*, which is a direct imitation of Ban Biao's work, describes her travels throught central Henan in the company of her son, who is about to take office in his first official post. The grandest travel poem of all is Pan Yue's "Rhapsody on a Westward Journey," which recounts in great detail his journey from Luoyang to Chang'an. The piece is rich in descriptive detail and full of comments on historical figures and places.

Visits to scenic spots or historical sites also were the occasion for the composition of other *fu* contained in the *Wen xuan*. The best known of these is Wang Can's "Rhapsody on Climbing a Tower," known by all Chinese school children. From the high vantage of a tower overlooking the Ju and Zhang rivers of Hubei, Wang longingly looks toward his home in the north, from which he has been absent for over ten years. Sun Chuo's "Rhapsody on Roaming the Celestial Terrace Mountains" recounts a journey of a slightly different kind, an imaginary mystical ascent of the Tiantai Mountains of Zhejiang. The piece is noted for its blending of Buddhist and Taoist concepts. More mundane and worldly is Bao Zhao's "Rhapsody on the Ruined City," which describes the once glorious city of Guangling (modern Yangzhou), which Bao Zhao finds deserted and destroyed. The piece is the first of many ruin poems in Chinese literature.

The *fu* that are most troublesome for the translator are the epideictic pieces. These poems are troublesome primarily because of their rich language, particularly the alliterative and rhyming descriptive binomes. In modern Chinese these binomes are customarily called *lianmianzi* 聯緜字 (compounds).[1] In early periods, if they were designated at all, they were called *shuangsheng* 雙聲 (alliterations) or *dieyun* 叠韻 (rhyming compounds).[2]

---

[1] The earliest known use of the term *lianman zi* is by the late Southern Song scholar Zhang You 張有 (1054–post 1124) in his *Fugu bian* 復古編 (Compilation of Restored Graphs), *Sbck*, C.1a. However, it is not clear how he understood the term. Other names for the alliterative or rhyming binome include *lianyu* 連語 (variant *lianyu* 讕語 or 聯語) or *pianyu* 駢語. See Gan Daxin 甘大昕, "Shuangsheng dieyun lianman zi yanjiu" 雙聲疊韻聯緜字研究, *Guowen yuekan* 50 (December 1946) : 1.

[2] The terms *shuangsheng* and *dieyun* achieved currency in the late Six Dynasties period. The *Nan shi* biography of Xie Zhuang 謝莊 (421–466) records an anecdote in which Wang Xuanmo 王玄謨 asks Xie what *shuang-sheng* and *dieyun* mean. He replied, Xuan-Hu 玄護 (*giwen-guo*) is *shuang-sheng*, and Queao 碻磝 (*k'ao-ngao*) is *dieyun*. (Xie obliquely alludes here to the disastrous defeat of Wang Xuanmo and Huan Hu by the Northern Wei at Queao in 451. See *Song shu* 5.99.) Liu Xie also uses the terms in the *Wenxin diaolong* (7.552–53).

Although descriptive binomes are common in earlier poetry, especially the *Classic of Songs* and the *Chuci*, writers of the *fu* delighted in using as many of these expressions as they could, and the rarer the word, the better. Unlike earlier poets, they did not hesitate to string eight, ten, even a dozen descriptive binomes together in a series.

To understand these words, one naturally consults the commentaries. Invariably, the commentators give what appears to the modern reader as frustratingly imprecise explanations. They tells us a word is *gao mao* 高貌 (descriptive of height), *luan mao* 亂貌 (descriptive of disorder), or if they really wish to be exact, *liu shui sheng mao* 流水聲貌 (descriptive of the sound of flowing water). Given this state of affairs, some scholars have claimed that such expressions make the *fu* impossible to translate. In the 1920's, Arthur Waley said the following about translating Sima Xiangru:

> I do not think that anyone who has read Hsiang-ju's poems will blame me for not attempting to translate them. Such a glittering torrent of words has never since poured forth from the pen of any writer in the world. Beside him Euphues seems timid and Apuleius cold. He sports with language as a dolphin sports with the sea. Such eloquence cannot be described, much less translated.[3]

Although Dr. Waley aptly characterizes Sima Xiangru's style, I believe he was wrong in suggesting that his *fu* are untranslatable. Indeed, since Waley made his pronouncement there have been three Western language translations of Sima Xiangru's most difficult composition, "Rhapsody on the Imperial Park," one in German by Erwin von Zach, one in English by Burton Watson, and one in French by Yves Hervouet.[4] Although von Zach did not make a special study of the binomial descriptives, he was aware of the problems of trying to translate them. In explaining why the *fu* was such a neglected genre in Western Sinology as of the 1920's, he comments:

> Der Grund dieser Vernachlassigung dürfte darin liegen, dass sich diese Literaturgattung durch eine gehäufte Anwendung seltener, sonst nicht oder wenig gebrauchter Worte resp. Wortcombinationen auszeichnete. Ob nun diese Binome Ellipsen vorstellen aus seinerzeit allgemein bekannten Versen oder dialektischen Ursprunges sind oder endlich als reine Kunstprodukte anzusehen sind, wage ich nicht zu entscheiden. Sicher ist, dass sie der Übersetzung grosse Schwierigkeiten entgegenstellen, besonders auch dadurch, dass die chinesischen Kommentatoren dieselben gar nicht oder nur sehr unbefriedigend erklaren. Gewöhnlich begnügen sie sich damit, eine allgemeine Umschreibung zu geben, sie sagen z. B. 相視貌 'eine Art, sich gegenseitig anzusehen', ohne aber nahere Bestimmungen hinzufugen (z. B. sich starr oder wild oder schweigend oder erstaunt etc. ansehen), was dem Leser aus dem Kontext zu schliessen überlassen bleibt. Bei vielen dieser Binome kann die damit verknüfpte

---

[3] See *The Temple*, pp. 43–44.

[4] See introductions to "Rhapsody of Sir Vacuous" and "Rhapsody on the Imperial Park."

Bedeutung erst aus deren Gebrauch in der spateren Literatur deduziert werden; er verbleibt dann aber immer noch eine nicht unberträchliche Anzahl von Doppelaus-drücken, die—soweit wir des wenigstens einstweilen mit unserem sehr beschränkten Rustzeug feststellen konnten- --*hapax legomena* geblieben sind, offenbar weil sie dem Chinesen selbst nicht ganz verstandlich waren and daher ihre neuerliche Verwen-dung nicht empfehlenswert schien.[5]

Like von Zach, Burton Watson shows an awareness for the difficulties the descriptive binomes pose to translators:

Though common enough in other types of poetry and prose, they are particularly numerous in the *fu*, helping to give them their musical, rhapsodic air. Here again commentators are often less then (sic) helpful, perhaps because they themselves were at a loss, offering only the vaguest glosses such as 'descriptive of high mountains' or the 'aspect of rushing water'. And again one wonders if such a wealth of epithets would have been easily intelligible to men of the Han; certainly they are hardly so today. Reading a Han *fu* is rather like reading 'Jabberywocky'. In most cases the characters themselves, with their water, wood, wind, or stone radicals, give the reader enough of a clue to their meaning that he may follow the general contour of the description. But even so, he would, without the aid of commentaries, be hard put at many points to say exactly what is going on. All this dazzling verbiage and ambiguity must, of course, disappear in translation, and the elusive, musical binomes must be reduced to explicit adjectives and adverbs.[6]

Although both von Zach and Watson chide the commentators for the vagueness of their explanations, neither made an effort to achieve a more precise understanding of them. The first Western scholar to undertake this task was Professor Hervouet, who in his 1964 study of Sima Xiangru devoted a twenty-two-page chapter to Sima Xiangru's "descriptive vocabulary."[7] In his copiously annotated translation of Sima Xiangru's *Shi ji* biography, published in 1972, Hervouet presents a detailed analysis of each of the binomial descriptives found in Sima's *fu*.[8] According to Hervouet, these words are a type of "vocal gesture" in which certain speech sounds, "like a gesture or mimicry, describe above all movements, but also sounds, odors, tastes, tactile impressions, or 'accompany the expression of colors, plenitude, degree, sadness, well-being, etc.'"[9] Hervouet especially emphasizes the "impressionistic" quality of these words, which evoke "by the direct im-pression produced in the ear an action, a scene, or a feeling."[10] Because of

---

[5] "Das Lu-Ling-Kwang-Tien-Fu des Wang Wen-k'ao," *AM* 3 (1926):467–68.

[6] *Early Chinese Literature* (New York: Columbia University Press, 1962), p. 272.

[7] *Un Poète de cour*, pp. 337–59.

[8] *Le Chapitre 117 du Che-ki (Biographie de Sseu-ma Siang-jou)*.

[9] *Un Poète de cour*, p. 346. The section in single quotation marks is from Lucien Lévy-Bruhl, *Les Fonctions mentales dans les sociétés inférieures* (Paris: Alcan, 1912), p. 183.

[10] *Un Poète de cour*, p 348.

4

their impressionistic nature, these *"impressifs,"* as Hervouet calls them, are highly ambiguous and difficult to define precisely.

Given this vagueness and imprecision, how does one determine what an *impressif* means? According to Hervouet, it is possible to find "in most cases a signific substratum" that lends the *impressif* "its consistency." In other words, the binome has a general sense that is determined by the component graphs. There are various possible combinations:

Tantôt l'un des deux caractères seulement donne un sens a l'expression totale, l'autre n'étant qu'une adjonction phonétique. Tantôt, et c'est le plus fréquent, les deux caractères apportent chacun leur signification propre et sur des voies qui peuvent être plus ou moins divergentes: la signification de l'ensemble est cependant une, même s'il est difficile de trouver dans la traduction un mot ou une expression qui corresponde à lui suel aux nuances distinctes du sens global. Le sens que l'on peut ainsi determiner ne suffit pas à remplir la place que tient l'impressif dans la phrase, car il reste ce rôle de geste vocal qui est donné par l'homophonie, partielle ou totale, des deux elements. Mais ce dernier emploi n'est pas traduisible et peut seulement être rendu de façon tres approximative par un jeu de sonorités, qu'il est d'une part difficile de trouver dans le système phonétique de la langue française et qui n'auront de toute façon pas cette valeur precise de mimique vocale." [11]

Hervouet thus finds in Sima Xiangru examples of *impressifs* composed of nearly synonymous elements (e.g. *zhaozhe* 昭晰, *tjah-tjad*, in which both elements mean *ming* 明 'brilliant'); impressifs with only one signific component (e.g., *leiluo* 磊砢, *lwei-la*, in which only the first graph seems related to the meaning 'piled up'); "purely phonetic" expressions in which the component graphs have no apparent relationship to the general sense (e.g. *bosu* 勃窣, *bhwet-swet*, 'lame').

Hervouet's study of specific words, presented in the notes to his translation of Sima Xiangru's biography, is the most detailed analysis of binomial descriptives in a Western language, and offers a useful corrective to the at times forced interpretations of Chinese commentators. In spite of his thoroughness, Hervouet's conclusion is not particularly encouraging for the translator:

Aussi souvent ne reste dans la traduction que la signification donnée par les caractères de l'impressif, qui est en même temps durcie, materialisée par la précision que lui donne son expression en une autre langue. Nous sommes loin de façon dont doivent être compris ces impressifs, qui sont proprement intraduisibles. . . . Dans la traduction de descriptions ainsi composées, il est bien évident que les limitations grammaticales et l'inguistiques ne permettent pas de rendre ces impressifs d'un façon qui corresponde à leur valeur propre.[12]

---

[11] *Un Poète de cour*, pp. 349–50

[12] *Un Poète de cour*, p. 350.

What Hervouet seems to be saying here is that since we cannot really understand the precise meaning of many of these words, we might as well devise a translation based on the meaning of the component graphs, even though the meaning of the graphs has only a tenuous connection with the apparent sense of the binome. As James Robert Hightower rightly has pointed out in his review of Hervouet's translation, many of Hervouet's formulations are "only a *pis aller*, a translator's convention."[13] By following this practice, Hervouet produces a number of ingenious, but linguistically unsupportable interpretations. As an example, Professor Hightower cites Hervouet's explanation of *yiyi* 裔裔 (**rjat-rjat*), which Sima Xiangru uses twice. The first, in "Rhapsody of Sir Vacuous," describes the movement of chariots and riders returning from the hunt:

纚乎淫淫
般乎裔裔

Hervouet's translation reads:

> Ils vont en rangs serrés, comme une eau qui s'écoule
> et se dispersent, ourlant au loin l'horizon.[14]

Hervouet faults the Chinese commentators for seeing in the term *yiyi* "only a description of the march of solidiers," and argues that the meaning of *yiyi* must be derived from the graph *yi* 裔, which means "the hem of a garment" and also has the sense of "edge" and "distant." Thus, *yiyi* is "an impressif that describes the soldiers who scatter afar to the limits of the horizon."[15] The second occurrence of *yiyi* is in the following line from "Rhapsody on the Imperial Park," in which Hervouet similarly reads into *yiyi* the "hem of the garment" metaphor:

淫淫裔裔
緣陵流澤

> comme l'écoulement de l'eau, comme l'ourlet de la robe,
> ils bordent les collines et s'écoulent dans les marais.

The question that Professor Hightower rightly raises about this interpretation is how relevant is the meaning of *yi* 'hem of a garment' to the sense of the binome *yiyi*. Other usages of the same *yiyi* clearly show that Hervouet's rendering of "ourlant au loin l'horizon" or "l'ourlet de la robe" is wide of the mark:
Zuo Si, "Shu Capital Rhapsody":

[13] See "Ein Standardwerk uber einen Han-Klassiker," p. 122.
[14] *Le Chapitre 117 du Che-ki*, p. 46.
[15] *Le Chapitre 117 du Che-ki*, p. 122, n. 18.

紆長袖而屢舞
翩躚躚而裔裔

Twirling their long sleeves, they dance again and again,
Lightly wheeling and turning, gracefully flowing.[16]

Sun Chuo, "Rhapsody on Roaming the Celestial Terrace Mountains"

覿翔鸞之裔裔

I view the graceful gliding of soaring simurghs.[17]

Song Yu, "Rhapsody on the Goddess":

步裔裔兮曜殿堂

Stepping graceful and slow, she illumines the hall.[18]

As Hightower observes, nowhere in these lines is the meaning 'hem of a garment' "even a subdued connotation."[19]

It should be clear from the examples above that the graphs used to write the word *yiyi* have no apparent connection with its meaning, which, depending upon the context, commentators variously gloss as *xing mao* 行貌 (descriptive of movement), *fei mao* 飛貌 (descriptive of flying), and *wu mao* 舞貌 (descriptive of dancing). They undoubtedly were aware that *yi* by itself means 'hem', but they did not choose to explain the word by invoking the common meaning of the components.

The graphs used to write the word *yiyi* (or more properly **rjat-rjat*) may have only a phonetic value and are irrelevant to the basic meaning of the word.[20] Thus, one must be wary of seeking the meaning of a binome by dissecting the component parts. Long before George Kennedy wrote about his famous "butterfly case" and doublets in the *Shijing*,[21] Chinese scholars have remarked on the indivisibility of certain bisyllabic expressions. For example, Guo Pu criticized an earlier commentator for his erroneous splitting of a binome to determine the meaning.[22] More recently, Gao Buying has pointed out disapprovingly Wang Xianqian's penchant for dissecting

---

[16] *Wen xuan* 4.23b; trans. from David R. Knechtges, *Wen xuan*, or Selections of Refined Literature, Volume one (Princeton: Princeton University Press, 1982), p. 363.

[17] *Wen xuan* 11.7a; "Rhapsody on Roaming the Celestial Terrace Mountains," L. 53.

[18] *Wen xuan* 19.7b.

[19] "Ein Standardwerk," p. 122.

[20] Zhu Qifeng (*Ci tong*, p. 174) equates *yiyi* with *qiqi* 祁祁 (**gjei-gjiei*), claiming that when *yi* is read in the level tone, it sounds similar to *qi*. I do not know on what authority Zhu bases his claim. The word *qiqi* commonly describes slow movement, a sense that aptly applies to the uses of *yiyi* cited above

[21] See Li Tien-yi, ed. *Selected Works of George A. Kennedy* (New Haven: Far Eastern Publications, Yale University, 1964), pp. 274–322 "The Butterfly Case (Part I)," and pp. 463–76, "A Note on Ode 220."

[22] See *Erya* 1B.17a.

binomes: "Generally, both parts of a *lianmian zi* form a single meaning and cannot be explained separately. In explaining such words, Wang often seeks a meaning for each part, and then tries to link them together. Thus, he misses the basic meaning of the term."[23]

There are of course many binomial descriptives in which the meaning of one or even both graphs is relevant to the general meaning of the word. However, the existence of numerous variants for even these types of expressions should at least caution one to hesitate before confidently assigning precise semantic values to the component elements, This caveat should be particularly observed for the Former Han period, when there was no standard way of writing many of the new expressions used by *fu* poets. For example, the *Shi ji* and *Han shu* versions of Sima Xiangru's *fu* contain numerous variant forms of the same word. The following variants are all from "Rhapsody on the Imperial Park":

Shi ji	*Han shu*
滂濞	彭湃
渾浮	渾弗
蜿灗	宛潬
湛湛	沈沈
玓瓅	的皪
潎洌	宓汨

Although such variants possibly are simply corrections by well-intentioned scribes, many of them may owe their existence to the fact that the written forms for these words were not yet fixed in Sima Xiangru's time.[24] One must remember that recitation was the primary medium of presentation for the *fu* throughout the entire Former Han period, and thus when transcribing their texts, *fu* poets were concerned with the sounds of the words. The extensive use of loan graphs not only confuses the modern reader, but apparently posed difficulties even for ancient readers. The sixth century literary critic Liu Xie aptly describes the problem:

Furthermore, when rhapsodizing on capitals and parks, most (*fu* writers) used loan graphs and phonetic compounds, and for this reason the philological studies of the Former Han were largely devoted to precious words. This was not only because (the writers) created so many unusual expressions, but also because they were difficult for most people to understand .... By the Wei dynasty when writers began to compose words of elegance, graphs had a common standard. When (the Wei writers) looked

[23] See *Wen xuan Li zhu yishu* 8.8b.

[24] For a complete list of variants, see Jian Zongwu 簡宗梧, *Han fu yuanliu yu jiazhi zhi shangque* 漢賦源流與價值之商榷 (Taibei: Wen shi zhe chubanshe, 1980), pp. 62–71. Professor Jian has an extremely illuminating discussion of the nature and function of these words, pp. 45–94.

back on the Han writings, they suddenly found them difficult and abstruse. Thus, Cao Zhi, in referring to the writings of Yang Xiong and Sima Xiangru, said that their aim was hidden and their purpose deep. Without a teacher the reader was unable to decipher the language, and without broad learning, he cannot comprehend their principles. It was not only because their talent was far-reaching, but also because the graphs they used were obscure.[25]

In spite of Liu Xie's sobering comments, which confirm what Waley, Watson, and Hervouet have said about the difficulties of understanding these "precious words," I am foolish enough to suggest that one attempt to produce English equivalents that represent as closely as possible the function and meaning of these words in the Chinese original. In order to understand the meaning of a word, one must consult the earliest commentaries. However, it is not enough simply to translate into English what the commentary says, for in many cases, the commentator is not explaining the precise meaning of the term, but rather what the term connotes in a particular context. For example, Mei Sheng's "Seven Stimuli" has the following line, which describes the condition of an ailing prince.[26]

紛屯澹淡

Li Shan explains the four-character line as *kuimao fanmen zhi mao* 憒眊煩悶 之貌 (descriptive of being muddled and woozy, annoyed and anxious). Translators of the line have more or less attempted to incorporate Li Shan's explanation into their renderings:

> von Zach: "Dein Geist is benommen, Du bist niedergeschlagen...."[27]
> John Scott: "You are pallid and afeared."[28]
> Hans H. Frankel: "Listless and without a will of your own."[29]

The rhyming binome *fentun* 紛屯 (*pjen-trjwen*) is not otherwise attested. Li Shan obviously derives the sense of 'muddled' from *fen*, which is a common component in binomes describing a state of confusion (cf. *fenlun* 紛綸 and *fenyun* 紛紜). It is more difficult to determine whether *tun* has any signific

---

[25] Cf. Hervouet, *Un Poète de cour*, p. 351: "Mais il semble bien que le plus souvent ce sont des copistes bien intentionnés qui se sont permis des corrections de graphie: la plupart sont absentes du *Han chou* mais existent dans le *Che ki*. Les variantes peuvent également ne pas être du tout des adaptions à un emploi dans un contexte donné et ne s'expliquer par aucune considération de signification, mais seulement par l'imprécision d'une graphie qui, à l'époque des Han, n'était pas encore fixée."

[26] *Wenxin diaolong zhu* 8.642.

[27] *Wen xuan* 34.1b.

[28] *Die Chinesische Anthologie* 2:607.

[29] *Love and Protest, Chinese Poems from the Sixth Century B.C. to the Seventeenth Century A.D.* (New York: Harper & Row, 1972), p. 36.

[29] *The Flowering Plum and the Palace Lady*, p. 187.

value.[30] Approximate English equivalents are "dazed and dizzy" or "wimbly-wambly" (unsteady, dizzy).[31]

The alliterative and rhyming binome *dandan* 澹淡 (**dam-dam*) is a much more common word. It clearly is the same as *dandan* 澹澹, which the *Shuowen* glosses as *shui yao mao* 水搖貌 (descriptive of the agitation of water).[32] Mei Sheng uses *dandan* elsewhere in the "Seven Stimuli" to describe the rushing waves that beat against the bank of a deep ravine:[33]

湍流遡波
又澹淡之

A turbulent flow and eddying waves
Also toss and tumble about it.

Other examples are:

Sima Xiangru, "Rhapsody on the Imperial Park," describing birds drifting with the current:[34]

羣浮乎其上
汎淫泛濫
隨風澹淡

In flocks they swim on the surface,
Freely floating, wandering at will,
Tossed and tumbled by the wind.

Ban Gu, "Western Capital Rhapsody," describing boats on the water:

靡微風
澹淡浮

Wafted by the gentle breeze,
Tossed and rocked, they sail across the water.[35]

Zuo Si, "Shu Capital Rhapsody," describing waterfowl bobbing on the water:

澹淡隨波

As they bob up and down with the waves.[36]

Zhang Heng, "Eastern Metropolis Rhapsody":

---

[30] Possibly *tun* means "confused." Cf. *tun* 芚 (stupid, confused) in *Zhuangzi jishi* 2.48: "The sage is stupid and muddled (*tun*)."

[31] See Nils Thun, *Reduplicative Words in English*, A Study of Formations of the Types *Tick-tick, Hurly-burly*, and *Shilly-shally* (Upsala. Carl Bloms Boktrycheri, 1963), p. 82.

[32] See *Shuowen* 11A.4980b–81a.

[33] *Wen xuan* 34.3b.

[34] *Wen xuan* 8.4a.

[35] *Wen xuan* 1.18a; trans. Knechtges, *Wen xuan*, p. 143.

[36] *Wen xuan* 4.5b; trans. Knechtges, *Wen xuan*, p. 321.

淥水澹澹
Its green waters, pitching and rolling...."[37]

Cf. Pan Yue, "Poem Composed for the Golden Valley Gathering"):

綠池汎淡淡
The green pond brimming full pitches and rolls.[38]

Although the English varies in each of these passages, in each case *dandan* describes a state of agitation. Thus, *dandan* in the first "Seven Stimuli" line is no different from the other usages and should be translated accordingly. A good approximation for the context would be "shivering and shaking" or "nitherty-notherty" (all of a tremble, from *nither* 'to shiver and shake').[39]

In interpreting descriptive binomes, one must pay particular attention to the sound glosses given by the commentators, for a sound gloss often provides an important clue to the meaning of the word. It may also help one distinguish between different binomes that are written with the same graphs. A case in point is a passage in Song Yu's "Rhapsody on Gaotang Mountain." The lines describe the surging flow of the numerous streams that converge around Wu Mountain:[40]

濞洶洶其無聲
潰淡淡而並入
The waters suddenly rise, surging and welling, without a sound;
They break forth calm and full, inflowing together.

Another translator has rendered these lines quite differently:

The roar of the rushing waters is deafening
As the torrents churn and race to their source.[41]

What the translator failed to notice was Li Shan's gloss on the graphs 淡淡, which he tells us should be pronounced 以冉 (Mandarin *yanyan*, Old Chinese *rjam-rjam*) and in this context describes the water "quietly flowing calm and full" 安流平滿貌.

The penchant for deciphering the graphs rather than identifying the word behind the graphs has resulted in ludicrous translations. For example, one translator renders a line from Mei Sheng's "Seven Stimuli" as follows:[42]

[37] *Wen xuan* 3 10b; trans. Knechtges, *Wen xuan*, p. 261.
[38] *Wen xuan* 20.34a.
[39] See Thun, *Reduplicative Words in English*, p. 81.
[40] *Wen xuan* 19.3a.
[41] Fusek, "The 'Kao-t'ang Fu,'" p. 415.
[42] *Wen xuan* 34.10a.

虹洞兮蒼天

A rainbow vaulting the blue skies.[43]

This line, which describes a view of a tidal bore as its waters blend with the blue sky, has nothing to do with rainbows. Li Shan, who surely knew a rainbow when he saw one, simply explains *hongtong* 虹洞 (**guang-duang*) as "descriptive of being interjoined." It clearly is the same word as *hongtong* 鴻洞 or *hongtong* 鴻絧, which describes a blending and joining of things. The *Huainanzi* uses it to describe a vast watery expanse:[44]

靡濫振蕩
與天地鴻洞

The waters spread and spill forth, stirring and shaking,
Mingling and merging with Heaven and Earth.

Yang Xiong uses it to describe a long line of chariots in a procession:

鴻絧緁獵

Mingling and merging, continuously connected.[45]

Wang Bao even uses *hongtong* to describe the sound of panpipes echoing in the wind:

風鴻洞而不絕

Continously carried by the wind, it never ceases.[46]

In some of the translations I have cited above, the binomes are represented by two English words. I use this method of translation not because I assume each word has a one to one equivalence with the graphs of the binome, but rather because I can convey through alliteration or repetition of synonyms something of the euphonic effect of the Chinese terms. The first scholar to suggest translating binomes in this fashion was Peter A. Boodberg, who even invented new English words where necessary.[47] In determining the meaning of binomes, I generally have sought to discover the signific element(s) of the word. In most cases, at least one graph of the compound offers a clue to the meaning. I refer to this element as the signific. In the annotations, I give a brief analysis of those binomes about which I at least dare to speculate. For some binomes I provide no annotations, primarily because I have nothing worthwhile to say about the word.

Since these binomes are important for their auditory effect, I give their

[43] Scott, *Love and Protest*, p. 44.
[44] *Huainanzi* 1.10b.
[45] "Rhapsody on the Plume Hunt" L. 75 (*Wen xuan* 8.19a).
[46] "Rhapsody on the Panpipes," *Wen xuan* 17.12b.
[47] "Cedules from a Berkeley Workshop in Asiatic Philology," *Tsing Hua Journal of Chinese Studies* 7.2 (1969): 3–4.

pronunciation in early Chinese. The transcription system used here is based on that of Professor Li Fang-kuei.[48] I use Li's system for its simplicity (it does not require as many diacritics as other systems), and also because the scholars who have done the most thorough studies of Han through Six Dynasties phonology use it. For Han time transcriptions, I have relied heavily on the careful study of Eastern Han sound glosses by W. South Coblin.[49] For the Wei-Jin finals, I have based my reconstructions on the phonological research of Ting Pang-hsin.[50] For determining Han dynasty rhymes, I have consulted the rhyme tables compiled by Zhou Zumo and Luo Changpei.[51]

[48] See Li Fang-kuei 李方桂, "Shanggu yin yanjiu" 上古音研究, *Tsing Hua Journal of Chinese Studies* 9.1 (1971) : 1–60; English translation by Gilbert L. Mattos, "Studies on Archaic Chinese," *MS* 31 (1974–75) : 219–87. I have used a simplified version of Li's system, eliminating all diacritics and using "*e*" for *schwä*.

[49] See W. South Coblin, *A Handbook of Eastern Han Sound Glosses* (Hong Kong: The Chinese University Press, 1983).

[50] Ting Pang-hsin 丁邦新, *Chinese Phonology of the Wei-Chin Period: Reconstruction of the Finals as Reflected in Poetry*. Institute of History and Philology, Academia Sinica, Special Publications No. 65. Taipei: Academia Sinica, 1975.

[51] Luo Changpei 羅常培 and Zhou Zumo 周祖謨, *Han Wei Jin Nanbeichao yunbu yanbian yanjiu* 漢魏晉南北朝韻部演變研究 (Beijing: Kexue chubanshe, 1958).

Wen xuan, or SELECTIONS OF REFINED LITERATURE

Map of Sweet Springs Palace Area

[1] Emperor Cheng reigned from 32 to 7 B C. This preface was not originally part of the piece. The editors of the *Wen xuan* have inserted it from Yang Xiong's "Autobiographical Postface," which is preserved in his *Han shu* biography (see *Han shu* 87A.3522).

[2] This retainer probably refers to Yang Zhuang 楊莊, who like Yang Xiong was from Shu. After hearing Yang Zhuang recite four of Yang Xiong's compositions, Emperor Cheng thought they so resembled the style of the great Shu writer Sima Xiangru that he summoned Yang Xiong to an audience. See Yang Xiong's "Letter in Response to Liu Xin," *Guwen yuan* 5.5b and David R. Knechtges, "The Liu Hsin/Yang Hsiung Correspondence on the *Fang yen*," *MS* 33 (1977):315–16.

[3] The Grand Altar (Tai zhi 泰畤) was the site of sacrifices to the Grand Unity. In 113 B.C., Emperor Wu established this altar at the foot of Sweet Springs Mountain. See *Shi ji* 28.1394; *Han shu* 6.185, 25A.1230; *Mh*, 3:490–91; *Records*, 2:53. The sacrifices at Fenyin 汾陰 (the old sacrificial mound can be found forty kilometers southwest of modern Wanrong 萬榮 *xian*, Shanxi) were performed in honor of Queen Earth (Hou tu 后土), the supreme earth spirit. Hou tu, which originally was a masculine deity, probably was considered female in the Former Han period. See *Mh*, 3:474–75, n. 3 and *Han shu* 22.1054.

[4] In 31 B.C., Emperor Cheng, on the advice of his advisers Kuang Heng 匡衡 and Zhang Tan 張譚, abolished the sacrifices at Sweet Springs Mountain and Fenyin, and moved them to the capital suburbs. In 16 B.C., because he was without an heir, he requested the Empress Dowager to issue an edict restoring the sacrifices to Sweet Springs Mountain and Fenyin. See *Han shu* 10.304, 10.323, 25.1253–59; *HFHD*, 2:406; Michael Loewe, "K'uang Heng and the Reform of Religious Practices (31 B.C.)," *AM* 17.1 (1971):1–27; rpt. in Michael Loewe, *Crisis and Conflict in Han China 104 BC to AD 9* (London: George Allen & Unwin, 1974), pp. 154–92.

[5] On the Hall of Received Brilliance, see "Western Capital Rhapsody," L. 234n.

[6] This probably was the first month (i.e., February/March) of 11 B.C. See Knechtges, *The Han Rhapsody*, pp. 113–16.

[7] The word I have translated "to sway" is *feng* 風, which as a verb should be read in the fourth tone. As used by Yang Xiong and other Former Han *fu* writers, it refers to the presentation of criticism and advice by indirection, usually in the form of subtle moral reprimands addressed to the emperor. Yang Xiong in LL. 108–10 warns the emperor about the dangers of extravagance. On the term *feng*, see Gibbs, "Notes on the Wind."

L. 1: This is the reign of Emperor Cheng.

L. 2: The Supreme Mystery (*Shang xuan* 上玄) is another name for Heaven. Cf. "Eastern Metropolis Rhapsody," L. 323n.

L. 3: Since Emperor Cheng restored the Grand Altar at Sweet Springs, Yang Xiong uses the word "establishes" (Gao Buying 7.5b).

L. 4: This literally reads "good (omens) from the spirits." I follow Yan Shigu (*Han shu* 87A.3523, n. 1) in reading *yong* 雍 as *yong* 擁 "to gather."

7

SACRIFICES

Sweet Springs Palace Rhapsody

YANG ZIYUN

During the reign of the Filial Emperor Cheng,[1] there was an imperial retainer who recommended my compositions as resembling those of Sima Xiangru.[2] His Highness was about to perform the boundary sacrifices at the Grand Altar in Sweet Springs and to Queen Earth at Fenyin,[3] in order to seek an heir and successor.[4] He summoned me to await appointment in the courtyard of the Hall of Received Brilliance.[5] In the first month,[6] I accompanied His Majesty to Sweet Springs. When I returned, I presented the "Sweet Springs Palace Rhapsody" in order to sway (the emperor's opinion).[7] The piece reads:

I

He is Han's tenth generation, and intending to offer the boundary sacrifices to the Supreme Mystery and establish the Grand Altar, He gathers

THIS RHAPSODY by Yang Xiong (zi Ziyun) describes an imperial progress to the Sweet Springs Palace, located three hundred li northwest of Chang'an (in modern Wudi cun 武帝村, north of Chunhua xian, Shaanxi). See "Western Capital Rhapsody," L. 103n. Sweet Springs Palace was the site of sacrifices to the supreme deity, the Grand Unity (see "Eastern Metropolis Rhapsody," L. 403n). The "Sweet Springs Palace Rhapsody," which is also found in Han shu 87A.3522–34, has been previously translated by Erwin von Zach, "Yang Hsiung's Poetische Beschreibung des Himmelsopfers im Lustschloss (Kanchuan fu)," Sinica 2 (1927): 190–93 and rpt. Die Chinesische Anthologie, 1:93–98; Elma E. Kopetsky, "Two Fu on Sacrifices by Yang Hsiung," Journal of Oriental Studies 10 (1972):110–14; Franklin M. Doeringer, "Yang Hsiung and His Formulation of a Classicism," Ph.D. dissertation, Columbia University, 1971, pp. 242–52; Knechtges, The Han Rhapsody, pp. 46–51; Obi Kōichi, Monzen, 1:366–81. This translation is a revised version of a translation that appeared in David R. Knechtges, trans., The Han shu Biography of Yang Xiong (53 B.C.—A.D. 18), Occasional Paper No. 14, Center for Asian Studies, Arizona State University (Tempe: Center for Asian Studies, 1982), pp. 17–24, 77–95.

L. 5: The "lustrous appellations" probably are the names of the gods (e.g., Grand Unity and Queen Earth), to whom the sacrifices were performed. See Wang Xianqian, *Han shu buzhu* 87A.9a.

LL. 6–7: See "Eastern Capital Rhapsody," L. 65n.

L. 8: I have followed Wang Xianqian (*Han shu buzhu* 87A 9a) here. Following the interpretation of Ying Shao (*Han shu* 87A 3523, n 2), the line would read: "He was concerned about the succession, and they (i.e., the gods) granted Him abundance."

L. 13: Yan Shigu (*Han shu* 87A.3523, n. 4) takes this line as a description of the procession, which "spread out like stars, moved like Heaven."

L. 14: On the Twinkling Indicator, see "Western Metropolic Rhapsody," LL. 487–88n. The Grand Yin (Tai yin 太陰) was another name for Tai sui 太歲 or the counter Jupiter. Also known as the Blue Dragon and the Celestial Unity, it was considered the most honorable of the celestial spirits. For a detailed discussion of this name, see Knechtges, *The Han shu Biography of Yang Xiong*, pp. 79–81, n. 87.

L. 15: On the Angular Array, see "Western Capital Rhapsody," L. 242n.

L. 16: Kanyu 堪輿 (Geomancer) literally is the "Container (of Heaven) and the Chariot (of Earth)." It is a common Han term for geomancy. See Needham, volume 2:359–60. Meng Kang (*Han shu* 87A.3523, n 6), however, says that in Yang Xiong's time Kanyu refers to the spirit who "created the books on planning a dwelling." Since the two preceding lines contain the names of star-spirits, Kanyu must be a spirit name as well, and possibly is the spirit of geomancy who attends to the building of the ramparts.

L. 17: Yang Xiong apparently has combined the names of two deities, Kui and Xu (my Demon Drought), into a binome. See "Eastern Metropolis Rhapsody," L. 571n. Xukuang 猦狂 (my Flying Frenzy) is a malevolent headless spirit about whom little is known. See Bodde, *Festivals*, p. 102.

L. 18: Yan Shigu (*Han shu* 87A.3524, n. 7) says the eight spirits are the spirits mentioned in the preceding lines (he apparently splits Kanyu and Kuixu into two names each). However, other commentators argue that Kuixu and Xukuang, who are in effect exorcised, cannot be included among the eight spirits. Thus, the eight spirits more probably refer to the spirits of the eight directions (cf. *Han shu* 6.192). See Wang Niansun, *Dushu zazhi* 4.13.26a.

L 19: Li Shan (7.2b) explains *zhen* 振 as "to rouse" (cf. Karlgren, "Glosses on the Ta Ya and Sung Odes," p. 150, #1083). However, Lu Xiang (7.3a) understands it in the sense of "numerous" (= thronging, swarming). Since all commentators (see *Han shu* 87A.3524, n. 7, and Li Shan 7.2b) explain the rhyming binome *yinlin* 殷轔 (*'jen-ljen*) as descriptive of the great numbers of chariots, Lu Xiang's interpretation is attractive. The signific probably is *yin* (numerous). I suspect the word is related to *yinzhen* 殷軫 (*'jen-tjen*), which also is used to describe the great numbers of marchers and soldiers in a cortege (see *Huainanzi* 15.4b; *Han shu* 87A.3544). The expression may be onomatopoeic. Note the reduplicative *yinyin linlin* 隱隱轔轔 in *Wen xuan* 3.18a, where *linlin* is glossed as "the sound of chariots."

L. 20: On Chiyou, see "Western Metropolis Rhapsody," L. 505n.

On the Ganjiang sword, see "Eastern Metropolis Rhapsody," L. 284n. and "Wu Capital Rhapsody," L 481n. The term Ganjiang originally might have meant any sharp-bladed weapon. See Hu Shaoying 9.11a–12a. According to Zhang Yan (*Han shu* 87A.3524, n. 8), the axe handles were studded with jade.

unto Himself divine blessings, honors the lustrous appellations, matches tally with the Three Emperors, registers merit equal to that of the Five Lords, shows concern for the succession, bestows largesse, broadens His pathway, and inaugurates new ventures. Thereupon, He orders the numerous officers to reckon an auspicious day and correlate an efficacious hour.

As the stars spread out and Heaven begins to move:

II

He summons Twinkling Indicator and Grand Yin,
15   Commands Angular Array to take charge of the troops,
Assigns Geomancer to the ramparts,
Cudgels Demon Drought and flogs Flying Frenzy.
The Eight Spirits race off, heralding and clearing the road:
Swarming in tumultuous throngs, in battle dress,
20   Peers of Chiyou
Girding on Ganjiang swords, grasping jade axes,

L. 21: The rhyming binome *mengrong* 蒙茸 (*mung-njung*), also written 蒙戎 (see *Mao shi* 37/3), originally meant a bushy, tousled appearance (see Karlgren, "Glosses on the Kuo Feng Odes," p. 123, #105). Yang Xiong here uses it to describe confused movement; hence, my "hurry-scurry."

The graphs used to write the alliterative binome *luliang* 陸梁 (*ljekw-ljang*) provide no clear guide to its meaning. Like *mengrong*, it describes disordered movement. Jin Zhuo (see *Han shu* 87A.3524, n. 8) glosses it as descriptive of wild leaping. I suspect that the significis *lu*, which in the form *lu* 踛, means "to leap." Cf. Guo Pu's "Rhapsody on the Yangzi River," L. 203 (*Wen xuan* 12.17a).

L. 22: Commentators explain the alliterative binome *jiaoge* 膠葛 (*kroh-kat*), also written 膠輵, 膠轕, and 轇轕 in widely divergent ways. In most contexts it describes complexity and confusion; cf. *Chuci buzhu* 5.7a; *Shi ji* 117.3060; *Han shu* 87A.3546. Yan Shigu (see *Han shu* 57A.2569, n. 2 and 87A.3524, n. 9) relates it to *jiaojia* 膠加 and *jiaojia* 交加, both of which have the sense of complicated, intricate, entangled. Some commentators also see in the word the sense of wild, unrestrained movement. See *Guangya shuzheng* 6A.30b; Hu Shaoying 6.17a–b. I suspect that the signific element is *jiao*, which probably is related to *jiu* 糾 (*kjioh*), "intertwined"; hence, my "twined and tangled."

L. 23: Jin Zhuo (see *Han shu* 87A.3524, n. 9) explains the rhyming binome *fangrang* 方攘 (*pjang-njang*) with another descriptive binome that means "to scatter" The element *fang* probably conveys the sense of "in every direction." I am less certain of the sense of *rang*. It appears in such binomes as *kuangrang* 俇攘 (see *Chuci buzhu* 8.5b) and *wangrang* 枉攘 (see *Chuci buzhu* 14.7b) where it evokes the idea of wild disorder. My "helter-skelter" is only an approximation. For *fen* 奮 in the sense of "to rush," see *Mao shi* 26/5.

L. 25: The virtually synonymous binomes *cizhi* 柴虒 (*tshja-drja*), my "higgledy-piggledy," and *cenci* 參差 (*tshem-tshja*), my "diversely disposed," both have the sense of "uneven." See *Han shu* 87A.3524, n. 10.

L. 26: *Meng* 蒙 is a variant for *meng* 雺 (brumous vapors). See Hu Shaoying 8.1b; Zhang Yun'ao 5.5b.

L. 27: The rhyming binome *pansan* 半散 (*phwan-san*) is a synonym compound with the literal meaning of "to separate and scatter." See Wang Xianqian, *Han shu buzhu* 57A.10b.

L. 28: The floriate mushroom is the elaborate mushroom-shaped canopy known as the Floriate Canopy (*Hua gai* 華蓋). The Floriate Canopy used by Wang Mang was constructed in nine layers and was eighty-one feet tall. See *Han shu* 99C.4169; *HFHD*, 3:413–14. Cf. "Western Metropolis Rhapsody," L. 493n (where it is called Flowery Baldaquin). The chariot was decorated with small phoenix-shaped figures. See Yan Shigu, *Han shu* 87A 3524, n. 1.

L. 29: These dragons are actually horses.

L. 30: The rhyming binome 蠖略 *huolue* (*ʾwak-ljak*) occurs in Sima Xiangru's "Great Man Rhapsody" (see *Shi ji* 117.3057; *Han shu* 57B.2593), where it describes the movement of dragons. Hervouet (see *Le Chapitre 117 du Che-ki*, p. 188, n. 1) thinks the primary meaning comes from *huo*, which is the word for looper caterpillar (i.e , "to move like a caterpillar"). However, none of the commentators mentions caterpillar as relevant to the meaning of the term, and thus I have simply rendered it as "coiling and uncoiling."

The rhyming binome *ruisui* 蕤綏 (*njwei-sjwei*), my "lush and luxuriant," possibly is equivalent to *weirui* 萎蕤 (*ʾjwai-njwei*) and its variants. The word describes luxuriant vegetation, frilled ornaments hanging from chariots, and in this line possibly the ornate trappings on the dragon-steeds. See Wang Xianqian, *Han shu buzhu* 87A.11a.

L. 31: Commentators do not agree on the meaning of the alliterative binome *sensi* 襂纚 (*srjem-srjai*). Yan Shigu (see *Han shu* 87A.3525, n. 3) says it describes the chariot ornaments. Li Shan (7.3a) says it describes the appearance of the wings hanging from the dragons. Wang Xianqian (see *Han shu buzhu* 87A.10a) equates it with *sensi* 襂欐 (see *Han shu* 57B.2597, n. 3,

20

Fly hurry-scurry, run leaping and lurching;
Jointly massed and mustered, grouped and gathered, twined and
        tangled,
Swift as whirlwinds, fleet as clouds, they rush helter-skelter;
Ranged in ranks, arrayed in columns, melding and merging like
        fishscales,
25 Higgledy-piggledy, diversely disposed, they leap like fish, glide like
        birds;
Bright and blazing, in a blinding blur, gathering like fog, closing in
        like mist,
Scattering and spreading, radiant and resplendent, they form an
        intricate pattern.

III

And then the Emperor thereupon
Mounts the phoenix car, shaded by a floriate mushroom,
With a four-in-hand of azure wiverns, a six-in-hand of ecru dragons:

30 Coiling and uncoiling, lush and luxuriant,
Streaming out, floridly festooned,

Zhang Yi's commentary), which evokes the sense of thick throngs of marchers. Since there are no clear parallel examples of the word, I cannot decide which, if any, of these interpretations is correct. "Floridly festooned" is my fanciful invention.

LL. 32–33: I follow Hu Shaoying (8.2a) in understanding shuaier 帥爾 (*srjwet-nja) in the sense of shuairan 率然 (*srjwet-nja), "sudden." Hu also shows that sha of sharan 霎然 (*srap-nja) is a variant for sha 渹 (srap), "rapid," in Shuowen (4A.1500a–b).

L. 34: The floating phosphors are luminous bodies in the highest reaches of the heavens. See L. 86n.

L. 37: The canopy was made of kingfisher plumes. See Hou Han shu, "Zhi," 29.3645, n. 7. The simurgh banners were made of plaited feathers and fur attached to the side of a staff. See Cai Yong, Du duan, 4.26b.

L. 40: According to Wang Niansun (see Guangya shuzheng 6A.23b–24a), the alliterative binome luli 陸離 (*ljekw-ljai) has two basic senses: a description of irregular appearance (cenci), and a description of length. In some contexts luli describes the dangling of jade pendants (see Chuci buzhu 2.13a), a long sword (see Chuci buzhu 4.7b), or long hair hanging down (see Chuci buzhu 9 11a). In other contexts it describes the scattering and dispersion of animals or people (see Chuci buzhu 1.23a; Wen xuan 4.4a, 4.24b, 8.8b, 8.9b). Wang Niansun thinks that in this line luli describes the irregular sounds of the chariots. I have adopted "echoing and re-echoing" for it in this context.

L. 42: Hu Shaoying (8.2a–b) notes the phonetic, and possibly semantic similarity between the rhyming binome yongsong 嶸嵷 (*zjung-sjung) and yongsong 踴竦 (*zjung-sjung), "to leap and rise upward"; hence, my "lofty heights."

L. 44: Chuanluan 橽欒 was a mountain located south of Sweet Springs. See Fu Qian, Han shu 87A.3524, n. 10.

L. 45: On Changhe, see "Western Metropolis Rhapsody," L. 97n and Major, "Notes on the Nomenclature of Winds," pp. 69–75.

L. 47: On the Sky-Piercing Tower, see "Western Metropolis Rhapsody," LL. 212–13n. Li Shan (7.4a) cites Xue Han's Han shi zhangju, which glosses the doublet yiyi 繹繹 (*rjak-rjak) as "splendid." However, elsewhere the same doublet is used to describe continous brightness: "Stars fell like rain, ten or twenty feet long. They continuously glittered (yiyi), and even upon reaching the ground they did not burn out" (Han shu 27B2.1510). Thus, in Yang Xiong's line I have rendered yiyi "continuous splendor."

L. 52: I follow Wang Niansun (see Dushu zazhi 4.13.26b–27a), who argues that tang 唐 is a descriptive term meaning "broad." The rhyming binome danman 潬曼 (*dan-man), also written danman 壇漫 (spaciously sprawling), conveys the idea of a broad, spacious expanse. See Gao Buying 7.12b–13a; Hervouet, Le Chapitre 117 du Che-ki, p. 22, n. 2

L. 53: Xin zhi 新雉 (*sjen-drjiei) probably is another name for xinyi 辛夷 (*sjen-rjiei), the tree peony (Paeonia lactiflora). See Zhu Jian 9.3a.

L. 54: The bagua 芭苦 (*pwat-kwat) probably is a variant for bo-he 薄荷 (*bak-ga), mint. See Bencao gangmu 14.917.

L. 55: The rhyming binome pili 被麗 (*phjai-liai) is a variant of pili 披離 (*phjai-ljai), "to spread and scatter." See Wang Xianqian, Han shu buzhu 57A.12a.

L. 56: The Shuowen (10A.4318a–b) glossed the rhyming binome po'e 駊騀 (*phwa-nga) as "descriptive of a horse shaking its head." Yang Xiong perhaps describes the hills as if they were proudly prancing horses; hence, my "proud hauteur."

L. 59: Great Peak (Feng luan 封欒) and Stone Gate (Shi guan 石關) are two viewing towers located on Shimen (Stone Gate) Mountain northeast of the palace. See Sanfu huangtu 5.94, which reads Shi que 石闕 (Stone Watchtower) for Shi guan. Hu Shaoying (8.3a–b) argues that Shi guan and Shi que are names for different parts of the viewing tower.

The rhyming binome yimi 施靡 (*jai-mjai) is a variant of yimi 迤靡 (*jai-mjai), also written

Suddenly they gather in darkness,
Abruptly they open to the light.
They overleap the pure empyrean, pass floating phosphors;
35 How the falcon and tortoise standards so straight and tall flap and
            flutter!
Spangled oxtail pennants streaming forth, flashing like lightning,
Blend with halcyon-plume canopies and simurgh banners.

Assembling a myriad riders in the central camp,
Mustering a thousand rigs of jade-encrusted chariots,
40 Their sounds rumbling and roaring, echoing and re-echoing,
Nimbly outpacing rapid thunder, outgalloping the swiftest wind,
He scales the lofty heights of a high plateau,
Crosses the crystalline clarity of winding waters,
Ascends Chuanluan and alights at Heaven's gate,
45 Gallops through Changhe and enters its trembling terror.

IV

At this time, while yet to reach Sweet Springs,
He gazes upon the continuous splendor of the Sky-Piercing Tower:
The base, submerged in shade, is chilly and cold;
The spire, a vast chaos, complexly conjoined,
50 Straight, tall and towering, reaches to Heaven:
Its height, alas, cannot be fully measured!
A level plain, broad and spaciously sprawling,
Is lined with peony trees in groves and thickets;
Clustered windmill palms and field mint
55 Rampantly spread and scatter without limit.

Lofty the proud hauteur of hills and barrows!
Deep moats, steeply scarped, form ravines.
Hither and thither, detached palaces outspread, lighting one
            another;
Great Peak and Stone Gate wind and weave, endlessly extended.

陁靡. Yan Shigu (see *Han shu* 87A.3526, n. 7) explains it as "descriptive of things joining one another." The same word appears in Sima Xiangru's "Rhapsody of Sir Vacuous" (L. 73), where it describes the plains stretching continuously south of the Yunmeng Preserve. My "wind and weave" is an approximation.

L. 61: Or, following Yan Shigu (*Han shu* 87A.3526, n. 1): "Precipitously piled, it achieves its form."

Meng Kang (see *Han shu* 87A.3527, n. 1) explains *zuizui* 崔嵬 (*tswei-tswei*) as "descriptive of timbers piled high." Wang Xianqian (see *Han shu buzhu* 87A.12a–b) equates it with *cuiwei* 崔嵬 (*dzwei-ngjwei*), "precipitously piled."

L. 64: The alliterative binome *liulan* 瀏灠 (*ljehw-lam*) possibly is a variant of *liulan* 流覽 (*ljehw-lam*), "gazing round," "panoramic view." I have understood it as describing the "full and flowing" sweep of the view.

L. 68: Wei Zhao (cited by Li Shan 7.5a) explains *ling* 軨 as "railing" and *xuan* 軒 as porch or verandah. Yan Shigu (see *Han shu* 87A.3527, n. 5) explains *ling xuan* as the lattice covering on the chariot. *Ling* unquestionably is the same as *ling* 櫺 (lattice). See *Shuowen* 14A.6421a–22a. *Ling* 櫺 *xuan* in several contexts is the lattice railing of a verandah. See *Wen xuan* 24.2a, 29.16a. However, Yang Xiong elsewhere uses *ling xuan* clearly to refer to chariots: "You use grilled chariots, banners, and pennons to distinguish them" ("Criticizing Qin and Praising Xin," *Wen xuan* 48.11a) Since the emperor probably still is in his chariot at this point, I have rendered *ling xuan* as "grilled chariot."

L. 70: On the jade trees, see "Western Capital Rhapsody," L 204n. Zhang Yun'ao (5.6b–7a) notes that *cui* 翠, rather than meaning "green," may be Shu dialect for "brilliant."

L. 71: The *Han shu* reads *bi* 壁 (wall) for *Wen xuan bi* 璧 (jade). Although good arguments can be made for either reading (see Gao Buying 7.15a–16a), I follow Zhu Jian (9.4a), who suggests that *bi* (jade), which is parallel to *cui* 翠 (green) in the preceding line, should be understood as *bi* 碧 (prase or prase-colored). Yan Shigu (see *Han shu* 87A.3527, n. 6) interprets *ma* 馬 as agate (*ma'nao* 馬腦) and *xi* 犀 as rhinoceros horn, which decorated the walls.

The rhyming binome *linbin* (*ljien-pjwen*) 璘瑸 (sparkling splendor) describes the glitter of gems. For variants, see Zhu Qifeng, *Ci tong*, p. 497.

LL. 72–73: The bronze (or gold?) men were ten-foot statues the Chinese captured from the Xiongnu in 120 B.C. They may have been Buddhist images. See Shiratori Kurakichi, "On the Territory of the Hsiung-nu Prince Hsiu-t'u Wang and His Metal Statues for Heaven Worship," *MTB* 5 (1930):1–77 (esp. 25–71); Homer H Dubs, "The 'Golden Man' of Former Han Times," *TP* 33 (1937):1–14, 191–92; James R. Ware, "Once More the 'Golden Man,'" *TP* 34 (1938):174–78. From the description here, I suspect that they wore armor similar to that of the mailed pottery figures discovered near the burial mound of the First Qin Emperor. See Albert E. Dien, trans., "Excavation of the Ch'in Dynasty Pit Containing Pottery Figures of Warriors and Horses at Ling-t'ung, Shensi Province," *Chinese Studies in Archeology*, 1.1 (1979):32–36.

LL. 74–75: Lu Yanji (7.6b–7a) thinks that these lines describe the dazzling luster of the palace buildings illuminated by the sun. However, the text clearly mentions a lighted torch. I follow Gao Buying (7.16b), who says the lines refer to the bronze statues.

LL. 76–77: On the Hanging Garden, see "Eastern Metropolis Rhapsody," L. 604n. It was located at the entrance to the dwelling of the Celestial Lord. See Major, "Notes on the Nomenclature of Winds," p. 70. The Grand Unity dwelled in the celestial Purple Palace. In some sources, the Grand Unity is considered another name for the Celestial Lord. See *Shi ji* 27.1290, n 3. Wang Xianqian (*Han shu buzhu* 87A.13a) says that these two lines describe the bronze figures. However, as Gao Buying suggests (7.16b–17a), they more likely apply to the Sweet Springs Palace, which would have been considered a terrestial replica of the Celestial Lord's palace.

L. 79: The Northern Pole (Bei ji 北極) is a five-star constellation, the fifth star of which (4339 Camelopardalis) was the pole star of Han times See Needham, volume 3:261.

V

60 And then
     A grand edifice, illusory as clouds, deceptive as waves,
     Precipitously piled, forms a tower.
     Raising and lifting His head to look on high,
     His eyes, blurred and blinded, see nothing.
     Straight ahead, the view full and flowing, vast and wide,
65 Points to a spacious sweep east and west.
     All dizzy and giddy,
     His soul is dazed and dazzled, confounded and confused.

     As he clutches the grilled dash and gazes all around,
     Suddenly the vista is broad and boundless, without limit.
70 Halcyon-colored the virescent luster of jade trees,
     Prase-hued the sparkling splendor of horses and rhinos.
     Bronze figures, brave and bold, upholding bell-stands,
     Cragged and crenate, scaled like dragons,
     Brandish lighted torches of lustrous brilliance,
75 Trail a fervid fulgor of luminous flame.
     All this befits the Hanging Garden of the Lord's abode,
     And images the majestic spirit of Grand Unity.
     The massive terrace thrusts itself upward in solitary prominence,
     Reaching the supernal heights of the Northern Pole.

L. 80: The *rong* 榮 (crests) are the wings of the roof that project upward. See *Han shu* 87A 3527, n. 11.

L. 81: The *chen* 栚 are the eaves of a roof. Wang Niansun (*Dushu zazhi* 4.13.27b–28b) proposes to emend *yang* 柍 to *yang* 央 "middle," claiming the wood radical was added on analogy with *chen*. He also suggests that *yang chen* actually means "halfway up the eaves."

L. 82: In the Han period, portions of a palace were built into a hill. Thus, the recesses of the palace literally were amidst "crags and crannies." Cf. "Rhapsody on the Imperial Park," L. 178.

The rhyming binome *yulu* 鬱律 (*°jwet-ljwet*), my "rumbles and roars," probably is an onomatopoeic expression for the sound of thunder. See Yan Shigu 87A.3528, n. 12) and Hervouet, *Le Chapitre 117 du Che-ki*, p. 196, n. 1.

L 86: The Upturned Phosphors (Dao jing 倒景) are luminous bodies in the highest part of the sky (4,000 *li* above the earth), above the sun and moon. Because the light of the sun and moon shone upward to it, it was called the region of the Upturned Phosphors. See *Han shu* 25C.1261, n. 3 and 57B.2599. On the Flying Bridge, see "Eastern Metropolis Rhapsody," L. 564n.

L. 87: I follow Hu Shaoying (8.5b) in reading *miemeng* 蠛蠓 as equivalent to *miemeng* 莧蒙 (Murky Mist), which refers to the fine dust and vapor collected in the highest regions of the sky. See *Hou Han shu* 59.1935, n. 16.

L. 88: Gouging Spear is the name of a comet. See "Eastern Metropolis Rhapsody," L. 157n. and Michael Loewe, "The Han View of Comets," *BMFEA* 52 (1980), 10. Mysterious Darkness (Xuanming 玄冥) is the guardian deity of the north. See Karlgren, "Legends and Cults," pp. 222, 239, 243–44, 246. This line is similar to a line in Sima Xiangru's "Great Man Rhapsody": "On the left is Mysterious Darkness, on the right Black Thunder" (*Shiji* 117.3058; *Han shu* 57B.2595). It is not clear whether Yang Xiong is referring to a statue of Mysterious Darkness, located on the west side of the palace (right is west in Han directions), or if he is continuing to describe the great height of the palace, which reaches into the supernal haunts of the gods.

L. 89: Jin Zhuo (*Han shu* 87A.3528, n. 1) notes that the Flaming Watchtower (Biao que 㯊闕) was red. Perhaps because of its color, it was located on the southern side of the palace complex (red is the color of south). Jin also notes that the Lord of the South was called Red Flaming Fury (see "Eastern Capital Rhapsody, "The Luminous Hall Poems," LL. 5–6). Possibly the tower was intended as a terrestrial replica of this god's celestial dwelling.

L. 90: On the Dark Capital, see "Eastern Capital Rhapsody," L. 208n. Cf. Liu Xin's "Sweet Springs Palace Rhapsody" (in *Yiwen leiju* 62.1113): "Its back is to Gonggong's Dark Capital." The emphasis is on the fact that the Sweet Springs Palace was located north of the capital.

LL. 92–93: The dragon must be the Azure Dragon, who was the guardian animal of the east. The White Tiger was the guardian animal of the west (where the Kunlun Mountains were located). See *Huainanzi* 3.3a–b. Yan Shigu (*Han shu* 87A.3528, n. 3) says that the Sweet Springs Palace had images of these creatures. However, he does not specify whether they were painted images or statues. Li Shan (7 5b) cites an apocryphon that says that the Azure Dragon and White Tiger occupied positions to the left and right respectively of the Grand Unity. Thus, it is possible that these were statues or mural paintings of figures associated with the Grand Unity, to whom sacrifices were performed.

L. 94: Lofty Radiance (Gao guang 高光) is a hall in the Sweet Springs Palace. See *Sanfu huangtu* 2.44.

The rhyming binome *jiulu* 樛流 (*°kjehw-ljehw*), which Yan Shigu (see *Han shu* 87A.3528, n. 4) glosses as "to bend," is equivalent to *zhoulu* 周流 (*°krjoh?-ljehw*), "roaming round." See Hu Shaoying 8.6a.

L. 95: The *Sanfu huangtu* (2.44–45) mentions a Panghuang 彷徨 viewing tower built in the

80 Constellations now stretch across the upper crests,
    The sun and moon pass through the middle eaves,
    Thunder rumbles and roars in its crags and crannies,
    Lightning darts and dashes in its walls and fences.
    Even ghosts and demons cannot reach the top;
85 Halfway up its long course, they tumble down again.
    It passes Upturned Phosphors, traverses Flying Bridge,
    Drifts through Murky Mist, and brushes Heaven.
    Gouging Spear left, Mysterious Darkness right,
    Flaming Watchtower front, and the receiving gate rear,
90 It shades the Western Sea and Dark Capital,
    Where bubbling wine spurts forth to form a stream.
    A dragon coils and curls along the eastern cliff;
    The White Tiger fiercely guards the Kunlun.

VI

    Gazing, roaming round at Lofty Radiance,
95 At ease, He lingers and loiters at a western repose.

27

Western Chamber of the Sweet Springs Palace. However, *panghuang* 方皇 (to linger and loiter) must be a verb here, and thus it cannot be the name of a building. The expression *xi qing* 西清 is not a proper noun, but simply designates a still place of repose in the western chamber. See *Han shu* 87A.3528, n. 4. Cf. "Rhapsody on the Imperial Park," L. 184.

L. 96: The front hall is the main hall of a palace.

L. 97: The walls of the buildings had gold discs fastened to the exposed wall laths. These discs were inlaid with jade and pearls. See *Han shu* 97B.3987. "Jade-of-He" simply is a common term for beautiful jade. See Hervouet, *Un Poète de cour*, p. 321. Meng Kang and Yan Shigu (*Han shu* 87A.3529, n. 5) say that *longling* 瓏玲 (*linglong* in You Mao) is the tinkling sound of the jade. However, Hu Shaoying (8.6a–b) cites evidence to show that the term can be used to describe the jade's luster.

L. 99: Yan Shigu (*Han shu* 87A.3529, n. 6) takes *momo* 莫莫 as *anmo* 闇莫 "darkness." Li Shan (7.6a), following the commentary to *Mao shi* 209/3, construes *momo* as "quiet." However, *momo* could be the same as *momo* 模模, which the *Erya* (A3.5b) glosses as "to exert oneself"; hence, my "mighty heaves."

L. 100: On *langlang* 閬閬 (*lang-lang*) in the sense of "hollow," "yawning," "gaping," see Hu Shaoying 8.6b.

L. 101: On the Purple Palace, see "Western Capital Rhapsody," LL. 164–65n.

The rhyming binome *zhenghong / zhengrong* 崝嶸 (*dzreng-rweng* or *dzreng-gweng*) can describe either sheer depths (see *Chuci buzhu* 5.11a, *Han shu* 57B.2598) or steep height (see *Wen xuan* 1.14b, 4.24b, 6.10b). It is difficult to decide which sense *zhengrong* has here. It could describe the chasmic hollowness of the gaping hall, or it could refer to the precipitous heights of the structure. My "precipitous profundity" is an attempt to combine both senses.

L. 103: I suspect that *tui* 崥 (*thweh*), which the *Pi cang* (cited by Li Shan 7.6a) explains as the long appearance of mountains, is a variant of *duo* 隋 (*dwa*). In *Mao shi* 296, *duo* describes the long and narrow shape of mountains. See *Erya* B7.3b.

The rhyming binome *zuiwei* 嶵隗 (*dz'wei-ngwei*), also written 崔嵬, undoubtedly is a variant of *cuiwei* 崔巍 (*dzwei-ngiwei*). See Zhu Qifeng, *Ci tong*, pp. 228–29. Here I have rendered it "tall and towering."

L. 105: Fu Qian (cited by Li Shan 7.6a) glosses menglong 蒙籠 (*muang-luang*) as *jiaoge* (see L. 22n above). However, I suspect that it is a variant of *menglong* 蒙蘢. Most commonly, it is used to describe a dense covering of vegetation (cf. *Han shu* 49.2296; *Wen xuan* 4.3a; 4.24b). Here, *menglong* has the derived sense of "densely obscured." According to Liu Liang (7.8b), the buildings blend in with the mountains as if naturally formed.

L. 106: The alliterative binome *liuli* 流離 (*ljehw-ljai*) probably is a variant of *luli* (see L. 40n above). Here it conveys the sense of the long, trailing stream of red color emanating from the hall.

L. 108: The Jade Chamber (Xuan shi 琁室) is a structure reputedly constructed by Jie, the last ruler of the Xia dynasty. On the Hundred-Acre Palace, reputedly built by Zhou, the last ruler of the Shang, see "Wu Capital Rhapsody," L. 351n. See *Yanzi chunqiu* 2.7b (where Xuan is written 璿); *Lüshi chunqiu* 23.6b (where the building of both structures is attributed to Jie); Li Shan 3.5b, citing the Old Text version of the *Zhushu jinian*. This line is a subtle warning to Emperor Cheng, whose obsession with lavish and ostentatious living, as in the case of the Xia and Shang, could bring about the fall of his dynasty.

LL. 109–10: Implied in these two lines, particularly in the reference to standing on the edge of an abyss, is that the emperor should take careful note of the great danger presented by his hedonistic activities. The words *wang guo* 亡國, which are in the *Wen xuan* text, are an interpolation from Ying Shao's commentary. See Hu Shaoying 8.6b–7a.

L. 112: Although *yiyang* 柂楊 can be the name of a single tree (either aspen or Chinese poplar), because of the parallelism with cinnamon and pepper, *yi* and *yang* must be separate

The front hall stands tall and towering,
With Jade-of-He glittering and glistening,
And flying rafters on floating posts raised aloft,
As if spirits, with mightly heaves, brace their collapse.
100 It spires upward, gaping and yawning, open and wide,
Like the precipitous profundity of Purple Palace.
Row by row, joined one to another, its buildings spread and sprawl,
Long and narrow, tall and towering, intertwining,
Climbing into cloud-capped turrets, rising and falling,
105 Tangling in a murky mass, as if from chaos formed.
Trailing a long stream of scarlet color,
Wafting a curling wreath of azure vapor,
It is heir to the Jade Chamber and the Hundred-Acre Palace,
And as He climbs this height to gaze afar,
110 He is awe-struck, as if poised on an abyss.

VII

A swirling whirlwind vents its pulsing fury,
Scattering cinnamon and pepper, gathering poplar and willow:

trees. The *yi*, which is also known as the *fuyi* 夫栘, is another name for the *changdi* 常棣, which is variously identified as *Populus tremula* (European aspen), *Amelanchier asiatica* (Asian shadbush), or *Populus cathayana* (Chinese poplar). See Lu Wenyu, p. 94, #105; Shi Shenghan, *Qimin yaoshu jinshi*, p. 837; Smith-Stuart, p. 347

L. 115: I follow Yan Shigu (*Han shu* 87A.3530) in reading *xiang* 薌 "fragrance" as *xiang* 響 "sound." See also Hu Shaoying 8.7a. Yang Xiong is describing the sound of the wind passing through the bells. The exact meaning of the rhyming binome *yixi* 呋肹 (*jwet-hjet*) is not known. Gao Buying (7.22b) thinks that it describes rapid movement; hence, my "rapidly reverberating." The *Han shu* reads *gen* 根 "trunk" for *Wen xuan*'s *pi* 批, "to strike." Gao Buying (7.22b) shows that *gen* should be understood as *gen* 揎, which also means "to strike."

L. 117: The door knockers (*jin pu* 金鋪, also called *pu shou* 鋪首), were large bronze figures usually shaped like tortoises and snakes. See *Han shu* 11.344.

L. 118: The *xiongqiong* (or *qiongqiong*) 莺藭 is *Conioselinum univattatum* (hemlock parsley). See Smith-Stuart, pp. 123–24.

L. 119: I have followed Hu Shaoying (8 7b–8a) in understanding the rhyming binome *penghong* 弸彋 (*phreng-grweng*) in the sense of "bulging and billowing."

The rhyming binome *fuyu* 拂汨 (*phjwet-gjwet*) is not otherwise attested. Li Shan (7.7a) explains it as descriptive of agitation; hence, my "shaking and shuddering."

L. 121: The *yin* and *yang* are the two groups into which the twelve pitches of the Chinese scale were divided. See Hart, "The Discussion of the *Wu-yi* Bells," pp. 397–401. Wang Yinzhi 王引之 (1766–1834), cited by Wang Niansun (see *Dushu zazhi* 4.13.28a–28b), shows that *mu* 穆 (majestic, solemn), also written *mu* 繆, is a term used in the *Huainanzi* (3.12b) for one of the so-called "altered notes" inserted in the regular pentatonic scale to create the heptatonic scale. See also *Dushu zazhi* 9.3.25b–27b; *Song shu* 11.207; *Jin shu* 16.476. To provide a contrast with *mu*, I have freely translated *yu* 羽, which is one of the notes of the pentatonic scale, as "gay." (Note that the *Bohu tong* A.38a associates *yu* with "repose.") Wang also suggests that *he* 和 should be understood as the *he* of *chang he* 唱和 "singing the lead and responding in chorus." The turbid and clear presumably are the low-pitched and high-pitched sounds respectively. All of this elaborate terminology is simply a way of describing the musical effect of the wind.

L. 122: On the music master Kui, see "Eastern Metropolis Rhapsody," L. 449n. Boya 伯牙 was a famous zither player. See *Lüshi chunqiu* 14.4a.

LL. 123–24: On Lu Ban and Wang Er, see "Western Metropolis Rhapsody," L. 186n. Chui 倕 was master of artisans under Emperor Yao. See Karlgren, "Legends and Cults," pp. 256–57.

L. 125: Zheng Qiao probably is the same as Zheng Boqiao 征伯僑 who is mentioned in Sima Xiangru's "Great Man Rhapsody" (see *Shi ji* 117.3058; *Han shu* 57B.2595). Virtually nothing is known about him. I assume Yang Xiong considered him an immortal. Wo Quan 偓佺 is an immortal whose biography is contained in the *Liexian zhuan* (A.5) The point of the line is that even famous immortals, who had seen many fabulous wonders, would be completely overwhelmed by the grandeur and majesty of the Sweet Springs Palace

L 130: Both *yuanwan* 蜿蜎 (*jwen-jwan*), my "crinkled and curled," and *huohuo* 蠖濩 (*wak-gwak*), my "scrolled and scalloped," are rhyming binomes used to describe the convolutions of the ornate carvings on the buildings. See Hu Shaoying 8.8b–9a. Hu thinks *huohuo* is a variant of *huolüe* (see L. 30n)

L. 132: I have followed the *Han shu*, which reads *si* 思 (thoughts) for *Wen xuan*'s *en* 恩 (bounty).

L. 134: The exact identity of the Three Spirits is not clear. Li Shan (7.7b) says they are Heaven, Earth, and Man. However, Gao Buying (7.25a) points out that Man is not a spirit. He suggests that they refer instead to the Three Unities (the Heavenly Unity, the Earthly Unity, and the Grand Unity) to whom sacrifices reputedly were made once every three years. See *Shi ji* 28.1386.

30

Fragrance, pungent and strong, arching upward,
Strikes the brackets, grazes the eaves.

115 Sounds rapidly reverberate with a clashing and clanging,
Musical echoes, pealing and chiming, pass through the bells;
It pushes jade doors open, joggles bronze knockers,
Whisking off thoroughwort, sweet basil, and hemlock parsley.

Curtains bulge and billow, shake and shudder;
120 Gradually all becomes dark and dim, deeply silent.
Yin and *yang*, clear and turbid, solemn and gay echo one another,
As if Kui and Ya were playing their zithers.

Ban and Chui would discard their knives and chisels;
Wang Er would throw down his compass and plumb.
125 Even to a Zheng Qiao or Wo Quan
It would be a vague vision as if in a dream.

VIII

And then, events change and things transform, His eyes start and ears whirr. The Son of Heaven then sedately stands in the midst of precious terraces, leisure lodges, jade finials, nephrite petals, all crinkled-and-curled, scrolled-and-scalloped. For this is a means to cleanse His mind, purify His soul, gather His vitality, and concentrate His thoughts, to influence Heaven and Earth, and receive blessings from the Three Spirits. Whereupon, He

31

L. 136: Gao is Gao Yao 皋繇, the wise Minister of Justice under Yao. See Karlgren, "Legends and Cults," p. 257. Yi is Yi Yin 伊尹, minister to Tang, founder of the Shang. See Karlgren, "Legends and Cults," pp. 328–29.

L. 138: The "Sweet Pear" is the title of *Mao shi* 16. According to the Mao School interpretation (see *Mao shi zhushu* 1.4.8a), this song praises the virtues of Shi 奭, Duke of Shao 召, a loyal associate of King Wu. Here "Sweet Pear" is metonymy for the Duke of Shao.

L. 139: The "Eastern March" alludes to the military campaign led by the Duke of Zhou to put down a rebellion of King Wu's two younger brothers and the son of the defeated Shang ruler. *Mao shi* 157/1 contains the line: "The Duke of Zhou marches east." Here "Eastward March" is metonymy for the Duke of Zhou."

L. 140: *Yang ling* 陽靈 probably is not the name of a specific place. It rather is a term applied to the sacred hall in which the emperor sacrificed to Heaven. Yan Shigu (see *Han shu* 87A.3531, n. 7) reads 齊 in the pronunciation *qi*, meaning "to congregate." Li Shan (7.7b) reads it as *zhai*(more commonly written 齋), meaning "to purify oneself."

L. 143: Following Hu Shaoying's suggestion (8.9a), I have emended *qing yun* 清雲 "pure clouds" to *qing yun* 青雲 "cerulean clouds," which occurs in Li Shan's commentary.

L. 144: The Ruo 若 is the name of a magic tree sometimes described as having ten suns on the top. The light from its blossoms illumines the earth below. See *Huainanzi* 4.3b; *Chuci buzhu* 1.21b; *Sahnhai jing* 17.7a (Guo Pu's commentary).

L. 148: The floriate sunshade probably is the Floriate Canopy. See L. 28n. above.

L. 149: The Jade Armil (Xuan ji 琁璣) is the name of an ancient astronomical instrument often identified as the armillary sphere. Originally, it probably was a disc-shaped sighting instrument used for determining the position of the celestial pole. The Jade Armil also refers to the four stars of the bowl of the Northern Dipper (α, β, γ, δ Ursae Majoris), which most likely is the usage Yang Xiong intended here. See Schlegel, *Uranographie chinoise*, 1:503; *HFHD*, 3:328–29; Needham, volume 3:333–39.

L. 150: The Sanwei 三危 (Triperil) is an ancient legendary mountain commonly located south of Dunhuang. See Gao Buying 7.26b–27a.

L. 153: The Dragon Pool (Long yuan 龍淵) may refer to a river of this same name over sixty *li* southwest of Shanggui 上邽 prefecture (northwest of modern Tianshui, Gansu). See *Shuijing zhu* 4.20.2; Zhu Jian 9.6a–7b. The Nine Divisions may be the nine layers of the Dragon Pool.

L. 156: The *Han shu* reads *yu rui* 御蕤 (chariot fringe) for *Wen xuan*'s *xian rui* 銜蕤 (holding fringe in the mouth). Yan Shigu (see *Han shu* 87A.3532, n. 13) claims that *xian rui* is a vulgar corruption of the text.

L. 157: The Weak River (Ruo shui 弱水) is the name of a legendary stream located in the northwest. Some sources claim that it is the home of the Queen Mother of the West (Xi wangmu) mentioned below. See *Han shu* 28B.1611; *Shi ji* 123.3164 (where Xi wangmu is a place name); *Hou Han shu* 86.2920. The Weak River was so named because it was believed that even a goose feather would sink in its waters. See *Shanhai jing* 16.6a, Guo Pu's commentary.

The rhyming binome *tingying* 渟濙 (*thieng-ghjweng*) describes small amounts of water (see Gao Buying 7.28a). I suspect that the signific is *ting*, which probably represents *ting* 渟 (stagnant). For variants, see Zhu Qifeng, *Ci tong*, p. 1561. I have rendered it as "shallow shoals" to fit this context.

L. 158: Buzhou 不周 Mountain, located in the northwest, was the peak that the rebel Gonggong 共工 butted, snapping the pillars of Heaven and the cords of Earth so that Heaven slanted northwest and Earth tilted southeast. See *Huainanzi* 3.1a–b; *Liezi zhu* 5.52; Karlgren, "Legends and Cults," p. 227. For a recent interpretation of the Gonggong myth, see William G. Boltz, "Kung kung and the Flood: Reverse Euhemerism in the *Yao tien*," *TP* 67 (1981): 141–53.

L. 159: The Queen Mother of the West, who dwelled in the Kunlun Mountains, was

seeks partners, searches for mates, cohorts like Gao and Yi, peerless ex-
emplars, superlative talents, who enfold the kindness of the "Sweet Pear,"
and embrace the intent of the "Eastward March," together to purify themselves in the palace of the *yang* spirit:

> He spreads fig leaves for mats,
> Snaps carnelian branches for their fragrance,
> Sips flowing mists in cerulean clouds,
> Drinks from the dewy petals of the Ruo Tree.
> 145 They assemble in the enclosure for rites to the gods,
> Ascend the hall for lauding the earth-spirits.
>
> He raises the long swallowtail streamers of dazzling brilliance,
> Displays the lush luxuriance of the floriate sunshade,
> Grasps the Jade Armil and downward looks,
> 150 Casts His roving gaze over the Triperil peaks.
> Deploying His many chariots over the eastern slope,
> He releases the jade wheel-locks and gallops downward;
> Drifting on Dragon Pool, circling the Nine Divisions,
> He peers under the earth and turns upward.
> 155 Winds, blasting and blustering, propel His axles;
> Simurghs and phoenixes tangle in His chariot fringe.
> Bridging Weak River's shallow shoals,
> Treading Buzhou's twisting tracks,
> He recalls Queen Mother of the West, and joyfully salutes her
>   longevity.

worshipped as the main figure in a Han dynasty immortality cult. See Homer H. Dubs, "An Ancient Chinese Mystery Cult," *Harvard Theological Review* 35 (1942):221–40; Kominami Ichirō 小南一郎, "Seiōbo to shichi seki denshō" 西王母と七夕傳承, *Tōhōgaku hō* 46 (1974): 33–81; Michael Loewe, *Ways to Paradise: The Chinese Quest for Immortality* (London: George Allen & Unwin, 1979), pp. 86–126.

L. 160: The Jade Maiden (Yu nu 玉女) is the goddess of Mt. Hua. She was a Taoist deity, probably identical to the Hairy Maiden (Mao nu 毛女) mentioned in the *Liexian zhuan* (B.47). According to tradition, she once was a palace lady of the First Qin Emperor. After the fall of Qin, she fled to the mountains where she prolonged her life eating pine needles. See *Pokora*, trans., *Hsin-lun*, pp. 247–48, n. 19. On Consort Fu, see "Eastern Metropolis Rhapsody," L. 127n. In his "Autobiographical Postface" (see *Han shu* 87A.3535), Yang Xiong comments on these lines: "At this time Brilliant Companion Zhao enjoyed great favor, and every time the emperor went up to Sweet Springs, she accompanied the Standard Cortege in the panther-tail section of the escort chariots. Thus, when I lavishly speak of the multitude of chariots and horsemen, the cortege of double and triple teams, this means that this is not the way 'to influence Heaven and Earth' or 'receive blessings from the Three Spirits'. When I say further, 'He rejects the Jade Maiden, expels Consort Fu,' this is a subtle warning to be grave and solemn in conducting affairs." Thus, it is clear that Yang Xiong intended the Jade Maiden and Consort Fu to stand for concubines who improperly accompanied the imperial carriage.

L. 162: Yan Shigu (see *Han shu* 87A.3518, n. 4) says that the expression *e mei* 蛾眉 is descriptive of beautiful eyebrows, which were shaped like silkworm moths. However, Duan Yucai shows that *e* simply is the word *e* 娥, "beautiful." Cf. Dai Zhen, *Fangyan shuzheng* 方言疏證 (Exegetical Evidence for the *Fangyan*), *Sbby*, 1.1b. See Duan's *Shi jing xiaoxue* 詩經小學 (Philological Studies of the *Classic of Songs*), in *Huang Qing jingjie*, 630.13.b–14a.

L. 167: The correct reading of this line is uncertain. The modern *Han shu* text reads *zhaoyao* 招繇, which Zhang Yan (see *Han shu* 87A.3532, n. 2) explains as the spirit Zhaoyao. The *Five Comm.* follows this same reading. Another version of the *Han shu* (presumably the one edited by Ru Chun in the third century) and the You Mao *Wen xuan* read *gaoyao* 皋搖. Ru Chun explains *gao* as *qiegao* 挈皋, which is a variant form for *jiegao* 桔橰, the name of a type of swape used to raise beacon-fires on high. Zhu Jian (9.6b–7a) cites a text (see *Shi ji* 28.1377 and *Han shu* 25A.1209) that mentions a type of pyre used to hoist the burnt offerings toward Heaven. Zhu also notes that parallelism with the preceding line requires the reading *gaoyao*. Although I have adopted this explanation in my translation, it is possible that the reading *zhaoyao* can be construed as a verb meaning "to shake" or "to agitate." In this sense, the sacrifice affects even the Grand Unity Star, which begins to twinkle and flicker in response.

L. 168: I can find no information about the *yi* 頤 banner. It possibly was emblazoned with Hexagram 27, *yi* (sustenance). My rendering of "Great Sustenance" is purely fanciful.

L. 169: The Sacred Pennant (Ling qi 靈旗) was used during ceremonies in honor of the Grand Unity. The pennant was painted with the sun, moon, Northern Dipper, and a soaring dragon to symbolize the Grand Unity. See *Shi ji* 28.1395; *Han shu* 25A.1231; *Mh*, 3:493; *Records*, 2:54.

L. 170: Yan Shigu (see *Han shu* 87A.3533, n. 3) explains *qiao* 樵 as firewood, and *zheng* 蒸 as hemp stalks used as fuel for the holocaust.

LL. 172–73: The Azure Sea (Cang hai 倉海) is another name for the Eastern Sea. The Flowing Sands (Liu sha 流沙) may refer to the Gobi.

L. 175: Fu Qian (see *Han shu* 87A.3533, n. 4) says that Danya 丹厓 (Cinnabar Shore) refers to the bank of the Dan River. However, to be parallel with the Dark Capital in the preceding line, Danya should refer to a place in the remote south, and all of the rivers named Dan are too far north. I suspect that Danya may be a variant name for Zhuya 朱崖 (Vermilion Shore), one of the names for Hainan Island. See Schafer, *Shore of Pearls*, pp. 8–9 There also is a Danya

160 He rejects Jade Maiden, expels Consort Fu.
    Jade Maiden has no place to gaze her limpid orbs;
    Consort Fu can no longer flaunt her pretty eyebrows.
    Now He grasps the essential firmness of the Way and Virtue,
    And equal to the gods, consults with them.

IX

165 And then
    Reverently He makes a burnt offering, devoutly prays:
    The holocaust perfumes the august heavens,
    Hoisted by pyre to Grand Unity.

    He raises Great Sustenance,
    Plants the Sacred Pennant.

170 Firebrands and burning stalks ascend together,
    Scatter into the four directions:
    Eastward illumining the Azure Sea,
    Westward dazzling the Flowing Sands,
    Northward brightening the Dark Capital,
175 Southward singeing the Cinnabar Shore.

Mountain mentioned in the *Shuijing zhu* 4.20.12, but its location in Henan is much too far north to be applicable here.

LL. 176–77: The ladle mentioned here is the *zan* 瓚, which was specifically used to pour millet wine libation. It had a capacity of five *sheng* 升 (about one liter) The handle was made of a jade *gui*. See *Zhou li zhushu* 20.20a, Zheng Xuan's commentary. According to Lu Wenyu (pp. 121–22, #129), *chang* 鬯 is turmeric, the stalk of which was mixed with the millet wine to give the wine a yellow cast. However, Ling Chunsheng 凌純聲 has argued that *chang* did not specifically refer to turmeric, and that several different types of plants were used as aromatics for the wine *Chang* by itself simply means aromatic wine. See his "Zhongguo jiu de qiyuan" 中國酒的起源, *BIHP* 29 (1958):896–905. See also Tjan Tjoe Som (Zeng Zhusen 曾珠森), trans., *Po Hu T'ung* 白虎通, *The Comprehensive Discussions in the White Tiger Hall*, 2 vols. (Leiden: Brill, 1949, 1952), 2:508–9. On turmeric, see Laufer, *Sino-Iranica*, pp. 309–23.

The rhyming binome *qiuliu* 觩樛 (*gjehw-ljehw*) describes the curved handle of the ladle. The signific is *qu* (cf. *Mao shi* 215/5), which means "curved."

The rhyming binome *handan* 泔淡 (*gam-dam*), which Ying Shao (see *Han shu* 87A.3533, n. 5) glosses as "descriptive of being full," may be related to *yanyan* 淡淡 (*rjam-rjam*), which also means full. See *Wen xuan* 19.3a. I have rendered it "fragrantly frothing."

L. 178: On *xixiang* (to scatter and spread), see "Shu Capital Rhapsody," LL. 390–91n.

LL. 180–81: The yellow dragon and the unicorn are auspicious omens.

L. 182: Shaman Xian (Wu xian 巫咸) was the diviner whom Qu Yuan consulted in the "Li sao." See "Li sao" couplet 141; *Chuci buzhu* 1.28b–29a.

L. 184: Technically *bin* 儐 should refer to the emperor's attendants, who escort guests into the hall and assist in the rites. See *Zhou li zhushu* 38.1a. Here, however, they seem to be the spirits' escorts, who descend on the altar in great numbers.

L. 188: Tri-Peak (San luan 三巒) Tower may be the same as the Great Peak (Feng luan 封巒) Tower. It was located inside the walls of the Sweet Springs Park. Cf. Liu Xin's "Sweet Springs Palace Rhapsody" (see *Yiwen leiju* 62.1113): "Great Peak forms its eastern wing." The Pear (Tangli 棠黎) Palace was located south of the Sweet Springs Park. See *Sanfu huangtu* 2.45.

L. 191: Changping 長平 was the name of a slope located on the bank of the Jing River southwest of Chiyang 池陽 prefecture (northwest of modern Jingyang 涇陽 xian, Shaanxi). See *Han shu* 8.271, n. 3.

L. 193: The clouds and rain are figures for imperial grace and favor.

L. 195: The circular mound is the altar used for sacrifices to Heaven. Its shape was intended to symbolize the roundness of Heaven. See Wang Niansun, *Guangya shuzheng* 9A.13.

L. 197: The rhyming binome *liyi* 刿㿁 (*lja-zja*), my "twisting and twining," is a variant for the more common *liyi* 邐迤 (*ljei-jiai*), which is used to describe landforms winding and stretching over a vast expanse. See *Erya* B6.3b and Hu Shaoying 8.10a-b.

L. 198: Reading 單 as *chan* 蟬 (sinuous, coiling). This sense matches with the *quanyuan* 埢垣 (*ghjwan-gjwan*), "curl and coil," which describes the contours of the mound.

L. 201: The rhyming binome *lingying* 岭嶸 (*ljeng-ghjweng*) (also read *linghong*) is not otherwise attested. Yan Shigu (see *Han shu* 87A.3534, n. 5) explains it as a descriptive meaning "deep." I have used "deep and steep" to suit this context.

The rhyming binome *linxun* 嶙峋 (*ljen-sgjiwen*) is a variant of *linxun* 鱗朐 (*ljien-sgjiwen*; see *Wen xuan* 2.6a). Yan Shigu (see *Han shu* 87A.3534, n. 5) explains it as descriptive of levels and stages. The basic meaning may be conveyed by *lin*, which may imply overlapping, imbricated (like fishscales). For a brief discussion of the term, see Gao Buying 2.16a.

L. 203: *Zai* 縡 (*tseg*) is a loan for *zai* 載 (*tseg*), "action." Cf. *Mao shi* 235/7: "The actions of high Heaven, / Are without sound, without smell."

L. 204: Commentators do not agree on the meaning of the alliterative binome *xuhu* 旭卉 (*hjuak-hywed*). Yan Shigu (see *Han shu* 87A.3534, n. 6) glosses it as "rapid and swift." Li Shan

In His Black ladle, curved and contoured,
The millet libation fragrantly froths,
Spreading and scattering, rich and full,
Savory and sapid, sweetly scented.
180 The flames stir the yellow dragon;
The blaze rouses the giant unicorn.
He selects Shaman Xian to hail the Lord's gatekeeper,
To open the celestial court and invite the spirit multitudes.

Visitants, thickly thronging, descend on the pure altar;
185 Auspicious omens, profusely abundant, heap into mountains.

X

And then
The service ended, and His merit expanded,
He wheels His chariot and returns,
Crossing Tri-Peak Tower, resting at Pear Palace:
Heaven's threshold is agape, Earth's boundary is open,
190 The Eight Barrens are in harmony, the myriad states are in accord.

He scales Changping and thunder drums rumble;
Their celestial sounds rise forth and brave warriors wax fierce.
Clouds fly and soar, rains swell and surge;
Now all are virtuous, to beautify a myriad ages.

XI

195 The finale:
Tall, so tall, the circular mound,
Arching upward, concealing the sky,
Climbing and plunging, twisting and twining,
Sinuously curls and coils.

Storied palaces, jaggedly jutting,
200 Stand abreast, peaked and pinnacled,
Deep and steep, towering tier upon tier,
Cavernous, without bound.

The actions of high Heaven,
Are mysteriously swift and sudden.

(7.10a) says it is "descriptive of obscurity and darkness." Neither of the graphs offers a clue to the meaning. Hu Shaoying (8.11a) proposes to equate *hui* with *xu* 欻 (*$hjwet$*), "sudden." Zhu Qifeng (see *Ci tong*, p. 2389) equates the binome with *shuhu* 倏忽 (*$hrjuk$-$hwet$*), "sudden," and its variants. The basic sense of the line is that the actions of Heaven are so fleeting, they are mysterious and hard to understand.

L. 209: The rhyming binome *shaoyao* 招搖 (*$djagw$-$zjagw$*) here is a variant of the more common *xiaoyao* 逍遙 (*$dzjagw$-$zjagw$*), "to wander free and easy." See Zhu Qifeng, *Ci tong*, p. 687.

L. 210: On the variant readings of this line, see Gao Buying 7.35a–b. The word represented by *qichi* 迟迟 is *qichi* 棲暹 (*$siei$-$drjiei$*), "to rest and repose." Cf. *Mao shi* 138/1.

LL. 1–2: The text reads *dingwei* 丁未, which is an error for *dinghai* 丁亥 (there was no *dinghai* day in the first month of that year). Both Zang Rongxu's *Jin shu* (cited by Li Shan 7.10b) and the standard history *Jin shu* "Annals of Emperor Wu" (3.56) say this plowing ceremony occurred on *dinghai* of the first month of the fourth year of Taishi 泰始 (19 February 268). A *hai* day, especially a *dinghai* day, was considered a particularly auspicious time for performing the plowing ceremony. In 485, six scholars presented opinions on the question of the *dinghai* day ceremony. See *Nan Qi shu* 9.142–43.

LL. 4–5: On the thousand-acre domain, see "Eastern Metropolis Rhapsody," L. 435n.

L. 6: The Master of the Domain (Dian shi 甸師) is a position described in the *Zhou li* (see *Zhou li zhushu* 4.14b–15a). Its holder was in charge of supervising the subordinate officials at the plowing of the Sacred Field. See Edouard Biot, trans., *Tcheou-Li, Rites des Tcheou*, 3 vols., (1851; rpt. Taipei: Ch'eng Wen Publishing Co., 1969), 1:84. The *Wen xuan* text reads Dian shuai 甸帥 instead of Dian shi. This reading was intended to avoid the taboo on the personal name of the Jin emperor Jing 景, Sima Shi 司馬師.

205 Our Sage Sovereign, solemn and stately,
   Truly is Heaven's compeer.

   Reverently He comes to sacrifice to the bounds;
   He is one on whom the gods rely.
   Wandering and wavering, rambling and roving,
210 The divinities now rest and repose.

   With a bright brilliance glistering and glittering,
   They send down their blessing:
      "Son after son, grandson after grandson,
      Forever, without end."

Rhapsody on the Sacred Field

PAN ANREN

I

It is the fourth year of Jin, the day *dinghai* of the first month, and personally leading his lords, the emperor plows in the thousand-acre domain. This is all in accord with the Rites.

And then He orders
The Master of the Domain to clear the imperial plot,

THIS RHAPSODY by Pan Yue (*zi* Anren) describes the imperial ceremony of plowing the Sacred Field, which grew the grain used for making wine and provided millet and other grains used in the state sacrifices. In the first or second month, the emperor went to the Sacred Field and plowed the first three furrows. He was then followed by the Three Ducal Ministers, who plowed five furrows. Their assistants and other ministers plowed nine furrows, the grandees, twelve, and the commoners finished the field. For further information on this ceremony in the Han, see *HFHD*, 1:281–83; Tjan Tjoe Som, *Po Hu T'ung*, 2:493; Bodde, *Festivals*, pp. 223–41. Pan Yue wrote his rhapsody in honor of the revival of the plowing ceremony by Emperor Wu, founder of the Jin dynasty. This ceremony took place on 19 February 268. On this day, the emperor rode a wooden cart to the field, where he sacrificed a bull, a sheep, and a pig to the First Husbandman, Shennong. He presumably performed the ceremony in the manner described above. See *Song shu* 14.583 and *Jin shu* 19.589. The "Rhapsody on the Sacred Field," which also is contained in *Jin shu* 55.1500–1503, has been previously translated by von Zach, *De Chineesche Revue* 1 (1927) and *Ostasiatische Rundschau* 10 (1929), rpt. in *Die Chinesische Anthologie*, 1:98–102; Obi Kōichi, *Monzen*, I:383–94. The title of this piece as cited in the *Jin shu* of Zang Rongxu is "Ji tian song" 藉田頌 or "Eulogy on the Sacred Field" (Li Shan 7.10b). Since the *song* and *fu* often were considered the same genre, this difference in title is not significant.

L. 7: The Director of Fields and Huts (Ye lu shi 野廬氏) is another *Zhou li* office (see *Zhou li zhushu* 36.18b). Its holder had charge of patrolling the roads and highways of the state as far as the borders of the royal domain. See Biot, 2:376.

L. 8: The Director of Mounds (Feng ren 封人) is a *Zhou li* office (see *Zhou li zhushu* 12.16a) the holder of which had charge of building the earthen walls surrounding the altars of the soil. See Biot, 1:261–62. Zheng Xuan (see *Zhou li zhushu* 12.16a–16b) explains *wei* 壝 as the altar and the low earthen walls. Pan Yue uses *wei* as a verb meaning "to surround with an earthen wall." The *gong* 宮 here is the name of the temporary residence used by the emperor when he was in the field. According to Zheng Xuan (see *Zhou li zhushu* 6.7b), when the emperor spent the night on flat terrain, his attendants built an earthen altar and piled up earth to make a low wall to form his "palace" (*gong*)

L. 9: The Director of Lodges (Zhang she 掌舍) was a *Zhou li* office (see *Zhou li zhushu* 6.7a), the responsibilities of which included erecting the barricades around the temporary camp used by the ruler when he was in the field. See Biot, 1:115.

LL. 10–11: The green and azure ("kingfisher blue") colors are symbolic of spring. The green altar is frequently mentioned in Six Dynasties poetic accounts of the plowing ceremony. Yan Yanzhi's "Poem on the Eastern Plowing" (in *Yiwen leiju* 39.703) says: "Drifting haze rises from the green altar." See also Zhang Zhengjian 張正見 (ob. ca. 575), "In the Entourage at the Sacred Field, Poem Written in Response to Jiao, Prince of Hengyang" (in *Yiwen leiju* 39.702): "Plants shoot up beyond the green altar" (poem three), and Jiang Zong 江總 (519–594), "Rhapsody on the Compensatory Wine" (in *Yiwen leiju* 39.704: "They open the green altar on the far-reaching domain."

L. 15: Cf. "Wei Capital Rhapsody," L. 195.

L. 19: Cf. *Mao shi* 203/1: "The Zhou road is smooth as a whetstone, / Straight as an arrow."

L. 20: According to Li Shan (7.11b), the leek green bullock (*cong jie* 繱犗) was a special ox that drew the imperial plow. The green color of the bullock presumably correlates with the color of spring.

L. 21: According to Bodde (*Festivals*, pp. 228–41), during the Han and several centuries thereafter, the ritual plowing was done with the foot plow. Pan Yue's line clearly indicates that already in the third century, the ox plow was used. The *Jin shu* (25.754) says that for the plowing ceremony, the emperor rode a chariot called the Geng gen ju 耕根車 (the Basic Chariot for Tilling the Fields?). It was an elaborate conveyance, drawn by four horses, covered by a three-tiered canopy, and flying a large scarlet banner and twelve streamers. The plowshare was placed on the crossbar. Citing Shen Yue as its authority, the *Sui shu* (10.209) gives essentially the same description of this chariot. It then comments: "This is what Pan Yue referred to as 'The violet shaft attached to the ebon plowshare.'" According to Shen Yue, who describes a plowing ceremony held in 443 (see *Song shu* 14.354), when the emperor reached the Sacred Field, the palace attendants kneeled and announced, "His Exalted Majesty shall descend from the chariot." As the emperor approached the altar (presumably the green altar), the Grand Minister of Agriculture announced, "The First Husbandman has been feted. May the August Emperor personally till the field." The emperor then plowed three furrows and turned the earth three times.

L. 22: Li Shan (7.11b) understands *jia* as an ellipsis for *jia niu* 駕牛 (harnessed ox). He says that the harnessed ox solemnly awaits the Son of Heaven to walk the field. Because the tilling was for the purpose of gathering stores (*chuchu* 儲畜), Pan Yue calls it the *chu jia* 儲駕 (the harnessed ox that gathers the stores?). Li Shan's explanation does too much violence to the grammar of the line. As Zhu Jian (9.8a–b) rightly shows, *chu* simply means "to assemble." The line thus describes the cortege gathering at the field to await the emperor's arrival. It is also possible to construe *yan* 儼 as a verb meaning "to prepare." Thus, an alternative translation of the line would read: "Coachmen ready the assembled chariots left of the settlement."

40

The Director of Fields and Huts to clear the roads,
The Director of Mounds to wall the palace,
The Director of Lodges to install the barricades.
10 The green altar, luxuriant, stands like a mountain peak;
The azure curtains, dark, spread like clouds.
They set the sacred site on its lofty foundation,
Place a broad receiving staircase opening to the four avenues.

The fecund fields are fat and rich;
15 The fertile soil is whetstone smooth.
Through turbid canals from the limpid Luo
They divert the flow and impel the waters.
Distant pathways are straight as marking lines;
Nearby walkways are straight as arrows.
20 A leek green bullock is hitched to a pale blue yoke;
A violet shaft is attached to an ebon plowshare.
Coachmen solemnly assemble the chariots left of the settlement,
Where they await the emperor personally to walk the field.

The centurial officers are placed first,
25 Positioned according to rank.

L. 26: This line is drawn verbatim from *Zhou yi zhushu* 4.30a (Hexagram 42, "Commentary on the Decision").

L. 27: Cf. "Eastern Metropolis Rhapsody," L. 259.

L. 29: The *you ju* (游車 or 斿車), or "excursion chariot," was a wooden chariot used for hunts and tours of the frontier There reputedly were nine of these chariots in the imperial procession. See *Zhou li zhushu* 27.17b, Zheng Xuan's commentary: *Guo yu* 6.2a, Wei Zhao's commentary; *Hou Han shu*, "Zhi," 29.3649; *Jin shu* 25.755. Cf. "Eastern Metropolis Rhapsody," L. 376n.

L. 32: Cf. *Mao shi* 238/2: "In holding their scepters they are stately and grand."

L 34: Cf. *Mao shi* 178/1: "Moist, moist is the dew; / Without the sun it will not dry." Li Shan (7.12a) explains that this is a metaphor for the lords' obedience and respect for the emperor. Like the morning dew that is subject to the morning sun, they comply with the ruler's commands and extend to him their reverence.

L. 35: Cf. *Lun yu* 2/1: "Governing by means of virtue may be compared to the northern pole star, which abides in its place while the various stars pay it homage."

L. 36: Cf. "Eastern Metropolis Rhapsody," L. 525n.

L. 38: The Changhe Gate was located on the north end of the western wall of Luoyang. See *Shuijing zhu* 3.16.74.

L. 39: Cf. "Western Capital Rhapsody," LL. 46–47n and "Western Metropolis Rhapsody," L. 314.

L. 40: The Permanent Chief (Chang bo 常伯) is an archaic name for the Palace Attendant (Shi zhong 侍中). He had charge of ceremonial functions. When the Grand Cortege left the palace on a tour, the Regular Palace Attendant carried the imperial seals and served as carriage attendant.

L. 41: The Grand Coachman (Tai pu 太僕) drove the imperial chariot. See *Hou Han shu*, "Zhi," 25.3581.

L. 42: According to Zheng Zhong (see *Zhou li zhushu* 7.18b), *tong* 穜 is the name of a grain that is planted early, but ripens late, and the *lu* 稑 (also written 穋) refers to grain that is planted late but ripens early. The *Zhou li* (see *Zhou li zhushu* 7.18a) says that at the beginning of spring, the empress leads the ladies of the palace to present seeds of these grains to the kind. See Biot, 1:148.

L 43: The Grand Minister of Agriculture was in charge of overseeing the Sacred Field. See *Jin shu* 24.737.

L. 44: The Holder of Vases (Qie hu shi 挈壺氏) is a *Zhou li* office (see *Zhou li zhushu* 30.15a), the responsibilities of which included holding vases of water to indicate the location of wells for military camps. The same officer held reins to mark the location of bivouacs and held baskets to mark the storehouses. See Biot, 2:201–2. The *Zhou li* says nothing about the Holder of Vases organizing the order of march (literally "the timing of the ascent and descent").

L. 45: The Regulator of the Palace (Gong zheng 宮正) is another *Zhou li* office (see *Zhou li zhushu* 3.18a–22a). One of its functions was to clear the way for the king when he left the palace. See Biot, 1:64–70.

L. 46: Cf. "Preface to the *Wen xuan*," L. 17n and "Western Capital Rhapsody," L. 397n.

L. 47: Cf. "Sweet Springs Palace Rhapsody," L. 28n.

L. 48: The *chongya* 衝牙 is one of the six ornamental pieces that hung from the top-piece (*heng* 衡) of a jade girdle pendant. It occupied the lower-center of the pendant. See Laufer, *Jade*, pp. 197–98, 206, 208.

L. 50: The Gilded Root (Jin gen 金根) is the name of a special chariot decorated with gold. It was drawn by four horses. See *Hou Han shu*, "Zhi," 29.3643–44; *Jin shu* 25.754. The meaning of the word *gen* ("root") is not clear. The chariot perhaps was constructed of a special auspicious wood. The Han dynasty apocryphon *Xiao jing yuan shen qi* (cited in *Yiwen leiju* 71.1235) mentions

From above down to those below,
All are titled lords.
Garbed in the sumptuous splendor of spring vestments,
They greet the rumbling and rattling of the excursion chariots.
30   A gentle breeze stirs within the light carriage curtains;
Fine dust rises from the vermilion wheels.
Thickly thronged, holding their scepters, they line up by rank;
Gazing at the imperial carriage, they quake with awe.
They are as the soaking dew dried by the morning sun,
35   Like the panoply of stars paying homage to the northern polestar.

II

And then
The vanguard lines up in fish-file;
The retinue chariots gather like scales.
The Changhe Gate opens cavernously;
On triple lanes quadrigae run side by side.
40   The Permanent Chief attends the chariot;
The Grand Coachman holds the reins.
The empress and consorts present the early and late ripening seeds;
The Minister of Agriculture prepares the sowing and planting tools.
The Holder of Vases determines the order of march;
45   The Regulator of the Palace directs the clearing of the gates and
            doors.

The Son of Heaven then
Mounts the Jade Carriage,
Shaded by a Floriate Canopy.
The pendent jades jingle and jangle;
The white silks rustle and swish.
50   The Gilded Root shines and glitters with a fiery glow;

a Root Chariot that was made from an auspicious tree that appeared in the mountains in response to a virtuous emperor.

L. 51: Cf. "Eastern Metropolis Rhapsody," L. 353. The rhyming binome *peiai* 沛艾 (**pwad-ngad*) first appears in Sima Xiangru's "Great Man Rhapsody" (*Shi ji* 117.3057; *Han shu* 57B.2593), where it is used to describe the "proud prancing" of the dragon-chargers that carry the Great Man on his celestial voyage. It probably is a variant for *po'e* 駊騀 (**phwa-nga*). See "Sweet Springs Palace Rhapsody," L. 56n.

LL. 52–53: In Chinese correlative thought, vermilion, black, green, and white are the colors of the south, north, east, and west respectively. To designate the directions, Pan Yue uses the names of the trigrams that correspond to the various directions: *Li* 離 (south), *Kan* 坎 (north), *Zhen* 震 (east), and *Dui* 兌 (west). Pan describes here the banners and chariots that correspond to the various directions. See "Eastern Metropolis Rhapsody," L. 364n.

L. 54: Yellow is the color of the center and earth. The *Jin shu* reads *hui* 輝 for *hui* 揮 of the *Wen xuan*. Zhu Jian (9.9a), who prefers the *Wen xuan* reading, explains *fa hui* 發揮 as describing the flying and waving of the banners.

L. 55: The *Chuci* poem, "Grand Unity, August One of the East" (see *Chuci buzhu* 2.3a) has a similar line: "The five notes gaily and richly blend."

L. 56: The five chariots are the five types of chariots mentioned in the *Zhou li* (see *Zhou li zhushu* 27 1b–5a). They include the Jade Chariot, Gilded Chariot, Ivory Chariot, Leather Chariot, and Wood Chariot. See also *Jin shu* 15.753–54; *Song shu* 18.494.

L. 57: The nine banners are the nine types of banners mentioned in the *Zhou li* (see *Zhou li zhushu* 27.16a). The banners were distinguished by their respective designs and component materials.

L. 58: The graph *se* 鈒 (**srjep*), which is a variant of *xi* 鍤 (**hjep*), is a type of halberd (see *Shuowen* 14A.6391). According to Xue Zong (cited in *Hou Han shu*, "Zhi," 29.3649, n. 2), four halberds were carried on the sides of the chariot. The *Jin shu* (25.758) mentions the Halberd Chariot (Xi ji ju 鍤戟車), which carries a long halberd tilted rearward.

L. 59: On the cloud-net cart, see "Eastern Metropolis Rhapsody," L. 376n. Shen Yue (see *Song shu* 18.499–500), who cites Pan Yue's line, rejects the explanation of the cloud-net as a type of banner. He speculates that originally the net (*han* 罕) was carried in a hunting cart. Later, it served only as an ornament.

LL. 62–63: Cf. "Western Metropolis Rhapsody," LL. 122–25 and note.

L. 67: On the Cicada Caps, see "Wei Capital Rhapsody," L. 228n.

L. 68: Lu Xiang (7.19a) claims that the *bi* 碧 refers to the jade carried by the officials. Gao Buying (7.44a) argues that carrying jade was not part of the plowing ceremony. However, he does not offer any explanation of its function here. Jin Sheng 金牲 (cited by Gao Buying 7.44a) says the *bi* (prase or blue) color refers to the color of the spring vestments. Pan Yue may have borrowed from the "Rhapsody on the Gaotang Terrace" (*Wen xuan* 19.4b): "Gaze upward at the mountain tops—how majestic their verdant luxuriance!"

L. 69: The famous jade of Bian He was cut from an uncarved jade found in the mountains of Chu (Jing). See *Hanfeizi jishi* 4.238.

L. 73: The term *zhi shang* 坻塲 is a general term for ant hill or molehill. See Dai Zhen, *Fangyan shuzheng*, 6.5b–6a.

L. 75: Scholars have interpreted *san tui* 三推 in two different ways. According to the most common interpretation, *tui* means "to plow a furrow." See Legge, *Li chi*, 1:255; *HFHD*, 1:283; Tjan, *Po Hu T'ung*, 2:493. However, Bodde (see *Festivals*, p. 238) has argued that *tui* means "to push the plow." Thus, *san tui* may mean "to push the plow three times." Since the plowing ceremony Pan Yue describes was done with an ox plow (see LL. 21–22 above), I assume that in this line, *san tui* means "to plow three furrows."

LL. 77–78: These lines refer to the classical form of the plowing ceremony stipulated in the

Dragon chargers, leaping and bounding, proudly prance.
They display the vermilion and black in the south and north,
Fly the green and white in the east and west.
The center-yellow resplendently issues forth its brilliance;
55 All the directional colors gaily and richly blend.
The five chariots sound their simurgh bells;
The nine banners fly their pennons.
Carnelian halberds are closely clustered;
Cloud-nets gather dark and dense.
60 Pipes and flutes toot and skirl;
Drums and tabors rattle and rumble.
Bell frames hang in the air poised for flight.
The great bell resounds beyond the mortal realm.

With a tumultuous tremor, a droning din,
65 And dust soaring and merging into the sky,
The emperor visits the sacred field.
The Cicada Caps glisten bright and brilliant,
Their prase-colored hues—how majestic their verdant luxuriance!
They resemble the night-glower cut from the Jing jade;
70 Are like lush pines resting on mountain tops.

III

And then our August Emperor
Descends from the sacred altar,
And grasps the imperial plow.
Molehills stain his slippers;
The great rein is in his hands.
75 After three furrows he stops;
The common people finish the acres.
Superior and inferior appear by rank,
Some make five furrows, some make nine.

At this time
Domiciles have no distinction between capital and frontier,

"Monthly Ordinances" (see *Li ji zhushu* 14.20a) in which after the emperor has made three furrows, the dukes (or ducal ministers) plow five furrows, and the ministers and lords plow nine furrows.

L. 82: Li Shan (7.14a) explains the binome *banbin* 頒斌 (**puan-pjen*) as "intermingled." It clearly is the same as *binbin* of Sima Xiangru's "Rhapsody on the Imperial Park" (see L. 196n). Just as it describes the mingling and blending of colors and patterns in stones, Pan Yue uses it to describe the "massing and merging" of people who attend the ceremony.

L. 89: There are two ways to punctuate this line, one with a stop after *yin* 音 (sounds), and the other with a stop after *guanzhe* 觀者 (spectators). I have followed the latter alternative, which is the punctuation used in the Zhonghua shuju edition of the *Jin shu* (55.1501). The rhyming binome *dongrong* 動容 (**dung-zjung*) conveys the sense of agitation and excitement. See *Ci tong*, p. 1122. Here I have rendered it "all atingle."

L. 92: Cf. "Western Metropolis Rhapsody," L. 343.

L. 96: Cf. *Zhou yi zhushu* 6.9b (Hexagram 58, "Commentary on the Decision"): "Joyously lead the people, and the people forget their toil."

L. 100: Cf. *Zhou yi zhushu* 4.27a (Hexagram 41, "Commentary on the Decision"): Decrease and increase, fullness and emptiness, they move together with time."

L. 102: Cf. *Laozi* 39: "The noble deems the mean as its root, and the high deems the low as its base."

L. 103: Pan Yue borrows a phrase from a speech by Li Yiji (see *Shi ji* 97.2694): "The king considers the people as his Heaven, and the people consider food as their Heaven."

LL. 104–5: The root and primary are agriculture and food. The branches and secondary refer to commerce. Cf. an edict of Emperor Wen of the Former Han: "Agriculture is the great root of the empire and is that upon which the people depend in order to live. Yet, some of the people do not devote themselves to the root but attend to the branches. Thus, the full span of their lives is not completed" (*Han shu* 4.118).

L. 107: The *Jin shu* reads *ye* 業 (profession) for *Wen xuan*'s *ren* 人 (people).

L. 108: Cf. *Li ji zhushu* 12.18b: "For three years' tilling there must be one year's surplus food. For nine years' tilling, there must be three years' surplus food.... Though there be baneful droughts and river floods, the people will not have famished expressions."

L. 109: Cf. *Li ji zhushu* 11.5b: "The lesser officers of the feudal lords were viewed as equal to a farmer of the highest degree Their salary was sufficient to replace earnings from tilling."

L. 111: The *Five Commentaries* reads *bi* 畢 (end) for You Mao *bi* 必 (certain) The expression *zi bi* 自必 is ambiguous. Li Shan (7.15a) seems to construe the line as an inversion: "Vainly does one confidently (*zi bi*) look forward to the harvest." Von Zach (*Die Chinesische Anthologie*, 1:101) reads it in almost the same way: "wie konnte man getrost (mit Selbstvertrauen; Legge 1:217) der bevorstehenden Ernte entgegenschen (Legge 5:739/2)?"

80   And the people do not distinguish between central plain and
              outland.
    Elders and youths, closely clustered, congregate;
    Gentlemen and ladies, massing and merging, all arrive.
    Dressed in homespun, shaking off their skirts,
    With hanging locks and bundled topknots,
85   They follow heel to toe, press shoulder to shoulder,
    Tug on each other's gowns, join sleeve to sleeve.
    They cause yellow dust to gather in all directions,
    And cause the bright sun to be hidden and veiled.
    The spectators, all atingle, uttering exclamations:
90   None fails to clap his hands and dance on the broad thoroughfares,
    Or sing and chant in praise of this sagacious reign.
    Their hearts happy and joyful in this toilsome labor,
    And they fervently desire to work hard at planting and seeding.
    Though no one oversees them, ever are they diligent;
95   No one exhorts them, for they inspire themselves.
    When the emperor personally leads them in toil, they are happy to
              work;
    Why control them harshly with stern punishments?

IV

    There are village elders and farmers.
    Some step forward and say:
100   "We opine that decrease and increase follow time;
    By virtue of the natural order this has always been so.
    The high takes the low as its base;
    The people take food as their Heaven.
    He who would rectify the branches first straightens the root;
105   He who would manage well the secondary first cares for the primary

    If the appropriate tributes of the nine lands are not supplied,
    The four professions will not concentrate on their work.
    If in the countryside there are famished expressions,
    The court will have no salary in lieu of working the fields.
110   If food is not stored in anticipation of calamity,
    How can one look for a good harvest with such self-confidence?
    The fall of the last rulers of the Three Dynasties
    Was entirely due to a neglect of these things.

L. 114: Cf. "Eastern Metropolis Rhapsody," L. 734.

L. 115: Cf. *Zhou yi zhushu* 1 3b (Hexagram 1, 9/3): "The gentleman all day is active and creative. At dusk he trembles with apprehension." He is apprehensive because he fears some task remains unfinished, or that some unexpected disaster might occur.

LL. 118–19: These lines are derived from an almost identical passage in the "Canon of Shun" (*Shang shu zhushu* 3.14a; Legge 3:39): "Be reverent! Be reverent! It is the punishments that should concern you "

L. 120: The three seasons are the three agricultural seasons of spring, summer, and autumn.

L. 122: Cf. Dong Zhongshu's "examination reply" (in *Han shu* 56.2412): "Your Majesty personally plows the Sacred Field and thereby shows the primacy of agriculture. He awakens early, arises at dawn, worries about overworking the people, thinks and ponders the ancient past, and ardently seeks for worthy men. Such is the devotion of a Yao or Shun."

L. 126: The *fu* 簠 is a rectangular bronze or wooden vessel; the *gui* 簋 was round. See Li Xueqin 李學勤, *The Wonder of Chinese Bronzes* (Beijing: Foreign Languages Press, 1980), pp. 11–13. The term *pu nao* 普淖 ("universal concord") is a kenning for millet. See *Yi li zhushu* 43.5a.

L. 128: Here *chang* 鬯 must be the name of the aromatic wine used in the sacrifices. See "Sweet Springs Palace Rhapsody," LL. 176–77n. The *Zhou li* (see *Zhou li zhushu* 4.15b) commentary of the grandee Zheng (Zheng Xing 鄭興, fl. A.D. 15–35) says that *xiao* 蕭 (*sjoh*) is sometimes written *suo* 茜 (*sr-*), which is read *suo* 縮 (*sr-*), "to strain wine through rushes." He explains that bundled rushes were placed in front of the offering, and wine was poured over it. "The wine seeped through it as if the spirits were drinking it." Du Zichun (see *Zhou li zhushu* 4.15b) says the reading *xiao* refers to a perennial plant (*Anapholis yedoensis*) that was suffused into the fat of the victim and mixed with millet to produce a strong odor. I am not sure how Pan Yue construed the term. For the sake of parallelism with *suo chang* ("filtered blend"), I have construed *xiao* in the sense of "to strain."

L. 129: Cf. the *Guo yu* (1.6b) description of the Sacred Field: "The sacrificial grain from it is produced."

LL. 130–33: Pan Yue borrows from *Zuozhuan, Huan* 6 (Legge 5:49), in which Ji Liang 季梁 explains the significance of the various types of sacrificial offerings: "In presenting the vessels of millet, (the sage kings) announced them as 'clean millet and abundant grain'. This meant that the three seasonal crops were not harmed, the people were concordant, and the harvest abundant. In presenting the wine and spirits, they announced them as 'fine wine of splendid solemnity'. This meant that both superior and inferior had excellent virtue and were without contrary minds. What was called the sweet fragrance meant there was no slander or evil.... Therefore, the people were harmonious and the spirits sent down to them blessings."

LL 135–38: Pan Yue alludes to *Xiao jing*, chapter 9 (see *Xiao jing zhushu* 5.1a): "Zengzi said, 'I venture to ask: Of the virtues of the sage, is there anything that surpasses filial piety?' The Master said, 'Of the natural endowments of Heaven and Earth, man is the most exalted. Of the acts of man, none is greater than filial piety.... Of the virtues of the sage, what could surpass filial piety?'"

L. 139: Cf. *Xiao jing*, chapter 8 (see *Xiao jing zhushu* 4.1a).

L. 140: Cf *Lun yu* 2/23: "Some of those who continue after the Zhou can be known even a hundred ages later."

L. 143: "This way" is the way of filial piety.

L. 144: Cf. *Mao shi* 235/7: "Make King Wen your example and pattern, / And the myriad states will put their trust in you."

L. 145: Cf. *Xiao jing*, chapter 2 (see *Xiao jing zhushu* 1.4b): "If love and respect are completely given in serving the parents, one's virtuous teachings will be extended to the common people."

Our present sage sovereign
At early dawn is greatly illustrious,
115 But at dusk he trembles with apprehension.
In the midst of plenty he plans for deficiency,
And in the midst of comfort he guards against shortage.
Oh reverent, reverent He is;
It is the grain that concerns Him!
120 He encourages the great tasks of the three seasons,
Brings the granaries and silos to overflowing fullness.
Truly this is the devotion of a Yao or Shun,
And is the essential method of preserving and aiding the people."

V

Now
At the ancestral temple there is a sacrificial service;
125 The invocator and master of rites reckon the day.
The vessels with the grain of universal concord,
From this sacred field are filled.
The filtered blend and the straining rushes,
Also are from it produced.
130 The sweet fragrance of the millet,
The splendid solemnity of the fine wine,
Befitting the concord of the people and the success of the harvest,
They are the blessings sent down by the spirits.

The ancients have a saying,
135 "Of the virtues of the sage,
Is there anything that surpasses filial piety?"
Filial piety is a natural endowment of Heaven and Earth,
And is what gives man his spiritual efficacy.
Anciently, the enlightened kings governed the empire by means of
filial piety,
140 But those who continued after them,
Few and rare indeed!

Now our august Jin emperor
Truly has illumined this way.
His example and pattern are trusted by the myriad states;
145 Love and reverence He completely gives to the ancestors.

L. 146: Cf. *Li ji zhushu* 49.3b: "The Son of Heaven personally tills in the southern suburbs in order to supply the sacrificial grain."

L. 147: Li Shan (7.16a) cites a lost work, the *Wu jing yao yi* 五經要義. (The Essential Meaning of the Five Classics), which says: "When the Son of Heaven plows the thousand acres of the Sacred Field, in this way he gives precedence to the common people and practices filial piety and reverence."

L. 149: Cf. *Shang shu zhushu* 7.5b (Legge 3:158): "The people are the roots of the state. When the roots are solid, the state is at peace."

L. 153: The two excellent results are "solidifying the roots and practicing filial piety."

LL. 154–55: Cf. *Lun yu* 8/7: "(The Gentleman) takes benevolence as his burden. Is it not heavy? Only with death does his path cease. Is it not heavy?"

LL. 157–58: Cf. *Mao shi* 299/1: "Oh, joyful the waters of Pan, / Here we gather its celery."

The *Jin shu* reads *fang* 芳 (fragrance) for the *mao* 茅 (rushes) of the *Wen xuan* text. Although some scholars have claimed that since *mao* (*mau) cannot rhyme with *nong* 農 (*nong), *fang* (*pjang) must be the correct reading. However, Zhu Jian (9.9b–10a) has shown that *mao* (which has a variant reading *mong) can rhyme with *nong*. On the other hand, Xu Sunxing (2.10b–11a) notes the reading *nau for *nong*. Thus, however one reads *nong* and *mao*, the lines rhyme, and there is no need to emend the text. The rushes are used for filtering wine. See L. 129n above.

L. 162: Cf. *Li ji zhushu* 39.14a: "(The emperor) tills the Sacred Field, and then the lords know the means of paying reverence."

LL. 163–64: The *Jin shu* reads *sui* 遂 (to complete) for *shi* 實 (fruits) of the *Wen xuan* text. Cf. *Mao shi* 212/3: "It rains on our Public Field, / Then it reaches our private plots."

LL. 165–66: How Pan Yue construes *zi* 齊 (variant *zi* 粢 or *zi* 齋) and *cheng* 盛 in these lines is not entirely clear. Zheng Xuan variously explains *zi* as millet or any of the five grains used as oblation in a sacrifice. See *Zhou li zhushu* 4.15a, 19.14a, 16.22a, 19.4a, 25.10a. *Cheng* is the name for the sacrificial grain in a vessel. As Duan Yucai shows (see *Shuowen* 5A.2121b), both terms are used singularly or together to refer to sacrificial grain. Thus, I have rendered *cheng* and *zi* respectively as "heaping oblations" and "sacrificial grains." The grain vessels mentioned here are the *fu* (my "paten") and *gui* (my "urn") mentioned in L. 126n above.

LL. 167–68: Cf. *Mao shi* 211/4: "The stacks of the descendent, / Are like islands, like hills." Cf. "Wei Capital Rhapsody," L. 482n.

L. 169: This line is cited verbatim from the "Counsels of the Great Yu" (*Shang shu zhushu* 4.6a; Legge 3:58), where it occurs in a speech by the Great Yu: "Oh, Lord, think of him. Think of this man here!"

L. 170: This line is drawn from *Mao shi* 243/3, where it is used to praise the Zhou king: "Ever does he think filial thoughts."

LL. 171–72: Cf. *Zuozhuan, Huan* 6 (Legge 5:48): Ji Liang said, "When the ruler on high thinks of benefitting the people, that is devotion. When the invocators' words are correct, that is faithfulness.... When (the ancient sages) offered their victims, they announced them as 'large, big, fat, and plump' This referred to the people's strength being everywhere preserved."

L. 174: This line is borrowed from *Mao shi* 186/3, where it is used in a *carpe diem* poem: "Be a duke, be a lord! / Enjoy yourself without end!" Gao Buying (7.51a) notes Pan Yue's inappropriate use of the line.

LL. 175–76: These lines are cited verbatim from the "Punishments of Lu" (*Shang shu zhushu* 25a; Legge 3:600). On the use of *lai* 賴 in the sense of "to benefit from," see Karlgren, "Glosses on the Book of Documents," p. 184, #2052.

Thus, personally tilling the land to supply the sacrificial grain is a means of practicing filial piety. Encouraging agriculture to bring sufficiency to the common people is a means of solidifying the roots. If the ruler is able to solidify the roots and practice filial piety, his splendid virtue and great deeds will be perfect indeed! This is but a single task, yet two excellent results are obtained. Is not the path long? Is not the burden heavy?

VI

I presume to compose the following eulogy:
Oh, joyful the imperial domain!
Here we gather the rushes.
The great lord arrives;
160 Now he plows his tilth.

His tilth is thrice furrowed,
And the myriad regions are thereby reverent.
He hoes our Public Field,
Its fruits extend to the private plots.
165 In our patens, heaping oblations;
In our urns, the sacrificial grain.
Our granaries are like hills,
Our stacks are like islands.

Oh, think on these things here!
170 May we ever think filial thoughts.
The people's strength is everywhere preserved,
And the invocators utter the correct words.
The gods and spirits are pleased with the offerings,
And our joy and ease shall last without end.
175 If the One Man has felicity,
The myriad people shall benefit from it.

L. 20: The area referred to here perhaps is the broad salt flat and marsh known as Haiyu 海隅. Located on the northern Shandong coast, Haiyu was one of the ten great preserves of the empire, which also included Yunmeng. See *Erya* B2.5a–b, Hao Yixing's commentary.

L. 23: The *mi* 麋 is the elaphure (Père David's deer). See Edward H. Schafer, "Cultural History of the Elaphure," *Sinologica* 4 (1956) : 250–74. Although *lin* 麟 often refers to a mythical one-horned animal usually identified as the unicorn, here it probably is the name of a large male deer. See *Shuowen* 10A.4360a–b; Lu Ji, *Mao shi caomu* B.49; *Erya yishu* C6.8a; Zhu Jian 9.10b–11a; Hu Shaoying 9.1b–2a.

L. 25: This line may also be rendered: "They carve the fresh meat and soak it on the wheels" (which are covered with salt). See Hu Shaoying 9.2a; Zhu Jian 9.11a–b; Gao Buying 7.55a–b; Hervouet, *Le Chapitre 117 du Che ki*, p. 13, n. 5.

Rhapsody of Sir Vacuous

SIMA ZHANGQING   Commentary by Guo Pu

I

When Chu sent Sir Vacuous as an envoy to Qi, the king of Qi mobilized all of his chariots and horsemen and went out to hunt with the envoy. When the hunt was finished, Sir Vacuous went over to boast to Master Improbable. Lord No-such was also present. After everyone was seated, Master Improbable asked, "Was today's hunt enjoyable?" Sir Vacuous replied, "Quite enjoyable." "Was your catch large?" He said, "It was small." "If this is so, then what did you enjoy about it?" Sir Vacuous replied, "I enjoyed the King of Qi's attempt to brag about his multitude of chariots and horsemen, while I replied to him with an account of our Yunmeng Preserve." Master Improbable said, "May I be permitted to hear it?" Sir Vacuous said, "You may."

"The King of Qi
With a cortege of chariots a thousand strong,
And choice entourage of a myriad horsemen,
Hunts on the strands of the sea:
20   Serried troops fill the marshes,
Snares and nets overspread the hills;
Netting hares, overrunning deer,
Shooting elaphures, hobbling stags,
They gallop over saline shores,
25   The fresh-carved kill staining the wheels.

THIS RHAPSODY by Sima Xiangru (*zi* Zhangqing) is an elaborate description of the huge Yunmeng hunting park in the old southern state of Chu. Sima Xiangru wrote this piece around 150 B.C. while he was residing at the court of Liu Wu, King of Liang. Later, around 137 B.C., Emperor Wu happened to read a copy of this rhapsody, and was so impressed he immediately summoned Sima to an audience. At the audience, Sima Xiangru offered to write a sequel in which he would describe the "excursions and hunts of the Son of Heaven." This piece is the

LL. 47–48: The Yunmeng marsh extended from modern Yiyang 益陽 (Hunan, south of Dongting Lake) in the south, north to Jiangling 江陵 and Anlu 安陸 (Hubei), and east to Wuhan. As Hervouet points out (see *Le Chapitre 117 du Che-ki*, p. 14, n. 2), the nine hundred-*li* size is an exaggeration. The marsh was closer to three hundred *li* square. For a detailed account of Yunmeng, see Hervouet, *Un Poète de cour*, pp. 245–54.

L 50: Guo Pu (cited in *Han shu* 57A.2536, n. 2) explains the rhyming binome *foyu* 岪鬱 (**bjet-ˈjwet*) as winding and twisting. The signific probably is *fo*, which has the sense of twisting. See *Chuci buzhu* 3 2b. I have rendered it "tortuously turning."

L. 51: The rhyming binome *luzu* 嶵崒 (**ljwet-dzwet*) describes precipitous heights. The signific may be *zu*, which the *Shuowen* (9B.4098a–b) glosses as "precipitously high." I have rendered it "precipitously piled."

L 52: The rhyming binome *cenyin* 岑崟 (**tshjem-ngjem*) and its variants (see Zhu Qifeng, *Ci tong*, p. 1085) describe steep heights. I have derived my "peaked and pointed" from Wang Yi's gloss on *yin* in *Chuci buzhu* 16.4b.

Arrows on target, the catch abundant, prideful, he congratulated himself. Looking over, he asked me, 'Does Chu also have level plains, broad marshes, and areas for excursions and hunts, which are as rich in pleasure as this? How would you compare the hunts of the King of Chu with mine?'

I dismounted my chariot and replied, 'I am a humble man from the state of Chu. I have been fortunate enough to serve as palace guard for over ten years. From time to time I have accompanied the King on his excursions as he roamed in his posterior park, and I caught a glimpse of what it contains. Even so I still have not seen it all. How then am I worthy to speak about the farther marshes?' "

The King of Qi said, 'Nevertheless, tell me roughly what you have seen and heard.'

I replied, 'Very well, very well. I have heard that Chu has seven marshes, but I have seen only one of them, and I have never seen the others. What I have seen is a only the very smallest of them. Its name is Yunmeng. Yunmeng is nine hundred *li* square. At its center are mountains.

50   The mountains:
Twisting and twining, tortuously turning,
Arch aloft, precipitously piled.

"Rhapsody on the Imperial Park," which follows "Rhapsody of Sir Vacuous" in the *Wen xuan*. The text of the "Rhapsody of Sir Vacuous" is also found in the *Shi ji* (117.3002–15) and *Han shu* (57A.2534–45). There are significant differences between the two texts, and the *Wen xuan* text selects from both versions. Technically, the "Rhapsody of Sir Vacuous" and "Rhapsody on the Imperial Park" form a single *fu*, and many scholars have criticized Xiao Tong for dividing the piece into two parts (see Gao Buying 7.52a–b for a summary of various opinions). The piece has been previously translated by von Zach, in *De Chineesche Revue* 2 (1928) and *Ostasiatische Rundschau* 10 (1929), rpt. in *Die Chinesische Anthologie*, 1:103–7; Watson, *Records*, 2:301–7; rpt. in *Chinese Rhyme-Prose*, pp. 30–37; Hervouet, *Le Chapitre 117 du Che-ki*, pp. 11–54; Obi Kōichi, *Monzen* 1:394–408. Hervouet's translation is copiously annotated and should be consulted for more detailed explanations of many of the terms in this notoriously difficult poem. My notes are intended as a supplement to Hervouet's monumental work. I also have consulted the notes in *Liang Han wenxueshi cankao ziliao*, pp. 27–40 and Shi Zhimian 施之勉, "*Shi ji* Sima Xiangru liezhuan jiaozhu" 史記司馬相如列傳校注 Part 1, *Dalu zazhi* 56.1 (1978):10–25; Part 2, *Dalu zazhi* 56.2 (1978):82–97; Pei Jinnan 裴晉南 *et al.*, eds. and comm. *Han Wei Liuchao fu xuan zhu* 漢魏六朝賦選注 (Shanghai: Guji chubanshe, 1983), pp. 17–30.

Guo Pu's commentary contains the most informative glosses on the difficult words of the "Rhapsody of Sir Vacuous" and the "Rhapsody on the Imperial Park." The *Sui shu* (35.1083) says that a one-*juan* text of this commentary, which existed in the Liang dynasty, was lost. However, the commentary must have survived in some form into the early Tang, for both Li Shan and the *Han shu* commentator, Yan Shigu, cite it. As Gao Buying (7.52b) points out, Li Shan does not cite the entire Guo Pu commentary, but rather in many places substitutes other commentary, notably that of Zhang Yi 張揖 (fl. 227–233) and Sima Biao 司馬彪 (ob. 306).

L. 56: The rhyming binomes *pituo* 龍池 (*bjai-da) and *potuo* 陂陀 (*pjai-da) probably are variants of the same word, which means "slanting and sloping." See Yan Shigu, *Kuang miu zheng su* 5.

L. 57: Or: "Below they join the rivers and streams."

L. 58: According to Zhang Yi (see *Shi ji* 117.3005, n. 4), the Shaoshi 少室 Mountains (north of modern Dengfeng 鄧封 *xian*, Henan) were the primary source of ochre (*zhe* 赭), also known as "red earth." The white clay (*e* 堊), also known as *bai e* 白堊, is the famous Chinese kaolin. See Read and Pak, p. 37, #57d.

L. 59: On *cihuang* 雌黃 (orpiment), see Read and Pak, pp. 32–33, #50; Edward H Schafer, "Orpiment and Realgar in Chinese Technology and Tradition," *JAOS* 75.2 (1955): 73–78. The milky quartz (*bai fu* 白坿), also known as *bai shi ying* 白石英, was a mineral commonly found in the Luyang 魯陽 Mountains (near modern Lushan 魯山 *xian*, Henan). See Zhang Yi, *Shi ji* 117.3005, n. 6; Read and Pak, p. 25, #40.

L. 63: The *meigui* 玫瑰 can refer to several different stones, including the ruby, mica, or the fire-regulating pearl (see "Western Capital Rhapsody," L. 195n). See Read and Pak, pp. 20–21, #35a; p 23, 37a; pp. 24–25, #39 I have invented the name rose stone for it, simply to match with red jade.

L. 64: Kunwu 昆吾 (also written 琨珸) is the name of a famous volcano that produced copper and gold. See Zhang Heng's "Rhapsody on Pondering the Mystery," *Wen xuan* 15.7a; *Hou Han shu* 59.1921. Sima Zhen (see *Shi ji* 117.3005, n. 10) cites a "River Diagram" text that mentions a Kunwu stone from Liuzhou 流州 (or 洲), an island of the Western Sea. It was used for making swords. I have freely rendered Kunwu as "vulcan stone."

Since it is parallel with Kunwu, *linmin* 琳珉 (*min* also written 瑉) probably is a binome here. (Cf. "Western Capital Rhapsody," L. 203n where the word is divided into two elements.) It probably was a pearl-shaped jade (see Hu Shaoying 9.2b–3a); hence, my "orbed jades."

L. 65: *Jianle* 瑊玏 is a variant of *jianle* 玪䤵, which the *Shuowen* (1A.174b–175a) glosses as a stone inferior to jade. The element *jian* possibly means "pointed" or "needle"; thus, my invention, "aculith."

On the *li* 厲 polishing stone, see *Shuowen* 9B.4162a–63a.

L. 66: On the *ruan shi* 礝石 (quartz), see "Western Capital Rhapsody," L. 202n.

"Warrior rock" is my invention for *wufu* 碔砆, a mineral found in Changsha. It is described as having white streaks on a red background. See *Han shu* 57A.2536, n. 10, Zhang Yi's commentary; *Shanhai jing* 1.7a, Guo Pu's commentary. Hervouet (see *Le Chapitre 117 du Che ki*, p. 18, n. 13) speculates it may be flaming opal.

L. 67: I do not know whether Hui pu 蕙圃 is a proper noun or simply should be understood as herb garden. See Hu Shaoying 9.17a–b.

L. 68: Zhang Yi (cited by Li Shan 7.19a) equates *heng* with *duheng* 杜衡, which is wild ginger (*Asarum forbesii*). This perennial woodland plant has large, heart-shaped leaves leaves, and a strong odor. See Zhu Jian 9.12a; Smith-Stuart, pp. 54–55; *Zhongguo gaodeng zhiwu tujian*, 1:542.

Zhi is *bai zhi* 白芷 (see *Shi ji* 117.3006, n. 14), *Angelica anomola* (angelica). This perennial plant with triangular leaves also is known for its strong fragrance. See Smith-Stuart, pp. 41–42; *Zhongguo gaodeng zhiwu tujian* 2:1088.

Ruo is *duruo* 杜若 (see *Shi ji* 117.3006, n. 14), which in modern Chinese designates the *Pollia japonica* This is a perennial plant with ovoid leaves and clusters of small white flowers. See Smith-Stuart, p. 338; *Zhongguo gaodeng zhiwu tujian* 5:396.

L. 69: *Changpu* 菖蒲 can refer to several varieties of Acorus. I have arbitrarily rendered it as sweet flag (*Acorus calamus*), a tall perennial marsh plant with swordlike leaves and strong fragrance. See Smith-Stuart, pp. 12–13, Shi Shenghan, *Qimin yaoshu jinshi*, pp. 787–88; *Zhongguo gaodeng zhiwu tujian* 5:359.

Peaked and pointed, jaggedly jutting,
They leave the sun and moon covered and eclipsed.

Multifariously merging, complexly conjoined,
55 Upward they invade the blue clouds.

Slanting and sloping, sloping and slanting,
Below they join the Jiang and He.

In their soil:
    Cinnabar, azurite, ochre, white clay,
    Orpiment, milky quartz,
60   Tin, prase, gold, and silver,
    In manifold hues glisten and glitter,
    Shining and sparkling like dragon scales.

Of stones there are:
    Red jade, rose stone,
    Orbed jades, vulcan stone,
65   Aculith, dark polishing stone,
    Quartz, and the warrior rock.
To the east there is Basil Garden,
    With wild ginger, thoroughwort, angelica, pollia,
    Hemlock parsley, sweet flag,

L. 70: Various sources differ on the identification of the *jiangli* 江蘺. Yan Shigu (see *Han shu* 57A.2537) cites Xu Zhicai's 徐之才 (5th century) *Yao dui* 藥對 (Dialogue on Medicines), which equates the *jiangli* with *miwu* 蘪蕪. The word *miwu* can refer to a type of *Selinum* or the young leaves of the *xiongqiong* (see "Sweet Springs Palace Rhapsody," L. 118n). See Smith-Stuart, pp. 402–3. Yan cites another authority that says the *jiangli* is a green saltwater plant produced in Linhai 臨海 prefecture (on the eastern coast of modern Zhejiang). This may be a type of seaweed that modern botanists identify as gracilary. See Li Shizhen, *Bencao gangmu* 14.841; Read, *Chinese Medicinal Plants*, p. 61, #231. Sima Xiangru clearly considered *xiongqiong*, *jiangli*, and *miwu* as different plants. Although neither *jiangli* nor *miwu* can be identified with any certainty, I agree with Hervouet (see *Le Chapitre 117 du Che-ki*, pp. 20–21, n. 4) that they are similar plants of the umbelliferous family. He gives the tentative translations of "ligustique" and "liveche." For *jiangli*, I have borrowed Hervouet's "liveche" (my "lovage") and use selinum for *miwu* (see "Southern Capital Rhapsody," L. 132n). For a full discussion of these names, see Zhu Jian 9.12a–13a and Hu Shaoying 9.4b–6a.

L. 71: *Zhuzhe* 諸柘 is another name for *ganzhe* 甘柘, the sugar cane. See *Shi ji* 117.3006, n. 17. The word *zhuzhe* (*tjah-tjag*) probably is of Austroasiatic origin. See Laufer, *Sino-Iranica*, p. 376, n. 5; Li, *Nan-fang ts'aomu chuang*, pp. 57–58. For a discussion of the Chinese words for sugar, see Matsumoto Nobuhiro 松本信廣, "Kanho meigi kō" 甘庶名義考, in *Gogaki ronsō* 語学論叢 (Tokyo: Keiō gijuku daigaku gogaku kenkyūjo, 1948), pp. 72–81; and Shi Shenghan, *Qimin yaoshu jinshi*, pp. 741–44.

According to Zhang Yi (cited in *Han shu* 57A.2537, n. 13), *baju* 巴苴 (written *boju* 猼且 in *Shi ji*) is *ranghe* or mioga ginger (see "Southern Capital Rhapsody," L. 124n). Yan Shigu (*ibid.*) asserts that only *boju* is mioga ginger, and the form *baju* is another name for *bajiao* 巴蕉, which is the banana. Zhu Jian (5.15a–b) presents a detailed argument to support Yan's identification. Hu Shaoying (9 6a–b), on the other hand, argues that *baju* and *boju* are variant names for mioga ginger I have arbitrarily followed Hu. See also Fang Yizhi, *Tong ya* 44.5a–6b, who argues for the equation with banana.

L. 76: Most commentators identify Shaman Mount as the famous Wushan 巫山 in eastern Sichuan near the Yangzi Gorges. See *Shi ji* 117.3006, n. 20 and *Han shu* 57A.2537, n. 16. Gao Buying (7.60a–b) argues that this location is too far from Chu. The "Rhapsody on the Gaotang Terrace" attributed to Song Yu mentions a Shaman Mount in Chu, which was the site of the Sun Terrace where a goddess resided (see *Wen xuan* 19.2a). According to the *Taiping huanyu ji* (132 7a), this terrace was located twenty-five *li* south of Chachuan 汊川 prefecture (north of modern Hanchuan 漢州 *xian*, Hubei). This location is close to the Yunmeng area.

L. 77: On *zhen* (wood sorrel), see "Western Metropolis Rhapsody," L. 419n.

According to Zhang Yi (cited by Li Shan 7.19a), the plant *si* 菥 (also written *si* 蕲 / 析) resembles *yanmai* 燕麥, which is a type of *Avena* (oats). According to the *Guang zhi* (cited in *Shi ji* 117.3007, n. 21), the *si* was a plant that grew in the region of Liangzhou 涼州 (modern Gansu), and was the same as the *yanmai* of China proper. I have thus rendered it as oats.

Zhang Yi (cited in *Han shu* 57A.2537, n. 17) equates *bao* 苞 with *piao* 藨, which is the wild bean plant *luhuo* (*Rhynchosia volubilis*). See "Southern Capital Rhapsody," L. 98n and *Zhongguo gaodeng zhiwu tujian* 2:507. My "twining snout" is a literal translation of *Rhynchosia volubilis*.

On *li* (iris), see "Western Metropolis Rhapsody," L. 420n.

L. 78: According to Zhang Yi (cited by Li Shan 7.19b), *xue* 薛 is another name for the *laihao* 賴蒿, which can designate common mugwort (*Artemesia vulgaris*). However, Lu Wenyu (pp. 91–92, #101) identifies it with the *Anaphalis margaritacea* (cadweed), a grayish-white perennial with fuzzy leaves. See *Zhongguo gaodeng zhiwu tujian* 4:468.

On *suo* (nutgrass), see "Western Metropolis Rhapsody," L. 419n.

On *qing fan* (sedge), see "Southern Capital Rhapsody," L. 98n. According to Zhang Yi (see *Han shu* 57A.1537, n. 18), the *qing fan* is similar to the *suo*, only larger. They are both a type of sedge. To distinguish them here, I have translated them as nutgrass and green sedge.

70   Lovage, selinum,
        Sugar cane, and mioga ginger.

    To the south there are:
        Level plains and broad marshes,
        Rising and falling, splaying and spreading,
        Steadily stretching, distantly extended.
75   They are hemmed by the Great River,
        Bordered by Shaman Mount.
    The high dry lands grow:
        Wood sorrel, oats, twining snout, iris,
        Cadweed, nutgrass, and green sedge.

L. 79: According to Guo Pu (cited by Li Shan 7.19b), *zanglang* 藏茛 is a grass used as fodder for horses and cattle. *Lang* in the word probably refers to the *langwei cao* 狼尾草, which is the forage grass *Pennisetum alopeucroides* (fountain grass, pearl millet). See Lu Wenyu pp. 81–82, #90 and *Zhongguo gaodeng zhiwu tujian*, 5:174.

On *jianjia* (marshgrass), see "Southern Capital Rhapsody," L. 99n.

L. 80: The *Qimin yaoshu* lists the *dongqiang* 東牆 and describes it as a greenish-black plant, similar to the *peng cao* 蓬草 (*Hydropyrum setaria*), and with seeds like those of the mallow It was used to make white wine. Shi Shenghan thinks it might be the *sha peng* 沙蓬 (*Agriophyllun arenarium*) that still grows in northeast and northwest China. See *Qimin yaoshu jinshi*, p. 728 and *Zhongguo gaodeng zhiwu tujian* 1:589. Zhu Jian (9.14a) thinks that the *dongqiang* of Sima Xiangru's line may be the same as *yultao* 虞蓼, which the *Erya* (C1.12b) gives as a synonym of *qiang*. Since this is a wetland plant (Smith-Stuart, p. 342, identifies it as *Polygonum flaccidum*, marsh smart-weed), I have followed Zhu's interpretation.

Diaohu 苀胡 is another name for *gumi* 菇米 (see *Shi ji* 117.3007, n. 25), the seeds of the *gu* (water bamboo, water oats). The seeds served as a food (Indian rice). See Smith-Stuart, pp. 210–11.

L. 81: Sima Xiangru actually uses the terms *lian* 蓮, which is the lotus fruit, and *ou* 藕, which is its root. See Smith-Stuart, p. 275.

Some commentators consider *hulu* 瓠蘆 a variant of *hulu* 壺蘆, the bottle gourd. See *Han shu buzhu* 57A.8b; Fang Yizhi, *Tong ya* 44.23a–b. However, as Zhu Jian (9.14a) points out, the bottle gourd is not a water plant. The *Shi ji* reads *gu lu* 菇蘆, which Guo Pu (see *Shi ji* 117.3007, n. 26) identifies as two water plants: *jiang* 蔣 (water bamboo) and *wei* 葦 (reed). To avoid repetition with water bamboo above, I have rendered *gu* in this line as water oats. See Gao Buying 7.62a.

L. 82: *Anlu* 菴閭, also known as *fulü* 覆閭, is *Artemisia keiskiana* (cottage thatch). Its stalks were used to thatch the roofs of houses. See Zhu Jian 9.14a–b; Smith-Stuart, pp. 51–52; *Zhongguo gaodeng zhiwu tujian* 4:532.

Zhang Yi (cited by Li Shan 7.19b) identifies *xianyu* 軒于 as *youcao* 猶草, which is variously identified as *Digitaria sanguinalis* (crabgrass), *Caryopteris divaricata* (spreading bluebeard), or possibly a *Potamogeton*. See Zhu Jian 9.14b; Smith-Stuart, pp. 150, 348. Since it is known for its foul smell (see *Zuozhuan*, *Xi* 4), I have dubbed it stink grass.

L. 87: *Furong* 芙蓉 is the lotus blossom (see *Han shu* 57A.2538, n. 25, Ying Shao).

On the *ling* (water chestnut, caltrop), see "Eastern Metropolis Rhapsody," LL. 219–20n.

L. 89: On *jiao* in the sense of crocodile, see "Western Metropolis Rhapsody," L. 646n.

On the *tuo* (alligator), see "Western Metropolis Rhapsody," L. 439n.

L. 90: The *daimei* 瑇瑁 is the hawksbill turtle. See Read, *Turtle and Shellfish Drugs*, p. 17, #202.

On the *bie* (soft-shell turtle) and *yuan* (trionyx), see "Western Metropolis Rhapsody," L. 439n.

L. 92: On *pian* (elm) and *nanmu*, see "Western Metropolis Rhapsody," LL. 411–12n.

L. 94: *Bo* 檗 is the *huangbo* 黃蘗, the *Phellodendron amurense* (the cork tree). See Smith-Stuart, pp. 316–17.

Zhang Yi (cited by Li Shan 7.19b) equates the *li* 離 with the *shanli* 山梨 (*Pyrus calleryana*, wild pear). See Zhu Jian 9.15a; *Erya yishu* C3.14a; Lu Wenyu, p. 75. #83.

L 95: The *zha* may be the *zhazi* 樝子 or *shanzha* 山樝, which is identified as the *Crataegus pinnatifida* (hawthorn). See Zhu Jian 9.15a–b; Smith-Stuart, pp. 120–30.

This *li* 棃 is *Pyrus sinensis* (Chinese pear). See Smith-Stuart, pp. 364–65.

The *yng* is *yingzao* or date plum. See "Southern Capital Rhapsody," L. 129n.

L. 98: *Tengyuan* 騰遠 may be equivalent to *teng yuan* 騰猿 "leaping gibbon." See Liang Zhangju 10.10b–11a; Hu Shaoying 9.10a–b.

60

The low wet lands grow:
    Fountain grass, marshgrass,
80   Smartweed, water bamboo,
    Lotus, water oats, reeds,
    Cottage thatch, and stink grass.
    So many things live here,
    They cannot all be counted.

85 To the west there are:
    Bubbling springs and clear ponds,
    Where surging waters ebb and flow.
    On their surface bloom lotus and caltrop flowers;
    Their depths conceal huge boulders and white sand

Within them there are:
    The divine turtle, crocodile, alligator,
90   Hawksbill, soft-shell, and trionyx.

To the north there is a shady grove:
    Its trees are elm, *nanmu*, camphor,
    Cinnamon, pepper, magnolia,
    Cork, wild pear, vermilion willow,
95   Hawthorn, pear, date plum, chestnut,
    Tangerine and pomelo sweet and fragrant.

In the treetops there are:
    The phoenix, peacock, simurgh,
    Leaping gibbon, and tree-jackal.

The *Fanyi mingyi* 翻譯名義 (The Meaning of Translated Buddhist Terms) by Fayun 法雲 (Song) equates *yegan* 射干 with *xiqeluo* 悉伽羅, which is the Chinese transcription for Sanskrit *Śrgala*, "jackal." See *Fanyi mingyi, Sbck, ji* 2, 51a–b. Although *yegan* (*zjak-kan) does not appear to be a Chinese word, I doubt that it is an equivalent of *Śrgala*. A closer Sanskrit equivalent is *jambuka*, which also means jackal. The *yegan* is particularly known for its ability to climb trees, and I have invented the name "tree jackal" for it.

L. 100: On the *Manyan*, see "Western Metropolis Rhapsody," LL. 707–12n.

Although some commentators treat *chuhan* 貙犴 (or *chu'an*) as the name of two different animals, it probably is the same as the *chuman* 貙獌 listed in the *Erya* (6.6a). Guo Pu (see *Erya yishu* 6.6a) says it is a term the mountain people use for large tiger. Schafer (see *The Vermilion Bird*, p. 111) thinks it might be the leopard cat (*Felis bengalensis*). It also may be a tapir or a mastiff. See Read, *Animal Drugs*, #353a.

L. 101: On Zhuanzhu, see "Wu Capital Rhapsody," L. 440n.

L. 102: It is not clear whether *bo* 駮 is the name of the mythical one horned tiger-eating horse (see "Wu Capital Rhapsody," L. 522n) or simply means piebald horse. I have given it the name hippogriff.

L. 104: On the fish-barbel staff, see "Wu Capital Rhapsody," L. 478n.

L. 105: On the luminous moon pearls, see "Western Capital Rhapsody," L. 192n.

L. 106: On the cock-halberd, see "Wu Capital Rhapsody," L. 483n. *Ganjiang* 干將 here simply means "sharp and pointed." See Hu Shaoying 9.11a–12a.

L. 107: On the Crow Caw bow see "Wu Capital Rhapsody," L. 480n.

L. 108: Xia may refer here to the famous archer Yi 羿 of the Xia dynasty (see *Han shu* 57A.2540, n 8), or as Gao Buying suggests (7.66a), it may mean summer, the season in which the quiver made in the spring was dried.

L. 109: The most likely identification of Master Yang is Sun Yang 孫陽, better known as Bo Le 伯樂, the legendary expert on horses. See Liang Zhangju 10. 11b; Hervouet, *Le Chaptire 117 du Che-ki*, p. 33, n. 1.

L. 110: Xian'e 孅阿 (or 纖阿) is known only as the "charioteer of the moon" (see *Shi ji* 117.3010, n. 7, Guo Pu).

LL. 113–14: The *qiongqiong* 蛩蛩 (or 邛邛) and *juxu* 距虚 probably are Xiongnu names for a type of wild ass. I have rendered them as "wild asses" and "wild mules" respectively. The *taotu* 騊駼 (my "tarpan") is a Xiongnu horse See Egami Namio 江上波夫, "Kyōdo no kichiku ni tsukite" 匈奴の奇獣に就きて, in *Yūrashia kodai hoppō bunka: Kyōdo bunka ronkō* エーラシア古代北方文化：匈奴文化論考 (1948; rpt. Tokyo: Yamakawa, 1950), pp. 193–203; "The K'uai-t'i, the T'ao-yu and the Tan-hsi, the Strange Donestic (sic) Animals of the Hsiung-nu," *MTB* 13 (1951), 103–11.

L. 117: The "swifter-than-wind" steed is my invention for *yifeng* 遺風. See *Lushi chunqiu* 14.7a; *Han shu* 64B.2324, n. 16.

L. 118: The *Erya* (C6.7b) mentions two types of wild horse, the *jun* 駽 (a horned steed), and the *qi* 騏 (an unhorned steed). *Qi* also designates a grey horse with black streaks. See Karlgren, "Glosses on the Kuo Feng Odes," p. 230, #364. I have rendered it as "piebald."

Beneath them there are:
The white tiger, black panther,
100   The *Manyan* and leopard cat.

II

And then, ordering peers of Zhuanzhu to attack these beasts with bare hands, the King of Chu then drives a quadriga of tamed hippogriffs, rides a chariot of carved jade. Waving withy pennants on fish-barbel staffs, trailing banners studded with luminous moon pearls, he raises a cock-halberd pointed and sharp. On his left is the carved Crow Caw bow, and on his right are strong arrows in a Xia quiver.

Master Yang is his chariot companion;
110   Xian'e is his driver.
With a measured pace, yet never slack,
They soon overtake the fleetest beasts.
The hooves trample wild asses,
The wheels crush wild mules,
115   They overrun wild horses,
Crush tarpans.
Mounted on swifter-than-wind steeds,
They shoot at roaming piebalds.

Swift and sudden, fleet and fast,
120   They move like thunder, arrive like a gale,
Course like stars, strike like lighting.

Their bows are not fired in vain;
Hitting the mark they are certain to split an eye,
Impale a breast, pierce a foreleg,
125   Or snap the heart's cords.
The catch, as if it had rained beasts,
Overspreads the grass, covers the ground.
Thereupon, the King of Chu then:
Slows his pace to dawdle and dally,
Roam and ramble, free and easy,
130   Scanning the shady groves;
He observes the violent ardor of the bold warriors,
And the fearful fright of the fierce beasts.

L. 135: The Zhou state of Zheng was famous for its beautiful women (see *Shi ji* 117.3011, n. 1). Ru Chun (cited in *Han shu* 57A.2541, n. 1) proposes that the Zheng *nü* 女 refers to the voluptuous Xia Ji (see "Western Metropolis Rhapsody," L. 769n), and that Man ji 曼姬 is another name for Deng Man 鄧曼, a concubine of King Wu of Chu. However, *man* simply means "fair of face." See Hu Shaoying 9.15a–b.

L. 136: The *e* 阿 (also written 綱) is a type of fine silk. See Wang Niansun, *Dushu zazhi* 3 5.11a–b. *Xi* 緆 (also written 錫) is a type of fine cloth. See Hu Shaoying 9.15b; Zhu Jian 9.18b.

L. 137: On *zhu* 紵 (ramie, grass cloth), see *HFHD*, 1 : 120, n. 2.

L. 140: The rhyming binome *biji* 襞積 (*pjak-tsjak*), also written *biji* 襞襀 (*piek-tsiek*), is a term for the pleat of a garment. See *Han shu* 57A.2541, n. 4 and Zhu Jian 9.18b. I have construed *qian zou* 蹇緅 as describing the crinkled folds of the dress. *Zou* (*tsogw*) probably is a loan for *cu* 蹙 (*tsjok*), "to constrict."

L. 143: The doublet *feifei* 裶裶 (*pjei-pjei*) is descriptive of the length of a garment. Cf. Qian Dazhao, cited in *Han shu buzhu* 57A.14a

L. 144: The word *yi* 袘 here refers to the hem of a garment. See *Yi li yishu* 40.11b, Zheng Xuan's commentary. The expression *xuxue* 戌削 (also written 卹削) is an alliterative binome (Old Chinese *smjet-sjakw*) used to describe the careful tailoring of a garment. See *Shi ji* 117.3012, n. 7; Hu Shaoying 9.16b; Hervouet, *Le Chapitre 117 du Che-ki*, p. 39, n. 8.

L. 145: Sima Biao (cited by Li Shan 7.21b) explains *xian* 襳 as a type of ornament on the woman's upper garment called *gui* 袿. Yan Shigu (see *Han shu* 57A.2541, n. 6) says it is a long belt. Guo Songtao (cited by Gao Buying 7 72a) argues that the *xian* is the lower portion of the *gui*, broad at the top and narrow at the bottom like a jade tablet (*gui*). See *Shi ming* 5.80. Guo explains the *shao* 髾 as a swallowtail-shaped ribbon attached to the bottom of the *gui*. For want of better English equivalents, I have loosely translated *xian* and *shao* as "apron" and "sash."

L. 146: Both *fuyu* 扶輿 (*bjah-zah*) and *yimi* 猗靡 (**jai-mjai*) are rhyming binomes used to describe the waving and fluttering of the garments. See Zhu Jian 9.19a and Hu Shaoying 9.16b–17a. I have rendered them as "flap and flutter" and "swirl and sway" respectively.

L. 147: The alliterative binome *xixia* 翕呷 (**hjep-hap*) describes the swelling and billowing of the clothes. See *Han shu* 57A.2542, n. 8 and Hervouet, *Le Chapitre 117 du Che-ki*, p. 40, n. 11. *Cuicai* 萃蔡 (**dzhjed-tshad*) is an onomatopoeic binome that indicates the rustling sound of the clothes. See Zhu Jian 9.19a.

L. 151: The graph *sui* 綏 possibly should be understood as *rui* 緌, which can mean streamer or ornamental cap ribbons. Zhang Shoujie (see *Shi ji* 117.3012, n. 12) says that this line describes the flying aprons and dangling sashes that entwine the carriage streamers. For a full discussion, see Gao Buying 7.73a.

L. 155: The rhyming binomes *panshan* (**bhwan-san*) 媻姍 (also written *pansan* 槃散; see *Shi ji* 76.2365) and *bosu* 勃窣 (**bhwet-swet*; also written *boxie* 勃屑, **bhwet-siet*), generally describe limping, halted movement. Cf. *Chuci buzhu* 13.9a, where Wang Yi explains *boxie* as "like *panshan*." As Hu Shaoying (9.17b) suggests, in Sima Xiangru's line both words describe slow movement; hence, my "sauntering slowly, lingering leisurely."

L. 156: On the term Metal Dike, see "Western Capital Rhapsody," L. 119n. The *Shuijing zhu* (6.34.26) mentions a metal dike located southeast of the ancient Chu capital of Jiangling. However, this dike was built in the mid-fourth century A.D.

L. 158: On the *junyi* (golden pheasant), see "Wu Capital Rhapsody," L. 555n.

L. 166: This would be one of the ponds mentioned in L. 93 above.

He intercepts the exhausted, seizes the spent,
And intently watches the changing aspects of all the creatures.

III

135 And thereupon Zheng maidens and comely consorts appear,
     Robed in thin silks and fine fabrics,
     Trailing garments of grass cloth and white silk,
     Wearing blends of delicate gauze,
     Draped in misty gossamer.
140 Their pleats and folds, crisped and crinkled,
     Ruffled and rumpled, creased and curled,
     Twist and turn like gorges and valleys.
     Long and trailing, full and flowing,
     Lifted hems of perfect tailoring,
145 Flying aprons and dangling sashes,
     Flap and flutter, swirl and sway,
     Surge and billow, rustle and swish,
     Grazing thoroughwort and basil below,
     Brushing feathered canopies above,
150 Entwining with the lush luxuriance of halcyon plumes,
     Tangling jade-studded streamers.

     Vaguely visualized, dimly descried,
     Apparitions, it seems, of goddesses.

IV

And then, together they hunt in Basil Garden. Sauntering slowly,
lingering leisurely, they ascend the Metal Dike.

     They net kingfishers,
     Shoot golden pheasants.
     Tiny arrows go forth,
160 Their fine cords unfolding,
     Darting the white swan,
     Entangling the wild goose.
     A pair of gray cranes falls;
     A black crane is hit.
165 Wearied, they set off again,
     To tour the clear pond.

65

L. 167: On the heron prow boat, see "Western Metropolis Rhapsody," L. 633n.

L. 168: Or, following the *Shi ji* text: "They raise the cinnamon-wood oars." The word *yi* 栧 can mean either oar or the poles on the side of the boat where banners were placed. See *Chuci buzhu* 2.7a, Wang Yi's commentary; Gao Buying 7.74b.

L. 169: According to Yan Shigu (see *Han shu* 57A.2542, n. 10), *cui* 翠 is the color of the curtains. Li Shan (7.22a) interprets *cui* as kingfisher feathers that decorate the curtains. Wang Xianqian (see *Han shu buzhu* 57A.16a) and Hervouet (see *Le Chapitre 117 du Che-ki*, p. 45, n. 4) concur with Li Shan.

L. 172: Sima Xiangru's account is purely fanciful here, for the purple cowrie is a saltwater shellfish. See Hervouet, *Le Chapitre 117 du Che-ki*, p. 45, n. 6.

L. 173: Guo Pu (cited by Li Shan 7.22a) says the *jin gu* 金鼓 is a *zheng* 鉦, or small bell-gong. The instrument is often called *jin zheng* 金鉦. See Gimm, *Das Yueh-fu tsa-lu*, p. 153, n. 3.

L. 180: *Benyang* 奔揚 (literally "the dashing and swelling") possibly is a kenning for waves.

L. 186: On the divine drum, see "Eastern Metropolis Rhapsody," L. 274n.

L. 187: On the beacon-fire system of the Han, see He Changqun 賀昌羣, "Feng sui kao" 烽燧考, *Guoli Beijing daxue sishi zhounian jinian lunwen ji*, 2.1 (1940): 77–102.

L. 190: According to Wang Xianqian (see *Han shu buzhu* 57A.16a), *xi* 纚 (also read *shi* and *li*) evokes the image of threads woven continuously together. Wang interprets *yinyin* 淫淫 as descriptive of gradual forward movement. Hervouet (see *Le Chapitre 117 du Che-ki*, p. 46, n. 17) says it describes the flowing of water. The doublet probably evokes the idea of a "streaming" procession.

L. 191: This line is similar to a line in one of the sacrificial songs composed in the Emperor Wu period of the Han. See *Han shu* 22.1052 (for translation see *Mh*, 3:613). According to Yan Shigu (see *Han shu* 22.1053, n. 9), *pan* 般 (*ban*?) should be read as *ban* 班 (to spread) On *yiyi*, see "Shu Capital Rhapsody," LL. 305–6n.

L. 192: According to Meng Kang (see *Han shu* 57A.2544, n. 4), the Sun Cloud Terrace (Yangyun tai 陽雲臺; Yunyang in *Wen xuan*) is the Gaotang Terrace described in Song Yu's "Rhapsody on the Gaotang Terrace." (In Song Yu's *fu*, the terrace is called Yang tai; see *Wen xuan* 19.2a.) The name Yangyun appears in the "Rhapsody of Great Words" and "Rhapsody of Small Words," both attributed to Song Yu (see *Guwen yuan* 1.6b–7a). The Sun-Cloud Terrace also is associated with Mount Wu in eastern Sichuan. The *Taiping huanyu ji* (148.7a) locates the Sun-Cloud Terrace associated with Song Yu in Wushan prefecture. A more likely location is near Chachuan prefecture. See L. 82n above.

LL. 193–94: Cf. *Laozi* 20: "I alone am calm and never reveal myself.... I am tranquil like the sea."

L. 195: On the blended sauce, see "Southern Capital Rhapsody," L 139n and Aoki Masaru 青木正兒, "Shakuyaku no wa" 芍藥之和, in *Aoki Masaru zenshū* 青木正兒全集, 10 vols. (Tokyo: Shunju sha, 1969–75), 8:64–76.

L. 200: *Luan* 將 is a variant of *luan* 臠 (sliced meat). The *Shi ji* reads *cui* 淬 (to stain) for *cui* 焠 (to roast) of the *Han shu* and *Wen xuan*. Yan Shigu (see *Han shu* 57A.2544, n. 7), who reads *cui* with the water radical, claims that the hunters sliced the meat and soaked it in the salt on the chariot wheels. In this way, the Chu envoy ridicules the practice, mentioned in L. 25 above, of eating meat soaked in salt caked to the chariot wheels Guo Songtao (cited in *Liang Han wenxueshi cankao ziliao*, p. 39, n. 97), who construes *cui* as "to roast," says the hunters cut a piece of meat and roasted it on the wheels. The line thus would ridicule the uncivilized habits of the King of Qi, who inelegantly eats in his chariot. Note that the King of Chu has a meal served to him in comfortable surroundings.

Drifting on figured heron prows,
They hoist banner poles,
Spread halcyon-plume curtains,
170 Raise feathered sunshades.
They net hawksbill turtles,
Angle for purple cowries.
They strike the metal bell-gongs,
Blow the singing panpipes.
175 The chief oarsman sings,
His voice fluid then sobbing.
The water creatures are startled,
Waves grandly surge,
While bubbling fountains spurt,
180 And the dashing swells converge.
Giant boulders scrape together,
Grinding and grating, clashing and clattering,
Like the noise of thunder and lightning,
Heard a hundred miles and beyond.

V

185 About to give the hunters rest,
They beat the divine drum,
Light the beacon fires.
Chariots fall into line,
Horsemen return to their squads,
190 Strung together in a steady stream,
Spread out in a catenating cortege.

And then the King of Chu
Ascends the Sun-Cloud Terrace:
Calm, he does not act;
Tranquil, he controls the self.
195 With the blended sauce prepared,
They serve the feast.

He is unlike Your Highness:
Who gallops and races all day long,
Never descending from Your chariot;
200 Whose meats sliced and carved, roasted on chariot wheels,

LL. 223–24: I have supplied these lines from the *Shi ji* and *Han shu*. Li Shan notes the similarity to lines in Yue Yi's letter to King Hui of Yan. See *Shi ji* 80.2430.

L 231: Yan Shigu (see *Han shu* 57A.2546, n. 6) understands these lines in the passive voice: "You certainly invite contempt from Qi and have been a burden to Chu." I follow Li Shan's explanation (7.23b).

L. 232: For *zhu* 陼 in the sense of "to border," see Hu Shaoying 9.20b–21a.

L. 233: Langye 琅邪 is Mount Langye located east of the Han prefecture of Langye (modern Jiaonan 膠南 *xian*, Shandong). The mountain rose up by the sea like a tall terrace. See *Shanhai jing* 13.2a. Both King Goujian of Yue and the First Qin Emperor built viewing towers on the peak. See *Han shu* 28A.1586; *Shi ji* 6.244, 28.1368, n. 11; *Mh*, 2:144, 190; Zhu Jian 9.20a–b.

L. 234: *Guan* 觀 here can mean "to build a viewing tower" (see Zhang Yi, *Han shu* 57A.2546, n. 8), or "to inspect" (see Zhu Jian 9.20b). Since it is parallel with *she* 射 (to shoot) in the next line, *guan* clearly means "to inspect." Mount Cheng 成山 was one of the eastern mountains scaled by the First Qin Emperor. It was located 180 *li* northeast of Wendeng 文鄧 prefecture (modern Wendeng *xian*), at the eastern tip of the Shandong Peninsula. See *Shi ji* 6.244, n. 3 (correct the *Kuodi zhi* to read 180 *li* northeast of Wendeng; see Gao Buying 7.78b); *Shi ji* 28.1368, n. 10; *Han shu* 28A.1585; *Mh*, 2:143, n. 4.

L. 235: Zhifu 之罘 is a mountain also once visited by the First Qin Emperor. It was located in Chui 腄 prefecture, 190 *li* northwest of Wendeng prefecture. See *Shi ji* 6.244, n. 3 (correct the *Kuodi zhi* to read 190 *li* northwest of Wendeng prefecture; see Gao Buying 7.78b–79a); *Han shu* 28A.1585; *Mh*, 2:143, n. 5.

L. 236: Boxie is another name for Bohai, the Eastern Sea. See "Wei Capital Rhapsody," L. 323n.

L. 237: Mengzhu 孟諸 is a marsh in the old state of Song. The *Yuanhe junxian tu zhi* (7.194) locates it ten *li* northwest of the Tang prefecture of Yucheng 虞城 (modern Yucheng, in eastern Henan).

L. 238: Yan Shigu (see *Han shu* 57A.2546, n. 12) claims *xie* 邪 (**zja*) should be read *zuo* 左 (**tsa*), "left," which he interprets as referring to the northeast. However, *xie* can simply mean in a diagonal direction. Sushen 肅慎 is the name of an ancient foreign state located in the northeast (modern Manchuria). The *Kuodi zhi* (cited in *Shi ji* 117.3016, n. 8) identifies it with the later Tungusic kingdom called Mohe 靺鞨. Some sources claim Sushen is an ancient transcription of Jurchen. See *Mh*, 5:341.

L. 239: On Dawn Valley, the eastern vale from which the sun rose, see "Eastern Metropolis Rhapsody," L. 603n. Li Shan (7.24a) proposes that *you* 右 (right) is a mistake for *zuo* 左 (left), which ordinarily designates east in Han texts. Zhang Shoujie (see *Shi ji* 117.3016, n. 9) explains the anomaly by saying that right is used to designate east because the vassal states face north toward the emperor.

L. 240: Qingqiu 青邱 has been variously identified. The *Shanhai jing* (1.3b–4a, 9.2a, 14.3b) mentions a Qingqiu located among the kingdoms of the Eastern Sea. It was famous for a nine-tailed fox. Some later sources claim that Qingqiu was located in Korea (see Gao Buying 7.80a–b). Since the next line mentions the land beyond the sea, Sima Xiangru probably is referring to the semi-mythical Qingqiu of the *Shanhai jing*.

You consider a pleasure.
But as I have observed it,
Qi hardly compares with Chu'.
At this, the King had no way of responding to me.''

VI

Master Improbable said, "How mistaken are your words! Your Excellency does not consider a thousand miles too far to travel, but comes to favor the state of Qi with his presence. The King has mobilized all of the soldiers in his realm and provided a multitude of chariots and horsemen, and has joined the hunt with the envoy. He has expended his entire effort obtaining a good catch to entertain his company. How can you call this bragging? When he asked what there was in the land of Chu, he wished to hear of the moral customs and achievements of your great state and any additional discourses that you might have. Now Your Excellency rather than praise the Chu king for the abundance of his virtue, lavishly extols Yunmeng, making it preeminent. You extravagantly speak of dissolute pleasures and vaunt wasteful ostentation. If I were you, I would not have adopted such a course. If the things you describe are actually as you say, they certainly are not to the credit of the state of Chu. If they exist, by speaking of them, you expose your lord's faults. If they do not exist, by speaking of them, you harm Your Excellency's credibility. To expose a ruler's faults and injure personal credibility are two things, neither of which can be allowed. Yet, by engaging in them, Your Excellency certainly has been contemptuous of Qi and has embarrassed Chu.

Moreover, Qi
On the east borders the great ocean;
To its south is Langye.
Our King inspects Mount Cheng,
235 Shoots at Zhifu,
Sails on the Boxie Gulf,
And roams the Mengzhu marsh.

Diagonally, Sushen is our neighbor,
On the right, Dawn Valley our border.
240 In autumn we hunt in Qingqiu,
Roam and ramble in the land beyond the sea.
Qi could swallow eight or nine parks like Yunmeng,

LL. 251–52: In his capacity as Yao's minister of works, Yu was an expert on geography, soils, plants, and animals. Xie 卨 (also written 契) was Yao's minister of instruction. Contrary to Sima Zhen's assertion (see *Shi ji* 117.3016, n. 12), Xie is not otherwise known for his computational skill. See Hu Shaoying 9.22b.

And they would not even be a splinter or straw in its throat.
As for
The unusual and uncommon, the precious and dear,
245 Exotic species from strange lands,
Rare and marvelous birds and beasts,
A myriad kinds gather like fishscales.
They so abundantly fill the park,
They cannot be completely recorded.
250 Yu would not be able to name them,
And Xie would be unable to tally them.

But one in the position of a vassal should not presume to speak of the joys of excursions and sports, the greatness of his parks and preserves. Moreover, Your Excellency had been received here as a guest, and thus His Majesty declined to reply to your words. How could it be that he had no way to respond?"

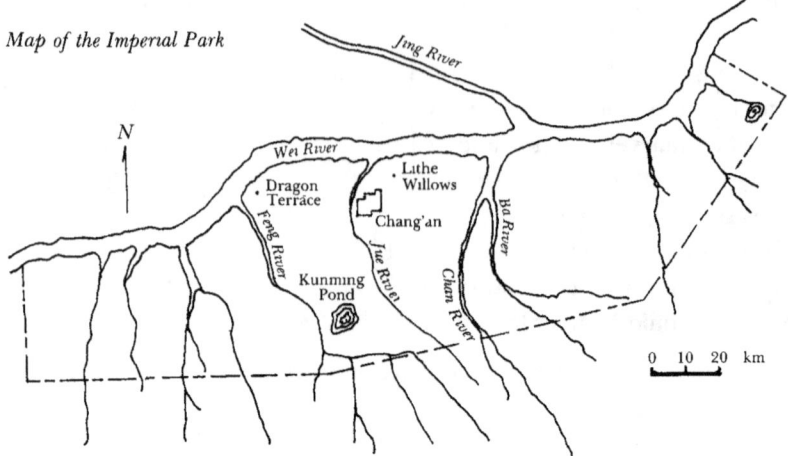

Map of the Imperial Park

L. 6: Cf. *Mengzi* 1B/4: "The vassal lords' visiting the Son of Heaven is called reporting on the administration of their offices."

8

HUNTING, PART II

Rhapsody on the Imperial Park

SIMA ZHANGQING

I

Lord No-such grinned and laughed, saying, "Chu has lost its case, but neither has Qi gained anything to its credit. Having the vassal lords present tribute is not for the articles and presents themselves, but is a means for them to report on the administration of their offices. Setting up boundaries and drawing borders are not for protection or defense, but are a means of prohibiting excessive territorial encroachment.

10   Now Qi

Has been placed as the eastern defensive barrier,
Yet externally it secretly consorts with Sushen,
Abandons its own territory, goes beyond its borders,
Crosses the sea to hunt.
In terms of its vassal duty, such things certainly should not be
      allowed.

THIS RHAPSODY by Sima Xiangru describes the Shanglin Park, the hunting park used by Former Han emperors (see "Western Capital Rhapsody," LL. 123–24n). Scholars do not agree on the exact date of this *fu*. Hervouet (see *Un Poète de cour*, p. 49, n. 5) places it "before 138 B.C." He Peixiong believes it was first written while Sima Xiangru was still in Chengdu (in He's dating 139 B.C.) and presented to Emperor Wu in 138 B.C. See "Shanglin fu zuo yu Jianyuan chunian kao" 上林賦作於建元初年考, *Dalu zazhi* 36.2 (1968) : 52–56. Jian Zongwu disagrees with He's dating and claims that it could not have been composed before 137 B.C. Jian dates the presentation to the emperor around 135 or 134 B.C. See "Shanglin fu zhuzuo niandai zhi shangque" 上林賦著作年代之商榷, *Dalu zazhi* 48.6 (1974) : 260–62 and *Sima Xiangru Yang Xiong ji qi fu zhi yanjiu*, pp. 58–63. I doubt that Sima Xiangru composed the *fu* while he was still in Chengdu, for his *Shi ji* biography (117.3002) reports that in his audience with Emperor Wu, Sima Xiangru requested "to compose a rhapsody on the excursion hunts of the Son of Heaven." The emperor then ordered the Master of Writing to give him brushes and bamboo slips with which to write his *fu*. Emperor Wu was so impressed with the composition, he appointed Sima Xiangru to the position of court gentleman. Professor Jian's careful chronology seems best to fit

L. 28: The following four lines contain place names that are virtually impossible to identify. Sima Xiangru probably is not using these names in any exact sense. Cangwu was the name of a mountain on which the legendary emperor Shun was buried. See "Wu Capital Rhapsody," L. 757n. Cangwu also was the name of a Han commandery in extreme southern China. Its administrative center was at Guangxin 廣信 (modern Wuzhou 梧州 City, Guangxi). See *Han shu* 28B.1629 However, since both of these locations are south rather than east of the Shanglin Park (left in Han directions indicates east), Wu Rulun 吳汝綸 (1840–1903) speculates that the Imperial Park had a replica of the southern Cangwu (see Gao Buying 8.4a–b). Other scholars have noted that there is a Cangwu Mountain located in Qu 朐 prefecture of Donghai 東海 (near modern Lianyungang 連雲港 City, Jiangsu). Guo Pu (see *Shanhai jing* 13.2a) says that according to tradition, this mountain was "transported here from the south" (see also *Shuijing zhu* 5 30.79). This location would be exactly east of the Shanglin Park. See Wu Renjie 吳仁傑 (ob. ca. 1200), *Liang Han kanwu buyi* 兩漢刊誤補遺 (Supplement to Errata in the Two Han Histories, *Wuyingdian juzhenban shu* edition, 6.10b–11a); Rao Zongyi, *Chuci dili kao* 楚辭地理考 (Shanghai: Shangwu yinshuguan, 1946), pp. 47–48. The main difficulty with accepting this explanation is that there is no evidence that this Cangwu is a Han place name. See Zhu Jian 10.1a and Hervouet, *Un Poète de cour*, p. 261, n. 4.

L. 29: Xiji 西極 or Western Limits is the name for the western terminus of the empire. According to the *Erya* (B5.12b), the Western Limits was the state of Bin 邠 (also written 豳) in west-central Shaanxi. This would place it north rather than west of the Imperial Park. The *Shuowen* (11A.4795a–96b) says that Bin 汃 is the river of the Western Limits. However, Gao Buying (8.4a–b) argues that Sima Xiangru actually is referring to a replica of the Western Limit's Bin River that flowed in the Imperial Park

L. 30: According to Ying Shao (see *Han shu* 57A.2549, n. 4), the Dan 丹 or Cinnabar River issued from the Zhongling 冢陵 Mountains of Shangluo prefecture (modern Shang 商 xian, Shaanix), flowed southeast to Xi 析 prefecture (near modern Xixia 西峽, Henan) where it entered the Jun 鈞 River. See also *Shuijing zhu* 4.20 11. Although the course of the river is southeast of the park, Wu Renjie (see *Liang Han kanwu buyi* 6.10a–b) argues that this location does not fit with Cangwu and the Western Limits, which are quite far removed from the park. He thus identifies the Dan River with Dan River of the Bohai Gulf mentioned in the *Shanhai jing* (1.9a). Cf. "Sweet Springs Palace Rhapsody," L. 175n.

L. 31: Zi yuan 紫淵 (Purple Gulf) may be the same as Zi ze 紫澤 (Purple Marsh), located northwest of Guluo 穀羅 prefecture (variously identified, but probably near modern Xing 興 xian, Shanxi; see Hervouet, *Un Poète de cour*, p. 264) See *Han shu* 57A.2549, n. 5. However, the equation of Zi yuan with Zi ze is not certain Zhang Shoujie (see *Shi ji* 117.3018) cites the *Shanhai jing*, which mentions a Purple Gulf River that issued from the Genqi 根耆 Mountains and then flowed into the Yellow River. This passage is not in the present version of the *Shanhai jing* (cf. Bi Yuan's commentary in *Shanhai jing* 3.3b).

LL. 32–33: On the Ba River, see "Western Capital Rhapsody," L. 36n. The Chan 滻 River had its source in Lantian Valley of Nanling 南陵 prefecture, southeast of Chang'an. It flowed north and joined the Ba River at Baling (see "Western Capital Rhapsody," LL. 72–73n). See *Shuijing zhu* 3.16.83.

L. 34: On the Feng River, see "Western Capital Rhapsody," L. 36n. On the Hao and Jue rivers, see "Western Metropolis Rhapsody," L. 49n. The Lao 潦 River, also written Lao 澇, originated in Lao Valley of the Southern Mountains west of Hu prefecture west of Chang'an. It flowed north into the Wei River. See *Shuijing zhu* 3.19.104.

L. 41: On *jiao* 椒 in the sense of "peaked," see Hu Shaoying 10.2a–b.

"Moreover, in your discourses both of you gentlemen do not strive to elucidate the duties of ruler and subject or to correct the ritual behavior of the vassal lords. You merely devote yourselves to competing over the joys of excursions and sports, the size of parks and preserves, wishing to overwhelm each other with wasteful ostentation and surpass one another in wild excesses. These things cannot serve to spread fame or enhance a reputation, but are enough to defame your rulers and do injury to yourselves. Furthermore, how are the affairs of Qi and Chu worth mentioning? Have you not seen what is truly great and beautiful? Have you alone not heard of the Imperial Park of the Son of Heaven?

II

"To its left is Cangwu,
To its right is Western Limits;
30   The Cinnabar River traverses its south,
The Purple Gulf intersects its north.

Here begin and end the Ba and Chan,
Exit and enter the Jing and Wei;
The Feng, Hao, Lao, and Jue,
35   Twisting and twining, sinuously snaking,
Crisscross within it.

Vast and wide, the eight streams separately flow,
Back to back, each in a different manner.
East, west, south, and north,
40   They gallop and dash hither and thither.

They emerge from gaps in the peaked hills,
Run along the banks of holms and isles,
Pass through the middle of cinnamon groves,

---

the circumstances of composition. The text of the "Rhapsody on the Imperial Park" also is found in *Shi ji* 117.3016–41 and *Han shu* 57A.2547–75. There are excellent notes in *Liang Han wenxueshi cankao ziliao*, pp. 40–66; and Shi Zhimian, "*Shi ji* Sima Xiangru liezhuan jiaozhu," Part 3, *Dalu zazhi* 56.3–4 (1978): 196–200; Part 4, *Dalu zazhi* 56.5 (1978): 247–50; Part 5, *Dalu zazhi* 57.1 (1978): 42–50; Part 6, *Dalu zazhi* 57.2 (1978): 91–100; Part 7, *Dalu zazhi* 57.3 (1978): 139–48; Part 8, *Dalu zazhi* 57.4 (1978): 192–96; Part 9, *Dalu zazhi* 57.5 (1978): 238–43; Part 10, *Dalu zazhi* 57.6 (1978): 287–92. Previous translations include Erwin von Zach, *De Chineesche Revue* 2 (Jan. 1928) and *Ostasiatische Rundschau* 10 (1929), rpt in *Die Chinesische Anthologie*, 1: 108–17; Watson, *Records*, 2: 307–21 and reprinted in *Chinese Rhyme-Prose*, pp. 37–51; Hervouet, *Le Chapitre 117 du Che-ki*, pp. 55–142; Obi Kōichi, *Monzen*, 1: 409–35.

L. 51: Sima Biao glosses the rhyming binome *xiongyong* 洶涌 (**hjung-djung*) as "descriptive of leaping and rising" (see *Shi ji* 117.3019, n. 13). The basic idea of the expression probably is conveyed by *yong*, which means "to leap" (see *Shuowen* 11A.4970a–b). *Xiong* does not occur independently. The *Shuowen* (11A.4970a) cites it in the reduplicative form *xiongxiong* and glosses it as *yong*. Thus, *xiongyong* may be a synonym compound.

The *Han shu* and You Mao version of the *Wen xuan* read *pengpai* 彭湃 (**brang-bwad*). Most editions of the *Shi ji* read *pang pei* 滂濞 (**pwrang-pwad*). These are obviously graphic variants of the same word. Although a signific element is difficult to identify, I suspect that the basic meaning is carried by the first graph, which conveys the meaning of "swollen." For other examples of *peng* in the sense of swollen, see William G. Boltz, "*Chuang Tzu*: Two Notes on *Hsiao Yao Yu*," *BSOAS* 43.3 (1980): 537.

L. 52: The alliterative and rhyming binome *bifei* 渾弗 (**pjiet-pjwet*) clearly is the same as *bifei* 觱沸 (**pjiet-pjwet*) of *Mao shi* 222/2 Karlgren construes *bi* as *bi* 彈 (to shoot) and understands the binome to mean "the rapid spurting (the ('shooting') of the spring water"; hence, my "spurting and spouting." See "Glosses on the Kuo Feng Odes," p. 232, #366.

Miyu 宓汩 (**mjiet-gjwet*) is a rhyming binome. The signific element probably is *yu*, which is the same as the *yu* 戾 in the *Shuowen* (11B.5142a–43a), which conveys the meaning of swift movement; hence, my "rushing and racing." See *Fangyan shuzheng* 6.4b.

L. 53: *Bice* 偪側 (**pjiek-tsrjek*) is a rhyming binome that is descriptive of waves pushing and pressing upon each other (see *Shi ji* 117.3019, n. 15). The signific element probably is *bi*, which is homophonous and synonymous with *po* 迫 (**pak*), "to press upon." Here I think it describes the waves "pressing and pushing" upon one another.

Bijie 泌瀄 (**pjiet-tsrjiet*) virtually echoes the preceding binome. Both Sima Biao (see *Shi ji* 117.3019, n 15) and Yan Shigu (see *Han shu* 57A.2550, n. 20) gloss it as "to strike one another"; hence, my "clashing and colliding."

L. 55. Meng Kang (see *Han shu* 57A.2550, n. 21) glosses *pielie* 滭冽 (**phjat-ljat*) as "to beat one against another." I suspect that the basic meaning is conveyed by *pie*, which is homophonous and possibly synonymous with *pie* (**phjat*) 撇 (to strike against). Hervouet translates it with the alliterative "claque et clapote" (see *Le Chapitre 117 du Che-ki*, p. 62). I have used "beating and battering."

L. 56: The *Shi ji* reads *pengpi* 澎濞 for *pangpi* 滂濞 of *Han shu* and *Wen xuan*. I assume with Hervouet (see *Le Chapitre 117 du Che-ki*, pp. 62–63, n. 7) that this word is a variant of *pengpai* in L. 51.

The alliterative binome *hangkai* 沆溉 (**gang-ghed*) rhymes with the preceding *pangpai*. Both Hu Shaoying (10.3a–b) and Wang Xianqian (see *Han shu buzhu* 57A.21b) consider this word related to *kangkai* 忼慨 (**khang-khed*), which means "agitated and disturbed." I have invented the alliterative "troublous and turbulent" for it.

L. 58: The rhyming binome *wanshan* 宛潬 (**'jwan-dzjan*), written *wanshan* 蜿灗 in *Shi ji*, describes turning and bending movement. The primary meaning is conveyed by *wan*, which means "to twist" or "to snake"; hence, my "sinuously snaking." See *Shi ji* 117.3019, n. 19.

Although Hervouet (see *Le Chapitre 117 du Che-ki*, p. 63, n. 9) claims that *jiaoli* 膠盭 / 膠戾 (**kroh-ljet*) does not alliterate or rhyme, I suspect that the *l/k* initial contact betrays some sign of alliteration. Since **l*-initial words often have contacts with gutturals (see Coblin, *Handbook*, pp. 48–49), perhaps *h* should be reconstructed **gliet*. None of the early commentators attempts to split the expression into its constituent parts. Guo Pu (see *Han shu* 57A.2550, n. 24) explains it as "pent and peevish, twining together." The expression is used in some contexts in the sense of "perverse" (see *Han shu* 36.1941). The word also describes twisting, winding movement (probably from "perverse," "awry," hence "crooked"). I have rendered it here as "twirling and whirling."

L. 60: The exact meaning of *lili* (**ljied-ljied*) 泣泣 is not known. Sima Biao (*Shi ji* 117.3019, n. 21) simply says it is the sound of water. My "lap, lap" is only an approximation.

Cross into broad and boundless wastes.
45 Swiftly, wildly flowing,
They descend along the slopes,
Enter mouths of narrow gorges,
Collide with beetling boulders,
Smash against winding sand mounds,
50 Frothing with violent anger.

Soaring and leaping, surging and swelling,
Spurting and spouting, rushing and racing,
Pressing and pushing, clashing and colliding,
Flowing uncontrolled, bending back,
55 Wheeling and rearing, beating and battering,
Swelling and surging, troublous and turbulent.
Loftily arching, billowing like clouds,
Sinuously snaking, twirling and whirling,
Outracing their own waves, they rush to the chasms,
60 Lap, lap, they descend to the shoals,

L. 62: The meaning of the rhyming binome *zhipei* 滯沛 (*drjad-phad) is not clear. Hervouet (see *Le Chapitre 117 du Che-ki*, p. 64) translates it "faisant jaillir des gouttelettes." I have followed Guo Pu (see *Shi ji* 117.3020, n. 23) in rendering it as "spraying and spuming."

L. 64: The *Zilin* 字林 (Grove of Graphs) of Lu Chen 呂忱 (4th century?) explains the alliterative binome *chanzhuo* 瀺灂 (*dzrjem-dzrjok) as "the little sounds of water" (see Li Shan 8.3a). It probably is onomatopoeic; hence, my "plashing and splashing."

L. 65: The *Shi ji* reads *chenchen* 湛湛 for *chenchen* 沈沈 of *Han shu* and *Wen xuan*. These are actually graphic variants for the same word. It conveys the sense of "deeply flowing"; hence, my "deep, deep." See *Shi ji* 117.3020, n. 27.

Hervouet (see *Le Chapitre 117 du Che-ki*, p. 65, n. 1) considers *yinyin* 隱隱 (*jen-jen) an onomatopoeic expression that evokes the sound of thunder or a great noise. Here, however, it is equivalent to *yinyin* 殷殷 (*'*jen-'jen*), with which it is interchangeable (see Li Shan 16.5b). *Yinyin* means "grand," and be extension conveys the idea of fullness, which is how Li Shan (8.3a) explains it. Thus, I have rendered it "full, full."

L. 67: The rhyming binome *chiqi* 潝濼 (*thjiep-tsjiep) is the same as *chiqi* 潝濕, which the *Shuowen* (11A.4970b–71a) glosses as "to froth"; hence, my "foaming and frothing."

LL. 71–76: According to Gao Buying (8.10a–b), these lines describe the gradual calming of the raging waters as they enter the lakes and ponds.

L. 77: Guo Pu (see *Han shu* 57A.2551, n. 35) says Tai hu 太湖 refers to the Zhen Marsh of Wu prefecture (see "Wu Captial Rhapsody," L. 65n). Shen Gua (see *Mengxi bitan jiaozheng* 4.48) considered the idea of the waters of the Shanglin Park reaching that far utterly preposterous and proposed to emend the text to read Da he 大河, the Great River, meaning the Yellow River. Zhu Jian (10.2b–3a) defends Guo Pu's interpretation, arguing that this kind of hyperbole is common in Sima Xiangru's *fu*. Whether this line is a case of hyperbole is difficult to determine. Several scholars accept the suggestion of Qi Shaonan 齊召南 (1706–1768) who proposed that Tai hu simply refers to a large marsh in the Chang'an area. See Zhang Yun'ao 5.26a–b; Wang Xianqian, *Han shu buzhu* 57A.22b; Gao Buying 8.10b.

L. 79: These may be crocodiles. See Read, *Dragon and Snake Drugs*, pp. 18–19, #104.

L. 80: On the *gengmeng* (beaked sturgeon), see "Wu Capital Rhapsody," L. 622n.

The *Shi ji* writes *qianli* 蟃離 for *Han shu* and *Wen xuan*'s *jianli* 漸離. The *Shuowen* (13A.6012b–13a) lists the *qianli*, but does not explain what it is. Guo Pu (see *Shi ji* 117.3021, n. 37) admits he has never heard of the *qianli*. Sima Biao (see *Wen xuan* 8.3b) says it is a fish. Hu Shaoying (10.4a–b) speculates that because it is preceded in the *Shuowen* by the word for tortoise and followed by the word for crab, it may be some sort of shellfish. I have arbitrarily called it a crayfish.

L. 81: On the *yong* (striped fish), see "Southern Capital Rhapsody," L. 90n.

The *Shi ji* reads *yong* 鱅 for *Han shu* and *Wen xuan yong* 鰫. They are variant names for the same fish, the bleak. See Gao Buying 4.16a–17a.

The exact identity of the *qian* 鰬 is not certain. The *Guangya* says the *qian* is a large *hua* 鯨, which Wang Niansun identifies as the eel. See *Guangya shuzheng* 10B.14a. This identification is confirmed by Guo Pu (see *Han shu* 57A.2551, n. 29), who says the *qian* is like an eel. See also Zhu Jian 10.3a–b.

Guo Pu (see *Han shu* 57A.2552, n. 39) equates the *tuo* 魠 with the *gan* 鱤, which is a name for the false salmon (see Read, *Fish Drugs*, pp. 22–23, #38). However, since Guo Pu also mentions that another name for the *tuo* is *huang jia* 黃頰 (the yellow jaw), a more likely identification is the golden catfish. See *Guangya shuzheng* 10B.12b–13a; "Western Metropolis Rhapsody," L. 441n.

L. 82: Guo Pu (see *Han shu* 57A.2552, n. 40) explains the *yongyong* 禺禺 as a fish with hairy skin, a yellow background, and black stripes, Xu Guang (see *Shi ji* 117.3021, n. 39) merely informs us it is the "fish-ox." This probably is the same as the *yongyong* 鱅鱅 fish mentioned in the *Shanhai jing* (4.1a). It is described as having the shape of a yak. Although some scholars have

78

Striking the bluffs, hurtling against the dikes,
Racing and swelling, spraying and spuming.
Nearing the sandbars, they pour into gullies,
Plashing and splashing as they tumble downward.
65 Flowing deep, deep, full, full,
Rumbling and roaring, ramping and raging,
Bubbling and boiling,
Foaming and frothing like a seething cauldron,
Speeding waves, flinging spray,
70 They swiftly swirl, furious and fast.

Far and wide, distantly heading homeward,
Still and silent, without a sound,
Unrestrained, they make their long return.
Finally
Broad and boundless, deep and diluvian,
75 Quietly gliding, slowly turning,
Brightly gleaming and glistening,
Eastward they pour into great lakes,
Spill and overflow into reservoirs and ponds.

Thereupon,
Scaly dragons and scarlet wiverns,
80 Beaked sturgeons, crayfish,
Striped fish, bleaks, eels, golden catfish,
Fish-ox, flounders,

attempted to equate this fish with the *yong* (bleak) of L. 81, it clearly is a different fish. See Zhu Jian 10.3b–4a. I have simply called it the fish-ox.

The *Shi ji* reads *xu na* 鱮魶 for *Han shu* and *Wen xuan's qu ta* 魼鰨. The *qu* is a name for flounder. See Read, *Fish Drugs*, p. 84, #177. *Ta* and *na* are variant names for salamander. See Read, *Fish Drugs*, pp. 76–77, #173. However, as Hu Shaoying (10.5a–6a) observes, to match with *yongyong*, *quta* should be a single fish. He notes that the *Shuowen* (11B.5214b–15a) list a fish called the *xuta*. Following Hu, I have called it a flounder.

L. 88: According to Shen Qinhan 沈欽韓 (1775–1831), the luminous moon (see "Western Capital Rhapsody," L. 192n) and the *zhuzi* 朱子 (pearlet) are two different things. He identifies the luminous moon with the *hai yue* 海月 (sea moon) or window shell, a clam shaped like a half moon and as large as a mirror. See Read, *Turtle and Shellfish Drugs*, p. 79, #242. Shen claims the pearlet is from the fresh water pearl mussel. See *Han shu shuzheng* 漢書疏證 (Exegetical Evidence for the *Han shu*), Zhejiang guan shuju, 1894 ed., 29.21b.

L. 90: Zhang Yi (see *Han shu* 57A.2552, n. 45) explains the stone of Shu (Sichuan) as inferior to jade. Nothing else is known about it.

L. 91: *Shui yu* 水玉 (my "water jade") is another name for *shui jing* 水精, rock crystal. See Guo Pu, cited in *Shi ji* 117.3021, n. 43; Read and Pak, *Minerals and Stones*, p. 23, #37. According to Guo Pu (cited by Li Shan 8.3b), *leiluo* 磊砢 (*lwed-la*) is a descriptive binome meaning "piled up high." However, Zhu Jian (10.4b) argues that to balance with rest of the line, *leiluo* should be the name of a stone. It could be the *leilei* 磊礧 pearl mentioned in the *Nanyue zhi* (cited in *Taiping yulan* 803 3567; *Chuxue ji* 27.649).

L. 95: On the *su* or *sushuang* (turquoise kingfisher), see "Western Metropolis Rhapsody," L. 445n.

L. 96: On *zhuyu* (egret), see "Western Capital Rhapsody," L. 381n.

L. 97: The *jiaojing* 交精 (or 鵁鶄) is the Chinese squacco heron. See Read, *Avian Drugs*, p. 21, #261.

Guo Pu (see *Han shu* 57A.2552, n. 48) admits he has never heard of the *xuanmu* 旋目 (or 䀛目). Yan Shigu (see *Han shu* 57A.2552, n. 48) mentions a red water bird from the area of Ying in Chu, with deep-set eyes, and long curly plumage around its eyes. He speculates that this might be the *xuanmu*. Sun Zhizu (see *Wen Lizhu buzheng* 1.28) attempts to identify it with the *zhen* 鵁 or serpent eagle, which some editions of the *Shuowen* (4A.1649b–50a) explain as *yunmu* 運目 (the turning eyes). Zhu Jian (10.4b–5a) disputes this identification on the grounds that the *yunmu* is a corruption for *yunri* 運日. He also notes that the serpent eagle is not a water bird. Hu Shaoying (10.6b–7a) notes that the *Qin jing* 禽經 (Avian Classic) mentions the *xuanmu* together with the *jiaojing*. He believes they are quite similar birds. Lacking a specific identification, I simply translate the name as "revolving eyes."

L. 98: According to Xu Guang (see *Shi ji* 117.3022, n. 47), *fanwu* 煩鶩 (*b'iwan-miug*) is also written *fanmeng* 番騖 (*b'wan-mung*). I suspect that these are variant names for the same bird. *Fanmeng* most likely is the Annamese water bird known as the *mengtong* 騺騼, or rhinoceros hornbill (see Read, *Avian Drugs*, pp. 9–10, #250).; hence, its name "borderland *meng* (hornbill)." See Zhu Jian 10.5a.

"Dike duck" is my invention for *yongqu* (modified from "Wu Capital Rhapsody," L. 111).

L. 99: Zhang Yi (see *Shi ji* 117 3022, n. 48) says the *zhenzi* 箴疵 (also written *zhenci* 鱵鱴) is a bluish-black bird similar to the blue kingfisher. The name probably means "needle beak" (cf. *zhen zi* 箴 觜), referring to its needle-sharp beak. See *Shuowen* 4a.1632a, Duan Yucai's commentary.

Although Guo Pu (see *Shi ji* 117.3022, n. 48) takes *jiaolu* 鵁盧 as the names of two birds (the *yujiao* 魚鵁 and *luci* 鸕鶿, both types of cormorants), the name should be understood as a binome. The *Shuowen* (4A.1630b–31b) lists it as a variant for the *jiaojing* (squacco heron). However, since Sima Xiangru has already mentioned the *jiaojing* in L. 97, *jiaolu* in this line must

Raising their dorsal fins, wiggling their tails,
Shaking their scales, flapping their fins,
85 Dwell submerged in the deep recesses.

Fish and turtles noisily sound forth;
Myriads of creatures throng in great numbers.
Luminous moons and pearlets
Gleam and glow on the river banks.
90 Shu stone, yellow quartz,
Water jade heaped high:

Spangling and sparkling, glittering and glistening,
Their colors and hues splendently shining,
Are thickly gathered within them.

95 Geese, kingfishers, swans, bustards,
Wild honkers, white egrets,
Squacco herons, revolving eyes,
Horn bills, dike ducks,
Needle beaks, and cormorants,

be another bird. Hu Shaoying (10.7b) and Wang Xianqian (see *Han shu buzhu* 57A.25a–b) think it is the cormorant.

L. 107: The *Shi ji* omits *chuchu* 矗矗 (spire on high). Wang Niansun (see *Dushu zazhi* 4.10.18b) observes that neither the *Wen xuan* nor the *Han shu* has a gloss on *chuchu*, and that *chuchu* does not appear in Li Shan's citation of the line in *Wen xuan* 1.7a. He suggests that it is an interpolation. In spite of Wang's strong evidence, I have retained *chuchu*, mainly on the grounds that *chuchu* is an extremely rare word and thus an unlikely choice for an interpolation.

L. 111: Yan Shigu (see *Han shu* 57A.2554, n. 3) construes *jienie* 巀嶭 (**dzhiat-ngiat*) as another name for Mount Cuo'e 嵯峨 located west of Sanyuan prefecture (cf. *Han shu* 28A.1545). However, Zhu Jian (10.5a–b) rightly points out that for reasons of parallelism with the following line, *jienie* must be understood as a descriptive expression. The exact meaning of *jienie* is not known. I suspect the signific may be *jie*, which without the mountain radical means "to cut"; hence, my "sheer and sharp." On Jiuzong (Nine Peaks), see "Western Capital Rhapsody," L. 102n.

L. 112: The Southern Mountains are the Zhongnan Mountains.

L. 113: Guo Pu (see *Shi ji* 117.3023, n. 5) explains *yanqi* (**ngjan-ngja*) 甗錡 as a binome describing twisting and bending of the mountains. *Yan* and *qi* are both names of types of cooking pots. The *yan* is a double-boiler steamer wide at the top and narrow at the bottom. See Li Xueqin, *Chinese Bronzes*, pp. 10–11. The *qi* (or *yi*) is a Chu dialect word for a wide-mouthed cooking pot. See *Fangyan shuzheng* 5.1a. Wang Xianqian (see *Han shu buzhu* 57A.26a) thinks that Sima Xiangru compares the mountains to cooking pots. In Wang's interpretation, the line says the mountains are steep and sheer like a double-boiler, recessed and hollowed like a cooking pot. Sima Biao (cited by Li Shan 8.4b) construes *qi* as *qi* 欹 (to lean). Thus, the mountains tilt like double boilers. I have attempted to preserve the cooking pot metaphor in my translation.

L. 114: Zhang Yi (cited in Li Shan 8.4b) explains the alliterative expression *jueqi* 崛崎 (**ngjwet-ngja*) as "steep and cut off." I have rendered it "bluff and bold."

L. 118: Sima Xiangru here describes the islands that rise from the streams like "mounds and barrows."

L. 119: Commentators variously explain the rhyming binome *weiwei* 崴魄 (**jwei-ngwei*) as describing uneven configuration of terrain, height (see *Chuci buzhu* 4.18a), or the aspect of piling up (see Li Shan 5.11a). It probably is a variation of *weihui* 嵔廆 (**jwei-gwei*) which follows. I suspect that both words essentially convey the meaning of imposing height. Cf. *wei* 威 (awesome) and *wei* 畏 (awful).

L. 120: The graphs used to write the alliterative binome *qiuqu* 丘虚 (**khjweh-khjag*) are also used to write the word *qiuxu* (same graphs), which means "ruins and wastes." Hervouet (see *Le Chapitre 117 du Che-ki*, p. 78, n. 11) thinks the primary meaning is carried by *qiu*, which means hill. The editors of the *Liang Han wenxueshi cankao ziliao* (p. 49, n 68) gloss it as the uneven appearance of the mounds. My "hillocky and hummocky" is an approximation of this sense.

Kulei 堀礨 (**khwet-glwei*) probably is a rhyming binome (although note that *ku* can also be read **khwei*; see *Shi ji* 117.3023, n. 11). It possibly is related to *weilei* 錕鐳 (**jwei-lwei*), which means "uneven." See *Guangya shuzheng* 6A.24b. It seems to describe the up and down movement of the hills. I have rendered it "rolling and rearing."

L. 121: Guo Pu (cited by Li Shan 8.4b) explains both *yinlin* 隱轔 (**jen-ljen*) and *yulu* 鬱嶍 (**jwet-ljwet*) as the uneven appearance of the hills and mounds Hu Shaoying (10.8b–9a) equates *yulü* 鬱律 (**jwet-ljwet*) in the "Western Metropolis Rhapsody," L. 46 (see *Wen xuan* 2.3a), where it occurs with *yinlin* in the sense of "irregular." To supply a subject for the lines, I have made nouns out of what grammatically are descriptive binomes.

L. 123: *Potuo* 陂池 (**pja-da*) is a variant for *potuo* 陂陀 (sloping and slanting). See "Rhapsody of Sir Vacuous," L. 56n.

The rhyming binome *pizhi* 陴豸 (**phja-drja*) echoes *potuo* that precedes. Duan Yucai (see

100 Swim in flocks on the surface,
      Freely floating, wandering at will,
      Tossed and tumbled with the wind,
      Bobbing and rocking with the waves,
      Resting and roosting on the river holms,
105 Nibbling at watergrass and horsetail,
      Chewing caltrop and lotus.

III

      And then the lofty mountains spire on high:
      Arching aloft, tall and towering,
      Densely forested with giant trees,
110 Steeply scarped, jaggedly jutting.
      Nine Peaks rises sheer and sharp,
      The Southern Mountains soar solemn and stately
      Their cliffs and ledges, like tottering cauldrons,
      Lie precipitously piled, bluff and bold.

115 They receive flumes, open to gorges,
      Which twist and twine with cloughs and channels,
      Stand yawning wide, gaping open.

      Mounds and barrows, each a separate islet,
      Rise awesome and awful, mighty and majestic,
120 Hillocky and hummocky, rolling and rearing.

      Their ragged ridges and creviced crests
      Rise and fall, wind and weave,
      Sloping and slanting, creeping and crawling.

Shuowen 9B.4253a) thinks that it is the same word. Li Shan (8.4b) glosses it as "descriptive of gradual leveling." I suspect that the basic meaning comes from the *zhi*, which means "to crawl, as feline beasts on prey or as reptiles"; see Bernhard Karlgren, *Grammata Serica Recensa* (1957; rpt. Kungsback: Elanders Boktryckeri Aktiebolag, 1972), p. 317, #1238b. For further details, see my review of Hervouet's *Le Chapitre 117 du Che-ki*, CLEAR 1.1 (1979), 106.

L. 124: Sima Xiangru makes an abrupt switch from the islands to the water Guo Pu's four-character gloss on the alliterative binomes *weirong* (also read *yanrong*) 沈容 (*zjwei-zjung, *zjwan-zjung) and *youyu* 淫鬻 (*zjoh-zjok) is utterly incomprehensible (see *Shi ji* 117.3024, n. 15). Wang Xianqian's effort to make sense of it (see *Han shu buzhu* 57A.26b) is quite forced. The binome *weirong* also appears in Yang Xiong's "Plume Hunt Rhapsody," L. 97 (see *Wen xuan* 8.20a), where it describes the march of the imperial cortege. In the same piece (see *Wen xuan* 8.22a), Yang Xiong uses the reduplicative form *weiwei rongrong* 沈沈容容 to describe the teeming throngs of beasts in the imperial park. The word thus must have something to do with abundance. In Sima Xiangru's line, it perhaps describes the spreading flow of the waters over the level ground; hence, my "flooding and flowing."

The meaning of *youyu* is even less clear than that of *weirong*. Following Xu Sunxing (see *Wen xuan biji* 2.13b–14a), Gao Buying (8.16b) claims it describes the slow-flowing appearance of the water. Although the evidence for this interpretation is slight, I have followed Gao for the lack of anything better to suggest.

LL. 126–27: Fu Qian (cited by Li Shan 8.4b) and Guo Pu (see *Shi ji* 117.3024) construe *ting* 亭 as post station. According to Fu, dikes had post stations every ten *li*. However, Wang Xianqian (see *Han shu buzhu* 57A.27a) convincingly shows that *ting* means "level." Cf. Sima Xiangru's "Rhapsody on the Second Qin Emperor" (in *shi ji* 117.3055 and *Han shu* 57B.2591), where *ping* 平 (level) is used instead of *ting*. Professor Serruys suggests translating these lines as "Pavilion (covered swamps) . . . stretch for 1000 li; there are none that have not been built"; see Paul L-M Serruys, "Remarks on the Nature, Functions and Meanings of the Grammatical Particle in Literary Chinese," *JAOS* 96.4 (1976):553. However, *ting* is not a pavilion in this context (as a building it should be rendered "post station"), and the verb *zhu* 築 in L. 127 does not mean "to build," but rather "to pound" (in the sense of pounding earth flat).

L. 128: Zhang Yi (cited by Li Shan 8.4b) equates *lü* 綠 with the *wangqu* or arthraxon (see "Western Metropolis Rhapsody," L. 421n). Yan Shigu (see *Han shu* 57A.2554, n. 13) takes *lu* in its ordinary sense of green. See Hu Shaoying 10.9a–b.

L. 129: On *jiangli* (lovage), see "Rhapsody of Sir Vacuous," L 70n.

L. 131: Although the *luyi* 留夷 usually is a name for magnolia, because Sima Xiangru is enumerating the names of plants, Yan Shigu (see *Han shu* 57A.2554, n. 14) notes that a tree would be out of place here. As the name of a plant, *liuyi* (*ljehw-zjiei) may be the same as the *luanyi* 欒夷 (*ljwa-zjiei), another name for the *shaoyao* or peony. See *Guangya shuzheng* 10A.5b–6a; Zhu Jian 10.5b; Hu Shaoying 10.9b–10a.

L. 132: The *jielu* 結縷 (my "knot-thread") is one of the Asian *Zoysia* grasses (Korean lawn grass); see *Zhongguo gaodeng zhiwu tujian*, 5:150. According to Yan Shigu (see *Han shu* 57A.2555, n. 15), wherever it grows, it produces fine roots that knot together like threads; hence, the name "knot-thread." For variant names, see *Erya* C1.23a.

L. 133: Commentators variously interpret the *lisuo* 戾莎. Zhu Jian (10.6a–b) cites a wide array of evidence to show that *li* is the name of a type of arthraxon used for making a greenish-yellow dye (see Smith-Stuart, p. 344, under *Polygonum tinctorium*). Because of its tinctorial properties, Wang Xianqian (see *Han shu buzhu* 57A.27b) concludes that *li* simply means green. *Suo* is the name of a plant of the *Cyperus* genus (galingale). See *Zhongguo gaodeng zhiwu tujian*, 5:242–47. Although *lisuo* possibly is the name of two plants, I have rendered it as "green galingale" to match with *jielu* in the preceding line. For further information on the *li*, see *Guangya shuzheng* 10A.26b.

Flooding and flowing, streaming slow,
125 The waters scatter and spread over a level plain,
And for a thousand miles of flat marshland,
There is nothing that has not been tamped smooth

The ground is covered with green basil,
Blanketed with lovage,
130 Scattered with selinum,
Strewn with peonies,
Spreading knot-thread,
Clustered green galingale.

L. 134: The *jieju* 揭車, also known as *qiyu* 艺輿, is a fragrant plant mentioned in the "Li sao" (see *Chuci buzhu* 1.8b and 1.32b). The *Erya* (C1.27a) lists it under the name *jieju* 蔼車. It has yellow leaves and white flowers, grows to a height of several feet, and is effective in repelling harmful insects from trees. No one has been able to identify it. The name "cart-halt" is David Hawkes' invention (see *Ch'u Tz'u*, p. 33, L. 163).

L. 135: The *gaoben* 藁本 is variously identified as *Nothosmyrnium japonicum* and *Ligusticum sinense* (Chinese lovage). It is an annual with small pinnate leaves. It has white flowers and yellowish-brown roots that are used in medicine. See Zhu Jian 10.6b; Smith-Stuart, pp. 286–87; *Zhongguo gaodeng zhiwu tujian*, 2 : 1086.

The *yegan* 射干 is *Belamcanda chinensis* (blackberry lily). This plant has long irislike leaves, bright orange red-spotted flowers, and clusters of black seeds that resemble blackberries. See Read, *Medicinal Plants*, p. 212, #653; *Zhongguo gaodeng zhiwu tujian*, 5 : 570; Cheung Siu-cheong (Zhuang Zhaoxiang 莊兆祥) and Li Ninghon (Li Ninghan 李甯漢), eds., *Chinese Medicinal Herbs of Hong Kong*, vol. 1 (Hong Kong: Commerical Press, 1978), pp. 194–95.

L. 136: The *zijiang* 茈薑 is another name for *shengjiang* 生薑, *Zingiber officinale* (ginger). See *Qimin yaoshu jinshi*, p. 188. *Zi* probably may refer to the purple (*zi*) color of the ginger shoots. See "Southern Capital Rhapsody," L. 144.

L. 137: It is not certain whether *zhen chi* 葴持 should be understood as two plants or one. *Zhen* is another name for the *hanjiang* 寒漿, *Physalis Alkekengi*, Chinese lantern or winter cherry. It is possible that *chi* (**djeg*) is equivalent to *zhi* 藏 (**tjek*), which according to Guo Pu (see *Erya* C1.27a) is similar to the *hanjiang*. This probably is the same as the *ku zhi* 苦藏, which is a smaller variety of the *hanjiang* (the *Physalis angulata*; see Smith-Stuart, p. 319) See Hu Shaoying 10.11a–b. Li Ciming 李慈銘 (1830–1894) thinks that *zhenchi* designates a single plant, the *hanjiang* (see *Han shu buzhu* 57A.28a–28b) However, there is no direct evidence that *zhenchi* is a binome. Thus, I prefer to take *zhen* and *chi* as names for two different varieties of *Physalis*.

On *sun* (sweet flag), see "Southern Capital Rhapsody," L. 132n.

L. 138: Sima Biao (see *Shi ji* 117.3024, n 27) equates the *xianshi* 鮮支 with the *zhizi* 支子 (or 梔子), the *Gardenia florida* (Chinese yellow berry or gardenia). However, this is a shrub and does not fit with the other plants mentioned in adjacent lines. Hu Shaoying (10.11b–12a) thinks that it is the *yanzhi* 樲支, which is a name for the wild jujube. However, the *yanzhi* tree is mentioned in L. 203 below, and it would be redundant for Sima Xiangru to mention it twice. The most likely equation is with the *yanzhi* 燕支, the *Basella rubra* or malabar nightshade, a plant with purple berries that produce a red juice used making dye and rouge. See Smith-Stuart, p. 66; Laufer, *Sino-Iranica*, pp. 324–28.

The identification of *huangli* 黃礫 is not certain. Li Ciming (cited in Gao Buying 8.19a–b) says that it may be a corruption for *huangyao* 黃藥, *Clematis recta* or virgin's bower. Its root was pounded into a yellow dye. See *Bencao gangmu* 18.1303. Sima Xiangru perhaps intended to match two tinctorial plants.

L. 139: On *jiang* (water bamboo) and *zhu* (chufa), see "Southern Capital Rhapsody," LL. 98n and 99n. On *qingfan* (green sedge), see "Rhapsody of Sir Vacuous," L. 78n.

L. 147: On *xixiang* (spreading and scattering), see "Shu Capital Rhapsody," LL. 390–91n.

L. 150: The rhyming binome *zhenfen* 繽紛 (**tsjen-pjen*) here describes profusion and abundance. See Meng Kang, cited by Li Shan 8 5b. Hu Shaoying (10.12b–13a) equates *zhen* with *tian* 闐 (**dien*), "abundant"; hence, my "plenteous profusion."

Guo Pu (cited in *Shi ji* 117 3024, n. 1) says the rhyming binome *yawu* 軋芴 (**ret-mjet*), also written *yawu* 軋沕, describes indistinctness. Meng Kang (cited by Li Shan 8.5b) says it means "close and dense" Hu Shaoying (10.12b–13a) argues that *wu* is equivalent to *hu* 忽 (**hwet*), "distant" Thus, the basic meaning is "long and far." The idea of indistinctness perhaps is related to the sense of things dimly seen far away Cf. Sima Xiangru's "Great Man Rhapsody" (*Shi ji* 117.3060): "Westward He gazes on the Kunlun, distantly descried, vaguely visualized." In this line, I have placed more emphasis on the boundless view with my "vast vista"

Cart-halt, wild ginger, thoroughwort,
135 Nothosmyrnium, blackberry lily,
Purple ginger, mioga ginger,
Winter cherry, ground cherry, pollia, sweet flag,
Malabar nightshade, virgin's bower,
Water bamboo, chufa, and green sedge
140 Spread and sprawl over the wide marsh,
Range and ramble over the great plain,
Tightly tangled, broadly stretching.

Bent and blown by the wind,
They emit fragrance, waft pungence,
145 Rich and redolent, sweetly-scented,
And a myriad perfumes issue forth,
Spread and scatter, permeating everything,
Thick and heavy, strong and sharp.

IV

And then
Gazing round, broadly viewing,
150 One sees such plenteous profusion, such a vast vista,
He becomes dizzy and dazed, confounded and confused

Look at it and it has no beginning;
Examine it and it has no end.
The sun rises from its eastern pond,
155 Sets at its western dike.
To the south
In deepest winter there are germination and growth,
Bubbling waters, and surging waves.

L. 158: Commentators identify the *yong* 㺄 as a name for the *fengniu* 犎牛 (humped-ox), which can refer either to the dromedary or the zebu. See Read, *Animal Drugs*, #330. It is impossible to tell which of the animals Sima Xiangru is referring to. I follow Hervouet (see *Le Chapitre 117 du Che-ki*, p. 86, n. 4) in translating *yong* as zebu.

On the *mao* 氂 or hairy yak, see Read, *Animal Drugs*, #357.

On the *mo* (tapir), see "Shu Capital Rhapsody," L. 343.

The *li* 犛 frequently is considered the same as the *mao*. It probably is the Tibetan yak. See Read, *Animal Drugs*, #356. Since Sima Xiangru considered it a different animal from the *mao*, I have rendered it as "grunting ox."

L. 159: On the plunging bull, see "Western Metropolis Rhapsody," L. 652.

On the identification of *zhu* 麈 as sambar, see Schafer, "Cultural History of the Elaphure," pp. 268–69.

L. 160: The redhead (*chi shou* 赤首) probably refers to a fabulous beast described in the *Shanhai jing* (4.8a). Known as the *gedan* 猲狙, this marvelous redheaded creature resembled a wolf, had the eyes of a rat, and made sounds like a pig.

The *yuan ti* 圜題／蹄 (for this emendation see Wang Xianqian, *Han shu buzhu* 57A.31a), or roundhoof, probably refers to the Chinese unicorn (*qilin*), which was known for its round hooves as well as its single horn. See *Han shu* 6.174, n. 2; *HFHD*, 2:57, n. 13.2.

L. 161: The *qiongqi* 窮奇 (my "extreme extraordinaire") is another fabulous beast mentioned twice in the *Shanhai jing* (2.27b and 12.2a) It most frequently is described as resembling a winged tiger. For further information, see Bodde, *Festivals*, pp 88–90.

L. 164: "Horn-snout" is my literal translation for *jueduan* 角端 (*kaktuan*), which possibly is related to Persian *kargadan* or rhinoceros. See Chunchiang Yen, "The *Chüeh-tuan* as Word, Art Motif and Legend," *JAOS* 89 (1969):578–92.

LL. 165–66: On the *taotu* (tarpan) and *qiongqiong* (here rendered as "chigetai"), see "Rhapsody of Sir Vacuous," LL. 113–14n.

Egami Namio tentatively identifies the *dianxi* 騨騱 (*tien-giai*) with the Mongolian *kulan* (= *qulan*), which is a type of wild ass quite similar to the *chigetai*. See *Yūrashia kodai hoppō bunka*, pp. 203–16; "The K'uai-t'i," pp. 111–23.

L. 167: The *jueti* 駃騠 (*kiwat-diai*) is applied both to the hinny (see *Shuowen* 10A.4343) and a powerful Aryan horse imported by the Xiongnu from the Aral and Caspian Sea region. See Egami, *Yūrashia kodai hoppō bunka*, pp. 180–93; "The K'uai-t'i," pp. 90–103. Professor E. G. Pulleyblank has suggested that *jueti* goes back to a Yenissean form "something like *kuti*," which presumably meant horse See his "Consonantal System of Old Chinese: Part II," *AM*, n.s., 9 (1962):245–46. Because it is mentioned together with other asslike creatures, the *lü* 驢 (ass) and the *luo* 贏 (mule), I have translated it here as hinny. It is impossible to know how Sima Xiangru understood the word.

L. 170: Wang Xianqian (see *Han shu buzhu* 57A.31a) thinks that *zhu* 注 (*tjuak*) is a loan for *zhu* 屬 (*tjuak*), "to connect." However, *zhu* may simply mean "to pour" in the sense of pouring out in the four directions.

L. 171: On *chongzuo* (double deck), see "Western Capital Rhapsody," L. 155n where it is rendered "double balcony." The twisting passageways are the elevated passageways that connected buildings. See "Western Capital Rhapsody," L. 253n.

L. 173: On the *nian dao* (carriage road), see "Western Capital Rhapsody," L. 252n.

L. 177: On *cheng* 成 in the sense of "layer" or "story," see Hu Shaoying 10.14b.

L. 178: Guo Pu (see *Shi ji* 117.3027, n. 5) explains that built into the cliffs and caves of the hills were rooms that secretly communicated with the terraces above. Cf. "Sweet Springs Palace Rhapsody," L. 82n. On *yao* 突 (recess, cranny), see Wang Niansun, *Dushu zazhi* 4.10.18b–19a.

L. 183: The green dragon, which is the guardian beast of the east, presumably is the great dragon steed that pulls the chariots of gods and immortals

Its animals are:
The zebu, hairy yak, tapir, grunting ox,
Plunging bull, sambar, elaphure,
160 Redhead, roundhoof,
Extreme extraordinaire, elephant, and rhinoceros.
To the north
In full summer it is enveloped in a freezing cold that cleaves the
           ground;
One just lifts his skirt to cross the iced-over streams.
Its animals are:
The unicorn, horn-snout,
165 Tarpan, camel,
Chigetai, kulan,
Hinny, ass, and mule.

V

And then
Detached palaces, separate lodges,
Stretch over the mountains, straddle the valleys:
170 Tall corridors pour out in four directions,
With double decks and twisting passageways;
Fitted with ornate rafters and jade finials,
Carriage roads are laced and linked together.
In the covered walkways to walk completely around,
175 Long is the course and midway one must halt for the night.

On leveled peaks they built the halls,
With tiered terraces rising story upon story,
And cavernous rooms in the crags and crannies.

Downward through the deep darkness nothing can be seen;
180 Upward, one may clutch the rafters to touch the sky.
Shooting stars pass through the doors and wickets;
Arching rainbows stretch over the rails and porches.

A green dragon curls and coils in the eastern chamber,

L. 184: It is not certain whether *xiang yu* 象輿 means ivory carriage or elephant-drawn carriage. According to Zhang Yi (cited by Li Shan 8.6b), the *xiang yu* was a naturally occurring object that appeared in the mountains as a propitious omen. Zhu Jian (10.8b–9b) argues on the basis of parallelism with "green dragon" in the preceding line that *xiang* must mean elephant here.

L. 185: Guo Pu (cited in *Shi ji* 117.3027, n. 9) says that Lingyu 靈圉 is another name for the immortal Chunyu 淳圉. Zhang Yi (cited in *Han shu* 57A.2558, n. 10) says that Lingyu is an appellation for the immortals. Sima Xiangru uses the expression in two other pieces (see his "Rhapsody on the Great Man," in *Shi ji* 117.3058 and "Essay on the Feng and Shan Sacrifices," in *Shi ji* 117.3065), where Lingyu clearly refers to the immortal multitudes (see Hervouet, *Le Chapitre 117 du Che-ki*, p. 92, n. 12 and p. 213, n 7).

L. 195: Guo Pu (see *Shi ji* 117.3028, n. 16) explains *pangtang* 旁唐 as a descriptive meaning "immense." Yan Shigu (see *Han shu* 57A.2559, n. 17), who interprets *tang* as *dang* 碭, says that *pangtang* is a type of *wen shi* 文石, or agate. Although *pangtang* does occur in other works in the sense of "immense," since Sima Xiangru often mentions related objects in the same line, I follow Wang Xianqian (see *Han shu buzhu* 57A.34a), who explains the expression as "large (*pang*) agates." Since *min* (cf. "Western Capital Rhapsody," L. 203n) also refers to a type of agate, I have rendered *pang tang* (or *dang*?) as "large carnelians."

L. 196: On *binbin* 玢豳 (striped and streaked), see "Rhapsody on the Sacred Field," L. 82n.

L. 199: I have followed Yan Shigu (see *Han shu* 57A.2559, n. 19), who explains *zhao cai* 晁采 (my "morning iridescence") as the white iridescent vapor that shoots from a beautiful jade in the morning. Duan Yucai (see *Shuowen* 1A.144b) thinks that *cai* is the *dacai* 大采 or great variegated jade tablet held by the Son of Heaven in presenting the solar sacrifice (*chao ri* 朝日). See *Guo yu* 5.8b; *Zhou li zhushu* 20.17a–18a; Biot, 1 : 484–85.

Both *wan* 琬 (round jade) and *yan* 琰 (pointed jade) are types of jade tablets. See Laufer, *Jade*, pp. 93–97. Guo Pu (see *Shi ji* 117.3028, n. 20) cites the *Ji zhong zhushu* 汲冢竹書 (Bamboo Book from the Ji Tumulus), which mentions two jades King Jie of Xia named after the maidens Wan and Yan whom he captured in an expedition in the Min Mountains. I have provisionally translated *wan yan* as "round and pointed jades."

L. 201: *Luju* 盧橘 literally means black orange. Guo Pu (cited in *Shi ji* 117.3029, n. 1) identifies it with the *jike cheng* 給客橙 (kumquat) of Shu. He says it is similar to the orange and pomelo, quite fragrant, and blooms and bears fruit winter and summer in succession. According to the *Guangzhou ji* 廣州記 (Records of Guangzhou, cited in *Shi ji* 117.3027, n. 1; cf. *Qimin yaoshu jinshi*, p. 737 for variants), its fruit is red in the ninth month, but turns greenish-black by the second month of the next year. Zhu Jian (10.10a–b) definitely has established that it is the kumquat. See also *Bencao gangmu* 30.1796; Smith-Stuart, pp. 111, 115.

L. 202: One of the most prized varieties of the *gan* 甘 (Mandarin orange, *Citrus reticulata*) is the yellow *gan*. Although many sources identify it as *Citrus nobilis* (sweet peel tangerine), Li Hui-Lin thinks it is the Mandarin orange. See *Nan-fang ts'ao chuang*, pp. 118–20. Cf. *Qimin yaoshu jinshi*, p. 737.

On the *cheng* (coolie orange), see "Southern Capital Rhapsody," L. 130n.

Zhang Yi (cited in *Han shu* 57A.2559, n. 2) identifies the *cou* 榛 as a small orange. Hu Shaoying (10.16b) cites evidence to equate *cou* with *zouzi* 皺子 (the wrinkled fruit), which is a vulgar name for the *you* 柚 or pomelo.

L. 203: On the *pipa* (loquat), see "Shu Capital Rhapsody," L. 158n.

The *yan* is the *yanzhi* (see L. 138n above), *Ziziphus vulgaris* (wild jujube). On this plant, see Laufer, *Sino-Iranica*, p. 385.

L. 204: On the *ting* (wild pear) and *nai* (apple), see "Shu Capital Rhapsody," L. 159n and L. 165n.

The term *hou po* 厚朴 literally means thick bark. It has been variously identified as *Magnolia*

The elephant carriage twists and turns through the western repose,
185 Immortal multitudes rest in the leisure lodges,
Wo Quan and his kind sun themselves in the southern eaves.
Sweetwater springs bubble amongst the cool rooms,
Freeflowing streams pass through the central courtyard.
Giant boulders line the shores,
190 Steeply scarped, leaning and listing,
Jaggedly jutting, peaked and pinnacled,
Carved and chiseled, precipitously poised.
Rose stone, prase, dark jade;
And coral grow in clusters.

195 Agate gems and large carnelians
Are striped and streaked like patterned fishscales.
Red jade, mottled and marbled,
Are mixed and mingled among them.
Morning iridescence, rounded and pointed jades,
200 Mr. He's jewel appear there.

VI

And then
Black kumquats that ripen in summer,
Yellow mandarins, coolie oranges, pomelos,
Loquats, wild jujubes, persimmons,
Wild pears, apples, magnolias,

hypoleuca (see Smith-Stuart, pp. 244–45) or *Magnolia officinalis* (Read, *Medicinal Plants*, p. 162, #511; *Zhongguo gaodeng zhiwu tu jian*, 1:787). On this tree, which is valued for its bark, see *Zhenglei bencao* 13.25b–26b.

L. 205: On the *yangmei* 楊梅 (*Myrica rubra*, box myrtle), see *Qimin yaoshu jinshi*, p. 750; Li Hui-Lin, *Nan-fang ts'ao-mu chuang*, pp. 117–18.

L. 206: This line contains the earliest mention of *putao* 蒲陶 (grape, *Vitis vinifera*) in Chinese literature. It in fact antedates by over a dozen years the reputed first introduction of the grape into China by Zhang Qian, who returned to the Han court with word of Ferghana grapes around 125 B.C. Subsequently (ca. 104 B.C.), Han envoys brought back from Central Asia grape seeds, which were planted by the detached palaces and lodges. See *Shi ji* 123.3173–74; *Han shu* 96A.3895; *Records*, 2:279–80; Hulsewé, *China in Central Asia*, pp. 132–36. The Shanglin Park even had a residence named Grape Lodge. See *Han shu* 94B.3816. Hervouet (see *Le Chapitre 117 du Che-ki*, p. 98, n.6) speculates that the *putao* mentioned by Sima Xiangru may be the Chinese wild grape (*Vitis pentagona, V. Davidi*), which existed in China long before the cultivated grape was brought to China. Since the word *putao* (**bag-dog?*) most likely is Ferghanian in origin, it seems strange that the Chinese would have used this word for the wild grape before the introduction of the cultivated grape. It is indeed possible that the cultivated grape was brought to China earlier than the Chinese sources claim. On the origin of the word, see Laufer, *Sino-Iranica*, pp. 225–28; Janus Chmielewski, "Yi putao yi ci wei li lun gudai Hanyu de jieci wenti" 以葡萄一詞爲例論古代漢語的借詞問題, *Beijing daxue xuebao* (1957:1):71–81. "The Problem of Early Loan-words in Chinese as Illustrated by the Word 'p'u-t'ao'," *Rocznik Orientalistyczny* 22.2 (1958):7–45; "Two Early Loan-Words in Chinese," *Rocznik Orientalistyczny* 24.2 (1961): 65–86.

L. 207: The identification of the *yinfu* 隱夫 is uncertain. I have followed Gao Buying (8.29a–b), who equates *fu* with *fuyi* (see "Sweet Springs Palace Rhapsody," L. 112n), the Chinese poplar. For a good summary of the scholarship on the name, see Hervouet, *Le Chapitre 117 du Che-ki*, p 98, n. 7.

The *yudi* 薁棣 (*Shi ji* reads 鬱) may be the name of two plants, but since it is matched with *yinfu*, I have taken it as the name of a single plant, variously known as *tangdi* 唐棣, *yuli* 薁李, and other names. This is the *Prunus japonica* (dwarf flowering cherry). See Gao Buying 8.29a–b.

L. 208: All we know about the *data* 荅遝 is that it is a plumlike tree from Shu. See *Shi ji* 117.3030, n. 9.

L. 219: Zhang Yi (see *Han shu* 57A.2560, n. 11) says the *shatang* 沙棠 is similar to the coarse pear, has yellow flowers and red fruit, tastes like a plum, and has no pit. Read (in *Medicinal Drugs*, p. 134, #439) identifies it as *Pyrus spectabilis* or crab apple. Hervouet (see *Le Chapitre 117 du Che-ki*, p. 100, n. 1) rejects this identification on the grounds that the fruit of the *Pyrus specatabilis* is yellow. He thinks it might be *Pirus baecata* (*baccata?*). In modern Chinese, the *Malus asiatica* (Asian apple) is called the *shaguo* 莎果 See *Zhongguo gaodeng zhiwu tujian*, 2:236. I have arbitrarily chosen crab apple. See also *Qimin yaoshu jinshi*, p. 751.

On *li* (serrated oak), see "Southern Capital Rhapsody," L. 52n.

Read (see *Medicinal Plants*, p. 198, #616) identifies the *zhu* 櫧 as *Quercus sclerophylla*. There also is the *ku zhu* 苦櫧 (bitter *zhu*), which is the name of the *Quercus myrsinaefolia* (see *Zhonguo gaodeng zhiwu tujian*, 1:439). *Zhu* also appears in the name of several types of *Lithocarpus* (tanbark oak) See *Zhongguo gaodeng zhiwu tujian*, 2:428, 436.

L. 220: The *hua* 華 or *huamu* 樺木 can refer to several different varieties of *Betula* or birch. See *Zhongguo gaodeng zhiwu tujian* 1:387–94.

On the *feng* (liquidambar), see "Western Metropolis Rhapsody," L. 412n.

The *ping* is the *pingzhong* or ginko (see "Wu Capital Rhapsody," L. 193n.

On the *lu* (sumac or Hungarian fustic), see "Southern Capital Rhapsody," L. 52n.

L. 221: There are several possibile identifications mentioned for *liuluo* 留落 Qian Daxin

205 Date plums, box myrtles,
    Cherries, grapes,
    Dark poplars, dwarf cherries,
    Plums, and litchees
    Are spread among the rear palaces,
210 Form rows in the northern orchards,
    Stretch over the hills and mounds,
    Descend to the level plain.

    They wave their emerald leaves,
    Sway their purple stalks,
215 Burst with red blossoms,
    Hang with vermilion blooms.

    Bright and brilliant, grand and glorious,
    They splendently sparkle in the vast fields.
    Apples, oaks,
220 White birch, liquidambars, ginkos, sumacs,
    Pomegranates, coconuts,

equates it with the *liuyi* 劉代 mentioned in the *Erya* (C3.11b). See his *Nianer shi kaoyi* 廿二史考異 (Variorum on the Twenty-two Histories), in *Qianyan tang congshu*, 5.22a. The *Qimin yaoshu* cites the *Nanfang caowu zhuang* 南方草物狀 (Description of Plants and Products of the South) by Xu Zhong 徐衷 (fl. ca. 281), which says it has sour yellow fruits as large as plums. Shi Shenghan (see *Qimin yaoshu jinshi*, p. 745) tentatively identifies it as *Rosa laevigata* or Cherokee rose. Cf. "Wu Capital Rhapsody," L. 254n. Sun Zhizu (see *Wen xuan Lizhu buzheng* 1.28a–b) equates it with the *fulu* (betel vine) of Zuo Si's "Wu Capital Rhapsody" (see L. 176n). Gao Buying (8.30b–31a) identifies it with the *shiliu* (pomegranate). Since there is no conclusive proof for any of these identifications, I have arbitrarily selected pomegranate, mainly to balance with coconut.

On the *xuye* 胥邪 or *ye shu* 椰樹 (coconut), see Li Hui-Lin, *Nanfang*, pp. 115–17; *Qimin yaoshu jinshi*, pp. 752–55.

L. 222: All commentators identify *renbin* 仁頻 as the *binlang* or betel palm (see "Wu Capital Rhapsody," L. 251n).

L. 223: Commentators (see *Shi ji* 117.3030, n. 15; *Han shu* 57A.2561, n. 14) identify the *chantan* 檦檀 as another name for the *tan* 檀, which can designate several different kinds of trees, including sandalwood, sanderswood, and dalbergia (see Smith-Stuart, pp. 394–95). The *chantan* (**dzram-dan*) of this line may be a Chinese transcription of Sanskrit *candana*, sandalwood. However, sandalwood reputedly was not brought to China until the introduction of Buddhism after the Han dynasty. See Schafer, *The Golden Peaches of Samarkand*, p. 137.

L. 224: On *yuzhang* (camphor) and *nizhen* (wax tree), see "Wu Capital Rhapsody," L. 189n and L. 192n.

L. 230· Sima Biao (cited by Li Shan 8 7b) explains the rhyming binome *ligui* 欐佹 (**ljai-kwiai*), which the *Shi ji* writes *leigui* 累佹 (*lwei-kjiwai*), as describing the branches massed (*lei* 累) in layers. Yan Shigu (see *Han shu* 57A.2561, n. 18) says it means "to brace, to support." Based on these glosses, later commentators have interpreted the word as a description of the layered bunching of the branches (Hu Shaoying 10.18a), or the joining (*li* = *li* 麗, "to attach") and splaying (*gui*) of the branches (Wang Xianqian, *Han shu buzhu* 57A.37a). I cannot decide which of these explanations, if any, is correct. My "clinging and cleaving" is a vague approximation.

L. 231: The word *bowei* 娑㧪 (**bat-'jwai*) is a variant for *bawei* 茇㧪 (**bat-'jwai*) that is used in the *Chuci* poem "Summoning a Hermit Scholar" (see *Chuci buzhu* 12.2b) to describe gnarled and twisted trees. See Hu Shaoying 10.18a

L. 232· The rhyming binome *kengheng* 坑衡 (**khrang-grang*) is a variant for *kangheng* (**khang-grang*) 抗衡 (to oppose, to resist); hence, my "locked as in combat." See Zhu Qifeng, *Ci tong*, p. 924.

Hu Shaoying (10.18a–b) shows that the rhyming binome *keluo* 閜砢 (**ha-la*) is a variant of *leiluo* (piled up high) of L 91 above. Hervouet (see *Le Chapitre 117 du Che-ki*, p. 103, n. 13) thinks it describes the spreading of branches, one above the other; hence, my "layered limbs."

L. 235: On the alliterative binome *xiaosen* (**sjoh-srjem*) 篇蔘 (closely clustered), see Zhu Jian 10.12a–b.

L. 237: Wang Xianqian (see *Han shu buzhu* 57A.37b) understands the alliterative binome *liuli* 薊茫 (**ljehw-ljiei*) as a variant of *liaoli* 憭慄 (**ljehw-ljiet*), "sad and sorrowful." Cf. *Chuci buzhu* 8.2a. However, Hervouet (see *Le Chapitre 117 du Che-ki*, p. 104, n. 18) thinks it is an onomatopoeia for the sounds of the wind in the trees. To combine the senses, I have translated it as "sigh and sough."

The alliterative binome *xuxi* 丗歙 (**hjwed-hjep*) probably is a variant of *xuxi* 欻吸 (**hjwet-hjep*), which describes the blowing sounds of the wind; hence, my "whistle and whiffle." See Hu Shaoying 10.19a.

L. 240: The rhyming binomes *cichi* 傑池 (**tshja-dja*) and *cizhi* 玭㢳 (**tshja-drja*) both describe irregular heights of the trees. Cf. "Sweet Springs Palace Rhapsody," L. 25n.

L. 241: These palaces presumably are the lodges used by the harem.

Betel palms, windmill palms,
Sandalwoods, magnolias,
Camphors, and wax trees:

225 Grow a thousand yards tall,
So wide only joined hands can span them,
Their blossoms and branches unfolding straight,
Their fruits and leaves lush and luxuriant.

Standing in thickets, reclining in copses,
230 Bent and bowed, clinging and cleaving,
Tangled and twined, twisted and gnarled,
Locked as in combat, in layered limbs,
Hanging branches spread and splay,
Falling petals fly and flutter.

235 Lush and luxuriant, closely clustered,
They swing and sway with the wind,
Which sighs and soughs, whistles and whiffles,
Like the sounds of bells and chimes,
Or the music of pipes and flutes.

240 Tall and short, high and low,
They surround the rear palaces.
Manifoldly layered, piled one upon another,
They blanket the mountains, hem the valleys,
Follow the slopes, descend into the depressions.
245 Look at them and there is no beginning;
Examine them and there is no end.

L. 248: On the *wei* (proboscis monkey, kahau), see "Western Capital Rhapsody," L. 357n.
On the *jue* (hoolock, great gibbon), see "Southern Capital Rhapsody," L. 67n (correct *que* to read *jue*).

The *fei lei* 飛鸓 is another name for the *wushu* or flying squirrel. See *Erya* C5.13a; Gao Buying 2.65a–b. Note: "Southern Capital Rhapsody," L. 69 and note. "Flying monkeys" should be corrected to read "flying squirrels."

L. 249: Guo Pu (cited in *Shi ji* 117.3032, n. 2) says he does not know the identity of *zhi tiao* 蛭蜩. It is not clear whether *zhi tiao* designates one or two animals. Yan Shigu (cited in *Han shu* 57A.3562, n. 3) deems quite inapposite for this context Zhang Yi's identification of *zhi* and *tiao* as leech and cicada respectively. The *zhi* possibly is the *longzhi* 蠪姪, which the *Shanhai jing* (4.5b) describes as a foxlike animal with nine tails and nine heads. However, it says nothing about it as an arboreal creature. Sima Zhen (see *Shiji* 117.3032, n. 2) cites the *Shen yi jing* 神異經 (Classic of Supernatural Wonders), which mentions the *tiao* as a tree-climbing animal whose fur is the color of a macaque. Wang Xianqian (see *Han shu buzhu* 57A.38b) shows that the *Shen yi jing* actually reads *zhou* 獨 for *tiao*. The extant *Shen yi jing*, *Han Wei congshu*, p. 15a, says the *zhou* is as large as a donkey and good at climbing trees. Read (＃400 A) identifies it as the dusky gibbon. Based on parallelism with *juenao* that follows, I suspect that *zhitiao/zhizhou* is a binome. I have thus rendered it as "dusky gibbon."

Both Sima Biao and Guo Pu (cited in *Shi ji* 117.3032, n. 2) consider *juenao* as a binome. Sima Biao says it is a *mihou* (monkey), and Guo Pu says it is yellow and similar to a monkey. I have simply called it "monkey."

L. 250: On the *chanhu* (macaque), see "Western Metropolis Rhapsody," L. 583n, where *canhu* should be corrected to *chanhu*.

On the *hu* (weasel), see "Southern Capital Rhapsody," L. 67n.

Guo Pu (cited in *Shi ji* 117.3032, n. 3) admits he has never heard of the *gui* 蚮. Several commentators (see Hu Shaoying 10.20b, Zhu Jian 10.13a) think that it is the turtlelike creature mentioned in *Shanhai jing* 5.43b. However, there is no mention of it living in trees. According to the *Lei pian* 類篇 (The Categorized Thesaurus), *Siku quanshu zhenben*, Series 6 (Taibei: Shangwu yinshuguan, 1975), 38.12a, the *gui* is a type of ape. For lack of a precise equivalent, I have called it "siamang," which is the largest of gibbons.

L. 254: Guo Pu (cited in *Shi ji* 117.3032, n. 5) explains the rhyming binome 夭蠮 *yaojiao* (*'*jahw-kjahw*) as "stretching repeatedly." Both elements means "to bend"; hence, my "bending and bowing."

I follow Gao Buying (8.35b) in reading *ge* 格 as *ge* 挌, which the *Yu pian* 玉篇 (Jade Thesaurus), *Sbck*, 15.6a, glosses as "branch."

L. 255: The *Guangya* (6A.20a) equates the rhyming binome *yanjian* 偃蹇 (*'*jan-kjan*) with *yaojiao* (see L. 257n above). Hervouet (see *Le Chapitre 117 du Che-ki*, p. 108, n. 6) thinks that it primarily describes a shamanistic dance posture, in which the shaman-dancer crouches and bends (from *yan*) while limping (from *jian*). The word indeed may mean "to crouch and to limp," but I doubt that in this context at least there is any connection with shamanistic dancing. I have simply translated it as "hunching and hunkering."

L. 260: The alliterative binome *laoluo* 牢落 (*lahw-lak) is a variant of *liaoluo* 遼落 (*liahw-lak), which has the primary meaning of "vacant and vast," and a derived sense of "sparsely scattered." I have adopted the secondary sense for this context. See Zhu Qifeng, *Ci tong*, p. 2498.

L. 261: The rhyming binome *lanman* 爛漫 (*lan-man) primarily means "to scatter." *Lan*, which literally means "ripe," may convey the sense of "dissolving." *Man* conveys the sense of "spreading." In this context, I have rendered it "dissolve and disperse."

L. 269: On *jiaolie* (barricade hunt), see "Wu Capital Rhapsody," L. 464n.

L. 271: Cf. "Sweet Springs Palace Rhapsody," L. 29.

VII

And then
Black apes and white she-apes,
Kahaus, hoolocks, flying squirrels,
Dusky gibbons, monkeys,
250 Macaques, weasels, and siamangs
Roost and repose amongst the trees.

With long howls and sad shrieks,
Gracefully gliding, they cross back and forth,
Bending and bowing on the boughs and branches,
255 Hunched and hunkered on the tree tops.
Overleaping unbridged streams,
They spring into diverse thickets,
Clutching hanging twigs,
Throwing themselves through the open spaces.
260 Sparsely scattered, helter-skelter,
The troupe dissolves and disperses, receding into the distance.

Places of this sort
Number in the hundreds and thousands.
The emperor sports and plays hither and thither,
And in whatever palace he spends the night or lodge where he rests,
265 His kitchen need not be transported,
His harem need not be moved,
And the centurial officers are completely staffed.

VIII

And then

As the year turns its back on autumn and edges into winter, the Son
of Heaven stages the barricade hunt:

270 He mounts a chariot of carved ivory,
Drawn by six jade-encrusted dragons,
Trailing rainbow streamers,
Waving cloud banners,

L. 274: The *pi xuan* 皮軒 perhaps was the Han equivalent of the classical leather chariot. According to Xu Guang (cited in *Hou Han shu*, "Zhi," 29.3649, n. 4), the *xuan* or awning was made of tiger skin. See Zhu Jian 10.13a–b.

L. 275: According to Yan Shigu (see *Han shu* 57A.2564, n. 5), *dao* 道 should be read *dao* 導 (to guide). This chariot and the excursion chariot are both mentioned in the *Zhou li*, where Zheng Xuan says that the guide chariot is an ivory chariot. See *Zhou li zhushu* 27.17a–b; Biot, 2:135.

LL. 276–77: The exact identity of Uncle Sun (Sun shu 孫叔) and Sir Wei 衛公 is not certain. A Master Zheng (cited in *Han shu* 57A.3565, n 6) says Sun shu is Gongsun He (courtesy name Zishu 子叔), who served as Grand Coachman under Emperor Wu of the Former Han. In this capacity he would have served as Emperor Wu's charioteer in processions of this importance. Zheng says Sir Wei is Wei Qing 衛青, General-in-chief under Emperor Wu. The General-in-chief customarily served as the emperor's chariot companion. See *Hou Han shu*, "Zhi," 29.3648. The main problem with this identification is that *fu* writers did not use the names of contemporary persons in their poems. The name of a charioteer or huntsman is always an ancient legendary or historical figure who is alluded to in much the same way Milton alludes to Triton or Aeolus. Thus, Wu Renjie (see *Liang Han kanwu buyi* 6.11b–12a) says that Sun shu and Sir Wei must be ancient charioteers, perhaps Sun Yang, more commonly known as Bo Le (see "Rhapsody of Sir Vacuous," L. 109n), and Duke Zhuang 莊 of Wei (reg. 480–478 B.C.), whom the *Guo yu* (15.5a) mentions as a chariot attendant for a Zhao noble. It is difficult to decide which explanation is correct. Perhaps Sima Xiangru indeed is referring to Gongsun He and Wei Qing, but did not dare refer to them by their proper names. Thus, he invented aliases that contemporaries would readily recognize as referring to these two distinguished officials.

L. 278: Commentators variously explain the term *hucong* 扈從. Feng Yan 封演 (*jinshi* 756) explains it as the "escort equipage of the officials," i.e., the imperial retinue. See *Fengshi wenjian ji jiaozheng* 封氏聞見記校證 (Master Feng's Record of Knowledge Collated and Verified) (Beiping: Harvard-Yenching Institute, 1933), 5.1a. Hu Shaoying (10.21b–22a) says *hu* should be read as *hu* 護 (protect). Thus, *hucong* could mean "guards and attendants."

L. 279: Commentators do not agree on the meaning of *si jiao/xiao* 四校. Wen Ying (cited in *Shi ji* 117.3034, n. 6) says they are the four brigades (*xiao*) of the five-brigade army. According to Wen, the fifth brigade accompanied the imperial procession. However, Yan Shigu (see *Han shu* 57A.2564, n. 7) says that *jiao* refers to the palisades that surrounded the hunting enclosure on four sides. Since the palisade was an important feature of this hunt, I have followed Yan's interpretation. I am less certain of how to construe the entire line. Does it mean "Emerged from the four-sided palisades" or "Emerged into the four-sided palisades"?

L. 280: Both Meng Kang (see *Han shu* 57A.2564, n. 8) and Zhang Yi (see *Shi ji* 117.3034, n. 7) explain *gu yan* 鼓嚴 as "drumming the warning drum." The warning drum was used to sound the advance. See "Eastern Metropolis Rhapsody," L. 383n. They both consider *bu* as an ellipsis for *lubu* 鹵簿, the imperial escort. However, Wang Xianqian (see *Han shu buzhu* 57A.41a) argues that grammatically *yan* modifies *bu*, and thus the line should be understood literally "they drummed in the solemn escort." I have followed Wang's interpretation.

L. 283: Gao Buying (8.38b) thinks that Tai shan here should be understood simply as great mountain, not Mount Tai.

L. 288: On *yinyin* (steadily streaming), see "Rhapsody of Sir Vacuous," L. 190n.
On *yiyi* (continuously coursing), see "Shu Capital Rhapsody," LL. 305–6n.

L. 291: The *pi* 貔, also known as the *zhiyi* 執夷, is variously described as a type of tiger, leopard, or bear. See Gao Buying 8.38b–39a. I have translated it as leopard to match the panther that follows. The use of *sheng* 生 here in the sense of "to capture alive" is unusual.

L. 293: The use of *shou* 手 as a verb meaning "to capture by hand" is unusual.

L. 294: The *ye yang* 羬羊 is explained variously as antelope, wild sheep, or goat. There is no

98

The hide-covered wagon at the fore,
275 The guiding and excursion chariots behind.

With Uncle Sun holding the reins,
And Sir Wei the chariot companion,
Guards and attendants marching on the flanks,
Emerge into the four-sided palisade.

280 To drumbeats from the solemn cortege,
They unleash the hunters.
The Jiang and He are the corral;
Mount Tai is the lookout tower.

Chariots and riders thunderously set forth,
285 Rumbling through the heavens, shaking the earth,
Front and rear, helter-skelter,
Scattered and dispersed, in separate pursuit;
Steadily streaming, continuously coursing,
They skirt along the mounds, flow into the marshes,
290 Spreading like clouds, showering like rain.

They capture alive leopards and panthers,
Pummel jackals and wolves,
Hand-capture black and brown bears,
Spurn wild goats.

good way to determine which identification is correct. For a detailed discussion of the possibilities, see Zhu Jian 10.14a. The use of *zu* 足 as a verb meaning "to trample, to spurn" is unusual.

L. 295: The *he* is the *he ji* 鶡雞, the Manchurian snow pheasant. See Read, *Avian Drugs*, #272. The bird was said to fight to the death without retreating, and for this reason its plumes were used as ornaments on warriors' caps. See *Hou Han shu*, "Zhi," 30.3670.

The word *su* 蘇 is explained as a bird's tail. See *Shi ji* 117.3035, n. 5.

L. 296: *Ku* 絝 probably represents *ku* 袴 (pants). See Yan Shigu, *Han shu* 57A.2565, n. 16. Sima Xiangru uses it as a verb (literally "panted in white tiger skins")

L. 297: This attire was worn by the Rapid-as-tigers cavalry, who dressed in unlined jackets with tiger patterns. See *Hou Han shu*, "Zhi," 30.3670.

L. 299: Guo Pu (cited by Li Shan 8.9b) identifies Sanzong 三嵕 as the name of a mountain located in Wenxi 聞喜 prefecture (modern Wenxi *xian*, Shanxi). However, Zhu Jian (10.14b) points out that Wenxi is in Hedong commandery, far from the Shanglin Park. Other commentators explain it as a three-tiered mountain. See *Shi ji* 117.3035, n. 9; *Han shu* 57A.2565, n. 19; *Han shu* 87A.3544, n. 11.

L. 300: I have followed Wang Niansun (see *Du shu zazhi* 4.10.20a–b) in construing *di* 坁 as "slope."

The rhyming binome *jili* 磧歷 (**tshjak-liak*) is not otherwise attested. Yan Shigu (see *Han shu* 57A.2565, n. 20) explains it as "descriptive of sand and stones." Zhang Yi (cited by Li Shan 8.9b) says it means "not level." My "rocky ridges" is an attempt to combine both senses.

L. 303: The *Shi ji* and *Han shu* read *tui* 推 for *Wen xuan*'s *chui* 椎. Yan Shigu (see *Han shu* 57A.2565, n. 22) says that *tui* is the correct reading and should be understood like *neng* 挼 (to bruise) in the following line. However, Hu Shaoying (10.22b) cites evidence to show that the graphs are interchangeable. In this context, *tui/chui* means "to strike with the fist." See Zhang Yun'ao 5.35a–b.

On the Feilian (my flying dragon-bird), see "Western Capital Rhapsody," L. 330n.

L. 304: Zhang Yi (see *Han shu* 57A.2564, n. 23) says the *xiezhi* 獬豸 (or 解廌) is a one-horned animal resembling a deer. According to legend, it had the ability to determine right and wrong in disputes. Thus, the judge's cap reputedly was made from this animal. See *Hou Han shu*, "Zhi," 30.3667. I have invented the name "sagacious stag" for it.

L. 305: None of the early commentators knows anything about the *xiage* 蝦蛤 (**gha-kep*). Zhu Ming (cited in Gao Buying 8.41a) says it is the same as the *jiajue* 蝦玃 (**gha-kjwak*) mentioned in the *Bowu zhi* (9.2a). This animal, which is found in the mountains of Shu, resembles a monkey, is seven feet tall, walks like a human, and is fond of kidnapping beautiful women. See also Gan Bao 干寶 (fl. A.D. 317), *Sou shen ji* 搜神記 (Notes on Exploring the Supernatural) (Beijing: Zhonghua shuju, 1979), 12.152–53. Lacking a precise identification, I have called it a yeti (Abominable Snowman).

L. 306: Guo Pu (cited in *Shi ji* 117.3035, n. 13) describes the *mengshi* 猛氏 as an animal from Shu which is like a bear only smaller. This explanation is virtually identical to his description of the *mengbao* 猛豹 in the *Shanhai jing* (2.5a). According to Hao Yixing (see *Shanhai jing* 2.5a), the *mengbao* is the tapir.

L. 307: The *yaoniao* 騕褭 (my "graceful galloper") is the name of a powerful horse described as having a gold snout and red body. See Zhang Yi, *Han shu* 57A 2565, n. 14.

L. 308: The giant boar is a supernatural creature See *Shanhai jing* 18.4b–5a, Hao Yixing's commentary; Granet, *Danses et legends*, 1 : 378–80.

L. 317: The rhyming binome *qinyin* 侵淫 (**tshjem-rjem*), which is more commonly written *qinyin* 浸淫, literally means "to soak and seep." In this context, it has the meaning of "gradually, little by little." See Zhu Qifeng, *Ci tong*, p. 1073; Hervouet, *Le Chapitre 117 du Che-ki*, p. 117, n. 3.

100

295 Capped in pheasant-tail hats,
    Dressed in white tiger skin pants,
    Garbed in striped pelts,
    Astride wild horses:

    They scale steeps of three-tiered peaks,
300 Descend slopes of rocky ridges,
    Cut across defiles, dash into scarps,
    Traverse gullies, ford rivers.

    They maul the flying dragon-bird,
    Bruise the sagacious stag,
305 Wrestle the yeti,
    Spear the fierce tapir,
    Rope the graceful galloper,
    Shoot the giant boar.

    Arrows do not wantonly injure;
310 They sever the neck, split the brain.
    Bows are not shot in vain;
    At the bowstring's twang down a beast falls.

IX

    And then the emperor
    Slackens the pace to wander about,
    Roam and ramble hither and thither,
315 To scan the movements of his regiments and companies,
    Review the changing gestures of generals and chiefs.

    Then, little by little He increases the pace,
    And suddenly He is off into the remote distance,
    Scattering fleet-winged birds,
320 Trampling nimble beasts,
    Axles crushing albino deer,
    Snatching nimble hares.
    Overtaking the scarlet lightning,
    Leaving its effulgent brilliance behind,
325 Pursuing strange creatures,
    He leaves the mundane realm.

L. 327: According to Wen Ying (cited in *Shi ji* 117.3036, n. 21), the Fanruo 蕃弱, also written 繁弱, was the name of an excellent bow used by the great archer Xia hou. According to Gao You (see *Lüshi chunqiu* 18.16b), Fanruo was the name of a place that produced excellent bows.

L. 329: Guo Pu (cited in *Shi ji* 117.3035, n. 23) says the *xiao* is the *xiaoyang*. Although *xiaoyang* is a name for the langur (see "Wu Capital Rhapsody," L. 223n), in this context Sima Xiangru probably conceived of it as a supernatural creature. The *Shanhai jing* (10.2a) describes it as having a human face, long lips, and a black hairy body. I have invented the name "roving simian" for it.

L. 330: Zhang Yi (cited in *Han shu* 57A.2566, n. 10) describes the *fei ju* 蜚遽 as a supernatural celestial beast that has a deer's head and a dragon's body. Guo Pu (cited in *Shi ji* 117.3036, n. 2) gives essentially the same description. The variant name *ju* 豦 appears in the *Erya* (C6.10b) as another name for the *xuntou* 迅頭 (the swift-head?). Under this entry Guo Pu says this animal is as large as a dog, resembles a monkey, is yellow-black in color, and has a beard and mane. It is always shaking its head and likes to throw stones at people. Read (see *Animal Drugs*, #400 B.) identifies it as *Inuus silenus*. Other sources identify the creature as akin to the giant boar. See Zhu Jian 10 15b–16a; Gao Buying 8.43a–b. Here it clearly is a supernatural beast. I have thus called it a "flying chimera."

L. 332: The *Shi ji* lacks the *er* 而, which makes for a more sensible reading. Otherwise, it would be necessary to emend the text to read 先命而中處.

L. 334: Yan Shigu (see *Han shu* 57A.2567, n. 12) explains *yi* (*ngjad) 藙 (written in the text as *yi* 藝) as *nie* (*ngiat) 臬 (bullseye). The text possibly should be understood as *nie* (*ngiat) 槷, which is a variant of *nie* meaning "bullseye." See Hu Shaoying 10.24a; Gao Buying 8.43b.

L. 340: Cf. "Rhapsody of Sir Vacuous," L. 173

L. 341: On the *kunji* (great fowl), see "Western Metropolis Rhapsody," L. 216n.

L. 344: The *yi niao* 鷖鳥 (my "canopy bird") is a type of variegated phoenix. See *Shanhai jing* 18.6a.

L. 346: On the *yuanchu* (rendered here "sea-argus"), see "Southern Capital Rhapsody," L. 68n.

L. 347: On the *jiaoming* (my "blazing firebird"), see "Wu Capital Rhapsody," L. 615n.

LL. 354–57: On the Stone Watchtower and Great Peak Tower, see "Sweet Springs Palace Rhapsody," L. 59n. The Zhique 鳷鵲 (Jaybird) Tower and Luhan 露寒 (Dewy Chill) Lodge were located in the Sweet Springs Park. See *Sanfu huangtu* 2.45.

L. 358: On the Pear Palace, see "Sweet Springs Palace Rhapsody," L. 188n.

L. 359: Yichun 宜春 (Befitting Spring) Palace was located east of Du prefecture (southeast of modern Xi'an). See *Sanfu huangtu* 3.60.

L. 360: The *Sanfu huangtu* (3.61) says the Xuanqu 宣曲 Palace was located west of the Kunming Pond (southwest of Chang'an). It claims that because Emperor Xuan frequently composed tunes here, it was called Xuanqu (Emperor Xuan's Tunes?). Gao Buying 8.45a–b remarks that the story of the invention of the name is an obvious concoction by some "later person." (The palace already had this name before the time of Emperor Xuan.)

L. 361: On Ox Head Lake, see "Western Metropolis Rhapsody," L. 398n.

Bending the Fanruo bow,
Drawn to the tip of the white-plumed shaft,
He shoots the roving simian,
330 Strikes the flying chimera.

Carefully selecting his game, he then shoots,
His first shot hitting the spot He names.
Just as the arrow leaves the string,
The quarry is killed and falls to the ground.

335 Then, raising His signal flag, He soars aloft,
Outdistancing the startling wind,
Cleaving the frightful gale,
Riding the empty void,
Companion of the gods.

340 He tramples the black crane,
Confounds the great fowl,
Harries the peacock and simurgh,
Torments the golden pheasant;

Strikes the canopy bird,
345 Clubs the phoenix,
Snatches the sea-argus,
Seizes the blazing firebird.

At journey's end, road's limit,
He wheels round his carriage and returns.

350 Rambling and roving, wandering and wavering,
He lands in the northern bounds.
Directly He advances straight ahead,
Suddenly reverses direction.

He treads the Stone Watchtower,
355 Courses by Great Peak,
Passes Jaybird Tower,
Gazes at Dewy Chill,
Descends to Pear Palace,
Rests at Befitting Spring.

360 Westward he gallops to Xuanqu,
Sculls the heron-prow on Ox Head Lake,

LL. 362–63: The Long tai 龍臺 (Dragon Terrace) Tower was located northwest of the Feng River near the Wei River. Xi liu 細柳 (Lithe Willows) was a viewing tower located south of the Kunming Pond. See *Han shu* 57A.2568, n. 8–9 and *Sanfu huangtu* 5.94.

L. 376: Lu Xiang (8.15a) explains *hao tian* 顥天 (vast Heaven) as the name of a terrace. However, since it is parallel with *jiaoge* (capacious) in the following line, it must be a descriptive expression.

L. 377: The use of *jiaoge* in the sense of "capacious" is different from its more common meanings. See "Sweet Springs Palace Rhapsody," L. 22n.

LL. 378–79: The *Zhanguo ce* (11.4a) also mentions a thousand-catty bell and a ten thousand-catty bell-stand. If this is the actual weight of the bell, it would weigh over 64,000 pounds! Sima Xiangru is indulging in typical *fu* hyperbole. According to the *Han yi* (= *Han jiu yi*?) cited in the *Jiu Tang shu* (29.1080), there were ten of these bells.

L. 382: Master Taotang is the name used by Yao when ruling the empire. Cf. "Wei Capital Rhaposdy," L. 149n. The music most commonly associated with Yao is "Xian chi" 咸池 or "The All-encompassing Pond." However, Yan Shigu (see *Han shu* 57A.2570, n. 6) cites what he claims is a correct version of a *Lüshi chunqiu* passage that names a Master Yinkang 陰康 together with Master Getian of the following line as the two earliest composers of music. Yan considers the versions of the *Lüshi chunqiu* (cf. 5.8a) that read Taotang corrupt. For a more detailed discussion, see Hervouet, *Le Chapitre 117 du Che-ki*, p. 125, n. 7.

L. 383: The *Lüshi chunqiu* (5.7b) describes the music created by the legendary emperor Master Getian as performed by three men holding an oxtail. They stamp their feet as they sing eight tunes.

L. 388: On the Ba-Yu dance, see "Shu Capital Rhapsody," L. 110n.

Song is most famous for the ritual songs performed by the Shang dynasty descendants. These pieces are found in the "Eulogia of Shang" section of the *Shi jing*. The *Li ji* (see *Li ji zhushu* 39.3a) describes the music of Song as licentious.

Cai 蔡 was a small state of central China. It was eventually absorbed by Chu in the mid-fifth century B.C. Virtually nothing is known of its music. As late as 7 B.C., there were three singers of Cai music employed by the bureau of music. See *Han shu* 22.1074. The music of Cai also is mentioned in the *Chuci* poem, "Summoning the Soul" (see *Chuci buzhu* 9.12a).

L. 389: Huainan is one of the largest and most powerful Han kingdoms. There were four musicians who performed Huainan music employed by the bureau of music. See *Han shu* 22.1073. Nothing is known about the "Ganzhe" 干遮 (or Yuzhe 于遮) tune.

L. 390: Wencheng 文成 was a prefecture in Liaoxi 遼西 commandery. See *Han shu* 28B.1625. It corresponds to modern Lulong *xian* in eastern Hebei. According to Wen Ying (cited in *Han shu* 57A.2570, n. 11), the people of this area were good singers.

Dian 顛 is the name of a non-Chinese kingdom of the southwest. See Hervouet, *Un Poète de cour*, pp. 113–13.

Climbs Dragon Terrace,
Reposes at Lithe Willows.

He observes the effort and prowess of his officers and men,
365 Evaluates the hunters' catch:
Those crushed and crumpled by foot-soldiers and chariots,
Those trampled and trod by infantry and cavalry,
Those squashed and flattened by the multitudes,
Together with those utterly and completely exhausted and fatigued,
370 In frightful panic, cowering in terror,
Who died without a single wound,
Heaped high, piled and pillowed,
Clog the ditches, fill the gullies,
Cover the plains, lie strewn over the marshes.

X

375 And then
Tired of excursion and sport,
He sets a feast for a terrace high as vast Heaven,
Prepares music for a capacious hall.
They beat thousand-catty bells,
Erect ten-thousand-catty bell-racks,
380 Raise banners adorned with kingfisher tufts,
And plant in place the drum of sacred alligator hide.

They present the dances of Taotang,
Perform the songs of Getian.
A thousand voices sing the lead;
385 Ten thousand sing the harmony.
The mountains and hills thus begin to quake and rock;
The streams and gorges thus begin to churn and billow.
The music of Ba-Yu, Song, and Cai,
The "Ganzhe" of Huainan,
390 Songs of Wencheng and Dian,
Are presented en masse, performed en suite.

Bells and drums alternately sound,
Their cling-clang and rat-a-tat-tat
Pierce the heart and startle the ears.

105

L. 395: Jing 荊 is another name for Chu. Liu Bang, the founder of the Han, was from Chu, and in the early Han, Chu music was the most common form of music played at the court. See *Han shu* 22.1043; Diény, *Aux Origines*, pp. 54–55.

The songs of Wu had yet to attain the popularity they achieved in the Six Dynasties. "Summoning the Soul" (see *Chuci buzhu* 9.12a) mentions songs of Wu together with the music of Cai.

The music of Zheng and Wei is synonymous with licentiousness. See Dieny, *Aux Origines*, pp. 17–40.

L. 396: The "Succession," "Salvation," and "Martial" are attributed to Shun, Cheng Tang, and King Wu respectively. On the "Succession" and "Martial," see "Eastern Capital Rhapsody," L. 244n. Several sources explain that the "Hu" 濩 ("Salvation") music received its name because Cheng Tang was able to "rescue" (*hu*) the people from their distress. See *Han shu* 22 1038; *Zhou li zhushu* 22.9a–b; *Guangya shuzheng* 4B.11b; *Bohu tong yi* A.21b (Tjan Tjoe Som, *Po Hu T'ung*, 2:393). The "Xiang" 象 or "Mime" dance is variously attributed to King Wu and the Duke of Zhou. According to the *Lushi chunqiu* (5.10b), when King Cheng succeeded to the Zhou throne, the people of the former Yin dynasty rebelled. They trained elephants (*xiang*) to rampage among the Eastern Yi. After the Duke of Zhou put down the rebellion, the "Three Xiang" (Three Elephant Songs?) were composed to praise his deeds. The *Li ji* twice mentions the "Xiang" as music played on the *guan* (pipes). See *Li ji zhushu* 20.27b, 31.7a. My translation of "Xiang" as "Mime" is based on the *Bohu tong yi*'s claim that King Wu composed the "Xiang" to "represent" (*xiang*) the achievement of peace. See *Bohu tong yi* A.21b; Tjan Tjoe Som, *Po Hu T'ung*, 2:394. It seems strange for Sima Xiangru to include these hallowed musical works with the notorious licentious music of Zheng and Wei. Hervouet (see *Un Poète de cour*, p. 283) speculates that Sima Xiangru may be objecting to the profane use of this religious music.

L. 397: On the rhyming binome *yinyin* 陰淫 (*·jem-rjem), "dissolute," see Wang Xianqian, *Han shu buzhu* 57A.47a.

L. 398: On Yanying, which was the old Chu capital, see "Wei Capital Rhapsody," L. 85n. According to Wang Xianqian (see *Han shu buzhu* 57A.47a), the alliterative binome *binfen* 繽紛 (*phjien-phjen) describes the mixed presentation of Chu dances and Chu songs.

L. 399: Commentators variously explain the expressions "Ji Chu" 激楚 and "Jie feng" 結風. According to Wen Ying (see *Shi ji* 117.3039, n. 10), *ji* means "turbulent." The tune title "Turbulent Chu" thus reputedly refers to the turbulent atmosphere of Chu that infuses the music. However, Hervouet (see *Le Chapitre 117 du Che-ki*, p. 128, n. 11) claims that the piece has nothing to do with Chu and simply means "Tristesse poignante." Although Hervouet's interpretation is possible, I have followed Wen Ying's explanation. It is not clear whether "Jie feng" is the name of a song or simply means "finale." It occurs in conjunction with "Ji Chu" in Mei Sheng's "Seven Stimulli" (see *Wen xuan* 34.7b), where it clearly means "finale." However, in Fu Yi's "Rhapsody on Dance" (see *Wen xuan* 17.16a) it seems to be construed as a song title. I have followed Gao Buying (8.49a–b) in translating it as "finale."

L. 401: According to Guo Pu (cited in *Han shu* 57A.2571), "Didi" 猩鞮 is the name of the music of the Western Rong. The same term appears in the *Li ji* (see *Li ji zhushu* 12.27a) as the name of the translator of the language of the western tribes. See also *Huainanzi* 11.4b. I suspect that Didi is a Chinese transcription of a Central Asian place name that can no longer be identified.

L. 405: Both the *Shi ji* and *Han shu* add 於後 to the end of this line. Li Shan (8.12b) claims this is an incorrect reading. I have followed him and the text as given by Gao Buying (8.50a) and in the *Liang Han wenxueshi cankao ziliao*, p. 43.

L. 406: Qing Qin 青琴 (Blue Zither) is the name of a goddess about whom nothing else is known. On Consort Fu, see "Eastern Metropolis Rhapsody," L. 127n.

L. 409: On *jingzhuang* (powdered and painted), see "Shu Capital Rhapsody," L. 249n.

106

The airs of Jing, Wu, Zheng, and Wei, the music of the "Succession," "Salvation," "Martial Dance," and "Mimes," melodies of dissolute dissipation, the mixed medleys of Yanying, the finale of "Turbulent Chu," jesters and dwarfs, girl singers from Didi, everything to delight the ears and eyes, gladden the heart and spirit, all in sumptuous splendor and garish glitter pass before Him.

405   Beautiful ladies of dainty delicacy,
      Like Blue Zither and Consort Fu,
      Truly extraordinary, unmatched in the world,
      Beguiling and bewitching, elegant and refined,
      Faces powdered and painted, hair sculpted and trimmed,

L. 410: The rhyming binome *pianxuan* 便嬛 (*bjan-hjwan*) is a variant of *pianjuan* 便娟, which is used in the "Great Summons" (see *Chuci buzhu* 10.6b) to describe the slender limbs of a beautiful women. I have translated it "lithe and lissome."

The rhyming binome *chuoyue* 綽約 (*tjakw-'jakw*) occurs in the *Zhuangzi* (1.14) to describe the gentle, modest quality of a virgin. The signific possibly is *yue*, which can mean "restrained." I have rendered it "decorous and demure " For other uses and variants, see Zhu Qifeng, *Ci tong*, pp. 2510–11.

L. 411: The assonant binome *rounao* 柔橈 (*njehw-njahw*) is not otherwise attested. It contains two elements: *rou* (soft) and *nao* (supple).

The *Wen xuan* mistakenly writes *manman* 嫚嫚. The text should read *yuanyuan* 嬛嬛. See Hu Kejia, *Wen xuan kaoyi* 2.10a; Gao Buying 8.50b–51a. Dictionaries merely gloss it as "beautiful." See *Guangya shuzheng* 6A.8b. I have translated it "gracile and graceful" to fit this context.

L. 412: The alliterative binome *wumei* 嫵媚 (*mjah-mekw*) is not attested earlier than Sima Xiangru. According to the *Pi cang* (cited by Li Shan 8.13a), it means "to enjoy," probably in the sense of "likeable, appealing, winsome." I have rendered it "winning and winsome."

L. 413: I follow the *Shi ji* text, which reads *yi* 袘 (hem) for *xie* 緤 (bridle) of *Wen xuan* and *yi* 袘 (sleeve) of *Han shu*. See "Rhapsody of Sir Vacuous," L. 144n. The *yu* is the *chanyu* 襜褕, a type of an unlined robe, usually with a straight lapel. See Zhang Moyuan, pp. 3, 7, n. 19, and pp. 84–85, illustrations #35 and #38.

What I have translated as "pure silk" literally is "solitary cocoon."

L. 414: The alliterative binome *yanyi* 閻易 (*rjam-rei*) is not otherwise attested. Guo Pu (cited in *Han shu* 57A.2572, n. 5) explains it as "descriptive of length of a garment." I cannot explain the component elements of the word. I have arbitrarily translated it as "flowing and falling."

On *xuxue* (perfectly tailored), see "Rhapsody of Sir Vacuous," L. 144n.

L. 415: The assonant binome *pianxian* (*bjan-sien*) 便姍 (also written 便姓 and 蝙姓) is a variant of *pianxian* 蝙躚, which in Zhang Heng's "Southern Capital Rhapsody" (see *Wen xuan* 4 8a; L. 201 of my translation) describes the whirling pirouettes of dancers. For other variants, see Zhu Qifeng, *Ci tong*, p 666. I have rendered it "wheel and reel."

The rhyming binome *piexie* 嫳屑 (*bjet-siet*) is a variant of *biexie* 蹩躠 (*bjat-siat*), which also occurs in the "Southern Capital Rhapsody" in the same line as *pianxian* above. It is similar in meaning to *pianxian*. For other variants, see Zhu Qifeng, *Ci tong*, p. 2423. Although I suspect that the word may have something to do with limping (cf. *bosu/boxie* in "Rhapsody of Sir Vacuous," L. 155n), I have rendered it here "whirl and twirl."

L. 417: *Ouyu* 漚鬱 (*'juh-'jwet*) may be an alliterative binome. It is not attested elsewhere. Guo Pu (cited in *Han shu* 57A.2572, n. 7) explains it as "the fullness of aromatic vapors." Each element has a relevant meaning. *Ou* means "to steep, to suffuse." *Yu* describes thick, dense vapors. I render it "profusely permeating."

L. 420: Wen Yiduo adduces an impressive array of evidence to show that *yi* of *yi xiao* 宜笑 should be understood as *yi* 齸 (exposing the teeth, toothy). See *Chuci jiaobu* 楚辭校補, 1942; rpt. in *Wen Yiduo Chuci yanjiu lunzhu shizhong* 聞一多楚辭研究論著十種 (Hong Kong: Weiya shuwu, n.d.), p. 193.

L. 431: Autumn was the season associated with punishment and destruction. In L. 268 above, Sima Xiangru mentions that the hunt took place in late autumn-early winter.

L. 435: Cf. *Mengzi* 1B/14: "A Gentleman creates achievements and passes down a tradition that can be continued."

LL. 440–41: As Hervouet points out (see *Le Chapitre 117 du Che-ki*, p. 135, n. 3), this section is reminiscent of *Mengzi* 1B/2, which describes the hunting park of King Wen of Zhou, in which woodcutters as well as hunters of pheasants and hares were allowed to enter.

410 Lithe and lissome, decorous and demure,
　　 Soft and supple, gracile and graceful,
　　 Winning and winsome, slender and slight,
　　 Trail the hems of their pure silk gowns,
　　 Subtly flowing and falling, perfectly tailored.
415 As they wheel and reel, whirl and twirl,
　　 Their garments seem not of this world.
　　 Their sweet fragrance, profusely permeating,
　　 Is strong and pungent, pure and thick.
　　 Their white teeth spangle and sparkle;
420 Their toothy smiles gleem and glitter.
　　 Beneath long eyebrows, coiling and curling,
　　 They coyly gaze, cast sidelong glances.
　　 Their beauty is offered, the spirit consents
　　 And the heart rejoices to be at their side.

XI

"And then, in the midst of drinking, during the rapture of music, the Son of Heaven becomes disconsolate, as if He had lost something. He says, 'Alas! This is too extravagant! During Our leisure moments from attending to state affairs, with nothing to do We cast away the days; following the celestial cycle, We kill and slaughter, and from time to time rest and repose here in this park. But We fear the dissolute dissipation of later generations, that once they have embarked on this course they will be unable to turn back. This is not the way to create achievements and pass down a tradition for one's heirs.'

"Thereupon, He dissolves the feast, ends the hunt, and commands His officials, saying, 'Let all land that can be reclaimed and opened up:

440 Be made into farmland
　　 In order to provide for the common people!
　　 Tear down the walls, fill in the moats,
　　 Allow the people of the mountains and marshes to come here!

　　 Restock the pools and ponds and do not ban people from them!
445 Empty the palaces and lodges and do not staff them!

LL. 446–47: Cf. *Mengzi* 1B/4: "(Duke Jing) for the first time opened up his granaries to supply the people's needs."

LL. 450–55: The suggestions for institutional and calendrical reform made in these lines would have been controversial in Sima Xiangru's time. Although Emperor Wu was interested in making these changes, he was opposed by his mother, the Empress Dowager. In 104 B.C., he established a new calendar, made yellow the official color, and standardized official titles. See *HFHD*, 2:99.

LL. 464–65: The "Wildcat's Head" ("Li shou" 狸首) and the "Zouyu" were names of musical pieces played as accompaniment for the archery performance of the emperor and vassal lords respectively. See *Li ji zhushu* 39.13b–14a, 62.2a; *Zhou li zhushu* 22.22b, 23.cb, 24.3b.

L. 466: The "Black Crane" ("Xuan he" 玄鶴) is the name of a dance attributed to Shun in the *Shang shu dazhuan* 尚書大傳 (Grand Commentary on the *Shang shu*), *Sbck*, 1B.14b. Note that the Black Crane is mentioned in L. 340 as one of the birds the emperor pursues on his celestial hunt.

L. 467: On the "Shield and Axe" dances, see "Wei Capital Rhapsody," L. 523n.

L. 468: On the cloud-net, see "Eastern Metropolis Rhapsody," L. 376n.

L. 469: There may be a pun on *ya* 雅, which means "refinement," but is homophonous with *ya* 鴉 (crow). The line refers to the emperor's efforts to recruit men of refinement and learning.

L. 470: "Cutting Sandalwood" is the title of *Mao shi* 112. It is traditionally interpreted as a poem criticizing greedy, incompetent officials who deprived worthy men of their positions. See *Mao shi zhushu* 5.3.9b.

L. 471: "Rejoicing All" is a phrase from *Mao shi* 215, which describes the vassal lords coming to court to receive favors. Following Zheng Xuan's interpretation (see *Mao shi zhushu* 14.2.8b), Yan Shigu (see *Han shu* 57A.2574) explains *le xu* 樂胥 as "to enjoy the talented." Yan thinks the allusion refers to kings who enjoy employing talented men. It is impossible to know how Sima Xiangru might have understood the *Mao shi* phrase.

LL. 474–75: Sima Xiangru perhaps intends here a reference to the practice stipulated in the *Classic of Changes* of leaving one side of an enclosure open to allow some animals to escape. See "Eastern Capital Rhapsody," L. 175n.

L. 476: On the Luminous Hall, see "Western Capital Rhapsody," L. 140n.

Open the granaries and storehouses in order to give relief to the poor
    and destitute!

Supply what they lack!
Pity widowers and widows,
Console the orphaned and childless!

450 Issue virtuous commands,
Reduce punishments and penalties,
Reform the institutions,
Alter the vestment colors,
Change the first month and day of the year,
455 Make a new beginning for the empire!'

XII

And then, calculating an auspicious day, he fasts and cleanses
    himself,
Dons His court robes,
And mounts the chariot of the Standard Cortege,
Flowery banners raised on high,
460 Jade simurgh bells jangling.
He sports in the preserve of the Six Classics,
Gallops over the road of Humaneness and Morality,
Goes sightseeing in the forest of the *Annals*,
Shoots to the "Wildcat's Head,"
465 Together with the "Zouyu."

His corded arrows catch the "Black Crane,"
He dances the "Shield and Axe."

Carrying in his cart a cloud-net,
He captures a flock of refinement.
470 He grieves at "Cutting Sandalwood,"
Delights in "Rejoicing All,"
Cultivates His comportment in the garden of the *Rites*,
Roams and rambles in the park of the *Documents*.

Transmitting the doctrine of the *Changes*,
475 He releases the strange beasts,
Ascends the Luminous Hall,

L. 477: The Pure Temple is the subject of *Mao shi* 266. It is the name of the main chamber of the Luminous Hall and also is a name for the Grand Temple. See Gao Buying 8.55a–b.

Sits in the Pure Temple.
One after another a multitude of ministers
Present advice and criticism,
480 And within the four seas,
No one is denied reward.
At this time, all in the empire greatly rejoice,
Face His virtuous wind and heed its sound,
Follow His current and are reformed,
485 Spontaneously promote the Way and revert to morality.
Punishments are discarded and no longer used.
His virtue is more lofty than that of the Three Kings,
His achievements are more abundant than those of the Five
                Emperors.
Under these conditions, hunting can be enjoyed.

490 As for
Galloping and riding all day long,
Tiring the spirit, straining the body,
Exhausting the utility of carriages and horses,
Sapping the energy of officers and men,
Wasting the wealth of treasuries and storehouses,
495 While depriving the people of generous beneficence;

Striving only for selfish pleasure;
Not caring for the common people,
Ignoring the administration of the state,
Craving only a catch of pheasants or hares:
500 These are things a benevolent ruler would not do.

"Looking at it from this perspective, are not the actions of Qi and Chu lamentable? Their territory does not exceed a thousand *li* square, yet their parks occupy nine hundred of them. This means the vegetation cannot be cleared and the people have nothing to eat. If someone of the insignificance of a vassal lord enjoys the extravagances fit only for an emperor, I fear the common people will suffer the ill effects."

"Thereupon, the two gentlemen paled, changed expressions, and seemed dispirited and lost in thought. As they retreated and backed away from the mat, they said, 'Your humble servants have been stubborn and uncouth, and ignorant of the prohibitions. Now this day we have received your instruction. We respectfully accept your command.'"

[1] This preface comes from Yang Xiong's "Autobiographical Postface," preserved in his *Han shu* biography. The plume of "plume hunt" refers to the plumes worn on the shoulders of the marchers in the emperor's entourage. See *Han shu* 87A.3541, n. 1 and *Guo yu* 7.6b. Instead of "during the reign of Emperor Cheng," the *Han shu* reads "in the twelfth month." The hunt probably took place in the twelfth month of Yuanyan 元延 2 (January 10 B.C.). For details on the problems of dating this piece, see Knechtges, *The Han Rhapsody*, pp. 113–116.

[2] The Two Emperors are Yao and Shun. The Three Kingships are the Xia, Yin, and Zhou.

[3] The ancient hunt theoretically had a threefold function: supplying cured meat for the sacrificial vessels, entertaining guests, and filling the ruler's larder. See "Eastern Capital Rhapsody," L. 175n.

[4] Yang Xiong alludes here to *Mengzi* 3B/4.

[5] These are all auspicious omens of good government. See *Li ji zhushu* 7.12a–b.

[6] Cf. the "Canon of Shun" (*Shang shu zhushu* 3.24b; Legge 3:46): "The emperor said, 'Who will attend to my uplands and lowlands, plants and trees, birds and beasts?' All said, 'Yi!'"

[7] See "Eastern Metropolis Rhapsody," LL. 539–40n.

[8] Yang Xiong alludes here to *Mengzi* 1B/2: "King Xuan of Qi asked, 'The enclosure of King Wen, was it really seventy *li* square?' Mencius replied, 'According to the records it is so.' The king said, 'Was it as large as that?' Mencius said, 'The people still regarded it as small.' The king said, 'My enclosure is forty *li* square, yet the people still regard it as large. Why?' Mencius replied, 'The enclosure of King Wen was seventy *li* square, but the gatherers of forage and fuel could enter it, and hunters of pheasants and hares could enter it. Since he shared with the people, was it not fitting that they considered it small?'"

[9] According to the *Sanfu huangtu* (4.65), Emperor Wu expanded the park in 138 B.C. On the expansion of the park, see *Han shu* 65.2847–51 and Hervouet, *Un Poète de cour*, pp. 224–48. On Befitting Spring Palace, see "Rhapsody on the Imperial Park," L. 359n. On Tripod Lake, see "Western Metropolis Rhapsody," L. 308n. The Yusu 御宿 (Imperial Overnight) was a park located on the Yusu River, thirty-seven *li* south of the Tang prefecture of Wannian 萬年 (modern Chang'an xian). See *Sanfu huangtu* 4.67 and *Yuanhe junxian tu zhi* 1 4. Kunwu 昆吾, located in the Lantian area, was the site of a famous pavilion. See *Han shu* 87A.3541, n. 7.

Plume Hunt Rhapsody

YANG ZIYUN

During the reign of Emperor Cheng a plume hunt was held, and I accompanied the imperial procession.[1] I believe that anciently under the Two Emperors and Three Kingships,[2] the palaces and lodges, terraces and towers, ponds and lakes, parks and enclosures, forests and foothills, preserves and marshes were just sufficient to provide for the boundary and temple sacrifices, to entertain guests and visitors, and to fill the larders and kitchens.[3] No one appropriated from the people's rich and fertile grain lands or mulberry and silkworm thorn areas, the women had surplus cloth, and the men had surplus grain.[4] The state was thriving and rich, and both superior and inferior were satisfied. Thus, sweet dew fell in the courtyards, sweet wine springs flowed in the temple paths, phoenixes nested in the trees, yellow dragons frolicked in the ponds, unicorns arrived in the enclosures, and holy birds perched in the forests.[5]

Anciently, when Yu employed Yi as forester, uplands and lowlands were in harmony, and the plants and trees flourished.[6] Cheng Tang loved hunting, yet the resources of the empire were sufficient.[7] King Wen's enclosure was a hundred *li* square, but the people thought it too small. King Xuan of Qi's enclosure was forty *li* square, but the people thought it too large. This is the difference between being generous with the people and appropriating from them.[8]

Emperor Wu expanded the Imperial Park southeast to Befitting Spring, Tripod Lake, the Imperial Overnight, and Kunwu,[9] west along the

THIS RHAPSODY by Yang Xiong describes an imperial hunt conducted in January, 10 B.C. According to the *Han shu* (10.327; see also *HFHD*, 2:412), the emperor invited guests from the Hu tribes of the northwest to participate in a hunting excursion at the Tall Poplars Palace in the Shanglin Park. Yang Xiong was a member of the imperial procession and was commissioned by the emperor to write a rhapsody to commemorate the event. Yang's *fu* is not solely a glorification of imperial power and virtue, but includes a subtle moral reprimand criticizing the extravagance of the hunt. For a more detailed discussion, see Knechtges, *The Han Rhapsody*, pp. 73–80. The text of this piece also is found in *Han shu* 87A.3540–3553. Previous translations include: von Zach, in *Sinologische Beiträge* 2, pp 14–16 and rpt. in *Die Chinesische Anthologie*, 1:117–25; Doeringer, "Yang Hsiung," pp. 259–72; Knechtges, *The Han Rhapsody*, pp. 63–73; Obi Kōichi, *Monzen*, 1:426–55. This translation is a revised version of the translation that appeared in my *The Han shu Biography of Yang Xiong*, pp. 27–38, 103–17.

115

[10] The Southern Mountains are the Zhongnan Mountains. On Tall Poplars Palace see "Western Capital Rhapsody," L. 382n. On Five Oaks Lodge, see "Western Metropolis Rhapsody," L. 397n.

[11] On the Yellow Mountains, see "Western Metropolis Rhapsody," L. 398n.

[12] Kunming 昆明 was the name of a non-Chinese state located in the area of the Southwestern Tribes. After the Kunming had attacked Han envoys, who were on their way to India, Emperor Wu in 120 B.C. ordered the digging of a Kunming Pond southwest of Chang'an to practice naval tactics to be used on the huge Dian Lake (see "Shu Capital Rhapsody," L. 352n) of the Kunming territory. The Kunming Pond was intended as a replica of this lake. Although some scholars have equated Dian Lake with the Kunming Lake located southeast of modern Kunming City, Yunnan (see *HFHD*, 2:63), because the state of Kunming was located near Dali, in western Yunnan, the Dian Lake imitated by Emperor Wu more probably refers to the Er 洱 River. Note that Yang Xiong does not call it a lake, but a river. See Quan Zuwang 全祖望 (1705–1755), *Jiqi ting ji* 鮚埼亭集 (Collection from Mussel Bank Pavilion), *Sbck*, 35.9a–11a; Hervouet, *Un Poète de cour*, p. 117, n. 3.

[13] On the Jianzhang Palace and the Phoenix Watchtower, see "Western Capital Rhapsody," LL. 256–57 On the Terrace of Divine Luminaries, see "Western Capital Rhapsody," L. 270n. On the Rapid Gallop Hall, see "Western Capital Rhapsody," L. 266n.

[14] On the Tower of Soaking Waters, see "Western Metropolis Rhapsody," L. 286n. On the Grand Fluid, see "Western Capital Rhapsody," L. 289n.

[15] In 47 B.C., Emperor Yuan of the Former Han ordered the lands of the parks under the office of the Chief Commandant of Waters and Parks, and the lower park of the Befitting Spring Palace, and the bird preserves abolished and lent to the common people. See *Han shu* 9.281; *HFHD*, 2:306; Hsu, *Han Agriculture*, p. 179

[16] For a similar use of the term *chuzhi* 儲偫 (stores and reserves), see *Han shu* 12.350.

[17] The word *yu* 禦 probably should be understood as *yu* 籞, another name for enclosure. According to Su Lin (cited in *Han shu* 8.249, n. 5), pieces of bamboo were tied together to prevent people from entering the forbidden area. In the Han Code, such places were designated *yu* (enclosures). The *Shuowen* (5A.1987b–89b) laconically explains *yu* as "forbidden park."

[18] On the three-sided battue, see "Eastern Capital Rhapsody," L. 175n.

[19] According to the *Chunqiu* (see *Wen* 16), Duke Wen destroyed the Spring Terrace (*Quan tai* 泉臺). The *Gongyang zhuan* (14.16a) condemned the destruction of the terrace, arguing that, since Duke Wen had not built it, his only duty was not to dwell in it. Yang Xiong implies that, since Emperor Cheng did not construct the Shanglin Park, he need not destroy it. However, he should not "revive former pursuits" by conducting elaborate excursions and hunts there.

[20] "Jiao lie fu" 校獵賦 ("Barricade Hunt Rhapsody") is Yang Xiong's original title for this piece. The title "Plume Hunt Rhapsody" is the title recorded in Ban Gu's "Appraisal" appended to Yang Xiong's *Han shu* biography (87B.3583). Both von Zach (see *Die Chinesische Anthologie*, 1:118) and Obi Kōichi (see *Monzen*, 1:438) punctuate this line to read: "Thus, using the opportunity of a the barricade hunt, I compose a *fu* in order to sway the emperor's opinion." However, there is overwhelming evidence that "Jiao lie fu" is a title. For details, see *The Han shu Biography of Yang Xiong*, pp. 106–8, n 249.

L. 1: Fu Xi and Shennong are ancient rulers known for their simplicity of government. Fu Xi invented the eight trigrams and taught the people how to fish and hunt. Shennong invented the plow and established markets. See Karlgren, "Legends and Cults," pp. 276–77.

L. 2: I have followed Gao Buying (8.62a–b) in emending *huo* 或 (perhaps) to *huo* 惑 (delude).

L. 6: Several texts mention seventy-two (or seventy) as the number of ancient rulers who performed the *feng* sacrifice on Mount Tai. See *Guanzi*, *ce* 2, 50.104; *Shi ji* 28.1361; *Mh*, 3:423; *Records*, 2:19; *Huainanzi* 11.9a.

L. 11: The divine sage is Emperor Cheng.

L. 12: The Dark Palace (Xuan gong 玄宮) probably is a ritual building similar to the Dark

116

Southern Mountains as far as Tall Poplars and Five Oaks,[10] north around the Yellow Mountains skirting east along the banks of the Wei,[11] for a circumference of serveral hundred *li*. They dug the Kunming Pond to replicate the River of Dian,[12] built the Jianzhang Palace, Phoenix Watchtower, the Terrace of the Divine Luminaries, and Rapid Gallop Hall.[13] At the Tower of Soaking Waters and the Grand Fluid, they replicated the sea flowing around Fangzhang, Yingzhou, and Penglai.[14] The excursion lodges were extravagantly lavish, most wonderful, and absolutely beautiful. Although the emperor ceded some territory from the three borders to provide for the common people,[15] when it came time for the plume hunt, the armored carts and war horses, implements and weapons, stores and reserves,[16] things constructed in the forbidden enclosures were still excessively ostentatious and grandiose,[17] and violated the intent of the three-sided battue of Yao, Shun, Cheng Tang, and King Wen.[18] In addition, fearing that later generations would revive former pursuits and would not strike a compromise on the example of the Spring Terrace,[19] I thus use the "Barricade Hunt Rhapsody" for the purpose of swaying the emperor's opinion.[20] The piece reads:

I

When someone praises Fu Xi and Shennong, could he be deluded by the increased material display of later emperors and kings?

One who would dispute this assertion says: No. Each determined what was right in accord with his own time. Why must they all be consonant and consistent with one another? Otherwise, why have there been seventy-two different ceremonies for the *feng* sacrifices on Mt. Tai? For this reason, all those who founded dynasties and handed down the succession could not perceive their deviations, and whether far from or near to the Three Kings and Five Emperors, who could determine right and wrong? Thus, I have composed the following eulogy:

Magnificent indeed the divine sage!
He abides in the Dark Palace.

Hall (Xuan tang 玄堂), the northern portion of the Luminous Hall theoretically occupied by the emperor the last month of winter. *Xuan* (dark, black) is the color of the north and winter. See *Li ji zhushu* 17.21a.

LL. 15–16: Duke Huan of Qi and Duke Zhuang 莊 of Chu (reg. 613–591 B.C.) both presided as hegemons over a league of states in the Zhou period. Zhuang is referred to as Yan here because of the taboo on Zhuang in the Later Han period.

L. 23: This is the peak of the *yin* pneuma.

L. 28: There was no park by this name in the Han period. Yang Xiong has borrowed a phrase from *Mao shi* 242/2. The Holy Park was the hunting park of King Wen of Zhou.

L. 30: Buzhou here refers to the wind that presumably blew from the Buzhou Mountain in the northwest. It was dominant during the first forty-five days of winter. See *Huainanzi* 3.4b; Major, "Nomenclature of the Winds," pp. 76–78.

L. 31: Zhuanxu is the ruler of the three months of winter, and Xuanming is their god. See *Li ji zhushu* 17.8a; *Lushi chunqiu* 10.1a. According to Ying Shao (see *Han shu* 87A.3544, n. 5), they are in charge of killing. The phrase *zhong shi* 終始, literally "beginning and end," often has the sense of "cycle." Cf. *Shi ji* 13.488 (*Mh*, 3:2) and *Fa yan* 10.1a for parallel examples. Here Yang Xiong uses *zhong shi* as a verb, probably in the sense of "to complete the cycle."

L. 33: Kun presumably is Kunming Pond.

L. 34: Changhe is the main gate of the celestial Purple Palace (see "Western Metropolis Rhapsody," L. 97). The Shanglin Park may have had a Changhe Gate that was considered an earthly replica of the heavenly gate.

L. 39: The Qian 汧 River flowed into the Wei River near modern Baoji, in western Shaanxi. See *Shuijing zhu* 17.3.94. There is a possible rhyme change here (see Jian Zongwu, *Sima Xiangru*, p. 314, n. 1).

L. 43: The *Wen xuan* reads *ta* 沓 (to join) for *Han shu*'s *yao* 杳 (vast). For requirements of rhyme, *yao* clearly is the superior reading. See Hu Shaoying, 11.3a.

L. 44: The word *huluo* 虎路 (my "tiger fence") is a variant for *huluo* 虎落, which was a type of barricade made of bamboo laths. See *Han shu* 49.2286, n. 4, Yan Shigu's commentary. On *sanzong* (three-tiered peak), see "Rhapsody on the Imperial Park," L. 299n. The major's gate designated the exterior gate of a palace where guards under the command of a major were stationed. See *Shi ji* 7.309, n. 3; *Han shu* 9.286, n. 10; 31.1806; *Mh*, 2:268, n. 4; *HFHD*, 2:316, n. 6.9.

His wealth having equaled Earth in riches,
His honor exactly matches Heaven in eminence.
15 Huan of Qi would be unworthy to steady His wheels;
Yan of Chu would be unworthy to be His chariot companion.
Stinted by the cramping confinement of the Three Kings,
Lofty and high He lifts himself, greatly inspired,
And traverses the vacant vastness of the Five Emperors,
20 Treks the ascendant grandeur of the Three August Ones.
He establishes the Way and Virtue as His teacher,
Takes Humaneness and Morality as His friend.

II

And then
In dark winter's final month,
When Heaven and Earth are waxing strong,
25 The myriad things,
Though germinating within,
Wither and wilt without.
The Emperor, contemplating a hunt in the Holy Park,
Opens the northern boundary,
30 Receives the rule of Buzhou's wind,
And thereby completes the cycle of Zhuanxu and Xuanming's rule.

Then He summons foresters to regulate the preserve, eastward stretching to the precints of Kun, westward galloping to Changhe Gate.

35 Stocking stores, preparing provisions,
The guard troop flanks the roads,
Chopping thorn thickets,
Mowing wild grass.

They begin the cordon from the Qian and Wei,
40 Mark and measure to the Feng and Hao,
To and fro, circling the entire park:
Here where rise and set the sun and moon,
It is vast as Heaven and Earth combined.

And then
They erect a tiger fence at a triple-tiered peak
45 To form a major's gate;

119

L. 49: The Gulf of Yu (Yu yuan 虞淵) is the legendary pool in the west where the sun was thought to set. See *Huainanzi* 3.10a.

LL. 53–54: White Poplar (Baiyang 白楊) Tower was located east of Kunming Lake. See *Sanfu huangtu* 5.94. The divine pool may refer to the Sacred Pond, which was located at Kunming Pond. Cf. "Western Capital Rhapsody," L. 130n.

L. 55: On Ben and Yu, see "Western Metropolis Rhapsody," L. 564n.

L. 57: Like Ganjiang (see "Sweet Springs Rhapsody," L. 20n), Moye may refer to any sharp weapon. Here "halberd" seems more appropriate. See *Han shu* 87A.3545, n. 15.

L. 61: The banner painted with the sun-and-moon design is the *taichang* banner. See "Eastern Metropolis Rhapsody," L. 350n.

LL. 63–64: Wei Zhao (cited by Li Shan 8.19a) explains *fen* 紛 as a banner streamer, and *xuan* 繯 as the ties or cords of a banner. However, both Hu Shaoying (11.3b–4a) and Zhu Jian (11.2b) have argued that *fen* and *xuan* are names of nooses and rope-snares. The *fen* may be the *fen* 分 that the *Erya* (B2.4a) equates with *lü* 律 (equals *lu* 率), "bird net." For *xuan* in the sense of noose, see *Hou Han shu* 60A.1959, n. 2 and *Shuowen* 13A.5819a–b.

L. 68: Hu Shaoying (11.4a) suggests that *yinyin* 淫淫 (*rjem-rjem) is equivalent to *yinyin* 忧忧 (*rjem-rjem), and *yuyu* 與與 (*rja-rja) is equivalent to *yuyu* 豫豫 (*rja-rja). The basic sense of the doublets is similar to that of *youyu* 猶豫 (halting, hesitant). Yan Shigu (see *Han shu* 87A.3545, n. 19) explains them as "descriptive of going and coming." My "to and fro, back and forth" is an approximation for this context. See L. 190n below.

L. 72: The Sparkling Deluder (Yinghuo 熒惑) is Mars, which was considered the Star of Punishment. It was charged with deciding the fate of miscreant beings. See Schlegel, *Uranographie chinoise*, 1:626–27; Schafer, *Pacing the Void*, pp. 215–16.

L. 73: On the Bow constellation (Celestial Bow), see "Western Metropolis Rhapsody," L. 491n.

L. 74: As Gao Buying (8.68a) shows, *xianpian* 鮮扁 (*sian-phjan) is a rhyming binome that has the sense of "fleet and fast."

L. 75: The rhyming binome *pianyan* 骿衍 (*bjen-zjan) perhaps is a variant of the more common *piantian* 骿田 (*bjen-dien), "closely clustered." See Gao Buying 2 51b.

L. 76: This line may also be translated: "The flag carts and nimble warriors."

L. 77: The rhyming binome *hongtong* 鴻絧 (*guang-duang), more commonly written 鴻洞, is used to describe a blending and joining of things. Cf. *Huainanzi* 1.10b, 7.1a. I have rendered it "mingling and merging."

The rhyming binome *jielie* 緁獵 (*dzjiep-ljep) means "following in sequence" (see *Han shu* 87A.3545, n. 23). I suspect that the signific is *jie*, which is synonymous and homphonous with *qi* 緝 (*tshjep), "to hem, to connect." Cf. *Guangya shuzheng* 1B.12a.

L. 78: On *yinyin zhenzhen* (rumbling and rattling in tumultuous throngs), see "Sweet Springs Palace Rhapsody," L. 19n.

L. 80: The *Han shu* reads *ming* 冥 (dark) for *Wen xuan's xiong* 夐 (far). I have followed the *Wen xuan* reading.

And enclose a hundred leagues
To form a palace portal.
Outside
Extending due south as far as the sea,
Diagonally bordering the Gulf of Yu,
50   All is wasty and wide, spaciously spread,
Marked by lofty mountains.

Only after the boundaries are closed and the enceinte is joined, do they begin to set things out south of White Poplar Tower, east of Kunming's divine pool. Peers of Ben and Yu, hidden by shields and bearing plumes, leaning on Moye halberds, form a phalanx ten thousand strong.

The rest
Shoulder fowling nets that span the sky,
60   Unfurl webbing that stretches across the plain,
Wave vermilion staffs hung with sun-and-moon flags,
Trail flying pennants of shooting stars.

Blue clouds forming a loop,
Red rainbows forming a noose,
65   Attach it to the Kunlun wastes.

Bright as a galaxy of celestial stars,
Grand as waves of a surging river:

To and fro, back and forth,
Front and rear, they intercept the game.

70   Comets form the covering wall,
The bright moon serves as lookout,
While Sparkling Deluder takes charge of life and death,
And Celestial Bow fires and shoots.
Fleet and fast, helter-skelter,
75   Closely clustered, they fill the roads.

Flag carts, light and sturdy,
Mingling and merging, continuously connected,
Rumbling and rattling in tumultuous throngs,
Blanket the hills, hem the slopes;
80   And upon reaching the farthest extremity, the remotest remove,
Line up together atop a high plateau.

L. 85: Meng Kang (cited by Li Shan 8.19b) explains the alliterative binome *leilu* 轠轣 (*lwei-lah) as a descriptive meaning "continuously joined." Yan Shigu (see *Han shu* 87A.3545, n. 20) glosses it as "to turn." Since it is difficult to determine the exact sense, I have followed Meng Kang in rendering it as "continuous cortege."

L. 93: On Chiyou, see "Western Metropolis Rhapsody," L. 505n.

L. 94: Fu Qian (see *Han shu* 87A.3546, n. 2) identifies Meng gong 蒙公 as Meng Tian, the famous Qin general. However, as Zhu Jian (11.3a–b) points out, Meng gong should be a star spirit like Chi You in the preceding line. He thus follows Ru Chun (cited by Li Shan 8.19b), who identifies Meng gong as Maotou 髦頭 (also written 庬頭), the "Shaggy-headed Star," which was another name for Mao 昴 (the Pleiades). See *Shi ji* 27.1305; *Mh*, 3:351. The *Jin shu* "Monograph on Astronomy" (11.302) mentions that when the emperor went out, Maotou drove in the vanguard. See also Ho Peng-yoke (He Bingyu 何炳郁), *The Astronomical Chapters of the Chin shu* (Paris and The Hague: Mouton, 1961), p. 101. Thus, Maotou's role as vanguard clearly is relevant to Yang Xiong's usage. The Shaggy Lord perhaps is a personification of Maotou. For Meng in the sense of "shaggy," see *Xunzi* 3.2a.

LL. 97–98: Lightning was thought to issue from cracks in an area of the sky 2,400 *li* from earth. See *Han shu* 57B.2599, n. 5; Zhu Jian 11.3b.

L. 99: The alliterative binome *cuicong* 萃㣚 (*dzjwet-dzjung) is a synonym compound each element of which means "to gather"; hence, my "grouped and gathered." See Hu Shaoying 11.4b.

On *weirong*, here rendered "in steady stream," see "Rhapsody on the Imperial park," L. 124n.

L. 100: The alliterative binome *linli* 淋離 (*ljem-ljai), also written 林離, possibly is related to *luli* in its sense of "long" (see "Sweet Springs Palace Rhapsody," L. 40n). See *Guangya shuzheng* 6A.23b–24a. I have loosely rendered it "continuously coursing."

L. 102: Feilian 飛廉 originally was the name of a master founder who forged cauldrons for the Xia ruler Qi 啟. He later beame equated with the god of the wind. See Karlgren, "Legends and Cults," pp. 317–19. On the Cloud Master, see "Western Metropolis Rhapsody," L. 245n.

L. 106: The *Han shu* reads *qiuqiu* 秋秋 for *Wen xuan*'s *qiuqiu* 啾啾. I have followed Yan Shigu (see *Han shu* 87A.3546, n. 7) in construing *qiuqiu* in the sense of "lightly leaping."

L. 108: Li Shan (8.20a) explains Shen guang 神光 (Divine Radiance) as the name of a palace. Nothing more is known about it

L. 109: On Peaceful Joy Lodge, see "Western Metropolis Rhapsody," L. 675n.

Plumed riders, buzzing and bustling,
Distinctly dividing their sundry tasks,
Race hurry-scurry, hither-thither.

85   The continuous cortege, unbroken,
Now bright, now dim,
Spreads out beneath the green woods.

III

And then

When the Son of Heaven on a sunny morn first comes forth from the
Dark Palace:

They strike the great bells,
90   Raise the nine-paneled flags,
Yoke six white tigers,
To carry Him in the divine chaise,
With Chiyou flanking the wheels,
And Shaggy Lord racing to the fore.

95   Raised standards cleave the heavens,
Trailing flags brush the stars,
Pealing thunder and the fiery fissures,
Spewing flames, ply their whips.
Grouped and gathered, in steady stream,
100 Continuously coursing, vast and wide,
They signal the eight outposts to open the gates.
Feilian and Cloud Master
Sniff and snort, huff and puff,
And in scalelike array, ranged in rows,
105 They mass as thick as dragon plumes.

Lightly leaping, proudly prancing,
They enter the western park,
Near Divine Radiance,
Gaze upon Peaceful Joy,
110 Cross bamboo groves,
Trample basil gardens,
Tread thoroughwort dikes.
With beacons raised and fires spread,

123

L. 116: The You Mao *Wen xuan* reads *jiao* 狡 (nimble) for *xiao* 校 (squad) of *Han shu* and *Five Comm.* I have followed the latter reading to maintain parallelism with the preceding line.

L. 123: The rhyming binome *yanman* 羨漫 (*zjan-man) clearly is a variant of *yanman* 衍漫 (*zjan-man), "spread and sprawl." See Zhu Qifeng, *Ci tong*, p. 1988.

L. 132: The *yan* here refers to the *manyan* monster. See "Western Metropolis Rhapsody," LL. 707–12n.

L. 141: Although some commentators attempt to explain *hou yi* 獲夷 as a proper noun, I have followed Hu Shaoying (11.5b) and Gao Buying (8.72a–b), who show that *huo* means "to catch" and *yi* means "to kill."

Holders of the reins display their skills,
115 Galloping abreast, a thousand fours-in-hand,
Riding in squads, a host of ten thousand.

This formation of howling tigers,
Lengthwise and crosswise twined and tangled,
Sobbing like whirlwinds, sharp as thunder;
120 Clop-clop, clap-clap,
They roar and rumble,
Causing Heaven to tremble and Earth to quake.
As they spread and sprawl, separately scattering,
All is desolate and deserted for thousands of miles beyond

IV

125 As for
Stout warriors, brave and bold,
Facing in diverse directions, dashing separate ways,
East, west, south, and north,
Chase whatever they please, pursue whatever they desire:
They drag down green boars,
130 Trample rhinos and yaks,
Crush roaming elaphures;

Cut down the giant *yan*,
Pummel black apes,
Spring into empty spaces,
135 Leap twining twists,
Vault bending boughs,
Cavort amidst brooks.
It is so dusty and dark, windy and wild,
In mountains and ravines they cause whirlblasts to blow,
140 And in woods and thickets sandstorms to rage.

Now for catchers and killers of game:
They topple pines and cypress,
Seize spiny caltrops,
Hunt bosky bushes,
145 Ride down the swift and fleet,
March over striped heads,

LL. 154–55: Grand Bloom is Mt. Taihua (see "Western Capital Rhapsody," L. 14n). Bear's Ear (Xionger) here probably refers to a mountain located northeast of Shangluo prefecture (modern Shang 商 xian, Shaanxi). See *Han shu* 28A.1549; *Shanhai jing* 5.10a; "Eastern Metropolis Rhapsody," L. 120n. The metaphors of the mountains serving as banners is typical *fu* hyperbole: the hunting procession is so large, it uses mountains for streamers and ties (the cords that secure the streamers to the staff).

LL. 161–62: Pang Meng 逢蒙 and Sir Yi (Hou Yi 后羿) are both famous archers. According to some sources, Pang Meng studied archery under Yi. See Karlgren, "Lengends and Cults," pp. 312–31.

L. 163: I have followed Gao Buying (8.74b–75a) in reading *huang* 皇 (imperial) as *huang* 煌 (resplendent). I also have accepted Hu Shaoying's suggestion (11.6a–b) that *youge* 幽輵 (*ˀjiehw-ˀjad*) is a variant of *youai* 幽藹 (*ˀjiehw-ˀad*), "densely arrayed."

L. 164: I have followed Wang Niansun, who reads *chun* 純 as *chun* 焞 (dazzle). See *Dushu zazhi* 4.13.31b–32a.

L. 165: Wang Shu 望舒 is the charioteer of the moon. Cf. *Chuci buzhu* 1.22a.

L. 166: On Shanglan, see "Western Capital Rhapsody," L. 333n.

L. 171: On the Ramparts, see "Western Metropolis Rhapsody," L. 512n. Note that there was a replica of the Ramparts constellation in the Shanglan Tower.

L. 177: Or, "The troops panic (the beasts), the hosts stampede (them)."

Turn long snakes into belts,
Hook scarlet panthers,
Snag elephants and rhinos,
150 Hurdle peaks and slopes,
Overleap dikes and banks.

Carts and riders converge as clouds,
Rising and falling, dark and dense.
Of Grand Bloom they make their streamers,
155 Of Bear's Ear they make their ties.
Trees are flattened, mountains whirl,
Sprawling far, beyond the heavens,
As they linger and loiter by the great banks,
Romp and rollick throughout the universe.

V

160 And then
As the sky clears and the sun shines forth,
Pang Meng stares with bulging eyes,
And Sir Yi draws his bow.

Gleaming chariots are densely arrayed,
Their luster dazzling Heaven and Earth.
165 As Wang Shu tightens the reins,
Relaxed, slow, they reach the Shanglan Tower.

They move the cordon, shift formations,
Little by little compressing the regiments,
So that companies and squads are solidly layered,
170 Each one dressed in files and columns.

As Ramparts rotates in the heavens,
Flailing like demons, striking like lightning,
They meet something and it is smashed,
They approach something and it is destroyed.

175 Birds cannot fly away in time;
Beasts can find no way to escape.
The troops are so surprised, the hosts so startled,
They scrape clean the fields, sweep down the earth

L. 182: On the roving simian, see "Rhapsody on the Imperial Park," L. 329n.

L. 183: On the Heavenly Treasure, see "Western Metropolis Rhapsody," L. 43n.

L. 188: According to some accounts, the Heavenly Treasure discovered at Chencang took the form of two children who, when chased by the people of Chencang, changed into male and female pheasants. See the *Jin Taikang dizhi* 晉太康地志 (Geography of the Taikang Era of Jin) cited in *Shi ji* 5.180, n. 4 and *Wen xuan* 8.22a, Li Shan.

L. 190: Following Wang Niansun (see *Dushu zazhi* 4.13.32b–33a), who interprets *jue* 噱 (**gjak*), "jaw," as *jue* 谻 (**gjak*), "fatigued," this line would read: "Lie far away spent within their nets." See also Hu Shaoying 11.7a–b; Zhu Jian 11.4a. I have supplied "pant and gasp" to clarify the sense.

L. 192: Wu Renjie (see *Liang Han kanwu buyi* 8.4a–b) proposes to read *yin* 冘 in the sense of *yinyu* 冘豫 (**rjem-rja*), "hesitant" (cf. *Han shu* 24.834 and 69.2242). Similarly, *yu* 與 should be understood as *yuyu* 與與 (faltering). Cf. *Huainanzi* 15.7b: "Strike the halting and hesitant, overrun the faint and faltering." See L. 68n above.

L. 193: The alliterative binome *yiyu* 紲隃 (**zjad-zjou*) is a variant of *yiyu* 跇踰 (**zjad-zjou*). See Zhu Qifeng, *Ci tong*, p. 0357. It seems to be a synonym compound, both elements of which mean "to leap." I have translated it "bounding and bouncing."

L. 196: On *lingju* 淩遽 in the sense of "quaking and quivering," see Hu Shaoying 11.8a–b.

L. 203: I follow Hu Shaoying's (11.8–9a) interpretation of this line.

L. 207: This pond could be the Dark Jade Pond (Lin chi 琳池), which was located near the Grand Fluid Pond. See *Sanfu huangtu* 4.76.

L. 208: On Mt. Qi, see "Western Capital Rhapsody," L. 444n. Mt. Liang 梁 was located northwest of Xiayang 夏陽 prefecture (south of modern Hancheng 韓城, Shaanxi). See *Han shu* 28A.1545, 1547.

At this time
Net carts rise in flight,
180 Mighty horsemen swiftly advance,
Trampling soaring leopards,
Roping the roving simian,
Chasing the Heavenly Treasure,
That comes from one direction,
185 Responding with a piercing call,
Striking with a streaming light.

Fields are scoured, mountains combed,
And they bag males and females,
In streaming swarms and teeming throngs,
190 Jaws agape, panting and gasping within the nets.

The three divisions, tired and worn,
Corner the hesitant, block the faltering.
All one sees are:
Bounding and bouncing of swift game,
Butting and bumping of rhinos and gaurs,
195 Gripping and grappling of brown and black bears,
Quaking and quivering of tigers and leopards.
Vainly thrusting with horns, striking with foreheads,
Kicking and rearing in fright and fear,
Animus gone, spirit lost,
200 They ram the spokes and entangle their necks.
Archers randomly shoot confident of hitting the mark;
Stepping forward or back, hunters trample or catch something
Beasts gashed by blades, wounded by wheels,
Are piled in hills, heaped in mounds.

VI

205 And then
When the game is depleted, shot to extinction,
They congregate at a lodge of still seclusion,
Overlooking a precious pond.
It is watered from Mts. Qi and Liang,
The overflow forms the Jiang and He.
210 One looks east as far as the eye can see;

129

L. 212: On the Sui pearls, see "Western Capital Rhapsody," L. 192n.

L. 214: The rhyming binome *qinyin* 礒嵒 (**dzrem-ngjem*), also read *jinyin*, is a variant of *cenyin* 岑嵒 (**tshjem-ngjem*), "peaked and pointed." See Zhu Qifeng, *Ci tong*, p. 1085; "Rhapsody of Sir Vacuous," L. 52n

L. 216: On the Han River nymphs, see "Eastern Metropolis Rhapsody," L. 574n and "Southern Capital Rhapsody," L. 29n.

L. 228: The tattooed swimmers are men from the area of Yue. They were known for their aquatic skills.

L. 232: *Bosuo* 薄索 (**bak-sak*) is a rhyming binome composed of two synonymous elements; hence, my translation "seeking and searching." See Hu Shaoying 11.9a–b.

L. 233: It is not clear whether *binta* 獱獺 should be construed as the name of one or two animals. The *ta* is an otter. Yan Shigu (see *Han shu* 87A.3551, n. 14) says the *bin* is a small *ta*. Other sources describe the *bin* or *binta* as a large animal with a head like a horse and resembling a bat below its waist. See *Guangya shuzheng* 10B.37a; Read, *Animal Drugs*, #384; Hu Shaoying 11.9b. Since the preceding line mentions two creatures, for the sake of parallelism I have rendered *bin* and *ta* as "otters and beavers."

L. 236: Jin Zhuo (see *Han shu* 87A.3552n, n. 16) identifies the Cavern as the Cavern of Yu (Yu xue 禹穴). This cave was located in Mount Wanwei 宛委 of the Guiji Mountains (central Zhejiang), near where the Great Yu was buried. See *Shi ji* 130.3294, n. 4; *Han shu* 28A.1591; *Shanhai jing* 1.7a, *Shuijing zhu* 6.40.116. The Cavern also could refer to the Dongting Cavern (see "Wu Capital Rhapsody," L. 671n).

L. 237: On Cangwu, see "Rhapsody on the Imperial Park," L. 28n.

LL. 240–41: On Pengli Lake, see "Wu Capital Rhapsody," L. 590n. Youyu 有虞 is Shun's title. I am not certain why Yang Xiong mentions Shun in connection with Pengli. Yan Shigu (see *Han shu* 87A.3552n, n. 18) suggests that they gaze afar on the site where Shun died (i.e., Cangwu).

L. 242: On *liuli* 流離 (beryl), which is a transcription of Sanskrit *vaiḍūrya*, see Paul Pelliot, review of Laufer's *Jade*, in *TP* 13 (1912):443. In later periods it is a term for glass. See Schafer, *Golden Peaches*, pp. 235–37.

L. 243: The luminous bright moon pearls were thought to come from the womb of the mussel. Cf. *Huainanzi* 16.13a.

LL. 244–45: On Consort Fu, see "Eastern Metropolis Rhapsody," L. 127n. On Wu Zixu, see "Wu Capital Rhapsody," L. 607n. Peng Xian 彭咸 reputedly was an official of the Shang, who drowned himself after his ruler failed to heed his advice. Qu Yuan twice refers to him in "Encountering Sorrow" (see *Chuci buzhu* 1.11a, 1.37a). The beating of Consort Fu probably represents the emperor's putative rejection of extravagance. The feasting of Qu Yuan, Peng Xian, and Wu Zixu, all of whom committed suicide after their loyal advice was not heeded by their rulers, represents the emperor's quest for wise officials, See Knechtges, *The Han Rhapsody*, pp 76–77.

Extending west is a boundless expanse.
Sui pearls and Master He's jade
Glitter and glisten on its banks.

Jade boulders peaked and pointed,
215 Dazzle and sparkle with a blue brilliance.
Han River nymphs lurking in its waters,
Strange creatures darkly obscured,
Cannot be described completely.
Black simurghs, peacocks,
220 Kingfishers shedding a glorious luster,
Ospreys screeching *gwa gwa*,
Geese shrieking *yee yee*,
Play in flocks within the pond,
Gio gio they call, singing in chorus.
225 Ducks, gulls, and flocking egrets,
Soar and dive, wings drumming,
With sounds like thunderclaps.

Then, He commands skilled swimmers from the tattooed tribes to seize
from the water scaly creatures.

Braving solid ice,
230 Defying forbidding depths,
They explore the cragged shore, push along the twisting banks,
Seeking and searching for krakens and wiverns,
Trampling otters and beavers,
Grabbing turtles and alligators,
235 Seizing sacred loggerheads.
Entering the Cavern
They come out at Cangwu.
Mounting giant orcs,
Riding monstrous whales,
240 They drift over Pengli,
Gaze on Youyu.
Now they bludgeon the beryl gem that glows in the dark,
Cleave the pearl embryo of the bright-moon jewel,
Flog Consort Fu of the River Luo,
245 Feast Qu Yuan, Peng, and Xu.

131

L. 247: The usual interpretation of *xuan mian* 軒冕 is "carriages and caps." However, Yang Xiong seems to be describing only the scholar's clothing, and carriages seem an intrusion into the description. I have thus followed the explanation of the third century *Han shu* commentator Deng Zhan 鄧展, who understands *xuan* as describing the low front and high rear of the cap. See *Han shu* 21B.1012, n. 1 and Yan Shigu's refutation of Deng's explanation.

LL. 249–50: The "Canon of Tang" refers to the "Canon of Yao," the first chapter of the *Shang shu*. The "Odes" and "Hymns" are the "Elegantiae" and "Eulogia" of the *Shi jing*. All Yang Xiong is saying here is these are scholars of the classics.

L. 254: On the (Northern) Di, see "Western Capital Rhapsody," L. 311n.

L. 255: The Southern Lin (Nan lin 南郯) could refer to the Jinlin, a south Asian state that cannot be precisely identified. See "Wu Capital Rhapsody," L. 468n. Hu Shaoying (11.10b) suggests that no specific place is intended and that Nanlin simply means "the south" or "the southern neighbors."

LL. 256–57: The wearers of felt and fur probably are the Xiongnu (see *Han shu* 94A.3473). The Mo 貉 may refer to the Northern Mo, a state in the northeast, probably in Korea. See *Han shu* 1A.46, n. 4

L. 261: According to Meng Kang as cited in the *Han shu* (87A.3553, n. 6) and in the *Wen xuan* (8.24a), Mount Lu 盧山 was located near the southern court of the Xiongnu *chanyu*. The *chanyu*'s southern court was located in the southern portion of modern Mongolia. Hu Kejia (see *Wen xuan kaoyi* 2.12a) claims the text should read "south of the *chanyu*'s court," i.e. near modern Ulan Bator.

L. 262: On the permanent chief, see "Rhapsody on the Sacred Field," L. 40n.

L. 263: Yang Zhu 楊朱 (395–340 B.C.) and Mo Di 墨翟 (480–390 B.C.) are both famous pre-Han philosophers. According to Yan Shigu (see *Han shu* 87A.3553, n. 7), they represent ancient worthies. For further discussion of what they might signify here, see Knechtges, *The Han Rhapsody*, p. 79

LL. 267–68: The Eastern Peak is Mount Tai. On Liangfu, see "Eastern Metropolis Rhapsody," L. 630n.

L. 272: The three numina are the sun, moon, and stars, emanations from which are interpreted as signs of the goodness of an emperor's rule. LL. 270–74 mention more of these auspicious omens.

L. 279: On Mengzhu, see "Rhapsody of Sir Vacuous," L. 237n.

L. 280: On the Terrace of Manifest Splendor, see "Eastern Metropolis Rhapsody," L. 23n.

L. 281: On the Divine Tower, see "Eastern Capital Rhapsody," L. 200n. Yang Xiong alludes to the Divine Tower built by King Wen of Zhou. *Mengzi* 1A/2 praises this building, which was constructed alongside a pond and a hunting preserve, because King Wen shared its pleasures with the people.

VII

Here then
Great masters and grand scholars
In peaked and canted hats,
Multicolored jackets and skirts,
Redactors of the "Canon of Tang,"
250 Correctors of the "Odes" and "Hymns:"

Bow and yield before Him,
Their lustrous resplendence shimmering and sparkling,
Swift and sudden as if spirit-borne.
His beneficent repute soothes the Northern Di;
255 His martial might shakes the Southern Lin.

Thus,
Kings of the felt and fur tribes,
Chiefs of the Hu and Mo:

Send treasures, come with tribute,
And with raised arms, declare themselves vassals.
260 The front of the cortege enters the cordon gate;
The rear of the line forms at Mt. Lu.

Assembled archons and permanent chiefs, peers of Yang Zhu and Mo
Di, gasp and declare: "Exalted indeed His virtue! Although rulers have the
eminence of Tang, Yu, the great Xia, Cheng, and Zhou, how could they
surpass this? Rulers of grand antiquity made visitations to the Eastern Peak,
performed the *shan* sacrifice at Mt. Liang's base. Other than this reign, who
can compare with them?"

VIII

The emperor still modestly declines and will not yet assent to this praise.
Now He will hunt above for emanations from the three numina, release
below moisture from the sweet wine springs, open the cave of the yellow
dragon, peer into the nest of the phoenix, approach the enclosure of the
unicorn, visit the park of the divine bird.

He considers Yunmeng too extravagant,
Deems Mengzhu too sumptuous,
280 Condemns Manifest Splendor,
Commends the Divine Tower.

133

L. 293: For *yu* 虞 in the sense of "preserve," see *Zhou li zhushu* 4.17b–18a and Hu Shaoying 11.11a.

L. 312: On the Ebang Palace, see "Eastern Capital Rhapsody," L. 334n.

He rarely goes to detached palaces,
And He ceases sightseeing excursions.
Earthworks are left unadorned,
285   Wood projects are left uncarved.

He aids the people in agriculture and sericulture, exhorts them not to be idle, matches men and women so that none is improperly wed. Fearing that the poor do not share in the overflowing abundance:

290   He opens the forbidden parks,
Distributes the public stores,
Constructs enclosures of the Way and Virtue,
Expands preserves of Humaneness and Kindness,
Gallops and fowls in enclosures of divine brilliance,
295   Examines and inspects the needs of his many subjects.

He releases pheasants and rabbits,
Stores nets and snares;
Elaphures and deer, fodder and hay,
He shares with the common folk.
300   And by this means he has attained his present success.

And then
Fostering a broadly permeating virtue,
Advancing standards of a flourishing age,
He toils more than the Three August Ones,
Strives harder than the Five Emperors.
305   Is this not the epitome of excellence?
Then
He devoutly reveres adherents of harmony and concord,
Establishes divisions between ruler and subject,
Exalts the deeds of worthies and sages.

He has no time for
The beauty of parks and enclosures,
310   The extravagance of excursions and hunts.

Thus
He wheels round his carriage,
Turns his back on Ebang,
Returns to the Everlasting Palace.

[1] These is some confusion about this date. It probably was presented in the autumn of Yuanyan 3 (September–November 10 B.C.). For further details, see Knechtges, *The Han Rhapsody*, p. 115.

[2] The Western Sustainer (Youfufeng 右扶風) was in charge of the capital district called Youfufeng (administrative center at Huaili 槐里, southeast of modern Xingping 興平 *xian*, Shaanxi). See Hans Bielenstein, *The Bureaucracy of Han Times* (Cambridge: Cambridge University Press, 1980), p. 87.

[3] On Bao-Ye, see "Western Capital Rhapsody," L. 15n. On Hongnong, see "Western Capital Rhapsody," L. 13n. Hanzhong 漢中 was a commandery south of Chang'an. Its administrative center was east of modern Hanzhong City. See *Han shu* 28A.1596.

[4] The Bear Shooting Lodge (She xiong guan 射熊館) was the principal hunting lodge in the Tall Poplars Palace area. See *Sanfu huangtu* 5.93–94.

[5] On the troublesome *zhi* 之 in this line, see *The Han shu Biography of Yang Xiong*, p. 118, n. 330. This preface is from Yang Xiong's "Autobiographical Postface."

136

9

HUNTING, PART II

Rhapsody on the Tall Poplars Palace

YANG ZIYUN

The next year,[1] wishing to boast to the Hu tribes of his numerous birds and beasts, in the autumn the emperor commanded the Western Sustainer to send people into the Southern Mountains,[2] and from Bao-Ye in the west to Hongnong in the east conduct a drive to Hanzhong in the south.[3] Spreading fowling and animals nets, they caught black bears, brown bears, porcupines, tigers, leopards, monkeys, hoolocks, foxes, rabbits, elaphures, and deer, which they loaded in cage carts and transported to the Bear Shooting Lodge at Tall Poplars Palace.[4] Using nets to make a circular corral, they released the birds and beasts into it, and commanded the Hu tribesmen to attack them barehanded and take for themselves whatever they caught. His Highness personally came to view them. At this time, the farmers were unable to harvest their crops. I accompanied the imperial procession to Bear Shooting Lodge, and upon my return, I submitted the "Rhapsody on the Tall Poplars Palace." Since I used brush and ink to create my composition, I thus borrow Plume Grove as host and Sir Ink as guest for the purpose of swaying the emperor's opinion.[5] The piece reads:

THIS RHAPSODY is a sequel to Yang Xiong's "Plume Hunt Rhapsody." In this *fu* Yang Xiong does not describe a hunt, but through the interlocutors Sir Ink and Plume Grove presents a debate on the merits of hunting extravaganzas. To counter Sir Ink's assertion that the hunt imposes unnecessary hardship on the peasants who live adjacent to the imperial park, Plume Grove presents a long argument, filled with historical examples, to show that the primary function of these spectacles is to impress the non-Chinese visitors with the might and power of the Han empire. Although Sir Ink acknowledges the merits of Plume Grove's exposition, there is evidence that Yang Xiong's own views are expressed in the persona of Sir Ink. For further details, see Knechtges, *The Han Rhapsody*, pp. 85–88. The text of this piece also is found in *Han shu* 87B.3557–65. Previous translations include von Zach, in *Deutsche Wacht* 14.6 (1928), 42–43, and reprinted in *Die Chinesische Anthologie*, 1:126–30; Doeringer, "Yang Hsiung," pp. 273–81; Knechtges, *The Han Rhapsody*, pp. 80–85; Obi Kōichi, *Monzen*, 1:456–68. This translation is revised from Knechtges, *The Han shu Biography of Yang Xiong*, pp. 39–45, 118–22.

137

L. 8: On Mt. Jienie, see "Rhapsody on the Imperial Park," L. 111n.

L. 17: On *chuxu* 儲胥 in the sense of holding pen, see Hu Shaoying 11.11b–12a.

L. 24: One of the three functions of the hunt was to provide meat for the sacrifices. See "Eastern Capital Rhapsody," L. 175n.

L. 28: Based on parallelism with the following line, Hu Shaoying (11.12b) suggests that *lu* 露 (to expose, to display) should be understood as "to weaken." Following Hu, the line should be translated: "Reveling in distant outings, thereby weakening one's awesome might."

L. 32: The *Han shu* text reads: "Is it really as you say?"

I

The guest, Sir Ink, asked the host, Plume Grove, "I have heard that a sage ruler in nurturing the people imbues them with benevolence, and steeps them in kindness. He does not act for his own sake. This year, when the emperor hunts at Tall Poplars:

> He first commands the Western Sustainer,
> With Taihua left and Bao-Ye right,
> To pound Mt. Jienie into a stake,
> Coil the Southern Mountains for a net,
> 10 Deploy a thousand chariots in forest brakes,
> Array a myriad riders in mountain nooks,
> Lead the army to gather at the corral,
> And grant game to the Rong, catch to the Hu.
> They seize black bears and brown bears,
> 15 Drag away porcupines.
> Wood pressed together, bamboo poles intertwined,
> Serve to form the holding pens.

"This is the greatest spectacle, the grandest sight in the empire. Nevertheless, it is a considerable disturbance to the farming folk. For three weeks and more their toil has been extreme, yet no results can be expected from it. I fear that one unfamiliar with the hunt, viewing it from outside, would simply consider it a pleasure excursion, or looking at it from inside would think it had nothing to do with the sacrifices. How is it done in behalf of the people?

Moreover, a true ruler of men embraces a spirit of mysterious silence, a virtue of placid tranquility. Now reveling in distant outings to display one's awesome might and wearing out chariots and armor with frequent rattling and shaking truly are not the most urgent tasks of a lord of men.

Although shrouded in ignorance, I am doubtful about it."

Host Plume Grove said, "Oh? Why do you say this? A person like you may be referred to as one who knows the first step but does not know the second, who sees superficialities, but has yet to recognize what lies beneath the surface. I am already weary of expounding on it and am unable one by one to explain the details. Please allow me briefly to present the generalities and let you examine the specifics for yourself."

The guest said, "Please do."

139

L. 41: The *Han shu* reads *shi* 士 (scholar) for *Wen xuan's tu* 土 (land). On the giant boar, see "Rhapsody on the Imperial Park," L. 308n.

L. 42: On the Yayu, see "Western Metropolis Rhapsody," L. 572n.

L. 43: The Chisel Fangs (Zuo chi 鑿齒) was a notorious man-eating monster. It had long fangs that resembled chisels. See *Huainanzi* 8.5b–6a; *Shanhai jing* 6.3b.

L. 48: The Dipper is the Northern Dipper (Ursa major). The Pole is the polestar. All stars were said to revolve around it. Cf. "Western Capital Rhapsody," LL. 164–65.

L. 49: The Celestial Barrier (Tian guan 天關) can refer to many different stars. According to the *Tian guan xing zhan* 天宮星占 (Divination by Means of the Celestial Office Stars), a lost astronomical work cited by Li Shan (9.3b), the Celestial Barrier is another name for the Northern Polestar. However, since Yang Xiong mentions the Polestar in the preceding line, he must have intended the Celestial Barrier to refer to another asterism. Thus, Li Shan (9.3b) cites another text, the *Xing jing* 星經 (Star Canon), that identifies the Celestial Barrier as the spirit of the Oxherd (six stars in Capricorn). There is no explanation why Gaozu would follow its revolutions.

L. 53: The *Han shu* omits *guo* 過 (to pass, to go). The *Han shu* reads *xian* 揃 for *shan* 揃 of the *Wen xuan*. Yan Shigu (cited in *Han shu* 87B.3560, n. 4) says *xian* means "to raise the arms and aim at something." Li Shan (9.3b) cites Zheng Xuan, who equates *shan* (*sram*) with *shan* (*sram*) 芟, "to mow down," "to destroy." See *Li ji zhushu* 23.22b. I have followed the *Wen xuan* text. See Wang Niansun, *Dushu zazhi* 4.13.33b–34a; Zhu Jian 11.6a–b; Hu Shaoying 11.13a.

II

40 The host said, "Of old there was mighty Qin,
   Which devoured the land like the giant boar,
   Oppressed its people like the Yayu.

Chisel Fangs and their kind, gnashing their teeth, vied against it, and
brave talents frothed like boiling congee, raged like storm clouds, and the
common people for this reason were not at peace. Thereupon, the Lord on
High turned a kindly nod toward Gaozu, and Gaozu received the mandate.

   Following the Dipper and Pole,
   Turning with the Celestial Barrier,
50 He traversed the giant sea,
   Shook the Kunlun.

   Grasping his sword, he shouted a curse,
   And wherever he went, he beckoned to the wall and destroyed the
         town,
   Defeated its generals, lowered its flags.
55 The battles of a single day,
   Cannot be fully described.

   While engaged in this toil:
   He had no leisure to comb his tousled hair,
   Though hungry he had no time to eat.
60 His leather casque teemed with lice,
   His armored helmet was soaked with sweat.
   Thus, for the sake of the people he begged for the mandate from
         August Heaven.

   Then, after releasing the people from suffering,
   Saving them from privation,
65 He made plans for a million years,
   And expanded the imperial enterprise.
   Within the span of seven years, the empire was at peace.

III

Next came sage Emperor Wen, who following the founder's customs
and riding in his wake, cast all his thoughts on perfect concord.

   He personally observed frugality and restraint,
   His silk gowns never wore out,

L. 73: The boots were made of untanned leather. See *Han shu* 65.2858. The idea is that Emperor Wen wore garments and boots of such durable material, new ones did not need to be made.

L. 83: The Jade Transverse (Yu heng 玉衡) is the fifth star of the Northern Dipper. It also was the name of a sighting instrument used together with the Jade Armil for locating the celestial pole. Shun reputedly used it to regulate the so-called Seven Directors (the sun, moon, and five planets). See Needham, volume 3:333–36. On the Grand Stairway, see "Wei Capital Rhapsody," L. 611n.

LL. 84–87: Xunyu 熏鬻 is an archaic name for the Xiongnu. The Eastern Yi here refers to the Koreans. The Qiang-Rong (proto-Tibetans) are tribes of the modern Qinghai area. The Min-Yue kingdom of the southeast was loosely allied with the Han. In the 130's B.C., members of the Min-Yue ruling family fought each other for the throne. See *Shi ji* 114.2981; *Records*, 2:253–54.

L. 91: This line is cited verbatim from *Mao shi* 241/6.

L. 92: The Swift Cavalry General is Huo Qubing 霍去病 (140–117 B.C.). He and Wei Qing 衛青 (ob. 106 B.C.) led successful expeditions against the Xiongnu in the 120's B.C. See *Shi ji* 111.2921–46; *Records*, 2:193–216.

L. 102: The Xuwu 余吾 (also pronounced Xiewu) River was a river in the Xiongnu territory. It may be the modern Tula River near modern Ulan Bator in Mongolia, or possibly the Ongin. See *Han shu* 6.176, n. 1 and Hulsewé, *China in Central Asia*, pp. 133–34, n. 332 (where the name of the river is wrongly given as Yu-wu).

His leather boots never had holes,
In grand buildings he would not live,
75 His wooden vessels had no ornamentation.

And then,
In the harem they disdained tortoise shells and shunned pearls,
Discarded ornaments of kingfisher plumes,
Removed handiworks that were etched or carved.
Loathing lavish luxury, he would not approach it;
80 Discarding sweet fragrances, he would not use them.

He banned the light, lascivious music of strings and reeds,
Hated to hear the delicate, dulcet tones of Zheng and Wei.
Thus, the Jade Transverse was correct and the Grand Stairway was
        well-ordered.

IV

Thereafter,
The Xunyu launched their brutal attacks,
85 The Eastern Yi rebelled at will,
The Qiang-Rong glowered in anger,
Min-Yue feuded with itself.
On this account the distant border peoples were insecure,
And the Central States suffered in their distress.

90 And then
Sage Emperor Wu rising in rage,
Marshalling his hosts,
And with the Swift Cavalry General and Wei Qing in command:

In teeming throngs and seething swarms
They gathered like clouds, brust forth like lightning,
95 Soaring like whirlwinds, flowing like waves,
Faster than snapping triggers, swifter than lances.
Swift as shooting stars,
Striking like thunderbolts:

They smashed the enemy's shielded carts,
100 Demolished their domed lodges,
Smeared their brains across the desert,
Filled the Xuwu River with their marrow.

L. 105: The word *mili* 焒蟁 (*miak-liai*) or *miluo* (*miak-lwa*), written *mili* 爄蟁 in *Han shu*, probably is Central Asian. Zhang Yan (cited in *Han shu* 87B.3562, n. 11) explains it as *gan luo* 乾酪, which is a dried form of soured milk or yoghurt. I have loosely translated it as "curds." The dried form was made by baking the *luo* under the sun. The skin was then skimmed off, and the remaining *luo* was baked until no more skin formed. See Shi Shenghan, *Qimin yaoshu jinshi*, 2:399.

L. 106: The *chanyu* 單于 (also read *shanyu*), my "khanate," is the title of the supreme Xiongnu leader. E. G. Pulleyblank reconstructs the Old Chinese form as *dan-hwah*, which he claims is a protoform for *targan* or *tarxan*. See "The Consonantal System of Old Chinese," p. 256.

L. 107: For a discussion of the dependent states, see Michael Loewe, *Records of Han Administration*, 2 vols. (Cambridge: Cambridge University Press, 1967), 1:60–64.

L. 113: For the alternative ways of understanding this confusing line, see Zhu Jian 11.8b–9a; Hu Shaoying 11.6b–17a; Wang Xianqian, *Han shu buzhu* 87B.5a–b.

L. 121: The Dark Capital refers here to the land of the Xiongnu.

L. 122: What I have translated "south" literally is "diagonally."

L. 123: In 112 B.C., Lu Jia 呂嘉, Chancellor to the King of Southern Yue (modern Guangdong, Guangxi, and southern Hunan), led a rebellion against the Han. Emperor Wu dispatched a large army to the area, and in 111 B.C. the Han forces routed the rebels. The Han then divided the Southern Yue kingdom into nine commanderies. See *Shi ji* 113.2972–77; *Han shu* 6.186–88, 95.3855–59; *Records*, 2:245–50; *HFHD*, 2:79–82.

L. 124: The token of credence (*jie* 節) was a long staff to which red oxtail or yaktail pennons were attached. See Ōba Osamu 大庭脩 "Kan no setsu ni tsuite—shōsei kasetsu no zentei" 漢の節について—将軍仮節の前提, *Tōzai gakujutsu kenkyūjo kiyō* 東西学術研究所紀要 2 (1969), 23–58; Hulsewé, *China in Central Asia*, p. 137, n. 351.

L. 125: They "galloped east" to surrender to the Han. The Bo 僰 was a non-Chinese tribe that lived in southwest Sichuan and northern Yunnan. See Hervouet, *Un Poète de cour*, pp. 125–28.

Then,
They marched into their king's courtyard,
Driving off his camels,
105 Burning his dried curds.

They cut the khanate in two,
Dismembered his dependent states,
Leveled slopes and valleys,
Plucked the saltland grasses,
110 Scraped down mountain rocks,
Trampled corpses, rode down the injured,
Fettered and bound the old and feeble.

Those scarred and gouged by sharp lances, gashed and wounded by
metal arrowheads, several hundred thousand:

Their foreheads bowed, their chins stiff,
Crept and crawled, cowering like ants,
And for twenty years and more
Never dared take even a quick breath.

120 Our celestial troops approach all four directions;
The Dark Capital was the first to fall.
When they turned their spears, pointing them southward,
The tribes of the Southern Yue destroyed themselves.
When we waved our tokens of credence and westward marched,
125 The Qiang and Bo galloped east.

Thus, in the realm of remote regions, exotic customs, alien districts, and
cut-off villages,

Where men had yet to be swayed by imperial benevolence,
Pacified by His flourishing virtue:

All lifted their feet, raised their arms,
130 And begged to present their tribute treasures,
Thus making the empire tranquil.
Never again would there be
Disasters at the border walls,
Concerns about clash of arms.

L. 155: Wuyi is an abbreviated form of Wuyishanli 獄山離 (*ʾah-drjek-san-ljaɪ), which probably is the Han name for Alexandria in Central Asia. See Hulsewé, *China in Central Asia*, p. 112

LL. 156–57: The lunar grotto and solar realm refer to the west and east respectively.

V

Now
Our court, embued with unsullied benevolence,
135 Follows the Way and manifests morality,
Embraces the grove of letters,
And its sagacious influence, spreading like clouds,
Wafted up and down like bright blossoms,
Floods and fills the eight regions,
140 So that everywhere covered by broad Heaven,
No one fails to be soaked or saturated.

If a scholar should not discourse on the way of kingship,
Even woodcutters would laugh at him.

Thus, it is my opinion that
There is nothing that upon reaching its apex of glory does not
decline,
145 And there is nothing that upon reaching its peak of splendor does not
deteriorate.
Therefore, in peace we cannot overlook peril;
Nor in security can we ignore danger.

Then in the proper season
After a bountiful year, we dispatched the army,
Readied the chariots, exhorted the batallions,
150 Marshalled the hosts at Five Oaks,
Drilled our steeds at Tall Poplars,
Tested our strength against mighty brutes,
Matched our valor against swift beasts.

Then en masse
We climbed the Southern Mountains,
155 Gazed at Wuyi,
Westward subdued the lunar grotto,
Eastward shook the solar realm.

Yet, we feared later generations, deluded by a one-time event,
Would always consider it a major endeavor of state,
160 And once they began lusting for the hunt and the chase,
The decay and deterioration could not be withstood.

L. 166: The Grand Ancestor is Liu Bang, founder of the Han.

L. 180: I follow Wang Xianqian (see *Han shu buzhu* 87B.6b) in understanding *shuai* 帥 as *shuai* 率 (fully, totally).

L. 184: The bellstand supports were shaped like crouching tigers. According to Meng Kang (see *Han shu* 97B.3565, n. 16), the rhyming binome *jiexia* 偈磍 (**jat-gat*) describes the fearsome appearance of the tiger-bellstands "in full rage." Thus, I have rendered it "raging and roaring."

L. 185: Yang Xiong uses what appears to be a modern text version of a *Shang shu* line. Cf. *Shang shu zhushu* 5.15a; Karlgren, "Glosses on the Book of Documents," pp. 138–139, # 1340; Zhu Jian 11.9a.

L. 186: This dance probably is the same as the Eight-File dance mentioned in *Lun yu* 3/1. Eight files of eight dancers each performed.

L. 187: Cf. *Mao shi* 293: "Oh, excellent are the king's hosts!"

L. 188: Cf. *Mao shi* 215/1, 2: "The gentlemen are joyful all."

L. 189: Cf. *Mao shi* 240/3: "Harmoniously concordant he was in the palace, / Solemn and serious he was in the temple."

L. 190: Cf. *Mao shi* 215/1: "The gentlemen are joyful all; / They shall receive Heaven's blessing."

L. 194: Cf. *Mao shi* 239/5: "Joyful and gay is the lord, / He is the one rewarded by the spirits."

Thus,
Without even braking the chariots,
And before the sun streamed across the banners,
The entourage, in a blinding blur,
165 Dissolved its ranks and returned home.
This also is a way
To uphold the glories of the Grand Ancestor,
To venerate the measures of Wen and Wu,
Revive the hunts of the Three Kings,
Restore the preserves of the Five Emperors.
170 It makes certain that
Farmers do not cease their harrowing,
Weavers do not leave their looms,
Marriages are done at the proper times,
With no man or woman missing the season.

Showing joy and gladness,
175 Acting with simplicty and ease,
The emperor commiserates with labor and toil,
Ceases corvee duty.

He visits the centenarians,
Consoles the orphaned and weak,
180 Totally sharing with them,
Partaking of their suffering and joy.

Then afterwards
They perform the music of bell and drum,
Sound the harmony of tabla and chime,
Erect the bellstand raging and roaring,
185 Strike the singing sphere,
Sway to the Eight File dance.
With 'true excellence' as their libation,
'Joy to all' as their viand,
They listen to the harmonious concord of the temple,
190 Receive blessings and fortune from the spirits.
The singing accords with the 'Hymns';
The music of the pipes is in tune with the 'Odes'.

Diligent effort like this truly shall earn reward from the spirits. Now He shall await a prime token:

L. 196: This is a way of saying they would build an altar at the summit to perform the *feng* sacrifice.

L. 208: Li Lou 離婁 is a man known for his keen eyesight. See *Mengzi* 4A/1.

L. 210: The Han used the hunt as a military review to impress the non-Chinese participants with its martial might.

195 In order to make a *shan* sacrifice at Liangfu's base,
    And increase Mt. Tai's height,
    Extending His brilliance to the future,
    Matching His glory with titled rulers of the past.

    How can He only crave:
200 Dissolute excursions and frivolous sightseeing,
    Dashing and galloping through fields of rice,
    Roaming and rambling through groves of pear and chestnut,
    Crushing and trampling fodder and hay,
    Boasting and bragging to the common multitudes,
205 Vaunting the crop of monkeys and hoolocks,
    Flaunting the catch of elaphures and deer?

    Moreover,
    The blind cannot see even a foot,
    Yet Li Lou could spy into a cranny a thousand miles away.
    You, my guest, merely begrudges that the Hu are catching our birds
        and beasts;
210 And does not know that we also already have captured their kings
        and lords."

Before the host's speech had ended, Ink Guest fell to the mat and kowtowing repeatedly said, "Grand indeed is your substance! Truly it is nothing this humble child could match. Today you have dispelled my ignorance, and now I see vast and clear."

L. 3: Although *yu* 聿 usually is a particle (see Serruys, "The Function and Meaning of *Yun*," pp. 305–9), Xu Yuan (9 9a) explains it as *shu* 述 "to transmit, to tell of." Pan Yue perhaps based his understanding of *yu* on the *Mao* commentary gloss to *Mao shi* 235/6, where *yu* is explained as "to transmit." See *Mao shi zhushu* 161.1.13a and Karlgren, "Glosses on the Ta Ya and Sung Odes," pp. 7–8, #762. Xu Yuan notes that one text reads *wei* 偉 (admirable) for *yu*. According to Xu Yuan (9.9a), *ying* 英 (bold) refers to the pheasant's "bold determination." Cf. L. 6 below.

L. 4: Classical lexicons explain the *hui* 翚 as a name people south of the Yi and Luo rivers use for a pheasant with five-colored plumage and plain underfeathers. See *Erya* C5.14b. Schafer identifies it as the pucras pheasant (*Pucrasia macrolopha*). See *The Vermilion Bird*, p. 243. Here, however, I think it is a general name for pheasant.

L. 5: On the pheasant as the bird of resolute integrity, see *Yili zhushu* 7.1b–2a; *Shishuo xinyu* 4.138 (Mather, *Shih-shuo Hsin-yu*, p. 276).

LL. 7–8: In these lines Pan Yue describes the pheasant as if he were a lord surveying his realm.

LL. 9–10: *Qing yang* 青陽 (Verdant Yang) and *Zhu ming* 朱明 (Vermilion Brilliance) are kennings for spring and summer respectively. See *Erya* B4.1b This pheasant hunt must have taken place in the fourth month (Xu Yuan 9.9b).

Rhapsody on Pheasant Shooting

PAN ANREN   Commentary by Xu Yuan

I

Through green groves I have roamed and gazed,
Delighting in the flocking flight of the feathered species,
And now I tell of the boldest and prettiest of the ornately plumed,
The famed pheasant of five colors:
5   Steeled with a steadfast heart of firm resolve,
Flaunting a splendrous figure of brave beauty,
He patrols hill and barrow, ordering and managing his realm,
Marks rise and flat, apportioning his domain.

II

Then
When Verdant Yang announces its departure,
10   And Vermilion Brilliance first receives its appointment,
There is not a tree that fails to flourish,
Not a plant that fails to germinate.

THIS RHAPSODY by Pan Yue (*zi* Anren) describes the ancient art of pheasant hunting as practiced in northeast China. According to Pan Yue's preface to this piece (cited by Li Shan 9.8b), he wrote the *fu* after moving with his family to the Langye area 琅邪 (in modern eastern Shandong). "By custom, the people of the area were truly skilled in archery. Making use of leisure moments from study, I learned the techniques of the decoy and the blind. I was subsequently so delighted, that I have composed a rhapsody on the subject." According to Xu Yuan 徐爰 (394–475), whose commentary to this *fu* is included with the *Wen xuan* text, the decoy or *mei* 媒 (literally "go-between") was a tame pheasant used to lure the wild pheasants within shooting range (see Li Shan 9.8b). The *Xijing zaji* (4.7a–b) mentions Wen Guyang 文固陽, a native of Langye, who was skilled in training pheasants as decoys for pheasant shooting. "Always in the third month of spring he made a blind of floss-grass which he used to

153

L. 14: The rare word *se* 槭 (withered, bare) also occurs in Pan Yue's "Rhapsody on Autumn Inspirations" (see *Wen xuan* 13.6a).

L. 15: Li Shan (9.9b) construes the doublet *yangyang* 泱泱 as interchangeable with *yingying* 英英 (bright and brilliant) of *Mao shi* 229/2: "Bright and brilliant are the white clouds " It is possible Pan followed the *Han shi* version of the *Classic of Songs*. See Zhu Jian 11.9b; Karlgren, "Glosses on the Siao Ya Odes," p. 52, #458. However, as Hu Shaoying (11.18b) notes, the element *yang* specifically describes the rising of cloud vapor. See *Shuowen* 11A.5031b–32a. Thus, I have translated *yangyang* as "swell and surge."

L. 17: Cf. the "Song of the Wheat in Bloom" attributed to the Viscount of Ji (*Shi ji* 38.1621; *Mh*, 4:231)· "The ears of wheat are peaked and pointed." For the association of wheat and pheasants, see also Mei Sheng's "Seven Stimuli" (in *Wen xuan* 34.4b): "The ears of wheat are pointed, pheasants fly at dawn." I suspect that *jianjian* 漸漸 (*tsjam-tsjam*), also written 蔪蔪, is related to *zhanzhan* 嶄嶄 (*dzram-dzram*), which is used to describe sheer mountain peaks. By analogy, *jianjian* describes the "peaked and pinnacled" appearance of the wheat spikes.

L. 18: According to the *Shuowen* (4A.1524a–25b and 4A.1647a–b), *yao* 鸙 is the call of the female pheasant, and *gou* 鴝 (also written 雊) is the cry of the male pheasant. Both words are found in the *Classic of Songs*; see *Mao shi* 34/2: "With the cry *yao*, the pheasant crows. . . . / The female pheasant crows, seeking her cock mate"; and *Mao shi* 197/5: "The pheasant is crowing (*gou*) at dawn, / He still seeks his hen mate." Yan Yanzhi (see Li Shan 9.9b), and Yan Zhitui after him (see *Yanshi jiaxun* A.46b; Teng, *Family Instructions*, pp. 102–3; Liang Zhangju 12.14b), criticize Pan Yue for wrongly using *gou* for the sound of the female pheasant. As both Li Shan and Duan Yucai (see *Shuowen* 4A.1524b) observe, this is an overly punctilious interpretation of the line, for *gou* is more probably simply a word for the call of a pheasant of either sex. See *Li ji zhushu* 17.21a.

L. 19: The alliterative binome *jiejiao* 揭驕 (*kjat-kjau*) is a variant of *jiejiao* 拮矯 (*kjet-kjau*), which is used in the *Chuci* poem "Distant Wandering" (Hawkes, *Ch'u Tz'u*, couplet 67) to describe elation and high spirits (both elements have the sense of "raised, high"). In this context, *jiejiao* means "elated and proud." For alliteration, I have rendered it as "with proud pleasure." For other discussions of this binome, see Jiang Liangfu 姜亮夫, *Qu Yuan fu jiaozhu* 屈原賦校注 (Hong Kong: Shangwu yinshuguan, 1964), pp. 550–51; and Hervouet, *Le Chapitre 117 du Che-ki*, p. 187, n. 8. According to Xu Yuan, there are two types of cage used for the decoys: the *xiang* 箱 (literally "box"), which was square and tightly enclosed so that the birds could not see any light; and the *long* 籠 (basket), which was round and open. I have loosely rendered the terms as "coops and cages."

L. 21: This line presumably describes the pheasants rubbing their legs together to sharpen their spurs.

L. 25. Although *xuan zhe* 軒翥 normally means "to soar aloft," in this line Pan Yue is describing the decoy pheasants getting ready to fly. Thus, I have translated *xuan zhe* as "rise and lift their wings."

L. 28: Xu Yuan (9.10a) says the alliterative binome *tingtong* 停僮 (*dieng-dung*) describes the blind. I have invented "dark and dense" for it. Hu Shaoying (11.18b–19a) notes its similarity to *tingtuan* 町疃 (*thiang-thwan*) of *Mao shi* 156/2, where it describes a clearing trampled by deer hoofs (cf. Karlgren, "Glosses on the Kuo Feng Odes," p. 240, #383). If Hu is right, the word may mean something like "tamped and trampled" (describing the clearing).

L. 33· The alliterative binome *liaoli* 料戾 (*liau-liei*), which describes the small holes in the wall of the blind through which the archer may look, is not otherwise attested. Neither of the two elements provides a clue to its meaning.

L 34: The rhyming binome *yanie* 厭𪘪 (*'jap-njap*), which is not otherwise attested, has the sense of "densely covered." The primary meaning probably comes from *ya* (to press down); hence, my "compactly compressed."

New stems are luxuriant in their dazzling freshness;
Aged branches, once bare, are transformed from their former state.
15 The sky swells and surges with drooping clouds;
Springs, burbling and bubbling, spurt and trickle.
The wheat, peaked and pinnacled, thrusts forth its spikes;
Calling "hock-hock," pheasants crow at dawn.

III

I peer into the coops and cages with proud pleasure,
20 Glance at the changing postures of the brave decoys inside.
They flex their powerful shanks, cutting at angles;
Stare through piercing eyes with a sideways squint.
With wings like patterned silk, ruddy rumps,
Throats of dazzling embroidery, dragon emblazoned backs,
25 They furiously rise and lift their wings, filled with unspent fury,
Anxious to crow a long crow and show their skills.

IV

And then
I sweep the clearing and erect a blind,
Which stands dense and dark, verdant and virescent.
Green cypress, randomly ranged,
30 Like patterned pinions, imbricating fishcales,
Lush and luxuriant, burgeon and flourish,
Twining and twisting, lithe and lissome.
The inside, cracked and creviced, allows a pervious purview;
The outside, compactly compressed, is finely woven.

---

screen himself. He shot them with ewe-horn arrows, and in a day was able to impale several hundred." According to Xu Yuan, after the fall of the Western Jin in 317, "this art" of pheasant shooting died out. However, Hao Yixing cites many examples of pheasant shooting in south China and accuses Xu Yuan of deliberately distorting the record. See his *Jin Song shu gu* 晉宋書故 (Notes on the Jin and Song Histories), *Yueya tang congshu* 粵雅堂叢書, pp. 21a–22a. As Zhu Jian (11.9b) suggests, the records that refer to pheasant shooting in the south do not mention the use of decoys and blinds, and thus Xu Yuan might have been right when he says "this art declined." For other translations of the *fu*, see J. Chalmers, "The Foo on Pheasant Shooting," *Chinese Review, Notes and Inquiries* 1 (1872–73):322–24; Obi Kōichi, *Monzen*, 1: 469–78.

L. 35: The word *you* 游 (**zjoh*) is a variant for *hua* 囮 (**ngwa*), also written *you* 圝 (**zjoh*). The *Shuowen* (6B.2736b–37a) explains *hua* as *yi* 譯, which Duan Yucai suspects is a miswriting of *you* (**zjoh*) 誘 (to entice). It then explains that the *hua* is a live bird decoy used to lure wild birds into a net. Duan Yucai's emendation is an attractive suggestion, for it shows that the root word for decoy should be read *you*, not *hua*, and that the basic meaning is "enticer" or "lure." For further information on the *you* , see Duan Gonglu 段公路 (fl. ca. 869), *Bei hu lu* 北戶錄 (Register of North-facing Doors), *Congshu jicheng*, 1.2–3

L. 36: The campestrian birds are the pheasants.

L. 39: The alliterative binome *qiaojie* 喬桀 (**kjau-kjat*), my "grand and glorious," possibly is an inversion of *jieqiao* in L. 19 above. See Hu Shaoying 11.19a.

L. 41: Xu Yuan (9.10b) explains that the hunter shook a cloth shaped liked a handkerchief to signal the decoy to begin its call to the wild pheasant.

L. 43: According to Xu Yuan (9.10b), the windows of the blind were covered with netting.

L. 46: The rhyming binome *peisai* 陪鰓 (**beh-seh?*) is a variant of *peisai* 毰毸, which describes the bristling feathers of a bird. See *Ci tong*, p. 0436.

L. 47: On *yue* 約 (to wrap, to envelop), see *Fangyan shuzheng* 13.6b.

L. 49: Xu Yuan (9.11a) explains *qiu* 鞦 as referring to the plumes "inserted between the tail (feathers?)." I assume it is a technical term for the coverts.

L. 50: Pan Yue must be comparing the color of the pheasant's breast with the purplish-red leaves and stem of the Chinese thoroughwort.

L. 54: This must be a type of tragopan pheasant, the male of which has two fleshy protuberances that resemble horns.

L. 59: On the yellow crossbow, see "Southern Capital Rhapsody," L. 213n.

L. 63: According to Xu Yuan (9.11b), the *bi* (**pjad*) 鷩 (golden pheasant) had a "testy" (*bie*/**pjat* 憋) nature.

35 Afraid my lure shall be late in springing,
Worried that the campestrian birds will be few in coming,
I cheer my weary heart through expectant anticipation,
Divert my tired eyes by intent watching.

V

How grand and glorious the trained fowl,
40 Far surpassing its kind, of extraordinary talent!
Awaiting the raising of the signal-cloth it then clearly calls;
Hearing the sound the wild bird responds to the decoy.
I lift the fine netting and after long gazing,
See a pheasant, hopping and halting, slowly advance.
45 It displays the scarlet splendor of its vermilion comb,
Spreads the ruffled quills of its ornate plumes.
Its head is enveloped in green and white,
From its body trails an embroidered design.
Its green coverts spread like sedge,
50 Its cinnabar breast is mottled like thoroughwort.

VI

Now kicking, now pecking,
It moves, then stops,
The hackles raised on its striped tail,
Its twin horns prominently raised.
55 My fine lure squawks and screeches
To draw him within shooting range.
Responding to the shriek, startled he stands,
Body erect, straight and still.
I raise the yellow crossbow and quietly bend it,
60 Fit the steel barb and stealthily take aim.
The downed bird suddenly falls to the ground,
Even before the trigger's reverberation has stopped.

VII

The golden pheasant of the mountains, fierce and ferocious,
Arrives swifter than a whirling gale.

157

L. 66: *Lin* 廩 apparently is another name for the blind. Cf. *Han Feizi jishi* 13.729–30.

L. 67: The *ya* 牙 is the name for the short forward prong of the crossbow behind which the bowstring is hooked. See K. P. Mayer, "On Variations in the Shapes of the Components of the Chinese *Nu-chi* (Crossbow Latch)," *TP* 52 (1965–66):1–7; A. F. P. Hulsewé, "Again the Crossbow Trigger Mechanism," *TP* 64 (1978):253.

L. 68: Pan Yue borrows terminology from the "Shooting Ceremonial" chapter of the *Li ji* (see *Li ji zhushu* 62.3a): "When one's inner feelings are upright, and his outer body is straight, he can grasp bow and arrow with careful aim and steady grip. Once he grasps the bow and arrow with careful aim and steady grip, he may speak about hitting the bullseye."

L. 77: Fearing that he will startle the wary golden pheasant, he puts down the signal cloth.

L. 78: On the term *ji yang* 技懩 (itching to test one's skill), see *Yanshi jiaxun* B.23b; Teng, *Family Instructions*, p. 166.

L. 87: The idea is that the fields have been taken over by weeds.

L. 94: The alliterative binome *shenshao* 滲躍 (*sjem-sjok) is not otherwise attested. Both elements have the sense of "excited, aroused"; hence, my translation of "pulsing and palpitating."

65 Crossing gullies, traversing ridges,
    Flying and screeching, it approaches the blind.
    I grasp the prong, lower the barbed arrow;
    Heart calmed, I watch and carefully take aim.
    Feathers and body fall asunder,
70 As sudden as ripping brocade.

VIII

    A cock pheasant far superior to his brood,
    Claiming the clearing for himself, seizes two hens.
    Jealous of the intruder, he strikes out at them,
    Swiftly running hither, now thither.
75 He is wary of the slight soughing of the wind above,
    Fearful of the glimmering glow of the shining sun.
    I remove the signal cloth and wait with bated breath,
    My heart fretful and itching to try my skill.
    When my valiant bird meets the enemy,
80 Scratching the ground, he screeches a piercing call.
    Hearing the cry, that wild bird directly advances,
    And suddenly they lock spurs in territorial combat.
    Its crimson form fills the shooting hole, and I get off a beautiful shot;
    Headless it falls in a blur, breast upward.

IX

    Sometimes when
85 Lofty embankments collapse and crumble,
    And farmers do not mend the field mounds,
    Barnyard grass and soybeans grow mingled and mixed,
    Rank and rampant, lush and luxuriant.
    The calling cock flaps its wings,
90 Following the crests of the mounds.
    In a flash it lands on a hummock and dashes toward the rival bird;
    Though its form is concealed, one sees the grass moving.
    When I see the bending and bowing of the straight stalks,
    My heart, pulsing and palpitating, leaps with excitement.
95 As he gradually emerges from the grass and enters the clearing,
    Increasingly my emotions tingle and my spirit shudders.

159

LL. 101–2: Pan Yue borrows from the *Guo yu* (3.1b) description of the way in which the cultivated gentleman uses his eyes to direct his hands and feet in the proper way: "For the Gentleman, the eyes thus steady the body, and the feet thus comply with the eyes. Therefore, by observing his demeanor, one can know his heart. The eyes thus focus on what is right, and the feet thus follow the eyes. Now, the Marquis of Jin's sights are set too far and his feet are planted too high, his eyes are not fixed on his body, and his feet do not follow his eyes. His heart must be disaffected indeed!"

L. 104: I follow Zhu Jian (11.11a) in reading *mo* 臀 as *mo* 脈 (to avert one's gaze).

L. 107: The handles presumably allow the person to rotate the blind like a turret.

L. 110: *Fu* 馥 (**biok*) is the sound the arrow striking the bird.

L 120: The rhyming binome *mili* 幎歷 (**miek-liek*) here describes the dense underbrush that conceals the pheasant. The basic meaning comes from *mi* (cover). I have thus rendered it here "copsy covert."

L. 121: Xu Yuan (9.13b) explains that behind the forward prong to which the bowstring is hooked there are markings (the *fen zhu* 分銖) which are used to determine the distance the arrow is to be shot.

L. 123: The *xuan dao* 懸刀 (literally "dangling blade") is the name for the trigger of the crossbow. See Mayer, "Variations," pp. 1–7; Hulsewé, "Again the Crossbow Trigger Mechanism," 253; Hayashi Minao 林巳奈夫, *Chūgoku In-Shu jidai no buki* 中国殷周時代の武器 (Kyoto: Jimbun kagaku kenkyūjo, 1972), pp. 301–20.

Against the black surroundings, the blind suddenly appears
           conspicuous,
And straightening his mantle, the pheasant whirls about.
Happily my concentration is keen and sharp;
100   I aim for his green forehead and I hit the neck.

X

There is one whose eyes do not follow his body,
And who gazes askance, glancing from side to side.
He hears nothing yet takes alarm,
Sees nothing yet averts his gaze.
105   As he whirls and swirls, round and round,
Twists and turns, reeling and wheeling,
I rotate the blind, spin the handles,
Follow him wherever he goes.
Starting and stopping, he halts in midcourse,
110   And *biok*, he is struck by my arrow.
In front it rends his thick breast,
On the side it severs his double quills.

XI

As for those pheasants that
Overcautious, weakwilled,
Poor in courage, timid of heart,
115   Inwardly lacking firm tenacity,
Outwardly afraid to engage in battle:
They come hither like virgin maids,
Depart like streaking lightning.
Peeping and peering from beneath the wheat stalks,
120   They suddenly reveal themselves from their copsy covert.

XII

And then
I calibrate the measurements,
Judge the distance,
Try the trigger,
And then display my superlative skill.

161

l. 125: Pan Yue borrows a line from *Mao shi* 177/5, which describes a well-balanced chariot that did not sag too low nor spring too high: "The war carts have been steadied, / As if falling, yet as if rising." The comparison with the flight of an arrow seems strained here.

ll. 133–36: The ugly Grandee of Jia took a beautiful girl for a wife. She was so depressed by her husband's ugliness, for three years she did not speak or laugh. One day in the hunting preserve she suddenly laughed when she saw him shoot a pheasant. See *Zuozhuan, Zhao* 28 (Legge 5:727); "Western Metropolis Rhapsody," l. 589n.

l. 143: The *Zhou li* (see *Zhou li zhushu* 8.7a; Biot, 1:163) mentions that two of the six types of robes worn by the empress were adorned with pheasant plumes

l. 145: Pan Yue alludes here to a *Zuozhuan* passage (see *Yin* 5; Legge, 5:727), in which a minister claimed that the ancient institutions specified that a ruler would shoot only those animals and birds that were "presented in feast stands." "The products of the mountains, forests, streams, and marshes ... and the affairs of underlings ..., the ruler does not concern himself." Pan Yue of course is arguing that pheasant-shooting is a legitimate undertaking for the ruler.

ll. 147–52· Cf. "Eastern Metropolis Rhapsody," ll. 674–77.

l 153: Cf. *Laozi* 12: "Galloping and racing, hunting and chasing, cause men's minds to go mad."

125 As if falling, yet as if rising,
 Neither too high nor too low,
 My arrows impale the beak straight through to the breast,
 Split the crop and smash the bill.

XIII

 With such varied terrain, both level and steep,
130 And diversity of birds, both docile and wild,
 At sunset one does not stop to eat,
 And at dusk does not mention fatigue.
 Of old, the Lady Jia went to the marsh,
 And smiled her first smile at a single arrow shot.
135 On this account a husband enhanced his appearance,
 And a resentful wife relieved her anger.

XIV

 Those who obtain catches in drives and hunts,
 All risk danger galloping and racing.
 How peaceful and relaxing this sport!
140 Ah, when the bird comes to me how enjoyable it is!
 We simply clear the path and proceed,
 Select a place and take up positions.
 Pheasant tails adorn bridles and the empress' vestments;
 Their meat, presented on feast stands, long has been imperial fare.
145 How is this something for underlings alone?
 This also is something a lord can do.

XV

 But if
 One rambles and revels, aimlessly drifting,
 Lets his mind stray, never altering his course,
 Forgets personal concerns,
150 Tends only to cocks and hens,
 Enjoying himself without restraint,
 His upright conduct perhaps may be harmed.
 This is something about which Master Lao warned,
 And something a Gentleman does not do.

Map of Ban Biao's Northward Journey

L. 1: The "overturning of the dynasty" refers to Wang Mang's usurpation and perhaps his subsequent overthrow.

L. 2: "Blockage and obstruction" refer to the failure of the Way of the true king to prevail.

L. 5: The gesture of flapping the sleeves suggests determination and courage.

L. 6: Cf. Liu Xin, "Rhapsody on Fufilling My Original Resolve," *Guwen yuan* 2.13a: "Detached from the world, I extinguish my traces and sally forth into the distance." The expression "extinguishing traces" usually implies cutting oneself off from the human world.

LL. 7–8: These two lines contain the common "morning and evening" formula of the *Chuci*. Cf. "Li sao" (*Chuci buzhu* 1.20b): "At dawn I depart from Cangwu, / At night I reach the Hanging Garden." The term "release the brake" simply means "to depart." Gourd Valley (Hu gu 瓠谷) probably refers to the preserve known as Hukou 瓠口, located north of the Han prefecture of Chiyang 池陽 (modern Jingyang 涇陽, Shaanxi). See *Shuijing zhu* 3.16.84; Zhu Jian 11.11b. I have been unable to identify the Dark Palace. Cf. Yang Xiong's "Plume Hunt Rhapsody," L. 12n.

L. 9: Cloud Gate (Yun men 雲門) must refer to a gate of the prefectural city of Yunyang 雲陽 (located northwest of modern Chunhua 淳化 *xian*, Shaanxi). The Sweet Springs Palace was located west of here.

L. 10: On the Sky-Piercing Tower, which was located at the Sweet Springs Palace, see "Western Metropolis Rhapsody," LL. 212–13n.

L. 12: Xun 郇 was the name of a Zhou state in which the sons of King Wen were enfeoffed (see *Shuo wen* 6B.2827b–28b). One of the Han Youfufeng prefectures was called Xunyi 栒邑 (located northeast of modern Xunyi *xian*, Shaanxi). West of Xunyi was the district town called Bin xiang 豳鄉 (also written Bin 邠), which was said to be the capital used by Duke Liu, the great-grandson of Houji and one of the illustrious ancestors of the Zhou ruling clan (see *Han shu* 28A.1547). *Yi* 邑 probably refers to Xunyi, and *xiang* 鄉 to Bin xiang. See Zhu Jian 11.12a.

L. 14: The "Rush by the Road" is the name of *Mao shi* 246. In Han times, this song often was interpreted as praising the benevolence of Duke Liu. See *Qianfu lun* 5.272, 8.373; Zhu Jian 11.12b.

L. 15: Cf. *Mao shi* 210/2: "Heaven increased it with drizzling rain; / It was abundant, it was rich."

L. 16: Cf. *Mao shi* 70/1: "In the later half of my life, I encounter these hundred misfortunes."

L. 17–18: Ban Biao here contradicts *Mao shi* 235/5, which says: "Heaven's decree is inconstant." The idea is that the fall of the dynasty occurred not because of any inconstancy on Heaven's part, but because the Han emperor failed to cultivate virtue. Ban Biao clearly

Rhapsody on a Northward Journey

BAN SHUPI

I

I have met the overturning of the dynasty,
Suffer the perilous calamity of blockage and obstruction.
My forebears' house has crumbled into hillock and waste,
And I cannot tarry even briefly.
5   So then, I flap my sleeves and travel northward;
Detached from the world, I extinguish my traces and distantly roam.

At dawn I release my brake at the Enduring Capital,
At night lodge in the Dark Palace of Gourd Valley.
Passing through Cloud Gate, I look back,
10   Gaze at the exalted heights of the Sky-piercing Tower.

Riding mound and ridge, I ascend and descend,
Rest at the towns and districts of Xun and Bin,
To admire Duke Liu's bequeathed virtue,
Which touched the roadside rushes and kept them from harm.
15   In that time, what plenty and abundance in their lives!
Now I alone meet these manifold misfortunes!
Certainly the changes and fluctuations of timely conjunctions
Are not because of the inconstancy of Heaven's decree.

AROUND THE YEAR A.D. 25, Ban Biao (*zi* Shupi) left the Chang'an area, which had been invaded by the Red Eyebrow rebels, to join the satrap Wei Ao 隗囂 (ob. 33) in eastern Gansu. Ban wrote the "Rhapsody on a Northward Journey" to recount his journey from Chang'an to Anding 安定 (modern Pingliang 平凉 *xian*, Gansu), 350 *li* to the northwest. Unlike earlier *fu* compositions, the piece does not portray an imaginary journey, but is a poetic record of an actual trip. The *fu* also is a good example of the *lan gu* 覽古 or "contemplation of antiquity" theme in Chinese poetry. (For an introduction to the subject, see Frankel, *The Flowering Plum and Palace Lady*, pp. 104–27.) In its common form, the poet describes his visit to

165

believed that misfortune was something man brought upon himself and was not necessarily determined by fate See his "Treatise on the Mandate of Kings," *Wen xuan* chapter 52.

L. 19–20: Yiqu dao 義渠道 was a prefecture located in Beidi 北地 commandery (west of modern Heshui 合水 *xian*, Gansu). See *Han shu* 28B.1616. Li Shan (9.16a) cites the *Shuijing zhu* (this passage no longer is in the present text; see Zhu Jian 11.11b–12a), which identifies Chixu 赤須 as a river that issued from Chixu Valley and flowed southwest into the Luo 羅 River (near modern Zhengning 正寧 Gansu).

L. 21–23: In the Zhou period, Yiqu was the kingdom of a Rong people. Empress Xuan 宣 was the mother of King Zhaoxiang 昭襄 of Qin (reg. 306–251 B.C.). She had illicit relations with the ruler of the Yiqu Rong and bore him two children. Later she had him murdered at the Sweet Springs Palace. Her son King Zhaoxiang then raised an army and captured Yiqu. See *Shi ji* 5.209; *Mh*, 2:76–77; *Han shu* 94A.3747.

L. 24: Cf. *Mao shi* 241/5: "Flushed with anger, the King was enraged at this." The subject of this line could also be "I": "Flushed with anger, northward I march."

L. 25: The old city is Yiqu.

L. 26: The expression *li zi* 歷茲 occurs twice in the "Li sao" (see *Chuci buzhu* 1.16a, 22b), where it means "to pass through these (difficulties)." In Ban Biao's piece, *zi* is less abstract: "this place."

L. 27: Li Shan (9.16b) cites the *Huainanzi* (1.3a) to explain the expression *shu jie* 舒節 (releasing restraint): "The great man ... gives free rein to his will, releases all restraint, and gallops throughout the great cosmos." However, Hu Shaoying (12.2a) thinks that *shu jie* should be understood in the sense of "slowing the pace." Cf. *Han shu* 57B.2599, n. 8. Following Hu, the line should read: "Then, with slackened pace, I go forth into the distance."

L. 28: Cf. "Li sao" (*Chuci buzhu* 1.35b): "I point to the Western Sea as my destination."

L 29: Cf. Liu Xin, "Rhapsody on Fulfilling My Original Resolve" (*Guwen yuan* 2.13b): "The road, long and distant, endlessly extends."

LL. 31–32: The route from Yiqu to Niyang 泥陽 (southeast of modern Ning 寧 *xian*, Gansu) actually took Ban Gu south and east, back toward Chang'an; hence, his description of a circuitous journey. During the Qin period, Ban Biao's ancestor Ban Yi 班壹 fled to the northern area of Loufan 樓煩 (modern Shenchi 神池 and Wuzhai 五寨 *xian*, Shanxi). Evidently some of the Ban family must have moved west to Niyang, where they established an ancestral temple.

L. 33: Pengyang 彭陽 (east of modern Zhenyuan 鎮原 *xian*, Gansu) was a prefecture of Anding commandery. See *Han shu* 28B.1615.

L. 36: Cf. *Mao shi* 66/1:

The sun is setting;
The sheep and oxen come down from the hills.
My lord is on campaign;
How can I not long for him?

LL. 37–38: Ban Biao may be referring here to *Mao shi* 33. According to the "Mao Preface" (see *Mao shi zhushu* 2.2.3a), this poem was a complaint about the hardships of military campaigns. "The officers were on duty for long periods. Husbands and wives complained of separation."

LL. 41–42: Sir Meng is Meng Tian, the Qin general who supervised the construction of the Great Wall. See *Shi ji* 88.2565–70; Derk Bodde, *Statesman, Patriot, and General in Ancient China* (New Haven: American Oriental Society, 1940), pp. 53–62. Note the pun on *zhu* 築 (build), which normally refers to building structures such as walls. These lines are similar to a line in Liu Xin's "Rhapsody on Fulfilling My Original Resolve" (*Guwen yuan* 2.12a): "Cruel was the tyranny of mighty Qin."

II

    I climb the long slopes of Chixu,
20 Enter the old walls of Yiqu.
    Outraged by the Rong king's licentious deceit,
    Disgusted by Empress Xuan's loss of virtue,
    I extol Zhao of Qin for punishing the bandits:
    Flushed with anger, northward he marched.

25 Bewildered, I depart this old city;
    My team, slowly, passes it by.
    Then, releasing all restraint, I go forth into the distance,
    Pointing off to Anding as my destination.
    Trekking the endless extent of the long road,
30 Distantly twining and turning, circuitously coursing,
    I pass Niyang and deeply sigh,
    Sad that our ancestral temple is in disrepair.
    I unhitch my horses at Pengyang,
    Briefly slowing my pace to reflect in myself.
35 As the sun, dim and darkling, nears evening,
    I see sheep and oxen come down from the hills.
    Awakening to the plaints at separation that so pain one's feelings,
    I condole with the poet who lamented his times.

III

    Crossing Anding, I amble about,
40 Following the spreading sprawl of the Great Wall.
    Cruelly Sir Meng wearied the people;
    For mighty Qin he built only resentment!

---

a place associated with a famous historical event or person. Many of the *lan gu* poems describe an ascent to a high place, from which the poet looks out into the distance and reflects upon the past. In "Northward Journey," Ban Biao relates his travel along a section of the Great Wall, which reminds him of the harsh Qin, who conscripted people to build the wall. Upon climbing one of its towers, he contrasts Qin's cruelty with the Han emperor Wen (the Civilized), who did not require defensive barriers to ward off invaders, but was able to conquer them through moral example. Ban is particularly critical of the builder of the wall, the general Meng Tian, who in spite of his loyal service, was imprisoned and forced to commit suicide. For other translations, see von Zach, in *Deutsche Wacht* 19 (1933) and rpt. in *Die Chinesische Anthologie*, 1 : 131–33; Obi Kōichi, *Monzen*, 1 : 479–86.

L. 43: Zhao Gao 趙高 was the eunuch who dominated the court of Hu Hai 胡亥, the Second Qin Emperor.

L. 44: In 215–214 B.C. Meng Tian led a successful military expedition against the northern tribes (Di). See *Shi ji* 6.252–53; *Mh*, 2:167–69. I can find no record of any expedition led by Meng against the southern tribes (Man).

LL. 47–50: One of Meng Tian's rivals was the eunuch Zhao Gao. Zhao was able to use his influence with the Second Qin Emperor to have Meng Tian arrested for plotting rebellion. Meng committed suicide in prison by taking poison. Just before swallowing the poison, he said, "How have I offended Heaven? Though guilty of no offense, am I to die? . . . My crime certainly is deserving of death. I began at Lintao and connected it with Liaodong, building walls and moats of more than ten thousand *li*. Perhaps in all of this I could not have avoided severing the earth's veins. This then was my crime." See *Shi ji* 88.2567–70.

L. 53: In Han times, the Xunyu were considered the ancestors of the Xiongnu. See *Shi ji* 110.2879; "Rhapsody on the Tall Poplars Palace," LL. 84–87n.

L. 54: In 166 B.C., the Xiongnu invaded Zhuna 朝那 (northwest of modern Pingliang *xian*, Gansu), one of the prefectures of Anding commandery, and killed Sun Ang 孫卬, the commandant of Beidi. See *Shi ji* 10.429, 110.2901; *Han shu* 4.125; *Mh*, 2:477; *Records*, 2:172–73; *HFHD*, 1:255–56.

LL. 55–58: The expression "mastering the art of yielding" alludes to one of the many laudatory epithets attributed to Yao in the "Canon of Yao" (see *Shang shu zhushu* 2.6b; Legge 3:15). Emperor Wen of the Han adopted a policy of winning the allegiance of foreign states through moral suasion rather than resorting to military force. Zhao Tuo 趙他 (Commandant Tuo) was the king of the Southern Yue. During the reign of Empress Lu, he declared himself Emperor Wu of the Southern Yue and began to harass the southern border area. When Emperor Wen assumed the throne in 180 B.C., instead of sending an army to punish Zhao Tuo, he summoned Zhao's brothers to court (Ban Biao actually says "father and brothers") and gave them high positions and lavish presents. He then sent the Confucian scholar Lu Jia as an envoy to Zhao Tuo. Lu was able to persuade Zhao to renounce his title as emperor and order his subjects to acknowledge the suzerainty of the Han emperor. See *Shi ji* 10.433, 113.2970; *Records*, 1:362, 2:241.

LL. 59–60: Liu Pi 劉濞, King of Wu (reg. 195–154 B.C.), was enraged when Emperor Wen's son killed his son during a chess game. Claiming illness, he refused to attend court. When Emperor Wen discovered that Liu Pi was not ill, rather than punish him, he sent him an armrest and cane, as official acknowledgment that Liu Pi was too old to attend court. See *Shi ji* 106.2823; *Records*, 1:467.

L. 61: The Grand Ancestor is Emperor Wen's temple name.

L. 63: Gaoping 高平 (Lofty Plain) possibly refers to Gaoping prefecture (modern Guyuan 固原 *xian*, Ningxia), which was located in Anding commandery. See *Han shu* 28B.1615.

L. 65: Cf. Liu Xin, "Rhapsody on Fulfilling My Original Resolve" (*Guwen yuan* 2.13a): "The wilds, deserted and desolate, are vast and vacant."

L. 66: Cf. Liu Xin, "Rhapsody on Fulfilling My Original Resolve" (*Guwen yuan* 2.13b): "Far, for hundreds of miles, there are no homes."

LL. 69–70: Cf. Liu Xin, "Rhapsody on Fulfilling My Original Resolve" (*Guwen yuan* 2.13b): "Tossed is the glistening whiteness of drifting snow, / And I trek the fallen frost frozen from dew." Although these lines seem perfectly parallel, the parallelism is misleading, for in each line there is a different subject. In L. 70, the subject of *she* 涉 (to cross, to trek) is "I," referring to Ban Biao's persona. Because of the ostensible parallelism between the two lines, one might assume that "I" also is the subject of *fei* 飛 (to fly) in L. 69. However, the absurdity of our poet flying through drifting snow makes this interpretation highly unlikely. The understood subject could be the geese of L. 71, but this interpretation requires the same birds as the

Dismissing pressing concern for Gao and Hai,
He attended to the remote dangers of the Man and Di.
45 He did not let virtue shine to tame distant reaches,
But rather strengthened strongholds, repaired fences.
His head was sundered from his body, but he did not comprehend;
But still tallied his exploits and denied the blame.
How absurd was that gentleman's speech!
50 Who could say the earth's veins caused his demise?

IV

I climb the fortress beacon tower and gaze into the distance,
For a brief moment to pause and ponder.
I grieve that the Xunyu disturb our Chinese land,
And lament Commandant Ang at Zhuna.
55 Ever since sage Wen mastered the art of yielding,
He did not toil his troops, but bestowed gifts instead.
By being magnanimous to fathers and brothers in Southern Yue,
He deposed the imperial title from Commandant Tuo.
He sent armrest and cane to a feudatory state,
60 And crushed Pi of Wu's perfidious treason.
Considering the spacious scope of the Grand Ancestor,
How could it be anything to which the late Qin could aspire?
I ascend Lofty Plain and survey my surroundings,
Gaze at the sheer scarps of mountain and gorge.
65 The wilds, deserted and desolate, spaciously spread;
Far, for a thousand miles, there are no homes.
A gale starts up, whirling and twirling;
Gorge waters pour down with swelling waves.

V

As the dark gloom of clouds and mist scuds past,
70 I trek the glistening whiteness of drifting snow,

subject of *she*, which cannot be used to refer to the flight of birds. Thus, I assume that what "flies" are the clouds and mist, which driven by the wind scud across the sky. The understood subject of *fei* in fact may be the wind (cf. L. 67), which "lets fly clouds and mist."

L. 73: The traveler is Ban Biao. The same statement was made by Han Gaozu when he returned to his home of Pei. See *Shi ji* 8.309; *Records*, 1:114.

L. 79: The dark storm is symptomatic of chaotic times.

L. 83: Ban alludes here to *Lun yu* 15/1: "Zilu said, 'Does the Gentleman also meet with adversity?' Confucius, said, 'The Gentleman is firm in adversity!'" The phrase *gu qiong* 固窮 can also mean "indeed meets with adversity" I am not certain which sense Ban Biao intended.

L. 84: Cf. *Lun yu* 7/6: "Let oneself roam in the arts."

L. 85: Cf. *Lun yu* 7/18, where Confucius characterizes himself as follows: "He bursts out with so much zeal, he forgets to eat. He is so joyful, he forgets sorrow."

L. 89: Cf. *Zhou yi zhushu* 5.27a (Hexagram 52, "Commentary on the Decision"): "When it is time to stop, one stops. When it is time to move, one moves. One's movement and rest do not miss their proper time, and their Way is bright and clear." Cf. *Kongzi jiayu* 8.14a: "The Gentleman in conducting himself ... bends when he can bend, straightens himself when he can straighten."

L. 90: Cf. *Zhou yi zhushu* (Hexagram 55, "Commentary on the Decision") 6.1b: "The fullness and emptiness of Heaven and Earth wax and wane with time."

L. 91: Cf. *Zhou yi zhushu* ("Great Commentary", Part I) 7.30b: "Treading the way of fidelity, one thinks on compliance."

L 93: Cf. *Lun yu* 15/5: "If one's words are loyal and true, and his actions are steadfast and cautious, even in the land of the Man and Mo, he may succeed."

While wild geese, honking in unison, soar by in flocks,
And the great fowl calls, squawking and screeching.
This traveler mourns for his old home;
My heart, sad and sorrowful, is pained with longing.
75   Stroking my long sword, sighing and sobbing;
I weep, and tears stream and fall, soaking my gown.

I wipe them away, choking and gasping,
And I sorrow for the people and their many afflictions.
Why has the dark storm not turned to sunshine?
80   Alas, long lost is the even measure!
Truly the cycle of time has made it so.
Long have I suffered—to whom can I make my plaint?

VI

The epilogue says:
The Master was firm in adversity,
And roamed in arts and letters.
85   To be so joyful one forgets sorrow—
Only the sage and wise can do so.
The discerning man in attending to affairs
Observes rules and standards.
Whether moving or stopping, bending or straightening,
90   He acts in accordance with the proper time.
The gentleman treads the way of fidelity;
There is nowhere he cannot live.
Even though he go to the land of the Man or Mo,
Why need he be worried or afraid?

171

CAO DAGU

Map of Cao Dagu's Eastward Journey

LL. 1–2: The text reads seventh year of Yongchu 永初, which is A.D. 113. However, there is good evidence that Yongchu is a mistake for Yongyuan 永元. According to Zhi Yu's commentary to the *Sanfu juelu* 三輔決錄 (Definitive Register of the Three Capital Districts), cited in *Hou Han shu* 84.2787, Cao Cheng was the son of Cao Shou 曹壽 (*zi* Shishu 世叔). His first appointment was as chief of Changyuan. When Ban Zhao became preceptor to the Grand Empress Deng 鄧 in 106, he was appointed palace attendant grandee. He later served as chancellor of Qi (a 2000-bushel post) and given the title of Marquis within the Pass (see *Hou Han shu* 84.2785). Ban Zhao mentions him in the preface to her "Instruction for Daughters": "I am constantly afraid Zigu will bring disgrace to our unsullied court. Sagacious beneficence has been generously bestowed, and he has undeservedly been given the golden seal and purple ribbon. This truly is something that a common man could hardly expect. Now that my son can provide for himself, I shall no longer consider him a source of worry." The golden seal and purple ribbon, which were given to officials of 2000-bushel rank, must refer to Cao Cheng's appointment as chancellor to Qi, which came sometime in the Yongchu period (106–113). Thus, Cao Cheng's appointment to Changyuan must have occurred much earlier. I follow Ruan Yuan (cited in Liang Zhangju 12.19b–20a) in emending Yongchu 7 to Yongyuan 7 (A.D. 95).

L 6: Yanshi 偃師 (modern Yanshi *xian*, Henan) was thirty *li* east of Luoyang.

L 7: Cf. "Nine Arguments" (*Chuci buzhu* 8.2a–b): "Fretful and worried, leaving the old, I advance toward the new."

L. 8: Cf. "Rhapsody on a Northward Journey," L. 74.

L 9: Cf. *Mao shi* 196/1: "Dawn breaks and I cannot sleep."

L. 10: Cf. *Mao shi* 35/2: "Traveling the road I am slow and tentative; / In my inner heart there is reluctance."

L. 12: Ban Zhao admonishes herself for her melancholy.

L. 13: This line alludes to the primordial period of pre-civilization, when people lived in nests and ate raw flesh. See *Wen xuan*, vol. 1, Xiao Tong's "Preface," LL. 3–4.

L. 14: Cf. *Lun yu* 16/1: "The Master said, "Qiu, Zhou Ren had a saying: When one can show his strength, he advances to the ranks.'" The line must refer to her son's imminent assumption of office.

L. 15: Cf. *Lun yu* 9/3: "The Master said, 'A hemp cap is the proper ritual. This (referring to the use of black silk) is simple and frugal. I follow the majority.'"

LL. 17–18: Ban Zhao refers to the roads in a double sense: one as the road actually traveled, and two as a metaphor for her son's career. He must follow the proper route and not take shortcuts and byways.

Rhapsody on an Eastward Journey

CAO DAGU

I

It is the seventh year of Yongyuan,
And I follow my son on an eastward journey.
The time is an auspicious day of early spring;
We choose a propitious hour for our departure.

5   Then, I stride forth to mount the carriage;
At dusk we lodge at Yanshi.
Then, leaving the old, we advance toward the new;
My heart, sorrowful and sad, is full of care.
As dawn brightly issues forth I cannot sleep;
10   I am slow and tentative—there is reluctance in my heart.
I pour a goblet of wine to ease my cares;
Sighing, I restrain my feelings and admonish myself.
Since we truly need not climb nests or crack open snails,
Must we not emulate others and show our strength?
15   Moreover, to follow the majority and advance to the ranks,
Is to heed what Heaven's decree ordains.
We follow the great way of open thoroughfares;
If we seek shortcuts, whom can we consult?

II

Then, as we go forth, swiftly advancing,
20   I let my gaze wander, my spirit roam.

THIS RHAPSODY by Cao Dagu (also known as Ban Zhao) is a poetic record of an actual trip that the poetess took probably in A.D. 95. She accompanied her son Cao Cheng 曹成 (*zi* Zigu 子穀) from Luoyang to Changyuan 長垣 prefecture (modern Changyuan *xian*, Henan) of Chenliu 陳留, where he was to assume his new post as chief of Changyuan. Like her father Ban Biao, whose "Rhapsody on a Northward Journey." she alludes to in LL. 71–72, Cao Dagu recounts the historical places she visits on this 530-*li* journey through central Henan. Most of the sites she mentions are associated with Confucius and his disciples. As she reflects on each of these places, she draws upon the *Lun yu* to offer advice to her son on his official career. Previous translations of the *fu* include: Nancy Lee Swann, *Pan Chao: Foremost Woman Scholar of China* (New York: The Century Co., 1932), pp. 113–29; von Zach, in *Deutsche Wacht* 19 (1933) and rpt. in *Die Chinesische Anthologie*, 1:133–35; Obi Kōichi, *Monzen*, 1:487–92.

L. 21: The seven towns should be the seven Zhou prefectures destroyed by the Qin. They include Henan, Luoyang, Gucheng 穀城, Pingyin 平陰, Yanshi, Gong 鞏, and Houshi 緱氏. See *Shi ji* 4.170, n. 3. However, to visit them all, she would have had to backtrack, for Gucheng, Henan, and Pingyin were west and northwest of Luoyang. For the first part of her journey, she followed the Luo River, passing through Yenshi, through Gong, to the confluence the Luo and Yellow Rivers, and from there to Chenggao.

L. 22: Gong (west of modern Gong *xian*, Henan) was a prefecture of Henan commandery. See *Hou Han shu*, "Zhi," 19.3390. "Much travail" can refer to physical hardships (see "Li sao," *Chuci buzhu* 1.11a) or the difficulties of the terrain (cf. "Li sao," *Chuci buzhu* 1.35b). Zhu Jian (11.15a) says the travail alludes to the suffering experienced by the people of the Gong area when it was invaded by the Qin in 250 B.C. The state of Han, which had control of Gong, was forced to cede it and Chenggao to Qin. Qin soon thereafter conquered all of China. See *Shi ji* 5.219; *Mh*, 2:97.

L. 23: The Luo River entered the He (Yellow River) northeast of Gong. See *Shuijing zhu* 3.15.55.

L. 24: Chenggao 成臯 (west of modern Sishui 汜水 *zhen*, Xingyang 滎陽 *xian*, Henan) was one of the Henan prefectures. The Turning Portal (Xuan men 旋門) was located ten *li* southwest of it. It was the location of a large slope that overlooked the Chenggao area. See *Shuijing zhu* 1.5.79 and "Eastern Metropolis Rhapsody," LL. 113–14n.

L. 26: Xingyang 滎陽 was a major Henan prefecture located about ten miles south of the Yellow River east of Chenggao. See *Hou Han shu*, "Zhi," 19.3389. Quan 卷 (located west of modern Yuanwu 原武 *xian*, Henan) was also one of the Henan prefectures. See *Han shu* 28A.1556; *Hou Han shu*, "Zhi," 19.3389.

LL. 27–28: Yuanwu 原武 (modern Yuanyang 原陽 *xian*, Henan) and Yangwu 陽武 (now incorporated with modern Yuanwu *xian*) were two Henan prefectures to the east of Xingyang. See *Hou Han shu*, "Zhi," 19.3389.

L. 29: Fengqiu 封丘 (modern Fengqiu *xian*, Henan) was a major prefecture of Chenliu commandery. See *Hou Han shu*, "Zhi," 21.3448.

L. 31: Cf. *Lun yu* 4/11: "The Master said, 'The Gentleman yearns for virtue; the petty man yearns for land.'" "Yearning for the land" usually is construed as referring to the desire for possessions Here, however, I think it means longing for one's home.

L. 34: Pingqiu 平丘 (southwest of modern Changyuan *xian*, Henan) was also a Chenliu prefecture. See *Hou Han shu*, "Zhi," 21.2447.

LL. 35–38: Kuang 匡 (known as Kuangcheng 匡城 in Cao Dagu's time, southwest of Changyuan *xian*) was a town through which Confucius once passed on his way to Chen. Mistaking him for the Lu brigand Yang Hu 陽虎, the people of the town surrounded his chariot. After five days, they released him. See *Lun yu* 9/5 and *Shi ji* 47.1919; *Mh*, 5:332–33.

L. 41: Changyuan was the Chenliu prefecture where Cao Cheng was to serve.

L. 43: Pucheng 蒲城 was a district town of Changyuan (see *Hou Han shu*, "Zhi," 21.3448). Confucius' disciple Zilu 子路 served here as grandee. See *Shi ji* 67.2193. Pucheng also had a shrine dedicated to him. See *Hou Han shu*, "Zhi," 21.3449, n. 17.

L. 47: Cf. *Lun yu* 17/23: "Zilu said, 'Does the Gentleman prize courage?' Confucius said, 'For the Gentleman, propriety is considered the most important. If a Gentleman has courage but no propriety, he becomes disorderly.'"

L. 48: Cf. *Lun yu* 16/12: "Boyi and Shuqi starved to death at the foot of Shouyang, and the people even till today praise them."

L. 49: Qu Yuan 蘧瑗, also known as Qu Boyu 伯玉, was an official of Wei whom Confucius admired (see *Lun yu* 15/6). Li Daoyuan (*Shuijing zhu* 2.7.40) cites the *Chenliu fengsu zhuan* 陳留風俗傳 (Commentary on the Customs of Chenliu), which refers to a Qu Bo District (*xiang*) in the Changyuan area. It had a Qu Pavilion, a Qu Boyu shrine, and a Qu Boyu tomb.

Through seven towns we view the sights;
But at Gong prefecture we encounter much travail.
We gaze at the confluence of the He and Luo;
See Turning Portal at Chenggao.

25 Having evaded and escaped the steep defiles,
We cross Xingyang and pass through Quan.
We eat and rest at Yuanwu,
Spend the night among the mulberries of Yangwu.
Edging into Fengqiu, we again tread the road;
30 Longing for the Capital, I sigh to myself.
A petty man by nature yearns for his home;
From ancient books we have had such a saying.
Then, advancing on the road, slightly ahead,
We reach the northern side of Pingqiu.

III

35 Entering Kuang's outskirts, I recall the distant past;
Ponder the Master's terrible adversity.
In that lawless age of decline and disorder,
They could torment and frighten even a sage.
Sadly pacing about, I make a long halt,
40 Oblivious of the setting sun and approaching dusk.
Reaching the borders of Changyuan,
I observe the residents of the farms,
Glimpse the ruins of Pucheng,
Growing thick clusters of thorns and stickers.
45 Startled, I awaken, and look back inquiringly,
And think of Zilu's majestic spirit.
The people of Wei admired his courage and propriety;
Even till the present he is praised.
Master Qu lived southeast of the city;
50 The people still honor his grave mound.

L. 51: Cf. *Zuozhuan, Xiang* 24 (Legge, 5:507): In explaining the meaning of the ancient saying "They died but did not perish," Mushu Bao said: "The thing of highest importance is to establish virtue. Next is to establish merit. After that is to establish good speech. If even after a long time they are not in disuse, one may say 'they are imperishable.'"

L. 55: Wu Zha is Ji Zha 季札, prince of Wu. In 544 B.C. the King of Wu sent him on a tour of the northern Chinese states. He visited the state of Wei where he met many Wei officers (including Qu Boyu). He was so impressed with the moral character of the men he met in Wei, he said, "Wei has many Gentleman. It will never have any disasters." See *Zuozhuan, Xiang* 30 (Legge 5:550); *Shi ji* 31.1458; *Mh*, 4:14.

L. 56: Cf. *Zuozhuan, Zhao* 8 (Legge 5:622): "The words of a Gentleman are true and verifiable."

L. 58: Wei's demise began with the ruler of Wei demoting himself to a marquis in 346 B.C. In 252 B.C., the state of Wei 魏 seized control by killing the Wei ruler and naming a successor. Finally, in 241 Qin conquered the area and divided its territory into commanderies. See *Shi ji* 37.1604–5; *Mh*, 4:212–13.

L 59: Cf. *Lun yu* 12/5: "Life and death involve fate. Wealth and honor depend upon Heaven."

L. 60: Cf. *Zhong yong* 中庸 (Doctrine of the Mean) 20/10: "The Master said, 'To love learning is to approach wisdom. To act vigorously is to approach benevolence.'"

L. 61: Cf. *Mao shi* 218/5: "The high hills—I look up at them; / The great road—I travel it."

L. 62: Cf. *Lun yu* 4/15: "Zengzi said, 'The Master's Way is nothing more than devotion and altruism.'" Cf. *Laozi* 79: "The Way of Heaven is not partial. It always associates with the good man."

L. 63: Cf. *Mao shi* 207/5: "Be respectful in your positions! / Love the straight and upright!" Cf. also *Mao shi* 239/6: "The joyous happy lord, / In seeking felicity he does not waver."

L. 64: Cf. Ban Biao, "Treatise on the Mandate of Kings" (*Wen xuan* 52.2a): "Through utter sincerity one affects the divine luminaries."

L. 69: Cf. *Lun yu* 5/25: "The Master said, 'Come, let each of you state his wishes.'"

L. 71: The expression *xing zhi* 行止 (literally "advancing and stopping") obviously alludes to Ban Biao's travels to the northwest, which was the subject of his "Rhapsody on a Northward Journey."

L. 73: Cf. *Lun yu* 12/1: "Yan Yuan said, 'Though I am not clever, I request to practice these words.'"

LL. 75–76: Cf. *Lun yu* 4/15: "The Master said, 'Wealth and honor—these are what men desire. If they can be obtained only by violating the Way, they should not be owned. Poverty and low position—these are what men detest. If they can be avoided only by violating the Way, they should not be avoided.'"

L. 83: Cf. *Mao shi* 253/3: "Be watchful and careful of your demeanor."

Verily, good virtue cannot perish;
The body dies but reputation survives.
This is what the classics and canons have extolled;
They honor the Way and virtue, benevolence and wisdom.

55 Wu Zha praised Wei's many Gentlemen;
These words are true and verifiable.
Later, Wei declined and met with disaster,
Gradually crumbling away, never to flourish again.

We know that life and fate rest with Heaven;
60 But through vigorous effort, one may approach benevolence.
Strive to gaze on high and tread in greatness;
Be fully devout and altruistic, associate with good men.
Love the straight and upright, do not waver,
And your pure devotion shall affect even the gods.
65 May the blessed spirits shine upon you;
For they bless the upright, assist the faithful.

IV

The epilogue says:
The thoughts of the Gentleman
Must take form in writing.
Let each one state his wishes,
70 Thus emulating the ancients.

My late father went on a journey,
And wrote a poem about it.
Though I am not clever,
How dare I not follow his example?

75 Honor and low position, poverty and wealth—
They cannot be sought.
Rectify the self, tread the Way,
And await the proper time.

The cycle—be it long or short—
80 Is alike for both stupid and wise.
Quiet and respectful one accepts fate—
Be it good fortune or bad.

177

L. 85: Cf. *Laozi* 45: "Being pure and tranquil, one may rule the empire."

L. 86: Cf. *Lun yu* 14/13: "Zilu asked about a consummate person. The Master said, 'Suppose the knowledge of Zang Wuzhong, the desirelessness of Gongchuo, the valor of Zhuangzi of Bian, the skills of Ran Qiu. Embellish them with the rites and music. I would consider this the consummate person.'" Meng Gongchuo 孟公綽 was the Lu official Confucius most respected. See *Shi ji* 67.2186. However, elsewhere in the *Lun yu* (14/12), Confucius said that Gongchuo was well-qualified to be elder of the Zhao and Wei families, but was not fit to be grandee in Teng or Xue. Ban Zhao probably mentions Gongchuo here as an example of a man free of excessive desires. She urges her son to emulate this quality.

Be watchful and careful, never negligent;
Think on modesty and restraint.

85 Be pure and tranquil, have few desires;
Take Gongchuo as your preceptor.

Map of Pan Yue's Westward Journey

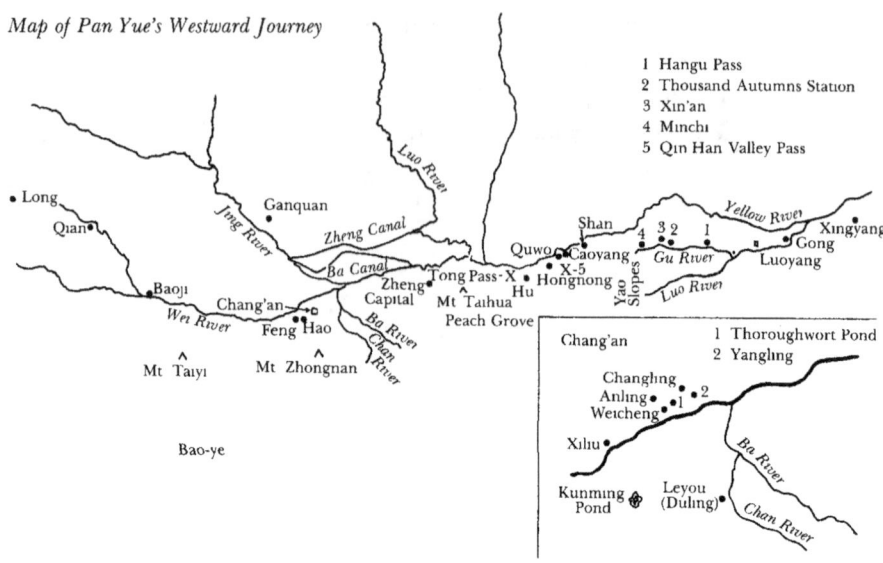

L. 1: Xuanxiao 玄枵 (Dark Void) is the astronomical name for the Jupiter station corresponding to the cyclical sign *zi* 子 and the lunar station Xu 虛 (Barrens: β Aquarii and α Equilei). See *Erya yishu* B4.11a–b; *Mh*, 3:654; Needham, Volume 3, p. 405; Schafer, *Pacing the Void*, p. 76. According to Pan Yue's "Lament for My Young Son" (cited by Li Shan 10.1a), his journey to Chang'an took place in Yuankang 2 (292), which was a *renzi* 壬子 year.

LL. 2–4: Ruibin 蕤賓, which I fancifully render as Festooned Guest, is the pitchpipe corresponding to the fifth month. *Bing* 丙 and *ding* 丁 are the cyclical signs for the days of the summer months. See *Li ji zhushu* 15.17a, 16.1a, 16.8a. *Yiwei* 乙未 was the nineteenth day of the fifth month (Li Shan erroneously gives it as the eighteenth). Thus, Pan Yue departed on 20 June 292.

L. 6: The Capital is Luoyang. Qin is the area of Chang'an, Pan's destination.

L. 10: This line is identical to a line of Jia Yi's "Rhapsody on the Owl" (see *Wen xuan* 13.19b).

LL. 14–15: Cf. *Zhou yi zhushu* 8.4a ("Great Commentary"): "The greatest virtue of Heaven and Earth is called life, and the greatest treasure of the sage is called position."

10

Rhapsody on a Westward Journey

PAN ANREN

I

Jupiter is stationed in the Dark Void,
The moon lodges in the Festooned Guest,
Bing and *ding* govern the days,
Yiwei controls the junction of the sun and moon:
5   And I, Panzi, leaning on my crossbar, journey west:
From the Capital, I go forth to Qin.

Sighing and sobbing, I say:
From the ancient past, to the recent present,
Oh how far, how distant!
10   Empty and vast, muddled and murky,
This primal pneuma was transformed to mold the Three Powers.

These Three Powers are:
The way of Heaven, Earth, and Man,
But only life and position
15   Does one call the greatest of treasures.

Life is ordained either long or short,
Position is fated for failure or success.
Just as ghosts and spirits cannot decree things to happen,
The sage and wise cannot forsee them.

THIS RHAPSODY is Pan Yue's account of his journey from Luoyang to the old Han dynasty capital of Chang'an. In 290, Pan had been appointed to the staff of Yang Jun 楊駿 (ob. 291), who had served as regent for the ailing Emperor Wu (reg. 265–290). Under the following emperor (Hui, reg. 290–306), the Empress Jia staged a coup to overthrow Yang Jun. On 23 April 291, the Duke of Dongan 東安, Sima You 司馬繇, led a troop of four hundred palace guards into Yang's headquarters, located south of the arsenal. They set fire to the building

181

L. 22: The *Mengzi* (5B/7) mentions the practice of summoning high officials to office with a banner appropriate to their status. The bow presumably had a similar function. See *Zuozhuan*, *Zhuang* 22 (Legge 5:103). The three legs of the tripod represented the three ducal ministers (see *Han shu* 27B2.1411). The treble platform (San tai 三台), which was also the name of a constellation, is an elegant expression for the highest ministerial posts. See *Jin shu* 11.293.

L. 23: Here Pan refers to his appointment on the staff of the Grand Marshall Jia Chong 賈充 (217–282), whom he served in the 270's.

LL. 24–25: Cf. *Lun yu* 17/15: "The Master said, 'The mean man—can one possibly work with him in serving one's lord? Before he has attained something, he worries about attaining it. When he has attained it, he worries about losing it.'"

LL. 26–27: Liu Ji 柳季 is Liuxia Hui (see "Western Metropolis Rhapsody," LL. 783–84n). Cf. *Lun yu* 18/2: "Liuxia Hui served as minister of justice, and thrice was dismissed. Someone said, 'Should you not leave?' He said, "If I uprightly serve men, where could I go and not be dismissed?"" Pan Yue was dismissed from his post as Referee to the Commandant of Justice (see Zang Rongxu's *Jin shu*, cited by Li Shan 10.2a).

L. 28: Mighty Augustus (Wu huang 武皇) is Sima Yan 司馬炎 (236–290), posthumously known as Emperor Wu (the Mighty). The death of an emperor was euphemistically called "ascending into the beyond." See *Li ji zhushu* 4.20b.

L. 29: According to the Old Text "Canon of Shun" (see *Shang shu zhushu* 3.18b; Legge 3:41), when Yao died "throughout the four seas they stilled and silenced the eight types of musical sounds."

L. 30: Sima Yan's successor was his second son, Sima Zhong 司馬衷 (259–306). He was an imbecile, and during his reign the court was controlled by Yang Jun and the empress, née Jia. According to the *Record of Rites* (see *Li ji zhushu* 20.18b–19a), following the example of Wuding of the Shang, a ruler mourning the death of his father spends three years in the mourning hut. See also *Lun yu* 14/43.

L. 31: According to the "Instructions of Yi" (see *Shang shu zhushu* 8.13b; Legge 3:191), after the death of the Shang ruler Cheng Tang, "the central officers gathered themselves together and heeded (the instructions of) the prime minister for three years." In Pan Yue's line, the prime minister refers to Yang Jun, who served as grand tutor and was in virtual control of the central administration. See *Jin shu* 40.1177–78.

L. 33: Yi is Yi Yin 伊尹, who deposed the Shang emperor Taijia 太甲 and served as regent for three years. See *Shi ji* 3.98; *Mh*, 1:188–89. Zhou is the Duke of Zhou, who served as regent during the minority of King Cheng. See *Shi ji* 4.132; *Mh*, 1:245.

L. 34: The seven nobles are the seven powerful consort clans of the Han: the Lu 呂, Huo 霍, Shangguan 上官, Ding 丁, Zhao 趙, Fu 傅, and Wang 王.

L. 35: Pan's point is that the power of consort clans is short-lived.

LL. 38–39: Yang Jun was overthrown in a coup led by forces loyal to the Empress Jia. Pan Yue cites a line from *Mao shi* 264/3 ("Disorder does not descend from Heaven; / It is engendered by women") to say that Yang Jun's fall from power was his own fault and had nothing to do with cosmic forces. Qu Shuiyuan (*Han Wei Liuchao fu xuan*, p. 74) notes the possibility of a double meaning in the *Mao shi* reference. It could either refer to Yang Jun, who was the cause of his own disaster, or Empress Jia, the "woman" who engineered the coup against him.

L. 40: Cf. *Lun yu* 7/10: "The Master said to Yan Yuan, 'When employed, to act, and when shunted aside, to retire—only you and I can do so.'"

II

20 Born in a flourishing age of blessed brilliance,
     I am endowed this shabby substance of meager talent.
     I received banner and bow on the treble platform,
     And assisted the various duties of the imperial chamber.
     Alas, I am a mean man who is eternally anxious;
25 Truly having attained what I want, I worry about losing it.
     Lacking the forthright manner of Liu Ji,
     As helper to the Minister of Justice I only once was dismissed.

     Mighty Augustus suddenly ascended into the beyond,
     And the eight musical sounds were silent throughout the four seas.
30 While the Son of Heaven slept in the mourning hut,
     The centurial officers heeded instructions from the prime minister.
     The burden he bore was unusually heavy;
     Even Yi or Zhou would have been imperiled.
     Look for the seven nobles from the Han court;
35 Which clan among them still survives?

     Lacking discernment of danger with which to secure his position,
     He simply dwelled nearer the throne to flaunt his authority.
     When he fell to the rebels and was put to death,
     This was not a misfortune descended from Heaven.
40 Confucius followed the changes of time in acting or retiring;

---

and stationed crossbowmen on the pavilion to prevent Yang's guards from leaving. Yang Jun fled to the stable, where a soldier ran him through with a halberd. The Empress Jia sent out a secret order to execute Yang's associates, and several thousand men were killed. See *Jin shu* 40.1178–79 As a protégé of Yang Jun, Pan Yue had his name removed from the official register. Although all members of Yang's entourage were condemned to death, Pan Yue escaped by leaving the capital on an emergency. His friend Gongsun Hong 公孫宏, who was in charge of the executions, was able to spare Pan's life by claiming that Pan was only an "acting official" on Yang Jun's staff. See *Jin shu* 55.1503–4. In the following year, Pan was appointed prefect of Chang'an He left Luoyang on 20 June 292. In his rhapsody, he provides a detailed account of his journey. Like the preceding rhapsodies by Ban Biao and Cao Dagu, "Westward Journey" is essentially a record of the historical sites through which Pan passed. His description of Chang'an is rich in detail and provides important information on third century Chang'an, which was no longer the glorious city it had been in the Former Han.

    This rhapsody has been previously translated by von Zach, *Aus dem Wenhsuan. Die Reise nach den Westen* (Hsi-cheng-fu, W. H. C. 10) von P'an Yo, gestorben 300 n. Chr. Frankfurt-am-Main: China Institut, 1930, and rpt. in *Die Chinesische Anthologie*, 1:136–58; and Obi Kōichi, *Monzen*, 2:5–59. There are also helpful notes in Qu Shuiyuan, *Han Wei Liuchao fu xuan*, pp. 70–117. For a study of this *fu*, see Fujiwara Takashi 藤原尚, "'Seisei fu' ni okeru ningenkan" 西征賦における人間観, *Nihon Chūgoku gakkai hō* 21 (1968), 210–33.

L. 41: Qu Boyu was a minister of the state of Wei (see "Rhapsody on an Eastward Journey, L. 49n). In *Lun yu* 15/6, Confucius praised him as follows: "A gentleman indeed is Qu Boyu. When the Way prevails in the state, he serves. When the Way does not prevail in the state, he can curl up and tuck himself away."

LL. 44–45: Cf. Ban Gu's "Appraisal for the Biographies of Wang, Gong, the Two Gong's and Bao" (*Han shu* 72.3097): "Once the scholar of the mountains and forests (i.e., the hermit) leaves (the court), he is unable to return."

L. 46: Pan's trammeled state is the pursuit of fame and fortune.

L. 50: Cf. "Wei Capital Rhapsody," L. 765n.

L. 51: Pan Yue alludes to a passage in *Zuozhuan*, *Xiang* 29 (Legge 5:550), in which an official's precarious position is compared to a swallow's nest built in a tent. As soon as the tent is taken down, the swallow's nest will be destroyed.

LL. 52–53: Cf. *Mao shi* 195/6: "Tremble, tremble, quake, quake, / As if standing over a deep abyss, / As if treading on thin ice."

L. 54: The night of the coup against Yang Jun, Pan was able to escape by returning home on an emergency. See *Jin shu* 55.1503–4.

LL. 56–57: Cf. "Wei Capital Rhapsody," L. 321.

L. 58: The "Wenyan Commentary" to the *Classic of Changes* (see *Zhou yi zhushu* 1.10a) defines the hexagram attribute *heng* 亨 ("success") as "a fortunate encounter." This line literally says: "I have met with the most fortunate encounter in a thousand years."

L. 59: Cf. *Zhou yi zhushu* 1.20a ("Wenyan Commentary"): "The great man matches his virtue with Heaven and Earth."

LL. 60–61: Autumn frost is a metaphor for severe punishment; spring moisture, for the emperor's mercy, which allowed Pan to escape punishment.

L. 63: Cf. "Li sao" (*Chuci buzhu* 1.13b): "I retire to fashion my former attire." The former attire is Pan's commoner's garb, which he donned after losing his official title.

L. 64: Pan borrows part of a line from the "Li sao" (*Chuci buzhu* 1.3b): "His august reflection discerned my natal signs, / And first granted me a favorable name."

L. 65: This secondary rank is his post as prefect of Chang'an.

L. 67: The Pass most likely is the Hangu Pass, which he had to cross in order to reach Chang'an.

L. 68: According to *Mengzi* (7B/17), when Confucius left Lu, he said, "I shall take my time in setting out."

L. 69: Ji is Liu Ji 劉季, better known as Liu Bang, founder of the Former Han dynasty. In 195 B.C. he passed his old home of Pei 沛, where he stopped and drank with old friends. In the midst of the celebration, he suddenly stood up and danced. With tears streaming down his face, he said to the Pei elders, "The traveler sorrows for his old home." See *Shi ji* 8.389; *Han shu* 1 74; *Records*, 1:113–14; *HFHD*, 1:136–37.

L. 73: The Hao Capital is the old Zhou capital near Chang'an.

L. 75: The expression "gatetower and court" is metonymy for the emperor.

Depending upon the condition of the state, Qu either stretched or
    curled.
If one is ignorant of the hidden and misinterprets the manifest,
He should worry that punishment for transgressions shall not be far
    off.
I now realize why the hermit scholar who hides in the mountains,
45   Standing aloof, departs forever, never to return.
I despise my own trammeled state,
Drifting like duckweed, tossed like a tumbleweed.

When official position collapsed I was cast from glory;
Name and character ruined, I tumbled into disgrace.
50   My situation was more precarious than a stack of white eggs,
Worse than that of the black swallow nesting on a tent.
I trembled with fear, quaked with dread,
As if on the brink of an abyss, as if treading thin ice.
At dusk I was able to return home outside the capital,
55   And before midnight calamity occurred.

Without choosing the right nest in which to roost,
Few birds can survive a forest fire.
I have met with the most fortunate age in a millennium;
Our august sovereign matches his virtue with Heaven and Earth.
60   Relaxing His stern demeanor as severe as autumn frost,
He let flow His grace as rich as spring moisture.
Having justice revealed to me, I understood my duty;
I returned home to don my former attire.

His august reflection discerned my loyal devotion,
65   And soon named me to a minor rank.
On my way to tend the weary folk of west China,
Leading old and young, I enter the Pass.

When Confucius left Lu, he looked back and sighed;
When Ji passed Pei, tears streamed down his face.
70   It was precisely this longing for home
That pains the inner hearts of sage and discerning men.
What about this simple man, long content in his own land,
Who now must take refuge in Hao Capital?
Like a dog or horse devoted to its master,
75   I convey my affection to gatetower and court.

LL. 76–77: According to the *Henan jun tu jing* 河南郡圖經 (Map Canon if Henan Commandery), a work of unknown authorship and date cited by Li Shan (10.4a), the grave of Pan Yue's father was located thirty-five *li* southwest of Gong prefecture. The *Shuijing zhu* (3.15.55) locates it on the Luo 羅 River, northwest of Yuangong wu 袁公塢 (fifteen *li* southwest of Houshi prefecture). Li Daoyuan reports that the stone inscription in front of the grave had broken and many characters were missing. Following the account in the *Shuijing zhu*, Zhu Jian (11.16a) concludes that the grave could not have been too far from both Yanshi and Gong prefectures. I assume that Pan began his trip from his home in Xingyang, and thus he mentions sites east of Luoyang.

LL. 78–79: The Tower of Peaceful Toy was located west of Luoyang. See "Eastern Metropolis Rhapsody," LL. 221–22n The Highway Station (Jie you 街郵) was an old relay station located on a plateau north of Zi Marsh 梓澤 (Zi Marsh, northwest of modern Luoyang, was the site of Shi Chong's Golden Valley estate, often frequented by Pan Yue.) It possibly is a variant name for Qian Station 贊亭. See *Han shu* 28A.1555; *Hou Han shu*, "Zhi," 19.3393, n. 40; *Shuijing zhu* 3.15.62; Hu Shaoying, 12.5b.

L. 80: Li Shan (10.4b) cites the *Shuijing zhu* (3.16.69), which identifies Marsh Gate (Gao men 皐門) as the stone sluice gate that controlled the flow of water from the Gu River to its old channel.

L. 81: Western Zhou refers to the fief of Henan 河南 (on the northwestern outskirts of modern Luoyang), which King Kao 考 (reg. 440–426 B.C.) of Zhou gave to his younger brother Jie 揭. See *Shi ji* 4.158; *Mh*, 1:300–1.

L. 82: The Ji was the ruling clan of the Zhou. For a similar phrase describing the Great Yu, see *Zuozhuan*, *Zhao* 1 (Legge 5:578).

L. 83: Jiang Yuan 姜原, the mother of Hou Ji 后稷, reputedly was the first wife of Di Ku 帝嚳, also known as Gao Xin 高辛. According to legend, she became pregnant after stepping in the footprint of a giant. Hou Ji was the first to take the Ji surname. See *Shi ji* 4.111–12; *Mh*, 1:209–10.

LL. 84–85: These lines are cited from *Mao shi* 275/1 and 245/1 respectively.

LL. 86–87: These lines refer to Danfu, King Wen of Zhou's grandfather. Cf. *Mao shi* 237/2:
The lord of old, Danfu,
At dawn galloped his horses.
He followed the West River's margin,
As far as Mt. Qi's base.
According to the *Shi ji* (4.113–14; *Mh*, 1:214), in order to escape an invasion of the Xunyu, Danfu led his people from Bin to the base of Mt. Qi See also *Shuijing zhu* 3.16 83.

L. 88: Chang 昌 is the name of King Wen of Zhou; Fa 發 is his son, King Wu.

L. 89: Cf. *Mao shi* 235/1: "Though Zhou is an old state, / Its mandate is new."

L. 90: King Wu's army defeated the forces of Zhou, the last Shang ruler, on the Plains of Mu 牧. See *Shi ji* 4.122–24; *Mh*, 1:228–34. The Plains of Mu were located south of modern Qi 淇 *xian*, Henan, about 120 kilometers northwest of Luoyang.

L. 91: Cf. *Laozi* 52: "Holding to softness is called strength." Pan also uses a phrase from *Mao shi* 274/1, which he seems to understand as saying "King Wu who maintains his strength."

LL. 92–93: Cf. "Nine Arguments" (*Chuci buzhu* 8.3a): "Alone, from nightfall to dawn, I do not sleep." According to the *Shi ji* (4.128–29; *Mh*, 1:241), when King Wu returned to his capital after defeating the Shang, he did not sleep all night because he was worried he had not yet obtained Heaven's protection.

L. 94: Hu Shaoying (12.6b) proposes that *wei* 惟 should be read *sui* 雖 (although).

L. 95: The Zhou dynasty actually ruled for 867 years.

LL. 96–97: The fallen king is Jie, the evil last ruler of the Xia. According to the "Announcement of Zhonghui" in the *Classic of Documents* (see *Shang shu zhushu* 8.6b; Legge 3:177), the

Gazing over Gong and Luo, I wipe my tears,
Thinking continuously of grave and burial ground.

III

And now
I cross Peaceful Joy,
Pass the Highway Station,
80 Graze my horses by Marsh Gate,
Rest my team at Western Zhou.
Far-reaching indeed Ji's virtue!
From Gao Xin it began.
Oh, how cultured was Hou Ji,
85 The first to engender our people!
Following West River's margin,
Transforming influence coursed through Qi and Bin.
Blessings of rule flourished under Chang and Fa,
And the old state was made new.

90 Wheeling toward the Plains of Mu, King Wu passed through here;
The more he held to softness the stronger he became.
From nightfall to dawn he did not sleep,
For he worried that Heaven's protection was not yet assured.
Though secure as Mt. Tai he felt imperiled;
95 Thus for eight hundred years there was a surfeit of blessings.
He took warning from the arrogance and dissipation of the fallen
                king,
Who fled to Nanchao and lost his life.

Shang founder Cheng Tang banished him to Nanchao 南巢 (modern Chao 巢 *xian*, Anhui). See also *Shi ji* 2.89; *Mh*, 3 : 170, n 2.

LL. 98–99: Cf. Zhao Yi 趙壹 (fl. ca. 178), "Rhapsody Criticizing the World and Condemning Evil" (*Hou Han shu* 80B.2631): "How is this any different from crossing the sea in a rudderless boat, / Or sitting on a pile of firewood waiting for it to burn." The *Shang shu dazhuan* (2.13a; cf. *Yiwen leiju* 1.44) records a dialogue between Yi Yin and King Jie at the Xia court. Yi Yin proclaimed to Jie, "There will be a day (*ri*) when your great mandate will perish." Jie scornfully laughed and said, "Heaven has a sun (*ri*), just as I have the people. Can the sun indeed perish? When the sun perishes, I shall perish!"

LL. 100–101: Cf. Sima Xiangru, "Dispatch Informing Ba and Shu" (*Wen xuan* 44.3a): "The disparity between their respective judgments, how far apart it is indeed!"

LL. 102–3: Cf. "Announcement of Shao" (in *Shang shu zhushu* 15.8b; Legge 3 : 428): "Having determined that the center of the land was located at this city (= Luoyang), King Cheng established the capital and ordered its construction." According to the *Shi ji* (4.133; *Mh*, 3 : 247), King Cheng of Zhou sent the Duke of Shao to rebuild the city of Luo. After divining the proper location, the Duke of Zhou began construction.

LL. 104–5: King Cheng of Zhou placed the famous nine tripods that reputedly once belonged to the Xia founder, the Great Yu, in the city of Jiaru. See "Eastern Metropolis Rhapsody," L. 128n. Through divination he determined that the Zhou would last thirty reigns, for a total of seven hundred years. See *Zuozhuan, Xuan* 3; Legge 5 : 283.

LL. 106–7: To escape incursions from the Rong, King Ping 平 (reg. 770–720 B.C.) of Zhou transfered the Zhou capital to Luoyi. In moving the capital east the Zhou reputedly were supported by the states of Zheng and Jin. See *Zuozhuan, Yin* 6 (Legge 5 : 21); *Shi ji* 4.149; *Mh*, 1 : 285, 292.

LL. 108–9: Cf. *Zuozhuan, Cheng* 8 (Legge 5 : 367): Han Jue 韓厥 said to the Marquis of Jin, "The good kings of the Three Dynasties for several hundred years all preserved the blessings of Heaven. How could there have been no wicked kings? They relied on their forebears' wisdom in order to escape (disaster)."

LL. 110–13: Sir Tui 子頹 was a son of Lady Yao 姚, one of King Zhuang 莊 (reg. 696–682) of Zhou's concubines. Ca. 674 B.C. five grandees, supported by the states of Yan and Wei, deposed King Hui 惠 (reg. 676–652 B.C.) and installed Tui in his place. Tui spent so much time indulging in music and dance, the Earl of Zheng accused him of "rejoicing over calamity." The states of Guoshu 虢叔 (or Guo) and Zheng then joined forces to attack Tui. Zheng entered through the Yu 圉 Gate, and Guo entered through the Bei (North) Gate. They killed Tui and reinstalled Hui as king. Later, the Earl of Zheng feted Hui west of the gateway, and another lord berated him for "imitating iniquity." See *Zuozhuan, Zhuang* 19–21; Legge 5 : 99–101; *Shi ji* 4.151; *Mh*, 1 : 289–90.

LL. 114–15: Dai is Shudai 叔帶, who plotted with the Rong and Di to attack his brother, King Xiang 襄 (reg. 651–619 B.C.) of Zhou. When the Di invaded the Zhou capital, King Xiang fled to Zheng, where he took up residence in the town of Fan 氾. Shudai then took the throne. In 635 B.C. King Xiang sought aid from Duke Wen of Jin (Chong of Pan Yue's line). Duke Wen captured Shudai and put him to death. He then restored King Xiang to the throne. See *Zuozhuan, Xi* 24–25; Legge 5 : 192–96; *Shi ji* 4.152–54; *Mh*, 1 : 290–94.

LL. 116–17: These lines allude to an event that reputedly occurred in the twenty-second year of King Ling 靈 of Zhou (550 B.C.). The Gu and Luo rivers, which flowed south and north of the Royal City (Luoyang), began "to rage" and threaten the Royal City. King Ling wanted to dam them, but crown prince Jin 晉 tried to dissuade him by arguing that ancient rulers did not reduce the size of mountains, raise marshes, dam streams, or dredge rivers. King Ling did not follow his advice. See *Guo yu* 3.5a–9a.

LL. 118–21: Just before his death, King Jing[3] 景 (reg. 544–520 B.C.) of Zhou named Chao

While sitting on a stack of firewood waiting for it to burn,
He pointed to the ascendant sun and compared himself to it.
100 The disparity in the judgments of different men,
How distant and divergent they are!

Having determined that the center of the land lay at this city,
King Cheng established his capital and planned its construction
Having secured the tripods at Jiaru,
105 He then drilled the tortoise and received the oracle.
When King Ping lost the Way and moved the capital here,
It was two states that came to his aid.
How could there have been no wicked kings in that time?
Thanks to their forebears' wisdom, long did they flourish.

110 Gazing at the two gates of Yu and Bei,
I recall how Guo and Zheng restored Hui.
Though the Earl of Zheng punished Sir Tui for rejoicing over
          calamity,
They blamed him for "imitating iniquity" west of the gateway.
Chong executed Dai in order to secure Xiang;
115 By promoting grand compliance, he became hegemon of his age
When King Ling dammed the rivers to halt the raging waters,
Expatiating on propriety, Prince Jin presented his advice.
Alas, from Kings Jing and Dao to Gai,
Government decayed and declined, ever nearing the end.
120 This caused the bastard son Chao to foment rebellion,
And through two reigns he sought the throne.

189

朝, a son of a concubine, as his successor. When King Jing³ died, a group of nobles and grandees attempted to replace him with Jing³'s eldest son, Meng 孟. After repeated clashes between the forces of Chao and Meng, Meng died. He was given the posthumous name of King Dao 悼 (The Lamented). With the aid of Jin, Meng's younger brother Gai 丐 was able to overthrow Chao. Gai's posthumous name was Jing⁴ 敬 (reg. 519–476 B.C.). See *Zuozhuan*, *Zhao* 22–23; Legge 5:694, 698–99; *Shi ji* 4.155–56; *Mh*, 1:297–98. It is possible that Pan Yue is referring to the tombs of the three Zhou kings located southwest of Henan. According to Li Daoyuan (see *Shujing zhu* 3.15.50), these were the tombs of Kings Dao, Jing⁴, and Jing³. Li also mentions a commentary to Pan Yue's *fu* by Cui Hao 崔浩 (ob 450), which says a text mistakenly reads Ding 丁 for Jing⁴ 敬 (the posthumous name of Gai). Thus, instead of Gai, the *Wen xuan* text possibly should read Jing⁴ to parallel the posthumous names of Jing³ and Dao. See Zhu Jian 11.16b–17a.

LL. 122–23: In the reign of King Nan 赧 of Zhou, which was ten reigns later than King Jing³, the Zhou royal domain was divided into two parts, West Zhou at Gong, and East Zhou at Henan. See *Shi ji* 4.160; *Mh*, 1:305. Cf. *Lun yu* 16/1: "His state was broken and collapsing, split and severed."

L. 124: The tiger's mouth is the Qin, who defeated the Zhou Cf. "Western Capital Rhapsody," L. 24.

L. 125: See "Eastern Metropolis Rhapsody," L. 146n.

LL. 126–27: The River of Filial Piety (Xiao shui 孝水), which is the "excellent name" to which Pan Yue refers, was located some ten *li* west of Henan. See *Shujing zhu* 3.16.66. Cf. "The Fisherman" (*Chuci buzhu* 7.2b): "When the Canglang River is clear, / I can wash my cap strings." Hu Shaoying (12.7b) proposes to read *ji* 濟 (to cross) for *zao* 澡 (to bathe) to avoid the redundancy with *zhuo* 濯 (to wash) in the same line. See also Zhu Jian 11.17a.

LL. 128–31: According to Pan Yue's "Lament for My Young Son" (cited by Li Shan 10.6b–7a), this son was born on *renyin* of the third month (28 April 292). Pan stopped at Xin'an 新安 (east of modern Minchi) on *renyin* of the fifth month (27 June), and the baby died on *jiachen* of the same month (29 June). The baby lived just sixty-three days, not quite seven weeks (the Chinese used a ten-day week). See Zhu Jian 11.17b. The Thousand Autumns Station (Qianqiu ting 千秋亭) was located south of Xin'an prefecture. See *Shujing zhu* 3.16.64.

LL. 132–33: When Yanling Jizi 延陵季子 (Ji Zha) went to Qi, his eldest son died on the return trip. He buried him between Ying 嬴 and Bo 博 See *Li ji zhushu* 10.18b. When the son of Dongmen Wu 東門吳 died, he did not grieve for him. His wife chided him, saying, "In your love for your son, there is no one in the world who can rival you. Now that he is dead, why do you not grieve?" Dongmen Wu replied, "I long was without a son. When I did not have a son, I did not grieve. Now that he is dead, it is the same as before when I did not have a son. Why should I grieve?" See *Liezi zhu* 6.75.

LL. 136–37: In 201 B.C., the Qin general Zhang Han 章邯 surrendered to Xiang Yu. The Qin soldiers and officers who had surrendered with Zhang Han began to doubt Xiang Yu's ability to defeat the Qin. Xiang Yu then in a night attack massacred over 200,000 Qin soldiers stationed at Xin'an. See *Shi ji* 7.310; *Mh* 2:272–73; *Records* 1:48–49.

L. 138: When Liu Bang conquered the Qin capital, he repealed most of Qin's oppressive laws and promised the vanquished people fair and kindly treatment. The Qin people immediately surrendered to him. See *Shi ji* 8.362; *Han shu* 1A.23; *Mh* 2:352–53; *HFHD* 1:58–59; *Records* 1:90.

L. 139. Lord Liu is Liu Bang. Cf. "Announcement of Zhonghui" (in *Shang shu zhushu* 4.3b; Legge 3:181): "We awaited our lord. Our lord has come, and we shall be revived."

LL. 140–41: After defeating the Qin, Xiang Yu tried to bring the entire empire under his sway, but was defeated by Liu Bang. He fled to the Wu River where he committed suicide. See *Shi ji* 7.336; *Mh* 2:319–20, *Records* 1:72–73. Cf. *Laozi* 30. "One who assists the ruler by

After ten eras came the reign of King Nan;
The state, broken and collapsing, split into two.
Finally, when swallowed into the tiger's mouth,
125 It transferred the sacred vessels of Wen and Wu.

IV

As I cross the River of Filial Piety and wash my cap strings,
I praise the excellent name I find here.
My infant son died at Xin'an;
We dug a pit by the roadside and buried him.
130 Though the post station was called Thousand Autumns,
My son had not even a span of seven weeks.
Though I try hard to emulate Yan and Wu,
In truth, I am deeply pained by my love.

I gaze over hills and streams, contemplating the past;
135 Disconsolate, in mid-road I pull in the reins.
How harsh the vicious cruelty of Xiang Yu!
He buried alive innocent surrendered soldiers,
Thus rousing the people of Qin to turn unto virtue,
And resulting in their revival by Lord Liu.
140 Deeds wicked and foul are wont to rebound;
In the end a clan was destroyed and the man himself butchered

means of the Way does not try to coerce the empire by force of arms. For such deeds are wont to rebound."

L. 142: Minchi 澠池 (or Mianchi) was a prefecture located west of modern Minchi *xian*, Henan.

LL. 144–45: These lines and the following allude to the story of Lin Xiangru 藺相如, a famous persuader of the Warring States period. When Qin tried to extort a valuable jade from Zhao, Lin went to the Qin court and by a clever ruse was able to induce the King of Qin into abandoning his effort to seize this jade. See *Shi ji* 81.2439–41; Yang and Yang, *Records*, pp. 140–42; LL. 526–27n below.

LL. 146–47: After Lin Xiangru had thwarted Qin's efforts to take the jade, the King of Qin proposed to meet the King of Zhao at Minchi. Although the King of Zhao was reluctant to go, both Lin Xiangru and Lian Po (see LL. 154–55n below) urged him not to show cowardice in the face of a threat from a powerful state. Accompanied by Lin Xiangru, the king journeyed to Minchi, where the King of Qin entertained the vistors with a grand feast. During the feast, the King of Qin asked the King of Zhao to play the zither. When he complied, the Qin scribe wrote in the records the insulting phrase, "On a certain day and month of a certain year, the King of Qin and the King of Zhao drank together. Our king ordered the King of Zhao to play the zither." To repay the insult, Lin Xiangru requested the King of Qin to play the pot, which the people of Qin used to mark time in singing. Angry, the King of Qin initially refused, and complied only after Lin Xiangru held a knife to his throat. Lin Xiangru then ordered the Zhao scribe to record that "on a certain day and month of a certain year the King of Qin played the pot for the King of Zhao." The officers of Qin then said, "We beg for Zhao's fifteen cities as tribute to the King of Qin." Lin Xiangru replied, "We beg for Qin's Xianyang (the Qin capital) as tribute to the King of Zhao." Because he was unable to get the better of Zhao, the King of Qin abruptly ended the feast. See *Shi ji* 81.2442; Yang and Yang, pp. 142–43.

LL. 148–49: East refers to Zhao, and west, to Qin.

L. 152: Minchi was located in the area south (hence "beyond") of the Western He (the modern Weinan area of Shaanxi) See *Shi ji* 2442, n. 2.

LL. 154–55: Sir Lian is Lian Po 廉頗, a Zhao general, who was so outraged when Lin Xiangru was appointed to a position above him, he vowed to insult him the next time they met. In order to avoid an embarrassing confrontation, Lin Xiangru stayed away from court. When his own stewards accused him of cowardice, Lin replied that it would be harmful to Zhao for two powerful leaders to fight. When Lian Po heard of Lin's noble behavior, he apologized to Xiangru by baring his shoulder and carrying thorns on his back. See *Shi ji* 81.2443; Yang and Yang, *Records*, pp. 143–44.

L. 156: Pan Yue here alludes to Sima Qian's comments made at the end of his *Shi ji* chapter on Lin Xiangru and Lian Po (81.2452): "Once Xiangru roused his spirit, his might extended to an enemy state. When he retreated and yielded to Po, his name was more honored than Mt. Tai. As for displaying craft and daring, one can say he possessed them both."

L. 160: These lines refer to the period before Liu Xiu 劉秀 (Emperor Guangwu) became emperor. After defeating Wang Mang's army at Kunyang (see "Eastern Capital Rhapsody," L. 50n), he sent Feng Yi 馮異 to the Minchi area to put down the Red Eyebrow rebels. The expression "covered with dust" is used to refer to the ruler when he travels in field. See *Zuozhuan*, *Xi* 24; Legge 5 : 193.

L. 161: Cf. "Eastern Capital Rhapsody," L. 33.

L. 162: Cf. "The Counsels of the Great Yu" (in *Shang shu zhushu* 4.12b; Legge 3 : 65): "I have received the charge to smite the felons."

L. 163: In A.D. 27, Feng Yi did battle with the Red Eyebrows, who occupied territory between Chang'an and Luoyang. After initial success, Feng was forced to retreat to Huixi 回谿 (northeast of modern Luoning 洛寧 *xian*, Henan, south of Minchi). Here Feng recouped his

V

As I pass through Minchi, I am long in thought;
I halt my chariot and do not advance.
Qin was a powerful state of tigers and wolves;
145 Zhao was a burnt-out tree weakened by invasion.
Calmly entering upon danger, Zhao met in grand assembly,
Relying upon the great Lin, the most renowned man of the age.
Shamed that the eastern zither was strummed alone,
He raised the western pot and thrust his blade.
150 Insulted by the prepostrous tribute of ten cities,
He lay claim to Xianyang and seized victory.
Beyond the borders, he extended his might beyond the He;
Oh, how his fierce temper roared and raged!
Within the court, he humbled himself before Sir Lian,
155 As if his four limbs had no bones.

He displayed profound excellence of craft and daring:
When matched against the fiery temper of the mean and stingy
    Lian Po,
Just as the brief changing day differs from the long turning year,
There is no common level on which to discuss them.

VI

160 When Guangwu was covered in dust,
He inflicted the royal punishment on the Red Eyebrows.
When Yi received the charge to smite the felons,
He first drooped his pinions at Huixi.

strength and inflicted a great defeat on the rebels on the slopes of the Yao Mountains south of Minchi. See *Hou Han shu* 1A.32–33; 17.646. In a letter congratulating him on his victory, Emperor Guangwu said, "Though at first your pinions drooped at Huixi, in the end you were able to flap your wings at Minchi" (*Hou Han shu* 17 646).

L. 168: See "Western Capital Rhapsody," L. 13n.

LL. 170–71: The You Mao edition reads *ji* 記 (record) for the *Five Comm.*'s *tuo* 託 (entrust), which clearly is the correct reading. In the Yao Mountains were two peaks, the southern peak, on which was located the grave of Lord Gao 皋 of the Xia dynasty; and the northern peak, where King Wen of Zhou once took shelter from a storm. See *Zuozhuan*, *Xi* 22; Legge 5:221.

LL. 172–73: In 628 B.C., Duke Mu of Qin sent out his three generals, Mengming Shi 孟明視, Xiqi Shu 西乞術, and Boyi Bing 白乙丙, to lead an attack against the state of Zheng. On the day of their departure, his adviser Jianshu 蹇叔 wept at the east gate, telling Mengming that they would be defeated at Yao. See *Zuozhuan*, *Xi* 22; Legge 5:221; *Shi ji* 5.191; *Mh*, 2:37–38. The next year the Qin army captured Hua 滑, a border city of Jin. Jin was in mourning for Duke Wen, who had just died. His successor Duke Xiang dressed in black-edged mourning robes, sent out his troops to attack Qin. As Jianshu predicted, the Jin army defeated Qin at Yao. See *Zuozhuan*, *Xi* 33; Legge 5:224–25; *Shi ji* 5.192; *Mh*, 2:39.

L. 174: This line refers to the utter defeat suffered by Qin. The phrasing is from *Gongyang Commentary*, *Xi* 33 (*Gongyang zhuan zhushu* 12 23a).

L. 175: When Jin defeated Qin at Yao, the three Qin generals were captured and taken back to the Jin capital. See *Zuozhuan*, *Xi* 33; Legge 5:225; *Shi ji* 5.192; *Mh*, 2:39.

L. 177: Shu is Jianshu, who had predicted the defeat of the Qin army.

LL. 178–79: Renhao 任好 is the personal name of Duke Mu of Qin. See *Shi ji* 5.185; *Mh*, 2:25. When his three generals returned to Qin, he accepted the blame for their defeat. See L. 164n above. Cf. *Mengzi* 2B/5: "Since I have neither office to hold nor responsibility to speak out, whether I advance or retreat, can't I afford to be generous in my magnanimity?"

LL. 180–81: Although Pan Yue says that Ming (i.e., the general Mengming Shi) was defeated three times, he actually was defeated only twice, once at Yao, and once at Pengya 彭衙 in an attempt to avenge the defeat at Yao. See *Zuozhuan*, *Wen* 2; Legge 5:233; *Shi ji* 5.192; *Mh*, 2:40. In 624 B.C., after receiving special honors from Duke Mu, Ming led the Qin to a great victory over Jin. See *Zuozhuan*, *Wen* 3; Legge 5:256; *Shi ji* 5.193–94; *Mh*, 2:43–44.

LL. 182–83: Cf. *Mao shi* 37/2: "Why does he stay so long? / There certainly must be a reason." After his victory over Jin, Duke Mu was acknowledged as hegemon over the Western Rong. See *Zuozhuan*, *Wen* 3; Legge 5:236.

LL. 184–85: The *Wen xuan* text reads Quyao 曲峣, but as Hu Shaoying (12.8a–b) points out, based on Li Shan's commentary (10.9a), the text probably should read Shiyao 石峣. It also is possible that *qu* is not part of the name, but means "winding." Guo 虢 (located near modern Sanmen xia City 三門峡, Henan), was a small state south of Jin. Yu 虞 (located near modern Pinglu 平陸, Shanxi) was a small state located between Jin and Guo. The two states were closely allied during the Chunqiu period.

LL. 186–89: Jin had sent to the ruler of Yu a precious Chuiji jade (see "Western Capital Rhapsody," L. 198n) and horses from Juechan 屈產 (southeast of modern Shilou 石樓 *xian*, Shanxi). In return, Yu was to allow Jin to pass through its territory to attack Guo. In 655 B.C., when Jin formally requested permission to pass through Yu territory, Gong Zhiqi 宮之奇, a Yu grandee warned that if it granted the request, Yu would perish soon after Guo. When the duke of Yu did not heed his advice, Gong Zhiqi fled with his family, saying, "Yu will not make it to the winter festival." That winter Jin troops destroyed Guo, and upon their return attacked Yu. They captured the duke of Yu and took back the Juechan horses. See *Zuozhuan*, *Xi* 2, 5; Legge 5: 136, 145–46; *Shi ji* 39.1649; *Mh*, 4:267–69.

LL. 190–91: Pan Yue borrows lines from *Zuozhuan*, *Wen* 5 (Legge 5:241): "Gaoyao

But Guangwu did not allow fault to obscure virtue,
165 And in the end Yi flapped his wings and soared on high,
Achieving prime merit helping to establish the mandate,
Retrieving the imperial guiderope and retying it.

VII

I ascend the tortuous twists of the Yao slopes,
Gaze up at the soaring scarps of the lofty peaks.
170 Gao entrusted his grave to the southern peak,
Wen fled the wind on the northern slope,
Jian wept for Meng and forsaw defeat,
Xiang donned black-edged mourning robes and took up his lance.
Not even a single horse and wagon returned,
175 And with three commanders in chains they crossed the He.

Had he met the swaggering obstinacy of a common ruler,
Shu's corpse assuredly would have been exposed in the market place
Renhao was generous in his magnanimity;
For he drew all the blame upon himself.
180 Though thrice defeated, Ming was never dismissed;
Finally he overran the Jin to wipe away his shame.
How could groundless fame be established?
Truly to attain hegemony there had to be a reason.

VIII

As I descend the winding Yao I grieve for Guo;
185 It trusted the doomed Yu as its ally.
Coveting gifts, Yu sold out its neighbor;
But before the winter festival, it too was seized.
The Chuiji jade was returned to its former storehouse;
The Juechan steeds were hitched to the Jin carriage.
190 With virtue not established and the people without assistance,
Sacrifices to Zhongyong suddenly ceased.

195

Tingjian, suddenly no one sacrifices to him. Alas, virtue has not been established, and the people have no assistance!" Zhongyong 仲雍, also known as Yuzhong 虞仲, was the second son of King Tai 太 of Zhou. He is considered the founder of the state of Yu. See *Zuozhuan*, *Xi* 55; Legge 5:145; *Lun yu* 18/8; *Mh*, 4:3, n. 1.

L. 192: Anyang 安陽 was a prefecture, located southwest of modern Xinyang 信陽 City, Henan. See *Shuijing zhu* 1.4.69.

L. 193: Shan 陝 prefecture is modern Shan *xian*, Henan.

L. 194: Man 漫 is Man Brook, which was the name given to the part of the Tuo 橐 River that flowed north of a valley located north of the Tuo Mountains. South of the old city of Shan prefecture it joined the Du 瀆 Valley River. See *Shuijing zhu* 1.4.69.

L. 195: According to the *Kuodi zhi* (cited in *Shi ji* 48.1955, n. 5), Caoyang 曹陽 was a post station located fourteen *li* south of Taolin 桃林 (modern Lingbao). In the Wei period, the name was changed to Haoyang 好陽. Zhou Wen 周文, one of Chen She's generals, committed suicide here after suffering a defeat by the Qin army. See *Shi ji* 48.1954; *Records*, 1:23. However, according to the *Yuanhe junxian tu zhi* (6.166), the Caoyang ruins, also known as Seven Li Brook 七里潤, was located seven *li* southeast of Shan prefecture. It was here where the last Han emperor (Xian 獻, reg. 190–219) camped out in the open after being abducted by Li Jue 李傕 and Guo Si 郭汜. See LL. 208–9n below. Clearly there were two Caoyangs in western Henan: one where Zhou Wen committed suicide, and the other the encampment of the last Han emperor. See *Shuijing zhu* 1.4.68, *Yuanhe jun xian tu zhi* 6.169; *Taiping huanyu ji* 6.11b; Zhu Jian 11.17b–18a. I assume it was the latter that Pan Yue visited.

L. 198: Zhou 周 and Shao 邵 were the younger brothers of King Wu of Zhou. When King Cheng took the Zhou throne, the Duke of Shao was given control over all territory west of Shan, and the Duke of Zhou assumed governance of the territory east of Shan. See *Shi ji* 34.1549; *Mh* 4:133–34; *Gongyang zhuan zhushu* 3.4a (Yin 5).

L. 199: The "Two Nan," which are the first two sections of the *Classic of Songs*, here must refer to the territory of Zhou and Shao.

L. 199: The "Unicorn's Foot" and the "Calling Ospreys" are the last and first pieces respectively in the "Zhou nan" section of the *Classic of Songs*.

L. 201: The "Zouyu" and "Magpie Nest" are the last and first pieces respectively in the "Shao nan" section of the *Classic of Songs*.

L. 202: Pan Yue here refers to the fall of the Later Han dynasty.

L. 204: Zhuo is the notorious Han minister Dong Zhuo 董卓 (ob. 192). In 189, he deposed the Han emperor and put Emperor Xian on the throne. He burned Luoyang and forced Emperor Xian to move to Chang'an. See *Hou Han shu* 72.2323–28.

L. 205:Cf. *Zuozhuan*, *Xuan* 12 (Legge 5:318): "Our lord has sent his vassals to remove all traces of your great state from Zheng."

LL. 208–9: Li Jue and Guo Si were two of Dong Zhuo's generals. After Dong Zhuo was killed, Li and Guo took the Han emperor hostage. Li Jue's general, Yang Feng 楊奉, tried to stage a coup against him, and in the confusion, the emperor was allowed to leave in order to return to Luoyang. When the emperor's entourage had barely reached the outskirts of Chang'an, Guo Si dispatched an army to bring him back. The emperor then fled to Yang Feng's camp, and Yang soundly defeated the pursuing army. Yang and the general Dong Cheng 董丞 then decided to accompany the emperor to Luoyang. Both Li Jue and Guo Si, at the head of their combined armies, pursued the emperor to Caoyang, where they inflicted a devastating defeat on Yang Feng's army. The emperor fled to Shan, crossed north over the Yellow River, and lost his baggage train. On foot, with only his wives, he finally took refuge in a person's house in the town of Dayang 大陽. See *Hou Han shu* 72.2339–40.

LL. 212–13: In the battle at Caoyang, Li Jue unleashed his soliders, who massacred the ministers accompanying the emperor. See *Hou Han shu* 9.378; *Sanguo zhi* 6.185–86.

IX

I go forth to Anyang,
And then cross the outer wall of Shan,
Trek to the confluence of Man and Du,
195 Rest at the ruins of Caoyang.
Oh, how beautiful, how distant,
This land so ancient!
Verily this is the fief apportioned to Zhou and Shao,
Where the Two Nan intersect.
200 "Unicorn's Foot" is confirmed by "Called Osprey,"
And "Zouyu" responds to "Magpie's Nest."

X

I lament the divisive turmoil in the house of Han:
Its court, scattering and fleeing, was split asunder.
Swelling up to Heaven, Zhuo widely ravaged the land,
205 Plundered palaces and temples, removing their every trace,
Forcing his supreme eminence, the lord of state,
To be humbled into longing for his distant home while on the march
He turned and begged Jue and Si to wheel about;
He no sooner obtained their assent than in midcourse they
       took alarm.
210 In pursuit of the imperial cortege they rushed into battle,
And even upon the jade wagon they let fly their arrows.

I grieve for the centurial officers who gave themselves for their king,
Expending every effort to the point of death.

197

LL. 216–19: When the emperor tried to cross the Yellow River, the bank was so high he could not get down to the river. His attendants made a litter from horse bridles and silk and carried him down to the water. There were not enough boats to carry all of the emperor's party, and many people tried to grab onto the boats. The men in the boats had to cut off their fingers to make them release their grip. They scooped up the fingers by the handful. See *Hou Han shu* 72.2340. The *locus classicus* for the phrase "scooping fingers by the handful" is *Zuozhuan, Xuan* 12; Legge 5:319.

L. 220: There are two places named Quwo 曲沃. Pan Yue must have visited the Quwo located east of modern Lingbao *xian*, Henan, which was part of the Zhou state of Wei. There was also a Quwo located northeast of modern Wenxi 聞喜 *xian*, Shanxi, which was a fief Marquis Zhao 昭 of Jin granted to his uncle Chengshi 成師 in 745 B.C. See *Zuozhuan, Huan* 2; *Shi ji* 39.1638; *Mh*, 4:253. In the following lines, Pan refers to events associated with the Jin fief. Whether Pan was confused in his geography, or simply using the name Quwo for its historical associations with the more celebrated Quwo in Shanxi is impossible to determine. See Zhu Jian 11.18a–b.

LL. 221–22: In 808 B.C., Marquis Mu 穆 of Jin (reg. 811–785 B.C.) took as a wife a lady née Jiang 姜 from Qi. In 805, while her husband was leading an attack on a small state, she gave birth to a son, who was named Chou 仇 (Enemy). In 802, when the Jin conquered another area, she gave birth to another son, who was named Chengshi 成師 (Successful Army). The king's adviser, Shifu 師服, admonished the marquis for selecting such names, claiming that they "portend strife and that the elder brother would be deposed." Later, in 745 B.C., when Marquis Zhao 昭 (reg. 745–740 B.C.) enfeoffed Chengshi in Quwo, Shifu said, "I have heard that when a state and clan are established, the roots should be large and the branches small. In this way, they may be secure. The Son of Heaven establishes states, and lords establish clans.... Now, Jin is a marquisate in the royal domain, but has established a state. Since its roots are so weak, can it long endure?" In 724 B.C., Count Zhuang 莊 of Quwo assassinated the Marquis of Jin. Again, in 709 B.C., Count Zhuang's son, Duke Wu 武 of Quwo, attacked Jin on the banks of the Fen River and captured Marquis Ai. In 706, he murdered Ai's son. In 679, his clan took over complete control in Jin. See *Zuozhuan, Huan* 2; Legge 5:40–41.

L. 223: Cf. *Zuozhuan, Huan* 18 (Legge 5:71): "Equal queens (i.e., a concubine made the equal of the queen), equal sons (i.e., the son of a concubine put on the same level as the queen's son), two administrations (i.e., favorites made equal to regular ministers), and equal cities (i.e., any other fortified city made as large as the capital)—these are the root of calamity."

LL. 224–25: Zang is Zizang 子臧, one of the sons of Duke Xuan 宣 of Cao 曹 (reg. 594–578 B.C.). After Xuan died, his younger brother Fuchu 負芻 (Duke Cheng 成, reg. 577–555 B.C.) seized power. Offended by this usurpation, the people of Cao wanted to put Zizang on the throne, but Zizang instead declared his intention to leave the state. Frightened that the people would follow him, Fuchu begged Zizang to stay. Zizang returned and surrendered his fief to Fuchu. See *Zuozhuan, Cheng* 13; Legge 5:383.

Zha is Ji Zha, the fourth son of King Shoumeng 壽夢 of Wu (reg. 585–561 B.C.). His father wanted to cede the throne to him, but he yielded in favor of his elder brother, Zhufan 諸樊. After Shoumeng died in 560 B.C., Zhufan wanted to abdicate the throne to Ji Zha, who again declined. In his speech declining the throne, Ji Zha mentioned the example of Zizang as that of a man "able to preserve his integrity " See *Zuozhuan, Xiang* 14; Legge 5:464; *Shi ji* 31.1449–50; *Mh*, 4:6.

L. 226: Zhuang and Wu were the Quwo nobles who usurped the throne in Jin.

L. 228: I assume that Pan Yue refers here to the old Qin Han Valley Pass located west of Shan See "Western Capital Rhapsody," L. 13n.

L. 229. Cf. "Western Metropolis Rhapsody," L. 814.

L. 231: The Ying clan was the ruling house of the Qin.

They sundered head from body with spear points and blades,
215 Impaled chest and side with streaming arrows.
Some lifted their gowns and dived from the bank;
Others raised their sleeves and raced for the water.
Sad indeed that the ruddercraft were narrow and small!
In the boats they scooped up fingers by the handful!

XI

220 Climbing to Quwo, I am sad and mournful,
Rueful of the sign portending strife and a brother's displacement.
When the branches are large, the roots split;
When a city equals a state disaster results.
Zang and Zha drifted high and far,
225 Yielded Cao and Wu to maintain integrity.
How shameless were Zhuang and Wu!
Merely to profit were they open and to propriety were they closed!

XII

I tread the layered fastness of Han Valley,
To view the "collars and belts" of the natural stronghold,
230 Explore the traces of bravery and cowardice among the vassal lords,
And reckon the benefit and harm incurred by the house of Ying.

LL 232–33: Pan alludes here to Jia Yi's "Finding Fault with Qin" (*Wen xuan* 51.3a): "The men of Qin opened the Pass and received the foe. The armies of nine states fled and skulked away, not daring to advance."

L. 235: Cf. *Zhanguo ce* 5.5a–b, where Fan Ju admonishes Qin for failing to pursue the enemy outside its borders. "Instead it closes its passes and does not venture to peek its troops east of the mountains."

L. 236: The cocks are small states that are most easily formed into a coalition to fight against a large state. Cf. *Zhanguo ce* 3.4b.

L. 239: Cf. "Wu Capital Rhapsody," L. 772.

LL. 240–41: Han's sixth ruler was Emperor Wu, who moved the Hangu Pass customs barrier from Hongnong to Xin'an. The old Hangu Pass prefecture became Hongnong prefecture. See "Western Capital Rhapsody," L. 13n.

L. 242: The emperor's palace was thought to be a terrestrial replica of the Purple Palace of Heaven. Pan Yue here calls it the Purple Pole.

LL. 244–47: Pan Yue alludes to a story contained in the *Wudi gushi* (cited by Li Shan 10.11b–12a). Emperor Wu was traveling incognito at Bogu and asked for lodging at the house of the canton chief, who would not receive him. He then spent the night at an inn. Mistaking the emperor for a brigand, the inn keeper recruited ten youths, all armed with bows and arrows, knives and swords, and told his wife to entertain the guests with food and drink. As soon as she saw the emperor, she knew he was no ordinary man. She then plied her husband and the youths with wine until they fell into a drunken slumber. She tied them up and then prepared a sumptuous repast for her guests. The next day the emperor returned to the palace and summoned the inn keeper and his wife He rewarded the lady with a thousand pieces of gold and appointed the husband to the plume grove guard. See "Histoire anecdotique et fabuleuse de l'empereur Wou des Han," pp. 45–46.

Bogu 柏谷 was a canton located in the western part of Lingbao prefecture. See *Shuijing zhu* 1.4.67.

LL. 248–51: Cf. Sima Xiangru's "Letter of Submission Admonishing Against Hunting" (*Wen xuan* 39.14b): "Moreover, though you clear the road before you travel, and though you gallop only in the middle of the road, still at times there are mishaps caused by slipped bits."

LL. 252–53: For this story, see "Eastern Metropolis Rhapsody," LL. 687–88.

LL. 256–61: Pan Yue recalls the story of Liu Ju 劉據, also known as Crown Prince Li 戾. His father, Emperor Wu of Han, named him crown prince in 122 B.C. In 91 B.C., the emperor suddenly fell ill, and suspecting someone was using black magic against him, sent Jiang Chong 江充 to investigate. Jiang Chong and Liu Ju long had been enemies, and Jiang Chong took the opportunity to search the crown prince's quarters, where he found a paulownia wood "voodoo" doll. He then charged the crown prince with conspiring to kill the emperor with black magic. Liu Ju then sent his retainers to arrest Jiang Chong, whom they immediately beheaded. Liu Ju's action was tantamount to revolt, and the emperor dispatched the Lieutenant Chancellor Liu Quli 劉屈氂 to punish Liu Ju. Liu Ju fled to the home of a friend in the village of Quanjiu 泉鳩 in Hu 湖 prefecture. The imperial soliders soon discovered his hiding place and surrounded the house. Rather than be captured, the crown prince committed suicide. When Emperor Wu later discovered that Liu Ju was innocent, he built the Palace of the Beloved Son and the terraces named Return! and Gazing and Longing. In 73 B.C., Emperor Xuan, Liu Ju's grandson, ordered that the Xie Village of Wenxiang 閿鄉 in Hu be made into a funerary park. This park was named Li Park (Crown Prince's Li's Park). See *Han shu* 45.2178–79, 63.2742–48; Watson, *Courtier and Commoner*, pp. 47–53; Michael Loewe, "The Case of Witchcraft in 91 B.C.," *AM*, n.s. 15 (1970), 159–96; rpt. in Loewe, *Crisis and Conflict in Han China*, pp. 37–90. Hu prefecture was located west of modern Lingbao *xian*, Henan. Quanjiu village was about twenty-five kilometers east of Hu. The Palace of the Beloved Son was twenty-five *li* northeast of Wenxiang See *Yuanhe junxian tu zhi* 6.173.

At times it opened the Pass to receive the foe,
Who sped off in skulking flight, fugitive evasion.
Other times, they shut tight the gates, opening to no one,
235 And refused to show its troops beyond the mountains.
A row of cocks cannot perch together;
But when small states unite, they form a great power.
Is it really strategic position that determines security and danger?
In truth it depends upon accord or discord in human affairs.

XIII

240 In Han's sixth reign the emperor expanded his domain,
Making Hongnong a prefecture and placing the Pass farther out.
Bored with the spacious comfort of the Purple Palace,
He preferred incognito traveling and roaming revels.
A canton chief was arrogant to him as guest in Bogu;
245 But the wife discerned his face and offered him a meal.
Rewarding the lowly wife was more than ample;
But why an underserved post for the husband?

Of old when the wise king toured his land,
He was sure to clear the road before departing.
250 Fearing mishap caused by slipped bits,
He disciplined his footmen and drivers with reward and punishment.
That white dragon in fish guise
Was caught in Yu Ju's tight mesh.
Since the emperor himself slighted the imperial dignity before the
        entire world,
255 How could such behavior be allowed to endure?

XIV

I grieve at Li Park in Hu district;
Truly did the fabled black magic affair occur!
When Emperor Wu delved into secrets lurking in the unknown,

L. 259: Before Liu Ju beheaded Jiang Chong, he cursed him as a "caitiff of Zhao." (Jiang Chong was a native of Handan in Zhao.) See *Han shu* 45.2179.

L. 260: Cf. "The Oath of Tai" (in *Shang shu zhushu* 11.13a; Legge 3:296): "Those whose merit is great shall have generous reward. Those who do not follow, shall have conspicuous punishment."

L. 263: Note that one of the terraces built by Emperor Wu in memory of Crown Prince Li was called the Terrace of Gazing and Longing.

L. 264: Quanjiu (also called Quanjiu 全鳩) was renamed Quanjie 全節 (Total Integrity) in honor of Liu Ju.

LL. 266–67: Peach Garden is Peach Grove, where King Wu of Zhou reputedly put his oxen to pasture after his conquest of the Shang. See *Shuijing zhu* 1.4.64–65; "Western Metropolis Rhapsody," L. 34n.

L. 269: Huangxiang 黃巷 is a long slope near the Yellow River where it flowed northeast of Tong Pass. This slope had to be climbed to cross Tong Pass. See *Shuijing zhu* 1.4.63. The *Yuanhe junxian tu zhi* (6.173) locates it thirty-five *li* northwest of Wenxiang. The Tong 潼 River flowed one *li* west of the Tong Pass. See *Yuanhe junxian tu zhi* 2.32.

L. 270: See "Western Metropolis Rhapsody," L. 35n.

L. 271: See "Western Metropolis Rhapsody," L. 36n.

LL. 272–73: In the autumn of 211 B.C., an imperial envoy from east of the Hangu Pass met a man at night on the Pingshu 平舒 Road of Huayin. The man handed him a jade and said, "Give it to the Lord of Hao Pond for me." He then left with a warning: "This year the proto-dragon shall die." The envoy took the jade and reported what he had heard to the First Qin Emperor. Upon examining the jade, he discovered that it was the same jade he had thrown into the Jiang eight years before, See *Shi ji* 6.259; *Mh*, 2:183–84. The Lord of Hao Pond has been variously identified, but Pan Yue seems to consider him a god of the Yangzi River. The Jiang envoy must be the Lord's emissary. See *Shi ji* 6.260, n. 4. The proto-dragon is the First Qin Emperor.

LL. 274–75: Confucius did not speak of wonders, feats of strength, disorder, and the supernatural. See *Lun yu* 7/20.

LL. 276–77: In Jian'an 16 (A.D. 211), the generals of the Liangzhou 涼州 area (in modern Gansu), Han Sui 韓遂 and Ma Chao 馬超, staged a revolt using Tong Pass as their base. Cao Cao put down their revolt. See *Sanguo zhi* 1.54–55.

L. 278: Wu of Wei is Cao Cao.

L. 281: The temple calculations are the estimates a commander makes about the chances for victory before he goes into battle. An abacus may have been used to tally the numbers. See *Sunzi* 1.25a.

L. 284: After his defeat, Ma Chao fled to Liangzhou, where he organized a force of barbarians and gained control of the northwest. See *Sanguo zhi* 1.42, 36.945–46.

L. 285: Cf. *Zuozhuan*, Xuan 12 (Legge 5:321): "In ancient times when wise kings punished the disrespectful, they took the worst villains and made a mound of them as the greatest humiliation Thus, there were giant towers for the purpose of warning the dissolute and depraved."

He trusted that slandering brigand, the caitiff of Zhao.
260 - He applied conspicuous punishment to his successor,
And cut off his own flesh and blood with nary a regret.
Later, when he built the mourning terrace of Return!,
Of what avail were his vain "gazing and longing"?

XV

Deeply troubled, far did I travel here to Quanjie;
265 Here I remain in fretful pacing.
I visit the ancient grove where King Wu released his oxen,
And am moved that its name is confirmed in the Peach Garden.

Leaving Wenxiang, I whip up my steeds:
Heading toward Huangxiang, I cross the Tong.
270 Gazing on the north slopes of the Hua Peaks,
I espy the traces of handprints reaching high.
I recall the Jiang envoy who returned the jade,
And announced the time of the proto-dragon's demise.
That one does not speak of such wonders to confirm the unusual,
275 I have heard from Master Kong.

XVI

I abhor the great perfidy of Han and Ma;
Blocking the Pass and Valley, they staged a revolt.
Wu of Wei, raging like quaking thunder,
Received the righteous charge and attacked the rebels.
280 Though their forces were many, what use were they?
For he had predetermined victory in temple calculations.
Peng—their waving drumsticks stirred the dust;
Kwa—the foe crumbled like tiles, melted like ice.
Chao then skulked away, escaping to the Di,
285 His armored troops transformed into giant towers.

XVII

Weary of the pressing confinement of the narrow road,
Its track, pitted and pocked, rising and falling,

LL. 290–93: These lines are similar to lines in Du Du's "Disquisition on the Capital, a Rhapsody" (see *Hou Han shu* 80A.2603):

Fertile fields for a thousand miles,
Plains and marshland fill the gaze.
Here they plant and tend the five grains;
Mulberry and hemp branch and burgeon.

LL 292–93: Cf. "Western Capital Rhapsody," L. 117n and "Western Metropolis Rhapsody," L. 42n.

L 295: Cf. "Western Metropolis Rhapsody," L. 42n

L. 296: Cf "Western Metropolis Rhapsody," L. 43n.

L. 297: The Sweet Springs Palace was located in Yunyang prefecture. see "Western Capital Rhapsody," L. 103n.

L. 298: Cf. "Western Capital Rhapsody," L. 14n.

L. 299: Cf. "Western Metropolis Rhapsody," L. 47n.

L. 300: Cf. "Western Capital Rhapsody," L. 102n.

L. 301: Cf. "Western Metropolis Rhapsody," L. 44n.

L. 304: On the Ba River, see "Western Capital Rhapsody," L. 36n. On the Chan, see "Rhapsody on the Imperial Park," LL. 32–33n.

L. 305: Li Shan (11.14a) cites the *Yongzhou tu* 雍州圖 (Map of Yongzhou), a work of unknown authorship and date, which mentions hot springs and spas in the areas of Xinfeng and Lantian. Perhaps Pan Yue is referring to the hotsprings of the Li Mountains.

L. 307: Thoroughwort Pond (Lan chi 蘭池), located twenty-five *li* east of Xianyang, was the site of an artificial lake constructed by the First Qin Emperor. It was filled by diverting water from the Wei River. In 216 B.C., while traveling incognito, the First Emperor was threatened by a band of brigands here. See *Shi ji* 6.251; *Mh* 2:164; *Taiping huanyu ji* 26.7b. This presumably was the site of the Thoroughwort Pond Palace, located northeast of the Han city of Weicheng 渭城 See *Han shu* 28A.1546; *Yuanhe jun xian tu zhi* 1.12. Zhous' Serpentine (Zhou qu 周曲) was located in the same area, thirty *li* east of Xianyang. According to the *Shuijing zhu* (3.19.117), it was the site of the graves of the Han ministers Zhou Bo 周勃 (ob. 169 B.C.) and his son Zhou Yafu 周亞夫 (ob. 143 B.C.) According to the *Taiping huanyu ji* (26.7b), Zhous' Serpentine was a pond thirteen *li* in circumference. Zhou Bo made his home here. Later, the emperor gave the pond to Zhuo Yafu for his meritorious service.

L. 308: On the Zheng and Bo canals, see "Western Capital Rhapsody," L 108n.

L. 309: Cf. "Western Capital Rhapsody," LL. 118–22.

L. 310: On Hu prefecture, see "Western Capital Rhapsody," L. 95n.

L. 311: On Lantian jade, see "Western Capital Rhapsody," L. 93n

L. 312: Cf. "Western Capital Rhapsody," L. 92.

L. 313: Cf. "Western Metropolis Rhapsody," L. 62n.

L. 314: These are the interlocutors of Ban Gu's "Two Capitals Rhapsody."

L. 315: These are the two interlocutors of Zhang Heng's rhapsodies on Chang'an and Luoyang

L. 317: Cf. *Lun yu* 9/27: "When the year turns cold, we know that the pine and cypress are the last to wither "

L. 319: The capital of the original state of Zheng was located near modern Hua 華 xian, Shaanxi. During the Eastern Zhou, a new state was established at Zhengzhou.

L. 320: Ji You 姬友, Duke Huan 桓 of Zheng (reg. 806–771 B.C.), served as minister of multitudes to King You 幽 of Zhou (reg. 781–771 B.C.).

L. 321: The "benighted lord" is King You of Zhou.

I tread into the Qin outskirts, where the land starts to open,
Spreading bright and high, broad and grand.
290　Yellow loam stretches for a thousand *li*,
Fertile fields fill the gaze,
Flowers and fruit rampantly spread,
Mulberry and hemp branch and burgeon.

Cater-corner it borders Bao-Ye,
295　Right it brinks Qian-Long,
Baoji resounds afore,
Sweet Springs bubbles behind.
Facing Zhongnan and with its back to Yunyang,
It straddles a level plain and joins Bozhong.
300　Nine Peaks rises sheer and sharp,
Taiyi stands tall and towering,
Exhaling the soughing sibilance of cool winds,
Inhaling the lush luxuriance of returning clouds.

South are the ebon Ba and pale Chan,
305　Boiling wells and warm vales.
North are the limpid Wei and turbid Jing,
Thoroughwort Pond and the Zhous' Serpentine.
To irrigate, they dredged the canals of Zheng and Bo;
Waterways haul grain from the Huai and the seacoast.
310　The groves luxuriate with bamboo of Hu;
Mountains extrude jade of Lantian.
Ban Gu described "precious treasures of the dry-land sea,"
Zhang Heng told of the "divine region and sacred refuge."
This is what the Western Guest spoke of to the Eastern Host,
315　And what Master Where-live heard from Sir Based-on-nothing
Can one say it is not true?

XVIII

The strong pine is most conspicuous in the cold of the year;
Loyal statesmen show themselves when the state is imperiled.
I enter the Zheng capital, clap my hands,
320　And extol Huan You's loyal counsel.
He exhausted limb and arms for a benighted lord,
Entered mud and coals but never wavered.

LL. 323–24: Duke Huan's son, Duke Wu 武, succeeded his father as minister of multitudes. According to the "Mao Preface" to the *Classic of Songs*, *Mao shi* 75 ("The Black Robe") praised Duke Wu's virtuous administration. See *Mao shi zhushu* 4.3.4a. Pan Yue alludes to this poem in L. 324: "Your black robe, how befitting! / When worn out, we shall make a new one."

LL. 325–30: Pan Yue refers to the invasion of the Zhou capital by the Quan-Rong 犬戎, a non-Chinese tribe that lived west of the Zhou. King You constructed a large beacon, which he lit to signal the vassal lords that an enemy attack was imminent. To entertain his favorite concubine, Bao Si 褒姒, who rarely laughed, King You ordered the beacons lit even when there was no attack. Bao Si laughed heartily at the joke. However, when the Quan-Rong attacked, and the beacons were lit, no vassal lords came to the king's rescue. The Zhou army was defeated at Xi, and King You was killed at the foot of Mt. Li 驪. See *Shi ji* 4.147–49; *Mh*, 1:284–85. The site of the Zhou army's defeat was traditionally located at Xiting 戲亭, on the west bank of the Xi River northeast of modern Lintong *xian*. See *Shuijing zhu* 3.19.120–21; *Yuan he junxian tu zhi* 1.7.

LL. 331–32: Cf. *Mao shi* 192/8: "Resplendent and majestic the Venerable Zhou, / Bao Si destroyed it."

LL. 337–40: Pan Yue may be basing his story of the First Qin Emperor's tomb on an account contained in a memorial by Liu Xiang (see *Han shu* 36.1954–55). When the Chu army led by Xiang Yu invaded Chang'an, he ordered the Qin palaces burned and the First Emperor's tomb dug up and its contents removed. Liu Xiang also tells the story of a shepherd boy who lost a sheep in a hole that led into the tomb. When he lit a torch to look for the sheep, he set fire to the coffin.

L. 341: This saying is found in *Zuozhuan*, *Xiang* 4; Legge 5:423.

L. 343: Cf. *Zhou yi zhushu* 7.3b–4a ("Great Commentary"): "Qian (= Heaven) knows things by being easy; Kun (= Earth) is able to act by being simple. Being easy, it is easily understood; being simple, it is easy to follow. Being easily understood, it has affinity with things; being easy to follow, it has efficacious results. Having affinity with things, it can endure; having efficacious results, it can become great." For an intepretation of this passage, see Willard J. Peterson, "Making Connections: 'Commentary on the Attached Verbalizations' of the *Book of Changes*," *HJAS* 42 1 (1982), 92–93.

L. 344: Cf. *Zhou yi zhushu* 1.23a (Hexagram 2, "Commentary on the Images"): "The power of earth is Kun. The gentleman uses its bountiful virtue to sustain things."

L. 346: Cf *Han shu* 100 4236: "August indeed Han Gaozu! Heir to the line of Yao, truly Heaven engendered his virtues: acute intelligence and divine might."

L. 347: Cf. *Han shu* 1.2: "(Gaozu) was generous, kind, and loving to people. His mind was open, and he always had a grand perspective."

L. 348: Cf. *Lun yu* 1/9: Zengzi said, "Carefully attend to final rites and commemorate the distantly departed."

His heir served well as minister of multitudes;
When his black robe was worn, they made him a new one.

XIX

325 As I tread the land invaded by the Quan-Rong,
I am angered by the treacherous deceit of Lord You:
He lit false beacons to demoralize the hosts;
Infatuated with his favorite Bao, he indulged her depravity.
His army was defeated above the River Xi;
330 He himself died north of Mt. Li.
Resplendent and majestic, the Venerable Zhou;
Destroyed, it became a defunct state.

XX

But there was another that followed it—
Oh, strange indeed, the First Qin Emperor's becoming overlord!
335 He depleted the empire to give himself lavish burial;
Ever since creation of such things no one has heard.
To the craftsmen's labors, he gave no thought,
But had them buried alive as recompense for their toil.
Without, the tomb was inflicted with calamity from West Chu;
340 Within, it suffered conflagration started by a shepherd boy.
A saying goes: "If one practices impropriety, his actions will redound
           upon him."
Is this not proof of this saying?

XXI

Qian and Kun, with their affinity to things, can long endure;
The gentleman, with earth's bountiful virtue, sustains life.
345 Behold the rise of Gaozu:
It was not only his acute intelligence and divine might,
Or his open-minded magnanimity and grand perspective.

For in truth he attended to final rites, commemorated the ancients,
Was steadfast and sincere, gentle and loving.
350 There was no place unpermeated by his kindness,

LL. 355–56: According to the *Sanfu jiushi* (cited by Li Shan 10.15b), Han Gaozu's father, a native of Feng 豐 in Chu, was unhappy living in the Chang'an area. Thus, Gaozu built the town of Xinfeng 新豐 (New Feng), to which he moved butchers, wine-sellers, pasta cooks, and merchants from the original Feng. Xinfeng was located north of Mount Li, northeast of modern Lintong *xian*. See *Han shu* 28A.1543; *Yuanhe junxian tu zhi* 1.6.

LL. 357–58: Fenyu 枌榆 (White Elm) was an altar of the soil deity located outside Gaozu's home city of Feng. When he began his insurrection against the Qin, Gaozu prayed at this altar. See *Shi ji* 28.1378; *Mh*, 3:448; *Records*, 2:31.

LL 358–61: A similar account is found in *Xijing zaji* 2.4a–b.

LL. 363–72: Xiang Yu, also known as Xiang Ji, invited Liu Bang (Lord of Pei) to banquet with him at Hongmen 鴻門 (east of modern Lintong). During the banquet, Fan Zeng 范增 signalled to Xiang Yu to have Liu Bang killed, but Xiang Yu did not respond. Fan then left and persuaded Xiang Zhuang 項莊 to stab Liu Bang while performing a sword dance. When Xiang Zhuang raised his sword and began to dance, Xiang Bo 項伯, a friend of Zhang Liang's, rose and danced to shield Liu Bang from Xiang Zhuang's attack. Alarmed by the danger to his master, Zhang Liang (Zifang) left the banquet tent and reported the situation to Liu Bang's general, Fan Kuai 樊噲. Fan Kuai angrily stormed into the tent with sword drawn. Impressed with his courage, Xiang Yu gave him a beaker of wine and shoulder of pork. After lecturing Xiang Yu for his treachery and ingratitude, Fan Kuai was able to aid his master's escape to Bashang 霸上 (east of modern Xi'an). See *Shi ji* 7.312–14; *Records*, 1:51–54.

L. 373: The serpent is Liu Bang, who after escaping from Xiang Yu's clutches, became a dragon who ruled the entire empire.

LL. 375–76: While Liu Bang was fleeing from Hongmen, he had Zhang Liang present Xiang Yu a pair of white jade discs and Fan Zeng with a pair of jade dippers. Enraged that Liu Bang had been allowed to escape, Fan smashed the dippers with his sword. See *Shi ji* 7.314; *Records*, 1:55.

LL. 377–78: See "Eastern Metropolis Rhapsody," L. 56n.

No place unreached by his beneficence.

Throughout the entire land he neglected nothing—
How much less his neighbors and home!
How much less his ministers and officers!

XXII

355 At this time
He replicated old Feng,
Built a new town.
The old soil-altar was relocated,
And the white elm transplanted.
Streets and avenues all seemed as before;
360 Courtyard and roof emulated the old.
Though they commingled fowl and dogs and randomly released
            them,
Each knew his home and raced into it.

XXIII

Xiang ji was filled with wrath at Hongmen;
Lord Pei, bent and bowed, came to pay him homage.
365 Fan Zeng plotted harm, but was refused;
Secretly handing over his sword, he made a pact with Zhuang.
Thrusting his naked blade, he performed a Wan dance;
Perilous it was as winter leaves awaiting the frost.
Lord Pei trod a tiger's tail, but was not bitten—
370 In truth, thanks to Zifang's plea to Bo!
Roused to anger, Fan Kuai drained a beaker of wine;
Chewing on a pork shoulder, he swelled with rage.
Suddenly the serpent transformed and uncoiled like a dragon;
Dominating Bashang, he soared on high.
375 Venting his anger on the dippers, Zeng furiously smashed them;
Though shattered, what real harm was there?

XXIV

Ziying, bound with cords on the Zhi road,
Dismounted his plain cart and bared his arm.

LL. 379–80: When Shu Guang 疎 (= 疏) 光 served as grand tutor to the heir apparent (ca. 67 B.C.), his nephew Shu Shou 疎受 was lesser tutor. After five years in office, Shu Guang proposed to Shu Shou that they resign on the grounds that they had enjoyed the peak of prestige and position for a sufficient time. The both retired to their home village. Before their departure, their fellow ministers and officials gave them a grand farewell banquet outside the Eastern Capital Gate of Chang'an. See *Han shu* 71 3039–40; Watson, *Courtier and Commoner*, pp. 162–64.

L. 381: Cf. "Western Metropolis Rhapsody," L. 279 and note.

L. 383: According to the *Chang'an tu* 長安圖 (Chart of Chang'an), cited by Li Shan (10.17a), the Horse Watering Bridge (Yin ma qiao 飲馬橋) was located on the Seven Mile Canal (Qi li qu 七里渠), which I have been unable to locate. The grave of Xiahou Ying 夏侯嬰 (ob. 172 B.C.), one of Liu Bang's loyal generals, was near here. See *Shi ji* 2667, n. 2.

L. 384: Proclaimed Peace (Xuan ping 宣平) was the northeast gate of Chang'an.

L. 391: "Spurring on my lassitude and stupidity" is a self-deprecating expression. There was no imperial court in Chang'an. Pan Yue uses "court" to refer to his prefectural office.

L. 392: Cf. *Zhou yi zhushu* 1.8a (Hexagram 1, "Commentary on the Images"): "The gentleman keeps himself strong and never rests."

L. 393: This is the seventh month of the lunar calendar.

LL. 403–6: Pan Yue mentions the names of the old Chang'an wards. Their exact location is not known.

L. 409: On the Palace of Enduring Joy, see "Western Capital Rhapsody," LL. 254–55n.

The Shus had a farewell feast at Eastern Capital Gate;
380 They feared the sumptuous fullness of supreme position.

A metal wall, massed a myriad spans,
Towers upward, sheer and steep, straight as a marking line.
When I reach Horse Watering Bridge on the south,
I tread the pristine threshold of Proclaimed Peace.
385 Within the capital, manifoldly mingled,
Are households in the thousands, people in the millions.
Gentlemen and ladies, both Chinese and Tartar,
Crowded and clustered, pressing and pushing.
I perform my initial civilities in this renowned metropolis,
390 Then go to my new station and assume my duties.
Spurring on my lassitude and stupidity, I approach the court;
I shall strive to keep myself strong and never rest.

XXV

And then,
As early autumn begins to recede,
On leisure days when free from hearings and reviews,
395 I make a tour to inspect the peasant's work,
Circumambulating their huts and houses.
Street wards are deserted and desolate;
Town dwellings are sparsely scattered.
The buildings and edifices, stations and bureaus,
400 Shops and markets, official storehouses,
Are now concentrated on a single corner of the wall—
Of a hundred barely one survives.

The wards called Esteemed Officialdom, Cultivation Perfected,
Yellow Thorn, Proclaimed Brilliance,
405 Established Yang, Flourishing Yin,
Northern Brightness, Southern Peace—
All have been leveled flat, swept away;
With their sites gone, only their names survive.

XXVI

And then
I climb to Enduring Joy,

211

L. 411: On the Grand Fluid Pond, see "Western Capital Rhapsody," L. 289n.

L. 412: On the Jianzhang Palace, see "Western Capital Rhapsody," LL. 256–57n.

L. 413: On the Hall of Rapid Gallop and Relaxation Hall, see "Western Capital Rhapsody," L. 266n.

L. 414: On Linden Hall, see "Western Capital Rhapsody," L. 267n. On Received Light, see "Western Metropolis Rhapsody," L. 254n.

L. 415: On Cinnamon Palace, see "Western Capital Rhapsody," LL. 254–55.

L 416: On Cypress Beams Terrace, see "Western Metropolis Rhapsody," L. 220n.

LL. 419–20: The thick millet growing in a ruin is a conventional image. Cf. "Wei Capital Rhapsody," L. 769n and *Mao shi* 65.

L. 423: Cf. *Mao shi* 197/2: "Tramped smooth is the Zhou road; / Everywhere has turned to thick grass."

L. 424: On these statues, see "Western Capital Rhapsody," LL. 158–59n. Pan Yue's *Guanzhong ji*, cited by Li Shan (10.18a), says that Dong Zhuo melted all but two of the statues into coins Emperor Ming of Wei wanted to transfer the remaining statues to Luoyang. They carried them as far as Bacheng 霸城, where they left them because they were too heavy to transport any further.

L. 425: See "Western Capital Rhapsody," L. 218n.

L. 426: Xin Qingji 辛慶忌, Li Guang 李廣, Wei Qing, and Huo Qubing were all Han generals who led expeditions against the Xiongnu. See *Shi ji* 109.2867–76, 111.2921–29; *Han shu* 54.2439–49, 55.2471–93, 69.2996–99; *Records*, 2:141–54, 193–216; Watson, *Courtier and Commoner*, pp. 12–23.

L. 427: Su, Director of Dependent States, is Su Wu, the Han official who served nineteen years as an envoy to the Xiongnu. See *Han shu* 54.2459–69; Watson, *Courtier and Commoner*, pp. 34–45.

L. 428: Zhang, Marquis of Bowang 博望, is Zhang Qian 張騫, the famous Central Asian explorer. See *Shi ji* 123.3157–69; *Han shu* 61 2687–98; Hulsewé, *China in Central Asia*, pp. 207–28.

L. 429: This line refers to the chancellors. Cf. *Shang shu zhushu* 12.2a (Legge 3:230): "I do not know how the constant norms should be properly ordered.".

L. 430: This line refers to the generals.

L. 431: This line refers to Zhang Qian.

L. 432: This line refers to Su Wu.

L. 433: The Marquis of Du 秺 is Jin Midi 金日磾, a Xiongnu noble who once saved Emperor Wu from assassination. See *Han shu* 68.2959–62; Watson, *Courtier and Commoner*, pp. 151–56.

L. 434: Lu Jia 陸賈 was a minister of emperors Hui and Wen of the Former Han. On a mission to Southern Yue, he received a gift of precious objects, which he converted into a thousand pieces of gold. He distributed the gold among his five sons, with the stipulation that they must entertain him and his entourage whenever he visited. Lu spent the remainder of his life traveling between his sons' homes. He always rode in a comfortable chariot, escorted by singers, drummers, and zither players, and carried a sword worth a hundred pieces of gold. See *Shi ji* 97.2699–2700; *Han shu* 43.2114; *Records*, 1:278.

L. 435: Zhangqing 長卿 is the sobriquet of Sima Xiangru; Yuan and Yun are short for Ziyuan 子淵 and Ziyun 子雲, the sobriquets of Wang Bao and Yang Xiong respectively.

L. 436: Zichang 子長 is the sobriquet of Sima Qian. Zheng and Jun are short for Zizheng 子政 and Zijun 子駿, the sobriquets of Liu Xiang and Liu Xin respectively. Sima Qian was the compiler of the *Shi ji*. Liu Xiang and Liu Xin compiled a catalogue of the imperial library.

L. 437: Zhao is Zhao Guanghan 趙廣漢, who served as governor of the capital district from 71–ca. 65 B.C. See *Han shu* 76.3199–3206; *HFHD*, 2:233, n. 13 4. Zhang is Zhang Chang

410 Ascend to the Everlasting Palace,
Drift on Grand Fluid,
Scale Jianzhang.
I wind through Rapid Gallop and reach Relaxation Hall,
Wheel through Linden Hall and Received Light,
415 Linger and loiter at Cinnamon Palace,
Sob and sigh at Cypress Beams.
Golden pheasants shriek on terraces and ponds;
Foxes and hares burrow beside the halls.
How lush and luxuriant the millet sprouts!
420 How tangled and twisted my thoughts!

Great bells have fallen in the ruined temple;
Bellframes have collapsed and hang no more.
The forbidden chancellory has turned to thick grass;
Bronze statues have been transported to Ba Stream.

XXVII

425 I yearn for the chancellors Xiao, Cao, Wei, and Bing,
And the generals Xin, Li, Huo, and Wei.
For carrying a commission, there was Su, Director of Dependent
        States;
For terrorizing distant lands, there was Zhang, Marquis of Bowang
When their teachings spread, the constant norms were properly
        ordered;
430 When they took up arms, imperial might extended far and wide.
Faced with danger, wisdom and courage were stirred;
In risking life, lofty integrity brightly shone.

As for
The Marquis of Du, whose loyalty and devotion were sincere
        and deep;
Lu Jia, who roamed and rambled, feasted and feted;
435 The writings of Zhangqing, Yuan, and Yun;
The histories of Zichang, Zheng, and Jun;
The Capital governors, Zhao, Zhang, and the three Wangs;

張敞, who served as governor of the capital from 61–ca. 53 B.C. See *Han shu* 76.3216–26. The three Wangs are Wang Zun 王遵 (capital governor 29–28 B.C.), Wang Zhang 王韋 (capital governor 25 B.C.), and Wang Jun 王駿 (capital governor 21 B.C.). See *Han shu* 72.3066–67; 76.3226–40.

L. 438: Dingguo is Yu Dingguo 于定國, who served as commandant of justice from 69 to 52 B.C. See *Han shu* 71.3041–45. Shizhi is Zhang Shizhi 張釋之, who served as commandant of justice around 177 B.C. See *Han shu* 50.2307–2312.

L. 439: Ji Zhangru 汲長孺 is Ji An 汲黯, a particularly acerbic and outspoken adviser to Emperor Wu. See *Shi ji* 120 3105–11; *Records*, 2:343–52.

L. 440: Zheng Dangshi 鄭當時 held high positions under Emperor Wu. It is said that each time he had an audience with the emperor, he recommended a worthy person for a position. See *Shi ji* 120.3111–13; *Records*, 2:352–55.

L. 441: Zhong Tong 終童 (The Lad Zhong) is Zhong Jun 終軍, a native of Ji'nan (in Shandong, "east of the mountains"). A child prodigy, at a young age he obtained appointment at the court of Emperor Wu. Because he died at the age of slightly over twenty, he was called The Lad Zhong. See *Han shu* 64B. 2814–21.

L. 442: Jia Sheng (Scholar Jia) is Jia Yi, a native of Luoyang. He was a child prodigy who died young. See *Shi ji* 84.2491–2503; *Han shu* 48.2221–65; *Records*, 1:508–16.

L. 446: The expression "wearing the hair loose and folding coats on the left" (cf. *Lun yu* 14/18) refers to the barbarian manner of dress. This line refers to Jin Midi, who was a Xiongnu.

LL. 448–49: These lines refer to Lu Jia. Pan Yue draws upon Ban Gu's "Judgment" appended to the *Han shu* biography of Lu Jia: "He insinuated himself between Chen Ping and Zhou Bo (two rivals at the court of Emperor Wen), and reconciled general and chancellor to strengthen the country" (*Han shu* 43.2131).

L. 450: This line refers to Zhao Guanghan, who was executed in 64 B.C.

L. 451: This line refers to Jia Yi.

L. 452: The You Mao text reads *lie* 烈 for *lie* 列. Lü Xiang (10.25a) construes 上列 as 上代 (superior ages). Qu Shuiyuan (p. 100, n. 23) takes it as "high position."

L. 453: Cf. *Mao shi* 235/2: "His fine renown never ends."

L. 456: Wang Yin 王音 and Wang Feng 王鳳 were from the family of Empress Wang, the wife of Emperor Yuan. They both served as regent at the end of the Former Han. See *Han shu* 98.4013–26. Hong Gong 弘恭 and Shi Xian 石顯 were eunuchs who gained high positions during the reigns of emperors Xuan and Yuan. See *Han shu* 93.3726–30; Ch'u T'ung-tsu, *Chinese Social Structure*, pp 430–37.

L. 457: Cf. *Han shu* 100A.4205: "Between the eras Jianshi and Heping, the eminences of Xu and Ban toppled and shook the former court, scenting and illumining the four quarters."

L 461: The *Five Comm.* text reads *ming* 名 (repute) for *cai* 才 (talent) of You Mao. Wang Niansun (see *Dushu zazhi*, "Zhiyu," B.29a–b) argues that *ming* is a better reading in this context on the grounds that though Wang Yin, Wang Feng, Hong Gong, and Shi Xian were illustrious while alive, after their deaths, "they had no repute." The line thus is a modification of *Lun yu* 8/20: "How true it is that talent is hard to find!"

L. 462: In October of A D. 23, troops opposed to Wang Mang seized Chang'an. Wang Mang set up a defense at the Tower of Soaking Waters (see "Western Metropolis Rhapsody," L. 286n) and was killed at the top of the tower. See *Han shu* 99C.4191; *HFHD*, 3:464–65.

L. 463: On this epithet for Wang Mang, see "Eastern Metropolis Rhapsody," L. 145n.

L. 464: Juan Buyi 雋不疑 was governor of the capital from 86 to 81 B.C. In 85 B.C., a young man claiming to be the crown prince appeared at the north gateway of the imperial palace. Unsure of his identity, none of the officials could decide what action to take. When Juan Buyi arrived, he ordered the man arrested. Later, it was discovered the man was indeed an imposter. See *Han shu* 71 3037–38; *Courtier and Commoner*, pp. 160–62.

Administrators of justice Dingguo and Shizhi;
Ji Zhangru, who was straight and upright;
440 Zheng Dangshi, who commended officials;
Zhong Tong, the blossoming talent of Shandong;
Jia Sheng, the genius from Luoyang:
Fluttering their azure cap-cords,
Trailing their singing jades—
445 They exited and entered the forbidden gates in great numbers.

Some, wearing their hair loose and folding their coats on the left,
Swiftly rose from the muck and mire.
Some using insinuation and reconciliation,
Scanned the surface and understood the core.
450 Some had conspicuous achievement, but suffered cruel punishment.
Some had great talent, but were denied noble service.
All wafted the purest breeze to the upper ranks,
Handed down fine renown that is never ending.
I imagine the lingering echoes of girdle-pendants,
455 Which seem to jingle and jangle in my ears.

When Yin, Feng, Gong, and Xian held sway,
They scented and illumined the four quarters,
Daunted and dazzled city and shire.
But on the day they died,
460 They could not even be ranked with the lackeys and servants of these
        ten-odd men.
How true it is that good repute is hard to keep!

XXVIII

I gaze at the Tower of Soaking Waters and grip my wrists;
Though they beheaded that giant deceiver, I still seethe with anger.
I bow to Buyi at north gateway,

L. 465: The Viscount of Shuli 樗里 was the younger brother of King Huı 惠 of Qin (reg. 337–307 B.C.). He was buried east of Zhang 章 Terrace on the south bank of the Wei River. Before he died, the viscount claimed that one hundred years later an emperor's palace would flank his grave. During the Han period, the Palace of Everlasting Joy and the Everlasting Palace were located east and west respectively of his grave, and the Arsenal was situated at the exact site of his grave. See *Shi jı* 71.2310.

LL. 466–67: Zhou Xin, the last Shang ruler, was so fond of food and wine, he had a wine pond and meat forest constructed. See *Shi jı* 3.105. In his "Judgment" to the chapter on the Western Regions ın the *Han shu* (96B.3928), Ban Gu claimed that Emperor Wu also "constructed a wine pond and meat forest to fete guests from the four tribes." Pan Yue chides Emperor Wu for failing to learn from the example of the prodigal Zhou Xin, who lost his kingdom because of his dissolute ways. The *Yuanhe jun xıan tu zhı* (1.6) locates Emperor Wu's wine pond at the Palace of Everlasting Joy.

LL. 468–69: Quyang 曲陽 refers to Wang Gen 王根, who was Marquis of Quyang. He was a member of the consort clan that dominated court at the end of the Former Han. A popular song satırized him for constructing a mansion that rivaled the White Tiger Palace. See *Han shu* 98.4023–24.

L. 471: Cf. *Laozı* 59: "This is called the way of deep roots, solid stalks, long life, and eternal vision."

L. 473: On Civılızed Accomplishment and Quintuple Benefit, see "Western Capital Rhapsody," LL. 303–4n (where Quintuple Benefit is rendered "Five Profits").

L. 476: Cf. "Western Metropolis Rhapsody," L. 298n.

L. 477: Cf. "Western Metropolis Rhapsody," L. 299n.

L. 479: The whale's eyes were thought to be luminous pearls.

L. 480: Cf. "Western Capital Rhapsody," L. 299n

L. 482: On Qiong bamboo, see "Shu Capital Rhapsody," L. 37n and L. 256n. On betel sauce, see "Shu Capital Rhapsody," L. 257n.

L. 484: See "Western Metropolis Rhapsody," L. 680n.

L. 485: Cf. "Western Metropolis Rhapsody," L. 676n.

L. 486: Cf. *Han shu* 7.233 and *HFHD*, 2:175.

L. 487: East Peak is Mount Tai. Suran, a mount located at the foot of Mount Tai, was the site of the *shan* sacrifices in the Former Han. Cf. "Eastern Metropolis Rhapsody," L. 74n.

L. 491: The rear yard is the locatıon of the harem.

L. 492: Once Emperor Yuan of the Former Han took the palace ladies to the animal pens to watch the wild animals fight. A wild bear broke out of its pen and headed for the emperor and his party. All of the palace ladies fled in terror, but Favorite Beauty Feng (Feng *jıeyu* 馮婕妤) walked directly toward the bear and blocked its path until attendants could kill it. See *Han shu* 97B.4005; Watson, *Courtier and Commoner*, p. 278.

L. 493: Emperor Cheng once invited his concubine Favorite Beauty Ban to ride with him in his hand-drawn cart. She refused on the grounds that the paintings of the ancient sage emperors never showed women by their sides. See *Han shu* 97B.3983–84; Watson, *Courtier and Commoner*, pp. 261–62.

L. 494: On Lady Wei, see "Western Metropolis Rhapsody," L 789n. Pan Yue borrows from *Zuozhuan*, *Zhao* 28 (Legge 5:724), which describes a lady's hair as "dark black and extremely beautiful. It was so lustrous it could be used as a mirror."

L. 495: On Lady Zhao, see "Western Metropolis Rhapsody," L. 790n.

L. 496: According to Zhang Xian (10.27b), this lıne refers to the ladies Feng and Ban, and the following line, to ladies Wei and Zhao. Li Shan (10.21b) apparently understands it as applying to court ladies in general, who first enjoyed prestige and power, only to lose them at the peak of their favor. I have followed Li's interpretation.

465 Salute Shuli at the Arsenal.
 The wine pond mirrored the lesson of Shang Xin;
 But Wu followed the overturned cart, unawakened to his folly.
 Quyang presumed *to imitate the White Tiger Palace;*
 He turned to extravagant dissipation and knew no limit.

470 Just as life has a beginning it has an inevitable end;
 Who can attain long life and eternal vision?
 Where now are Wu's grand strategems?
 Near, he was deluded by Civilized Accomplishment and Quintuple
   Benefit;
 He imitated the Fashioner in his constructions,
475 And he probed the dark secrets of mountain and sea.
 The divine Ruo frolicked on sacred isles;
 A darting whale, carried by a wave, washed ashore,
 Exposing its scaly skeleton on a broad sandspit,
 Letting fall a pair of bright-moon pearls.
480 He also hoisted immortals' palms to catch the dew;
 Invading Cloud-Han, they reached on high.
 Importing Qiong bamboo and betel sauce—was it hard?
 If only "We" desired it, the whim was fulfilled.
 He indulged idle play in competitive games,
485 Strung A-rank and B-rank tents with pearls and halcyon plumes.
 He could bear to reduce the population by half,
 And though he inscribed his feats on East Peak, for nought was the
   praise.

XXIX

 Now, after long contemplation and distant reflection,
 All seems like a turning wheel that never ceases.
490 Having inspected the blazing splendor of the facing court,
 I come next to the dainty delicacy of the rear yard.
 Admirable was the loyal courage of blocking the bear;
 Profound was the bright wisdom of declining the hand-cart.
 Wei's ebon hair glistened like a mirror;
495 Zhao of light form was slender and beautiful.
 All skillfully established themselves and their fame spread;
 But at favor's peak their misfortunes were many.

L. 498: The Access Gate (Bian men 便門) bridge was located west of Chang'an. The bridge crossed the Wei River and provided access to the mausoleum town of Mouling. See *Han shu* 6.158, n. 1; *Yuanhe junxian tu zhi* 1.13.

LL. 500–507: In 159 B.C., the Xiongnu invaded the northern border area. Emperor Wen ordered the general Zhou Yafu to encamp at Xiliu 細柳 west of Chang'an to await the Xiongnu attack. To encourage the troops, the emperor himself visited the camp. When he tried to enter Xiliu, the sentries refused admission to his vanguard. Only after receiving orders from General Zhou did they allow the entourage to enter. The camp guards then ordered the emperor's driver to slow his pace, for General Zhou had commanded that there be no galloping in the camp. When Zhou Yafu came out to greet the emperor, he gave only a single bow, claiming an officer in armor need not observe full ceremony, even before an emperor. Emperor Wen fully approved of Zhou Yafu's strict adherence to military regimen. See *Shi ji* 57.2074–75; *Records*, 1:434–35. The *Yuanhe jun xian tu zhi* (1.4 and 1.12) locates Xiliu twenty *li* southwest of Xianyang.

L. 508: Before coming to Xiliu, Emperor Wen had visited camps at Jimen 棘門 (northwest of Chang'an) and Bashang 霸上 (east of Chang'an), where he was admitted immediately. After departing Xiliu, Emperor Wen remarked that the armies at Bashang and Jimen "were like children at play," for they were vulnerable to suprise attack. See *Shi ji* 57.2075; Watson, *Records*, 2:435.

L. 509: Zhou Yafu was enfeoffed as Marquis of Tiao 條. On Zhou Yafu's "proud nobility," see *Shi ji* 122.3133; *Records*, 2:421.

LL. 510–11: Du Station 杜郵 was located seventeen *li* west of Xianyang. The name was later changed to Filial Hamlet. It was the location of a shrine dedicated to the Qin general Bo Qi 白起. See *Shuijing zhu* 3.17.106.

L. 513. Wuan 武安 is Bo Qi, who was Lord of Wuan.

L. 514: Bo Qi had led the Qin army to many victories over enemy states. The Qin chancellor Fan Ju, who was jealous of Bo Qi's success, devised a scheme to demoblize the army and seek a peaceful settlement with Zhao. Later, when Qin launched an attack against the Zhao capital of Handan, Bo Qi pleaded illness and declined to take command, predicting that Qin would not be victorious. Though the Qin army besieged Handan for eight or nine months, it could not defeat Zhao. King Zhao then tried to force Bo Qi into taking command of the Qin army. When Bo refused, the king demoted him to a commoner and banished him to Yinmi 陰密. Three months later, when Zhao repeatedly repulsed the Qin assault, King Zhao conspired with Fan Ju to summon Bo Qi to Du Station. There he was presented with a sword with which he committed suicide. See *Shi ji* 73.2335–37.

L. 515: Cf. L. 28 in above.

L. 522: Weicheng 渭城 was another name for Xianyang. See *Shi ji* 5.203, n. 4

L. 523: When Qin constructed Xianyang in 350 B.C., they built the Ji Gatetower 冀闕. See *Shi ji* 5.203; *Mh*, 2:65; J. J. L. Duyvendak, *The Book of Lord Shang* (1928; rpt. Chicago: University of Chicago Press, 1963), p. 17, n. 3.

LL. 526–27: The Zhao envoy is Lin Xiangru (see LL. 144–45n). When Qin tried to extort a valuable jade from Zhao, ostensibly in exchange for fifteen Qin cities, Lin offered to take the jade to Qin. After presenting the jade to the King of Qin, Lin saw that he had no intention of turning over the cities to Zhao. Pretending to show the king a flaw in the jade, Lin seized it and threatened to smash it against a pillar unless the king held to his agreement. Lin was then able secretly to return the jade to Zhao. Although chagrined over Lin Xiangru's deception, the king allowed him to return to Zhao. See *Shi ji* 81.2439–41; Yang and Yang, *Records*, pp. 139–42.

LL. 528–29: Jing Ke tried to assassinate the First Qin Emperor while presenting him a map of territory the state of Yan offered to cede to Qin. When the emperor opened the map

XXX

I cross Access Gate and then wheel right,
To survey the limits of my district.
500 At Xiliu, I stroke my sword,
And rejoice at the commander named by Filial Wen.
Once General Zhou received command he forgot self,
Thus confirming the unflinching determination of martial regimen.
He blocked the floriate canopy at the camp entrance,
505 Drew the honorable reins of the imperial carriage.
Though solemn in the presence of celestial majesty,
He followed martial etiquette and bowed a long bow.
Emperor Wen belittled the child's play of Ji and Ba,
And honored the proud nobility of Lord Tiao.

XXXI

510 I search for Du Station, but where is it?
They say it is the former name of Filial Hamlet.
Disconsolate, I halt my carriage and linger here;
Grieving for Wuan, sadness wells inside me.
He opposed attacking Zhao and thus died for his state;
515 For he had determined the chances of victory in temple calculations.
The king repulsed his solemn words and would not accept them;
Instead, nursing resentment, he turned the blame on Bo.
He was not even ten miles on his exile journey,
When they gave him a sword with which to sever his head.
520 Alas, when the lord is benighted and a minister is jealous,
What disaster could not occur?

XXXII

I peer at the Qin ruins in Weicheng;
Ji Gatetower has completely disappeared.
I search for the remains of the palace foundation;
525 Now, collapsed and crumbled, it is a ragged remnant.
I recall the Zhao envoy who held tight to the jade;
Eyes blazing, he glanced at the pillar, roused with wrath.
Once the Yan map was unrolled, Jing revealed his dagger;
Befuddled, the emperor ripped his sleeve and recoiled in terror.

219

container, with his right hand Jing Ke snatched the dagger he had hidden inside the map, and with his left seized the emperor's sleeve. Alarmed, the emperor drew back and tore the sleeve from his robe. See *Shi ji* 86.2534–35; Watson, *Records of the Historian*, pp. 63–64; Yang and Yang, *Records*, pp. 399–400.

LL. 530–31: Jing Ke's friend, Gao Jianli 高漸離, was a skilled musician. After Jing Ke failed in his attempt to kill the First Qin Emperor, Gao performed on his zither before distinguished families. The emperor soon heard of his skill and had him brought to the capital. Knowing Gao's former association with Jing Ke, he had Gao's eyes put out. He then commanded him to perform for the court. Eventually, Gao was able to sit directly before the emperor when he performed. One day he fastened a heavy piece of lead inside his zither, and as he approached the emperor to play, he swung the zither at his head, but missed. Gao was immediately executed. See *Shi ji* 86.1536–37; Watson, *Records of the Historian*, pp. 65–66; Yang and Yang, *Records*, p. 401.

Li Shan (10.23a) cites the *Lun heng*, which says that Gao struck the King of Qin in the kneecap, inflicting a mortal wound. Cf. Liu Pansui, *Lun heng jijie* 4.90, which reads "throat" for "kneecap."

L. 536: Shang Yang 商鞅 (fl. 359–338 B.C.) was a Qin minister who instituted the Qin law code. One of the laws stipulated that anyone who threw ashes on the road would be punished. See *Shi ji* 87.2555; Bodde, *China's First Unifier*, p. 40.

L. 537: After the First Qin Emperor died, Li Si conspired with the eunuch Zhao Gao 趙高 and the First Emperor's second son, Hu Hai 胡亥, to forge an edict ordering the heir-apparent, Fu Su 扶蘇, who was in exile on the northern border, to commit suicide. See *Shi ji* 87.2547–51; Bodde, *China's First Unifier*, pp. 25–33.

LL. 538–39: On Li Si's advice, the First Qin Emperor ordered the classics burned and Confucian scholars thrown into pits and killed. See *Shi ji* 6.255, 258; *Mh*, 2:181–82.

LL. 540–41: Both Shang Yang and Li Si were executed by the successors to the rulers they had faithfully served. Shang Yang was torn to pieces by chariots, and all members of his family were killed. See *Shi ji* 68.2237; Duyvendak, *Book of Lord Shang*, p. 30. Li Si was cut in two, and his parents, brothers, wife, and children were put to death. See *Shi ji* 87.2562; Bodde, *China's First Unifier*, p. 52.

L. 542: When Shang Yang tried to flee arrest, he sought refuge at an inn, but was refused by the innkeeper, who informed him that according to Lord Shang's law, anyone who accepts guests into his inn without identification will be punished. See *Shi ji* 68.2236–37; Duyvendak, *The Book of Lord Shang*, p. 29.

L. 543: Just before his execution, Li Si said to his son, "Though I wished again to go with you outside the east gate of Shangcai, leading a yellow dog in pursuit of the wily hare, could I do so?" See *Shi ji* 87.2562; Bodde, *China's First Unifier*, p. 52.

LL. 544–45: Li Shan (10.23b) cites the *Fengsu tong* (*yi?*), which tells the anecdote of the eunuch Zhao Gao, who had so terrorized the officials at the court of the Second Qin Emperor he could call a bundle of rushes dried meat and point to a deer and call it a horse with no one daring to contradict him. The present edition of the *Fengsu tongyi* does not have this passage. The portion of the anedote about the rushes is preserved in the *Yiwen leiju* (82.1407; *Mh*, 2:211), but is attributed to the *Shi ji*. However, the *Shi ji* (6.273) has only the deer-as-horse episode. For other sources of the anecdote, see Hu Shaoying 12.14b–15a.

L. 546: The slandering traitor is Zhao Gao.

LL. 548–49: When a rebel band stormed the palace and entered the throne room, the Second Qin Emperor turned to a eunuch and asked, "Why did you not tell me about this sooner?" The eunuch replied, "Your servants did not dare to speak. Thus, we have been able to save ourselves. If your servants had spoken earlier, we all would have been condmemmed to death. How could we have lived until now?" See *Shi ji* 6.274; *Mh*, 2:214.

530 While the zither's sounds pierced the air, Gao bestirred himself,
     Waiting to deposit the lead and sever a kneecap.
     To occupy the celestial throne like this,
     So perplexed and panicked, how sad!

     Qin chose good men to assist it;
535 They called Li Si loyal and Shang Yang wise.
     Shang Yang stipulated harsh measures for discarding ashes;
     Li Si deceived Fu Su at the northern border.
     Ruist scholars filled pits and holes;
     The *Songs* and *Documents*, burning brightly, were reduced to ashes.
540 Their fiefs were destroyed, thereby cutting off their posterity;
     They themselves were dismembered by chariots, thus presaging the
           ruin of Qin.
     How did Lord Shang's laws find him a place to stay?
     How could Li Si again lead a yellow dog?

     Wild rushes turned into dried meat;
545 A deer from the park transformed into a horse.
     An emperor lent a slandering traitor his celestial authority,
     Muzzled the people's mouths yet sat in a puppet's seat.
     Only when the executioner's blade touched his neck did he turn and
           ask,
     "Why did you not tell me sooner?"

LL. 550–51: Yan Le 閻樂, the leader of the palace coup, asked the Second Qin Emperor to choose how he preferred to die. When his requests to be named king of a commandery and marquis of a myriad households were denied, he then begged to live as a commoner "like the other lords." When this request was also denied, the emperor committed suicide. See *Shi ji* 6.274; *Mh*, 2:214–15.

LL. 552–53: Ziying succeeded the Second Qin Emperor as king (not emperor) of Qin. One of his first acts was to put the traitor Zhao Gao to death. See *Shi ji* 6.275; *Mh*, 2:215–16.

L. 555: Cf. LL. 377–78 above.

L. 556: When Liu Bang's army overran the Xianyang capital, all the generals dashed about fighting over the gold and silk in the Qin storehouses. However, Xiao He went ahead and gathered up the regulations, maps, and documents that had belonged to the Qin chancellors and secretaries. See *Shi ji* 53.2014; *Records*, 1:125–26.

L. 558: When Xiang Yu entered Xianyang, he set fire to all the palaces and buildings and then left. See *Shi ji* 7.215; *Records*, 1:55 Pan Yue criticizes him for failing to make use of the opportunity to hold the Qin capital. For the phrase "what Heaven bestows," see *Shi ji* 89.2580; *Records*, 1:181.

L. 559: When Xiang Yu refused to accept advice to remain in Xianyang, the person who offered the advice said, "People say that men of Chu are merely monkeys who wear hats. Now I know it is true." (Xiang Yu was a native of Chu.) See *Shi ji* 7.315; *Records*, 1:55.

LL. 562–63: The left adjunct Han Yanshou and the grandee secretary Xiao Wangzhi, who were political enemies, issued a series of accusations against each other. The emperor eventually condemned Han to be executed in the market. See *Han shu* 76.3214–16. The hemp-stalks were used for fuel

L. 564: When Han Yanshou was led to the execution ground, several thousand of his clerks accompanied him to Weicheng. When he was executed, the people wept. See *Han shu* 76.3216. Li Shan (10.25a) points out that Pan Yue actually draws from the account of Zhao Guanghan's execution, which is recorded in *Han shu* 76.3204. This account specifically mentions clerks and gatetower guards offering to substitute themselves for Zhao Guanghan.

L. 565: Cf. *Mao shi* 131/1:

That azure Heaven—
It destroys good men.
If we could ransom him,
His life would be worth a hundred men.

LL. 568–69: Cf. *Lun yu* 17/24: "I detest anyone who accuses others and considers that forthrightness."

L. 570 "This man" is Han Yanshou.

L 575: Xiao Wangzhi was grand tutor to the heir-apparent.

L. 576: Chang Mount 長山, or Changling 長陵, was the site of Han Gaozu's grave. It was located north of the Wei River, forty *li* from Chang'an. See *Han shu* 1B.80.

L. 577: Cf. *Han shu* 1.2: "Gaozu was a man with a protruding nose and a dragon countenance."

L. 578: Cf. *Han shu* 1.2. "(Gaozu's) mind was open."

L. 579: Cf. Ban Biao, "Discourse on the Mandate of Kings" (*Wen xuan* 52.5a): "Brave heroes displayed their efforts, and hosts of strategems were all presented."

L. 581· Gaozu's tomb was ransacked by the Red Eyebrow rebels at the end of the Former Han See *Hou Han shu* 1A.28.

550   He wished to become a commoner, but who could allow it?
      Only when he begged for death was his request approved.
      Strong indeed was Ziying's bold determination!
      He dared to punish the rebel and expel calamity.
      Qin's power collapsed like a landslide and no one could save it;
555   Ziying became a surrendered king by the roadside.
      Xiao gathered maps to assist Liu,
      And to judge steepness of terrain and population.
      What Heaven bestows, Yu did not accept,
      This monkey wearing a hat let the fire rage.
560   Even piercing the Three Luminants and penetrating the nine springs
      Would be insufficient to illustrate the gulf between them.

XXXIII

      Moved by the sight of hemp-stalk stalls in the city market,
      I sigh at the old site where Han was turned to a corpse.
      Deputies and subordinates wailed as they guarded the gatetowers;
565   A hundred men offered themselves to ransom him.
      How could they so easily give their lives?
      Truly, because his compassion and love were everywhere known.
      But when he accused Wangzhi in the pursuit of forthrightness,
      Even I detest this to the bottom of my heart.
570   I ponder this man's method of government:
      Verily was he a good instrument for guiding the age.
      However, Xiao simply set forth the law to unleash his vengeance;
      Nor did he cherish talent with which to complete the empire's tasks.
      Broadly viewing the whole with lofty nobility,
575   Was something one could not expect from Tutor Xiao.

XXXIV

      Upon reaching Chang Mount, I am stirred to sadness;
      Great indeed the heroic lord of the dragon countenance!
      Within his heart he magnanimously opened himself;
      All the good fellows who flocked about him were sure to be
               employed.
580   Alive, his majesty reached the celestial precincts;
      Dead, his grave was exhumed and no one could protect it.

L. 584: Anling, located thirty-five *li* north of Chang'an, was the grave mound of Emperor Hui 惠 (reg. 194–188 B.C.). See "Western Capital Rhapsody," LL. 72–73n.

LL. 586–87: Yuan Si 爰絲 is Yuan Ang 爰盎, who retired to his home in Anling after loyally serving as adviser to Emperor Wen. Once Emperor Jing asked Yuan's advice about naming the King of Liang heir to the throne, and Yuan recommended against it. Angered, the King of Liang sent assassins to Anling, and they stabbed Yuan to death outside the outer wall gate of Anling. See *Shi ji* 101.2744–45; *Records*, 1:526–27.

L. 588: Yang Hillock is Yangling, the location of Emperor Jing's tomb, located forty-five *li* northeast of Chang'an. See *Han shu* 5.153.

LL. 590–91: Once the crown prince of Wu was playing chess with the heir apparent, the future Emperor Jing. During an argument over the game, the heir apparent picked up the chess board, hit the prince over the head, and killed him. See *Shi ji* 106.2823; *Records*, 1:466–67.

LL. 592–93: One of the leaders of the Rebellion of the Seven Kingdoms in 154 B.C. was Liu Pi, King of Wu (reg. 195–154 B.C.), who long had harbored a grudge against Emperor Jing for killing his son. Wu and six other kingdoms rose in revolt to resist attempts by the emperor to reduce their power. This policy had been suggested to Emperor Jing by Chao Cuo 晁錯, who was executed on trumped up charges after the rebellion broke out. For a convenient summary of the important events of the rebellion, see *HFHD*, 1:292–97.

L. 594: "The guilty" here is Yuan Ang, who advised Emperor Jing to execute Chao Cuo to assuage the anger of the kingdoms. Pan Yue is criticizing Emperor Jing for eliminating his wisest counselor. See *Shi ji* 106.2830–31; *Han shu* 49.2273; *Records*, 1:476–77.

L. 596: Wei Tumulus is Weiling 渭陵, located 50 *li* north of Chang'an. It was the site of Emperor Yuan's tomb. See *Han shu* 9.298; *HFHD*, 2:336.

L. 597: The eunuchs refer to Hong Gong and Shi Xian, who dominated Emperor Yuan's court.

LL. 598–99: In 40 B.C., Emperor Yuan abolished the funerary parks of Empress Si and the crown prince Li. He also probably abolished other funerary parks. See *Han shu* 9.292; *HFHD*, 2:326.

L. 600: Yan Gate was at Yanling 延陵, sixty-two *li* west of Chang'an, the site of Emperor Cheng's tomb. See *Han shu* 10.330; *HFHD*, 2:417.

LL. 602–3: Wang Zhang 王章 served as governor of the capital from 25–24 B.C. After criticizing the powerful minister Wang Feng, Wang Zhang was charged with various crimes and sent to prison, where he died. See *Han shu* 76.3238–39; *HFHD*, 2:388.

L. 604: Qu Shuiyuan (p. 109, n. 7) suggests that *tai* 忕 should be emended to *she* 伏 (to be accustomed to). Cf. *Shi ji* 17.802: "They were accustomed to (*she*) the plans and counsels of evil ministers and engage in depraved and disorderly conduct." I have translated *she* as "indulged."

L. 605: The depraved favorite is Emperor Cheng's concubine, the Brilliant Companion Zhao. She was responsible for ordering the killing of newborn sons of other concubines. See *Han shu* 97B.3988–89; Watson, *Courtier and Commoner*, pp. 267–72.

L. 606: The uncle's clan refers to the Wang clan. Wang Feng was Emperor Cheng's uncle. The usurper Wang Mang came from this clan.

L. 608: Yi is Yiling 義陵, located forty-six *li* west of Chang'an. It was the site of Emperor Ai's tomb. See *Han shu* 11.344; *HFHD*, 3:38.

L. 609: The Lord Gao'an 高安 was Dong Xian, Emperor Ai's catamite. See "Western Metropolis Rhapsody," L. 327n.

Overlooking the covered pit, I repeatedly wring my hands;
Walking along the ruined wall, long do I linger.

XXXV

Crossing Anling, there is nothing to mock;
585 But in truth Hui's fame is unsung.
I lament Yuan Si, a man of rectitude and principle,
Who fell to the Liang swordsman in the eastern suburb.
I seek Jing Augustus at Yang Hillock;
Why did he trust slander and vaunt frivolity?
590 When he felled the Wu heir with a chessboard,
His angry outburst was over a single game!
However, having given the Seven Kingdoms cause to declare
        rebellion,
Instead, he aided their treason by executing Cuo.
Regretably, he failed in judgment and did not punish the guilty;
595 This thwarts goodness and abets evil.

XXXVI

I reprove Filial Yuan at Wei Tumulus;
His reliance on eunuchs clearly deserves blame.
But I praise this lord's good deeds;
For he abolished parks and towns to honor frugality.
600 I pass Yan Gate and berate Emperor Cheng;
For what crime were loyal men executed?
When they incriminated the defender of the state, Wang Zhang,
He was given a prison death that no one investigated.
He indulged the viscious cruelty of a depraved favorite,
605 Who destroyed newborn offspring of the imperial line.
He opened the way for the traitorous encroachment of the uncle's
        clan;
And thus caused the Han house to topple and fall.

XXXVII

I revile Lord Ai at the precincts of Yi;
He improperly conferred celestial rank on Gao'an.

225

L. 610: Cf. *Lun yu* 13/22: "If one is inconstant in his virtue, he will bring shame upon himself." Emperor Ai thought he would imitate Yao's act of abdicating to Shun by transfering the throne to Dong Xian. See "Western Metropolis Rhapsody," LL. 800–802n.

L. 612: Kang Park is Kangling 康陵, 60 *li* north of Chang'an, the site of Emperor Ping's tomb. See *Han shu* 12.360; *HFHD*, 3.86. The tumulus is solitary because Emperor Ping, the last Former Han emperor, was buried alone.

L. 613: Emperor Ping's Empress Wang was Wang Mang's daughter. Her *Han shu* biography (99B.4010) describes her as "docile, serene, and a person of moral integrity." After Wang Mang's usurpation, she claimed illness and refused to attend court gatherings. When Han loyalists overthrew Wang Mang and set fire to the Everlasting Palace, she said, "How do I have the face to look upon the Han house?" She then committed suicide by throwing herself into the fire. See *Han shu* 99B.4011.

L. 616: "Settling matters herself" is a euphemisim for committing suicide.

L. 620: The Guang Bridge 横, which spanned the Wei River, was located two *li* north of Chang'an. See Pan Yue's *Guanzhong ji*, cited by Li Shan 10.27a.

LL. 622–23: On the Ebang Palace see "Eastern Capital Rhapsody," L. 334n. According to the *Sanfu huangtu* (1.46), magnolia wood was used for its beams, and it had gates constructed of lodestones, which were used to detect weapons hidden on anyone who entered the palace. The *Yuanhe junxian tu zhi* (1.12) says this gate was located fifteen *li* southeast of Xianyang, and it served as the north gate to the Ebang Palace.

L. 624: In 212 B.C., the First Qin Emperor ordered the construction of a covered passageway from the Ebang Palace to the Southern Mountains. The summit of (a peak of?) the Southern Mountains was built into a gatetower ("arc de triomphe"). See *Shi ji* 6.256; *Mh*, 2:175.

L. 625: The Fan River 樊, also called the Qin 秦 River, was located directly south of Chang'an. See *San Qin ji*, cited by Li Shan 10.27a.

LL. 626–27: When the Rong envoy Youyu (see "Eastern Metropolis Rhapsody," LL. 9–10n) visited Qin, Duke Mu tried to impress him with his lavish palaces. Youyu replied, "If you have had the spirits do this for you, you have tired the gods. If you have had men do it, you have tortured the people." See *Shi ji* 5.192; *Mh*, 2:41.

LL. 632–33: In A.D. 20, Wang Mang constructed nine temples in honor of his putative ancestors, including the Yellow Lord and Shun (Yu). See *Han shu* 99B.4162; *HFHD*, 3:398–99.

LL. 634–35: As the rebel armies moved closer to the capital, Wang Mang became frightened. An adviser told him that according to the *Zhou li* and the *Zuozhuan*, whenever there was a great calamity in the state, the ruler should weep in order to suppress it. Wang Mang then led his court officers to the southern suburbs, set out all of his talismans, beat his breast, and wailed loudly. He appointed over five thousand of the best wailers palace squires. *Han shu* 99C.4187–88; *HFHD*, 3:457–58. I have followed Zhu Jian's explanation of the line (11.21b).

L. 636: On Wang Mang's promotion of the classics, see *Han shu* 99A.4069; *HFHD*, 3:192–94. Pan Yue draws from Ban Gu's "Judgment" appended to the Wang Mang chapter in the *Han shu* (see 99C.4194; *HFHD*, 3:473).

L. 637: The expression "facing the wall" implies ignorance. Cf. *Lun yu* 17/10: "To be a man and not study the 'Zhou nan' and 'Shao nan' is like standing directly facing the wall, is it not?"

610 Though wishing to emulate Yao, he only brought shame upon
          himself;
For all eternity this indignity cannot be erased!
As I gaze over the solitary tomb of Kang Park,
I grieve for Emperor Ping's empress who was true and pure.
Afflicted by her father's traitorous usurpation,
615 She was covered in shame and could not wash it away.
Inspired by right and truth, she settled matters herself,
Dashed toward the vermilion flames to prove her integrity.
She threw herself in the palace conflagration and burned into
          nothing;
Together with ashes and flames her life was extinguished.

XXXVIII

620 I rush to the Guang Bridge, wheel about,
And pass through the southern edge of my humble district.
With gates of lodestone and beams of magnolia,
They constructed the winding wonder of Ebang.
They opened the Southern Mountains to site a gatetower,
625 Widened the Fan River to water the ponds.
Even if they used spirit workers, it would be wrong;
How much worse it was made with human labor!
Before craftsmen could finishing their carving,
Loyal armies furiously galloped hither and thither.
630 Even the ancestral temples were defiled and reduced to ponds;
This edifice was not destroyed alone.

XXXIX

I come from the nine temples of the false Xin,
Where Wang Mang boasted of his ancestry to Yu and Shun.
He drove forth wailers and weepers to perform their devilish
          lamentation,
635 Searched for artful mourners to appoint as squires.
He chanted the Six Classics to gloss over his villainy;
The First Emperor burned the *Songs* and *Documents* so that people
          stood "facing the wall."

227

L. 638: Cf *Zuozhuan*, *Xi* 24: "A heart that does not follow the standards of virtue and morality is perverse."

L. 639: Cf. *Han shu* 99C.4194 (translation derived from *HFHD*, 3:473): "Of old (the First Qin Emperor) burned the *Songs* and *Documents* to establish his personal proposals, and Wang Mang chanted the Six Classics to gloss over his evil words. They returned together, but by different roads; and both thereby perished."

L. 640: Leyou 樂游 was the temple of Emperor Xuan. It was located at Duling, the site of Emperor Xuan's tomb, fifty *li* south of Chang'an. See *Han shu* 8.262; *HFHD*, 2.243.

L. 641: Cf. *Han shu* 8.275: "Xuan's accomplishments glorified his ancestors, and his feats were handed down to his posterity. One may call his reign a restoration."

L. 642: Emperor Xuan was the son of Liu Jin 劉進, who was put to death together with his father, Crown Prince Li, in the black magic affair of 91 B C. See LL. 256–61n above. Emperor Xuan was a baby at the time and thus never had a chance "to honor or nurture" his parents. For details, see *Han shu* 8.235; *HFHD*. 2:109.

LL. 644–45: Fengming 奉明 (Upholding Brilliance), originally known as Guangming 光明, was the burial place of the Imperial Grandson Shi (Shi Huangsun 史皇孫), Emperor Xuan's father See *Han shu* 8.254; *Han shu* 63.2747–49. According to Pan Yue's *Guanzhong ji* (cited by Li Shan 10.28a), Emperor Xuan's grandmother, Empress Si 思, née Wei, was buried at a place called Thousand Men Village (Qianren xiang 千人鄉). The village received this name because a thousand musicians and acrobats were stationed here "to add joy to the park." See also *Han shu* 97A.3951, n. 3.

L. 647: Xun 詢 was the personal name of Emperor Xuan.

LL. 648–49: Both Lu Yanji (10 35b) and Qu Shuiyuan (p. 112, n. 7) interpret *wang mu* 王母 as referring to Emperor Xuan's mother, Lady Wang 王夫人. However, *wang mu* also is a term for grandmother (see *Erya yishu* A4.1b). Since Emperor Xuan installed musicians at his grandmother's grave, I have translated *wang mu* as "grandmother."

L. 651: This line is a paraphrase of *Lun yu* 4/7

L. 652: According to the *Chang'an tu* (cited by Li Shan 10.28a), the High View Mound (Gaowang dui 高望堆) was located eight *li* south of the Yanxing 延興 Gate (the west gate of Tang dynasty Chang'an).

L. 654: The lodges cool in summer were located at Sweet Springs. Cf. "Western Metropolis Rhapsody," LL. 56–59.

L. 655: On Five Oaks Lodge, see "Western Metropolis Rhapsody," L. 397n.

L. 658: On Kunming Pond, see "Western Capital Rhapsody," L. 130n.

L. 661: Cf. "Western Capital Rhapsody," LL. 400–402n.

L. 663: Cf. "Western Metropolis Rhapsody," L. 437.

L. 664: On Dawn Valley, see "Eastern Metropolis Rhapsody," L. 603n.

L. 665: On the Gulf of Yu, see Yang Xiong's "Plume Hunt Rhapsody," L. 49n.

L. 666: On Camphor Lodge, see "Western Capital Rhapsody," L. 399n.

L. 667: Cf. "Western Metropolis Rhapsody," LL. 429–34.

L. 668: The Phosphor Star (Jing xing 景星), or Star of Virtue (De xing 德星), was a large yellow light shaped like a half moon. It was not really a star, but reflected sunlight from the earth ("earth shine"). See Ho Peng Yoke, *The Astronomical Chapters of the Chin shu*, p. 129; Schafer, *Pacing the Void*, pp. 180–82.

L. 669: See "Western Capital Rhapsody," LL. 400–402n.

Their hearts did not follow the standards of virtue and morality;
Though differing in method, alike they perished.

XL

640   I honor Filial Xuan at Leyou;
Though heir to a failing line, he restored the dynasty.
Since he could not attend to honoring and nurturing his parents,
He spent his all exalting funerary parks and grave mounds.

The grave, it was Upholding Brilliance;
645   The town was called Thousand Men.
I inquired of ancient elders,
And learned they were built by Emperor Xun.
Grieving at his grandmother's wrongful death,
He had music played to soothe her soul.
650   Although this did not conform to ancient canons,
By observing his fault, we can perceive his goodness.

XLI

Resting atop the southern slope of High View Mound,
I inspect the heights and basins of river and land.
I open my collar in the cool summer lodges,
655   Wander my gaze over Five Oaks Lodge.
Crisscrossing canals direct water transport;
Turbulent rapids generate wind.

Then, there is Kunming Pond in their midst.
Its waters, roiling and raging, profusely pouring,
660   Swelling and surging, vastly spread,
Grand as the Sky River.
The sun and moon clinging to the sky,
Exit and enter east and west.
At sunrise it resembles Dawn Valley;
665   At dusk, it is like the Gulf of Yu.

Of old, the famous edifice of Camphor Lodge
Prominently rose from the dark flow.
Replicating the Phosphor Star in the Celestial Han,
They placed Oxherd and Maid as twin statues.

L. 671: What I have translated as "decade" is *ji* 紀, which actually is a twelve-year period.

L. 674: This line is drawn verbatim from *Mao shi* 278/1.

L. 681: *Qing fan* 青蕃 probably is a variant for *qing fan* 青蘋 (green sedge). See "Southern Capital Rhapsody," L. 98n.

L. 684: The phrase "toil in the distance" is adopted from *Zuozhuan*, *Xi* 9 (Legge 5:154), where it has the sense of "devoting oneself to remote schemes." In Pan Yue's line, it refers to distant military campaigns.

L. 689: Cf. *Zuozhuan*, *Cheng* 2 (Legge 5:346): "The former kings in demarcating and ordering the empire, examined the fitness of the land so as to distribute the benefits."

L. 692: This line alludes to *Lun yu* 13/19: "Ran You said, 'Since (the people) are numerous, what else can one do for them?' 'Enrich them.' 'Once enriched, what else can one do?' 'Teach them.'"

L. 699: Li Shan (10.29a) says the wheels refer to the carts used to pull in the fishing lines. He adds that *lun* 輪 is also written *lun* 綸, which means "fishing line." I have adopted this reading.

L. 703: Li Shan (10.29b) explains that this net was made with white feathers plaited together with thin webbing stretched over them. The net was placed in the water, with a man pulling each end.

L. 704: This pole was struck on the sides of the boat to drive the fish into the nets.

670   They hoped it would not fall for ten thousand years;
       Suddenly it crumbled and collapsed after ten decades.
       What they created as a storied tower of a hundred fathoms,
       Now is only a ruin of several yards.

       Flocking egrets go flying by;
675   Ducks glide and geese skim the waters;
       Riding the clouds they soar and dive;
       On waves they toss and tumble.
       Pitching and plunging in the startling waves,
       They peck and nibble at caltrop and fox nut.
680   Flowering lotuses shimmer on emerald ponds;
       Green sedge burgeons on azure ripples.

       This pond was first dug
       To train for river battles on wild frontiers.
       The aim was to toil in the distance to maximize military might;
685   Truly they did not seek future blessings.
       Yet, its vegetables, potherbs, greens, and fruits,
       And aquatic products of sundry kinds,
       Were more abundant than those of plain and field.
       Now again in this august age we "examine the land";
690   Thus, what was once destroyed, we restore.

XLII

       All of my district officers
       Both enrich and teach the people.
       Leading the poor and idle,
       Together they ready sweeps and oars.
695   They haul in the nets and judge the catch,
       Pull in the arrow cords and hold up the prize.
       Widowers again have wives,
       Grieving folk now are joyful.

       Just behold the pounding sweeps and winding lines,
700   The scattering hooks, cast nets,
       Dangling bait bobbing up and down,
       And gaffs thrusting back and forth!
       Thin webbing is interlaced with white;
       Whistling poles sharply echo.

L. 707: The *kun* 鯤 fish cannot be identified.

L. 712: Cf. "Eastern Metropolis Rhapsody," L. 485n.

LL. 719–20: Cf. *Zuozhuan*, *Zhao* 28 (Legge 5 : 728): "I wish the belly of the petty man would become as the heart of the gentleman—to be sated when full."

L. 723: On Feng and Hao, see "Western Capital Rhapsody," L. 332n.

L 724: Cf. *Kong Congzi* 孔叢子 (Kong's Collectanea), *Sbby*, 3.2a: "The lord as if starved and thirsty awaits worthy men."

L. 727: Cf. *Lun yu* 7/5: "The Master said, 'Extreme indeed is my decline. Long indeed has it been since I dreamed of seeing the Duke of Zhou.'" The three sages are King Wen, King Wu, and the Duke of Zhou.

L. 728: Pan Yue alludes to the "Great Declaration" of the *Classic of Documents* (see *Shang shu zhushu* 11.9b; Legge 3 : 292), which reports King Wu of Zhou as declaring, "I have ten vassals capable of governing." See also *Lun yu* 8/20.

LL. 729–30: On the Divine Tower, see "Eastern Capital Rhapsody," L. 200. Cf. *Mao shi* 242/1: "He planned and built (literally "began") the Divine Tower. . . . / In less than a day (the people) finished it."

L. 733: Cf. *Mao shi* 242/1: "The people came like children."

705 They impale the gills, snag the tails,
Lift them in twos, haul them in threes.

And then they release blue *kun* from the net barbs,
Free ruddy carp from the sticky mesh.
Speckled bream flick their scales;
710 Whitish carp flap their dorsal fins.
A cook cuts them into threadlike shreds;
His simurgh knife seems to fly.
Upon meeting the blade, the flesh falls to the cutting board,
Flurrying and fluttering fine and fast.
715 As soon as the fresh red morsels are carried in,
Guests leap up eagerly awaiting to be served.
After eating, they are full and sated;
Quiet and tranquil, they have no desires.
This turns the bellies of petty men
720 Into the minds of gentlemen.

XLIII

And then
I lift the whip, brush the cushion,
Flick my cap, shake my clothes,
Lingering at Feng and Hao,
As if thirsty, as if starved.
725 My heart leaping excitedly, I gaze in wonder;
No extra deference is required, for I am naturally reverential.
How presume I dream of the three sages?
Perhaps I dare aspire to be like the ten capable officials.

King Wen planned and built the Divine Tower;
730 They finished it in less then a day.
And in Feng and in Hao,
They continued to enlarge the houses.
The commoners all arrived like children,
And the gods sent down blessings upon them.
735 Through accumulated virtue the Zhou prolonged its rule;
There was no double, only single, loyalty.

Though men long have pondered this state,
Who now can comprehend it?

233

LL. 741–42: Cf. Jia Yi's reference to this concept of morality in the Qin (*Han shu* 48.2244): "Lord Shang neglected rites and propriety, discarded kindness and mercy.... When a son lent his father a harrow or hoe, he thought he should show a virtuous face."

LL. 742–43: Li Shan (10.30b) cites a passage from the *Shang shu dazhuan* (2.16b), which tells of the visit of men from Yu 虞 and Rui 芮 to King Wen of Zhou for the purpose of having him arbitrate their dispute over ownership of a field. When they arrived in Zhou, they saw that everyone practiced yielding to the point that the farmers left their fields idle so as to avoid contention between neighbors.

L. 745: Su and Zhang are Su Qin and Zhang Yi, renowned persuaders of the Warring States period. As Zhang Xian (10.39b) suggests, Su Qin and Zhang Yi were pleased with the political machinations encouraged by Qin.

L. 746: Cf. LL. 742–43n above.

LL. 749–50: Cf. Dong Zhongshu's examination response (in *Han shu* 56.2501): "The superior's transforming the inferior and the inferior's following the superior are like clay in a potter's wheel. It is something only a potter can make."

LL. 751–52: Cf. *Han shu* 28B.1642: "Thus, (the people of) the five regions are so mixed and varied, our customs and mores are not pure."

LL. 753–54: Pan Yue alludes to the "Pan Geng" chapter of the *Classic of Documents* (see *Shang shu zhushu* 9.6a; Legge 3 : 227): "If the lazy farmer takes his ease and does not exert himself performing labor, and does not work his fields and acres, he shall have no millet." Pan Yue implies that farmers have become merchants.

L. 755: The Xianyun is the ancient name for the Xiongnu.

L. 756: Cf. *Laozi* 46: "When the empire is without the way, war horses breed in the countryside."

LL. 757–58: Cf. Jia Yi's memorial submitted to Emperor Wen (*Han shu* 48.2233): "If one wields a knife, he must cut."

L. 761: Cf. *Lun yu* 13/4: "If the superior loves fidelity, none of the people will dare show bad faith."

L. 762: Cf. *Lun yu* 12/18: "If you sir were without desires, even if you offered them a reward to do so, people would not steal."

L 765: "These thoughts" refer to fidelity and no desires.

L. 766: This line is based on an almost identical line in *Zuozhuan*, *Wen* 18 (Legge 5 : 283).

LL. 767–68: These lines are quoted verbatim from *Lun yu* 11/25.

Only in outline can he know it;
740 Hard it is to reach the core.
When a son lent a spare hoe to his father,
As taught by Qin law, he showed a virtuous face.
To avoid contention over boundaries, farmers left fields idle;
For imbued with Zhou's teachings, they even let thorns grow.
745 Overjoyed, Su and Zhang gave free rein to deceit;
Shamed, Yu and Rui ceased their litigation.
From this one can see:
Though a land has no constant customs,
Teachings have set standards.
The superior transforms those below him,
750 As the potter kneads his clay.

When the five regions mingle and merge,
Customs and mores become muddled and confused.
Lazy farmers fond of profit
Do not strive to perform labor.
755 Near, close, are the Xianyun;
War horses breed in the countryside.
Yet, if the person in charge is to do the cutting,
Truly he must know how to handle the knife.

The rise and fall of human kind
760 Follows the glories and declines of government.
If one relies on fidelity, no one will show bad faith;
If one is without desire, even if you reward him, he will not steal.
Although I am not wise enough to govern,
And not intelligent enough to be discerning,
765 If I put trust in these thoughts,
Perhaps I can avoid transgression.
As for promoting the rites and music,
I shall wait for gentlemen wiser than I.

235

Map for Wang Can's "Climbing the Tower"

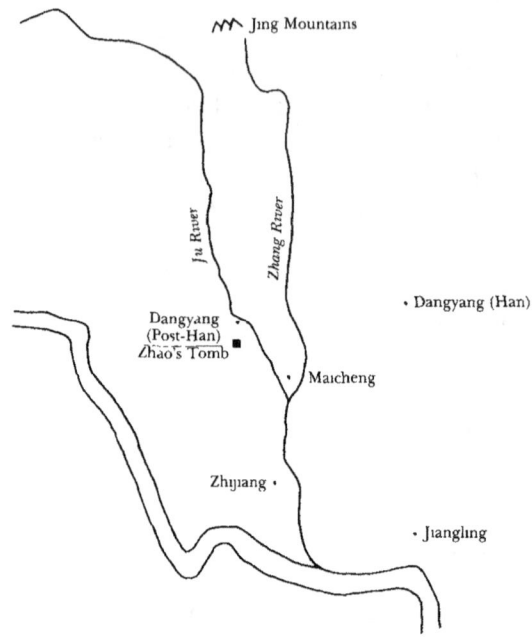

L. 1: There are conflicting reports about the location of this tower. Sheng Hongzhi's *Jingzhou ji* (cited by Li Shan 11.1b) says it was a wall tower in Dangyang 當陽 prefecture (south of modern Jingmen 荊門 City, Hubei; note that the Han dynasty Dangyang was located about 35 kilometers east of the post-Han Dangyang). The Tang *Wen xuan* commentator Liu Liang (11.1a) asserts that Wang ascended a wall tower in Jiangling, where he was on the staff of Liu Biao. This location does not fit with LL. 5–6, which clearly locate the tower between the Zhang 漳 and Ju 沮 rivers. The *Shuijing zhu* (5.32.105) gives the most precise location: a wall tower on the southeast corner of Maicheng 麥城, located at the confluence of the Zhang and Ju Rivers (southeast of modern Dangyang *xian*, Hubei). Maicheng fits exactly the location Wang specifies in LL. 5–6. The *Taiping huanyu ji* (146.20a) also confirms the Maicheng location for the tower. For additional discussion of the question, see Zhang Yun'ao, 6.21a–22a.

L. 2: Or: "Whiling away leisure days to dispel sorrow." Li Shan's text reads *xia* 假 (leisure), but in his commentary, Li notes that *xia* is also written *jia* 假 (to borrow). The phrase *liao jia ri* 聊假日 (literally "briefly borrowing days") is a common *Chuci* formula; see *Chuci buzhu* 1.36b; 4.24a, 15.4b, 16.30a. Thus, I have followed the *jia* reading. For a justification of *xia*, see Hu Shaoying 13.1a–b.

LL. 5–6: According to the *Shuijing zhu* (5.32.105), the Zhang River had its source in the Jing 荊 Mountains of northern Hubei (southwest of modern Nanzhang 南漳 *xian*), and flowed southeast through Dangyang prefecture east of Maicheng and joined the Ju River about a hundred *li* to the south of Dangyang, near Zhijiang 枝江 (northeast of modern Zhijiang *xian*). The Ju River had its source in the Jing 景 Mountains (southeast of modern Fang 房 *xian*, Hubei), flowed south just west of Maicheng. The combined Zhang-Ju stream flowed south and entered the Yangzi River at Ziangling. See also Zhu Jian 12.1a–b.

According to the *Yangxian feng tu ji* 陽縣風土記 (Record of Customs and Geography of Yangxian) of Zhou Chu 周處 (4th century), *Suxiang shi congshu* 粟香室叢書, p. 2a, the word

11

SIGHTSEEING

Rhapsody on Climbing the Tower

WANG ZHONGXUAN

I

I climb this tower and gaze in the four directions,
Briefly stealing some time to dispel my sorrows.
I scan the site on which this building rests:
Truly spacious and open, rare is its peer!

5 It hugs the intersecting channel of the clear Zhang,
Rests upon the long sandbars of the twisting Ju,
Backs upon a broad stretch of hillock and plain,
Faces toward the rich flow of river margin and marsh,

WANG CAN (*zi* Zhongxuan) composed this *fu* sometime between 193 and 208 while he
was residing in the area of Jiangling, where he had moved to escape the political and military
turmoil that afflicted his home area in Chang'an. The poem is a typical example of the
"climbing high" *topos* in which the poet climbs to a high vantage point and expresses his
personal feelings, in this case Wang's nostalgic longing for his home in the north.

    A partial text of this *fu* has been discovered among the Dunhuang manuscripts. See Chen
Zuolong 陳祚龍, "Dunhuang xieben 'Deng lou fu' jiaozheng" 敦煌寫本登樓賦斠證, *Dalu
zazhi* 21.5 (1960):173–78; Rao Zongyi, "Dunhuang xieben 'Deng lou fu' chongyan" 重研,
Dalu zazhi 24.6 (1962):167–69.

    Other translations of the piece include: Margouliès, *Le Kou-wen chinois*, pp. 110–11;
Watson, *Chinese Rhyme-Prose*, pp. 53–54; Itō Masafumi and Ikkai Tomoyoshi, *Kan Gi Rikuchō
Tō Sō sambun sen*, pp. 74–75; Obi Kōichi, *Monzen*, 2:60–64; Ronald Miao, *Early Medieval Chinese
Poetry: The Life and Verse of Wang Ts'an (A.D. 117–217)* (Wiesbaden: Franz Steiner, 1982),
pp. 273–75. I also have consulted the texts and notes in *Liang Han wenxueshi cankao ziliao*,
pp. 84–87; *Wei Jin Nanbeichao wenxueshi cankao ziliao*, 1:133–37; Qu Shuiyuan, *Han Wei Liuchao
fu xuan*, pp. 58–62; Xu Shiying, *Gujin wenxuan* 2:513–16; Yu Shaochu 俞紹初, ed. *Wang Can ji*
王粲集 (Beijing: Zhonghua shuju, 1980), pp. 19–20; Pei Jinnan, *et al.*, eds. and comm. *Han
Wei Liuchao fu xuan zhu*, pp. 97–102; Wu Yun 吳雲 and Tang Shaozhong 唐紹忠, eds. and
comm. *Wang Can ji zhu* 注 (Xinyang, Henan: Zhongzhou shuhuashe, 1984), pp. 46–51.

pu 浦 designates the small outlet of a large river that joins with another river. Thus, perhaps the tower overlooked a small tributary of the Zhang, near where it intersected with the Ju.

L. 9: Tao is Lord Zhu of Tao 陶朱公, the name assumed by the Yue minister Fan Li 范蠡 when he left court and became a merchant. See *Shi ji* 41.1752; *Mh*, 4:441. Li Shan (11.2a) cites Sheng Hongzhi's *Jingzhou ji*, which locates Lord Zhu of Tao's grave west of Jiangling. It also quotes the grave inscription as saying: "This is Fan Li of Yue, who died in Tao." However, the grave probably referred to here is not that of Fan Li, but one Fan 范, prefect of the Western Rong. Li Daoyuan (see *Shuijing zhu* 5.32.106) cites various sources that locate his grave southwest of Huarong 華容 prefecture, which was about thirty-five kilometers east of Jiangling. He also cites Guo Zhongchan 郭仲產, who personally visited the grave, as locating it ten *li* east of Huarong and citing the grave inscription as saying that Fan was a descendant of Fan Li. Clearly this grave cannot be the grave of Lord Zhu of Tao. The actual location of Lord Zhu's grave was five *li* south of Mount Tao, near modern Dingtao 定陶, Shandong, which is nowhere near the area of the tower. See *Shi ji* 41.1753, n. 2; *Yuanhe junxian tu zhi* 11.318. Judging from the confused accounts about a putative grave of Lord Tao around the Jiangling area, I suspect that Wang Can was relying on a local account that placed the Grave of Lord Zhu of Tao north of Maicheng.

The Dunhuang manuscript reads *mu* 沐 for *mu* 牧 (pasturage) of the *Wen xuan*. Rao Zongyi ("Dunhuang xieben," p. 169) suggests that the Dunhuang manuscript *mu* should be understood as *mu* 木 (tree), referring to the trees on Lord Zhu's grave mound.

L. 10: King Zhao 昭 (reg. 515–489 B.C.) of Chu became ill on a campaign against Chen and died at Chengfu 城父 (north of modern Pingding shan 平頂山 City, Henan). See *Shi ji* 40.1717–18; *Mh*, 4:379–81. According to Sheng Hongzhi's *Jingzhou ji* (cited by Li Shan 11.2a), his tomb was located seventy *li* southeast of Dangyang. The *Shuijing zhu* (5.32.105), which cites this line, says that his tomb was on the Ju River facing east toward Maicheng. The present location of the tomb is thirty-five kilometers southeast of Dangyang, right near the confluence of the Ju and Zhang rivers. See *Zhongguo mingsheng cidian* 中國名勝詞典 (Shanghai: Shanghai cishu chubanshe, 1981), p. 756.

LL. 13–14: Cf. Wang Can's "Poem of Seven Laments" (in *Wen xuan* 23.16a: "The land of the Jing tribes is not my home; / Why have I been mired here so long?"

L. 16: Wang refers to the insurrections that occurred in the Chang'an area in the 190's. The word *ji* 紀, which I have loosely translated as "decade," actually is a twelve-year span. It is not clear what span of time Wang is referring to here. It could cover the time since he left Chang'an, which would mean he wrote the *fu* around 204, or "until now" could mean the time since he first ascended the tower. See Miao, *Early Medieval Chinese Poetry*, p. 292, n. 204.

L. 22: Wang looks north, but his view is blocked by the Jing Mountains, which act as a barrier that does not even allow him a glimpse of his homeland.

L. 24: Li Shan (11.2b) cites the Han version of *Mao shi* 8, in which *yang* 漾 is used for *yong* 永 (long) of the *Mao shi* text. Xue Han glosses *yang* as "long." This *yang* clearly is a miswriting for *yang* 羕, which both *Erya* (A1.23b) and *Shuowen* (11B.5155a–b) explain as "long." See Hu Shaoying 13.1b.

LL. 27–28: Father Ni is Confucius. Wang alludes to *Lun yu* 5/21: "When the Master was in Chen, he said, 'Let us return! Let us return!'"

L. 29: Zhong Yi 鍾儀, a native of Chu, was a prisoner in Jin. One day the Marquis of Jin happened to see him and asked, "Who is the bound man?" The man in charge said, "He is a prisoner from Chu presented to us by Zheng." The Marquis had him untied and asked about his family. Zhong Yi replied, "We are musicians." The Marquis had someone give him a zither, and he played a southern tune. Fan Wenzi commented: "The prisoner from Chu is a gentleman.... He played the music of his land, proving that he has not forgotten the past." See *Zuozhuan, Cheng* 9; Legge 5:371.

238

North extends to Tao's pasturage,
10 West touches Zhao's barrow.
Flowers and fruit cover the plain,
Millets fill the fields.
Though truly beautiful, it is not my home!
How can I remain here even briefly?

II

15 Encountering tumult and turmoil, I wandered afar;
A long decade has passed until now.
With my heart longing and languishing, I cherish a return;
Who can bear such anxious thoughts?
Leaning on the grilled railing, afar I gaze,
20 Face the north wind and open my collar.
The plain distantly stretches as far as the eyes can see,
But it is obscured by Jing Mountains' high ridges.
Roads sinuously snake, distant and far;
Rivers are long, fords are deep.
25 I am sad to be blocked and cut off from my homeland;
Tears stream down my face, and I cannot hold them back.
Of old, when Father Ni was in Chen,
There was his sad cry "Let us return!"
When imprisoned, Zhong Yi played a Chu tune;

L. 30: *Shi ji* 70.2301 tells the story of Zhuang Xi 莊舄, a native of Yue who was a high officer in Chu. Suddenly he became ill, and the king of Chu asked, "Xi is a former commoner of Yue. Now that he serves Chu, holds the jade insignia, has wealth and honor, does he think of Yue?" A eunuch replied, "Generally when men long for their homes, it is when they are sick. If he is longing for Yue, he will sing the sounds of Yue. If he is not longing for Yue, he will sing the sounds of Chu." The king sent someone to listen to him, and indeed he was moaning the sounds of Yue.

L. 37: Cf. *Lun yu* 17/7: The Master said, "How can I be a gourd? How can I be hung up and not be eaten?"

L. 38: Cf. *Zhou yi zhushu* 5.16a–b (Hexagram 48, 9/3): "The well is cleaned but no one drinks from it. This makes my heart sad! For it can be used to draw from. If the king were wise, all might enjoy its blessings." The basic point is that like the well with clean water that is not drunk, Wang's pure character has not been appreciated.

30   Though eminent, Zhuang Xi intoned the songs of Yue.
       All men share the emotion of yearning for their lands;
       How can adversity or success alter the heart?

III

       Thinking how days and months pass quickly by,
       I wait for the River to clear, but it does not.
35   I hope for the King's Way at last to be smooth,
       And to take the high road to try my strength.
       I fear hanging uselessly like a gourd,
       Dread being a cleaned well from which no one drinks.
       Walking slow and sluggish, I pace to and fro;
40   The bright sun suddenly is about to set.
       The wind, soughing and sighing, rises all around;
       The sky, pale and pallid, has lost all color.
       Beasts, wildly gazing, seek their herds;
       Birds, crying back and forth, raise their wings.
45   The plains and wilds are deserted, unpeopled;
       Yet wayfarers march on, never resting.
       My heart, sad and sorrowful, bursts with pain;
       My mood, somber and sullen, is doeful and drear.
       As I descend the steps,
50   I feel my spirit troubled and tormented within my breast.
       The night reaches midpoint, yet I do not sleep;
       Pensively brooding, I toss and turn.

[1] For Fangzhang and Penglai, see "Western Capital Rhapsody," L. 289n

[2] Four Luminaries (Siming 四明) is the name of a range of over 280 peaks adjacent to the Celestial Terrace Mountains. They are famous for one peak, Square Rock (Fang shi 方石), which opened on four sides like a natural window to allow the light from sun, moon, and stars to filter through. See Xie Lingyun's "Rhapsody on Mountain Dwelling," *Song shu* 67.1758.

[3] Sun Chuo has borrowed a phrase from *Mao shi* 259/1: "Lofty and tall is the Peak, / Towering and pinnacled in the sky."

[4] On the Five Peaks, see "Eastern Capital Rhapsody," L. 319n.

[5] The layered depths are the sea.

[6] Li Shan (11.4b) says the exotic records refer to a text called the *Nei jing shan ji* 內經山記 (The Mountain Record of the Inner Canon), an unknown work, but which sounds similar to the *Shanhai jing*. Richard Mather ("Mystical Ascent," p. 236, n. 45) notes that the *Shanhai jing* (15.5a) mentions the high mountains of the Celestial Terrace into which the waters of the sea enter.

[7] What I have translated as "levitate" is literally "lightly rise" (*qing ju* 輕舉). In Taoist texts it refers to the technique of lightening the body so that it could float through the air. See *Baopuzi* 4.4b: "The ninth cinnabar is called 'Gold Cinnabar.' Take one spatula a day for one hundred days, and one will become an immortal. Boy and girl immortals will come to wait upon you, you will fly and levitate without using wings."

[8] Sun Chuo is referring to the state of mystic detachment.

Rhapsody on Roaming the Celestial Terrace Mountains

SUN XINGGONG

I

The Celestial Terrace Mountains indeed are the divine eminence of all mounts and peaks. Cross the sea and there will be Fangzhang and Penglai.[1] Climb the plateaus and there will be the Four Luminaries and Celestial Terrace.[2] All are places where mystic sages roam and transform themselves, sites of the grotto dwellings of sacred immortals. In their form of towering pinnacles,[3] and the goodliness of their fair omens, they possess all the precious wealth of mountains and seas, contain the grandest beauty of man or god. As for the reasons they are not ranked among the Five Peaks,[4] and lack a notice in the standard canons, could it be because the place they stand is dark and obscure, and the road to them secluded and remote? Or is it because they cast their shadows into the layered depths,[5] or hide their peaks among a thousand ranges? One begins by traversing the paths of sprites and goblins, and ends by treading a realm devoid of men. In the whole world there are few who can ascend or scale them, and among the kings, none has observed devout offering there. Thus, accounts about them are omitted from ordinary documents, and their name is signaled only in exotic records.[6] Yet, the flourishing of charts and illustrations, how could this be fanciful? If one is not a man who abandons the world to "play with the Tao," who shuns grains to dine on mushrooms, how can he levitate in order to dwell in them?[7] Unless one "confers himself afar" and "darkly explores,"[8] steadfastly and sincerely communes with the gods, how dare he presume to preserve them in

THIS RHAPSODY by Sun Chuo (*zi* Xinggong) portrays a mystical journey to the Celestial Terrace Mountains (Tiantai 天台) of eastern Zhejiang. The mountain range extended through five prefectures of Guiji commandery: Yuyao 餘姚, Yin 鄞, Juzhang 句章, Shan 剡, and Shining 始寧. The area had just become an important scenic attraction as well as a Buddhist and Taoist center. Sun Chuo's *fu* is the earliest known tribute to these mountains. Sun begins by describing the physical features of the peaks, focussing particularly on the two most prominent sights, the Scarlet Wall, a cragged cliff towering over three hundred meters, and the Cascade, a huge waterfall located in the southwestern part of the range. As he progresses up the slopes, Sun's account becomes more philosophical as he imagines himself roaming the slopes with Taoist immortals and Buddhist arhats. The poem ends in the realm of pure philosophy, in which Buddhist and Taoist concepts are perfectly blended.

[9] This first section, written almost entirely in parallel prose, serves as the preface to the piece.

L. 1: The Grand Void (*Tai xu* 太虛) is the undifferentiated state of the Tao prior to the emergence of concrete forms. In Taoist thought, non-existence (*wu* 無) is prior to existence (*you* 有). "Sublime existence" (*miao you* 妙有) is a term for describing the potential existence that is latent in non-existence. Li Shan (11.5a) explains: "One wishes to speak of Existence (*you*), but cannot see its form. Since it is not (true) Existence (*you*), one calls it sublime Existence. One wishes to speak of things being produced by it. Since it is not Non-existence (*wu*), one calls it Existence. This is none other than Existence within Non-existence."

L. 7: The Oxherd constellation was the celestial coordinate governing the area of Guiji in which the Tiantai Mountains are located. See *Jin shu* 11.310.

L. 9: Hua is Mount Hua in Shaanxi. Dai is Mount Tai in Shandong.

L. 10: On Jiuyi Mountain, see "Wu Capital Rhapsody," L. 492n.

L. 11: The "Tang Canon" is the "Canon of Yao" in the *Shang shu*. As Professor Mather points out ("Mystical Ascent," p. 237, n. 58), the expression "counterpart of Heaven" (*pei tian* 配天) does not occur in this chapter. Yao, however, is compared with Heaven in *Lun yu* 8/19.

L. 12: See n. 3 above.

L. 17: Cf. *Zhuangzi* 6.6a: "The reason the summer insect cannot be told about ice is that it is confined to a single season."

L. 19: Cf. *Lienu zhuan* 5.19b, referring to the conduct of the Loyal Concubine of the Lord of Zhou: "There was nothing so slight in her reputation that could not be made known; in her conduct, there was nothing so obscure to leave unmanifest"

distant imaginings? The reason I gallop my spirit and turn my thoughts over and over, sing by day and rise at night, is that in the space of a nod, it seems I have already ascended them twice. Now I shall release my ropes and bonds, and forever entrust myself to these peaks. Being unable to bear the extremes of recitation aloud and silent thought, I shall resort to literary elegance to dispel my feeling:[9]

II

The Grand Void, vast and wide, unhindered,
Propels sublime Existence, which is naturally so.
Melting, it forms rivers and waterways;
Coalescing, it forms mountains and hills.
5   Ah, the wondrous protrusion of Terrace Peaks,
Verily things upheld by the gods!
Sheltered by the Oxherd, which illumines their crests,
Resting upon numinous Yue, which squares their base,
They set roots broader than those of Hua and Dai,
10   Point straight up, taller than the Jiuyi.
They match "the counterpart of Heaven" of the "Tang Canon,"
Equal the "towering pinnacle" of the "Zhou Odes."

III

So far is that trackless realm,
So dark and deep, secluded and sequestered,
15   Men of shallow knowledge, because of their guarded vision, do not
         go there;
And of those who go, because the path is cut, none knows it well.
Scorning the summer insect for doubting ice,
I preen my light wings longing to soar.
No Noumenon is so obscure to remain ever unmanifest;

Other translations of the *fu* include: von Zach, in *Deutsche Wacht* 15 (1929), and rpt. in *Die Chinesische Anthologie*, 1:159–62; Richard Mather, "The Mystical Ascent of the T'ien-t'ai Mountains," *MS* 20 (1961), 226–45; Watson, *Chinese Rhyme-Prose*, pp. 80–85; Obi Kōichi, *Monzen*, 2:65–75. There are useful notes in Qu Shuiyuan, *Han Wei Liuchao fu xuan*, pp. 162–71. For a seventeenth century account of Mount Tiantai, see Li Chi, trans. *The Travel Diaries of Hsu Hsia-k'o* (Hong Kong: The Chinese University of Hong Kong, 1974), pp. 29–42.

L. 20: The dual wonders are the Scarlet Wall and the Cascade mentioned below.

L. 21: The Scarlet Wall (Chi cheng 赤城) is a southwest peak of the Tiantai range. (It is about 3.5 km northwest of modern Tiantai *xian*, see *Zhongguo mingsheng cidian*, p. 401.) From a distance, the red rocks of its three-hundred-meter high cliff resemble a scarlet wall. According to Zhi Dun's 支遁 (314–366) "Tiantai shan ming xu" 天台山銘序 ("Preface to an Inscription on the Tiantai Mountains")," cited by Li Shan (11.6a), in going to Tiantai, "one must follow the Scarlet Wall Peak as the main path." Kong Lingfu 孔靈符 (n.d.) in his *Guiji ji* 會稽記 (Records of Guiji), cited by Li Shan (11.6a) says "its color is completely scarlet. Its appearance resembles rosy clouds."

L. 22: According to Kong Lingfu's *Guiji ji* (cited by Li Shan 11.6a), the Cascade (Pubu 瀑布) is an 8,000 (sic) foot high waterfall that cascades from Scarlet Wall. Li Shan (11.6a) cites another work, the *Tiantai shan tu* 天台山圖 (Chart of the Tiantai Mountains), which identifies the Cascade as a southwestern peak of the Tiantai range. According to Gu Zuyu 顧祖禹 (1631–1692), *Dushi fangyu jiyao* 讀史方輿紀要 (Essentials of Geography for Reading History) (Beijing: Zhonghua shuju, 1955), 92.3884, the Cascade Mountain was forty *li* west of Tiantai prefecture. It had a cataract 1,000 feet high.

L. 25: Sun Chuo has borrowed this line from the *Chuci* poem "Distant Roaming" (see *Chuci buzhu* 5.5a). The plumed men are the immortals. Cinnabar Hill is an imaginary land inhabited by the immortals.

L. 28: The Storied City (Zeng cheng 增城) is the highest peak of the Kunlun Mountains. According to the *Huainanzi* (4.2b), it is 11,000 *li*, 114 paces, 2 feet, 6 inches high.

L. 29: The term "realm-within" (*yu zhong* 域中) comes from *Laozi* 25. I assume Sun Chuo uses it here to mean the profane world.

L. 32: The metal staff is the staff (*xi zhang* 錫杖) or *khakkara* carried by Buddhist monks. The tip has a metal ring.

L. 35: You Stream 楢溪 (also written You 油), located thirty *li* east of Tiantai prefecture, was one of the forbidding barriers one must cross to enter the mountains. According to Xie Lingyun (see *Song shu* 67.1758), "to go back and forth one must cross Stone Bridge and You Stream. Among the perils of human pathways, nothing surpasses this."

L. 36: One presumes that Sun Chuo here is referring to the boundaries of the five prefectures through which the Tiantai Mountains stretch: Yuyao, Yin, Zuzhang, Shan, and Shining.

LL. 37–38: The Hanging Ledge is the Stone Bridge. The commentary to Gu Kaizhi's 顧愷之 (ca. 345–406) *Qimeng ji* 啓蒙記 (Records for Dispelling Ignorance), a no longer extant lexicon (cited by Li Shan 11.6b), explains that the path of the Stone Bridge "is not a full foot wide and several tens of paces long. Each step is extremely slippery. It looks down on a brook of absolute darkness." The *Zhongguo mingsheng cidian* (pp. 400–401), which locates the Stone Bridge in the Middle Fangguang 方廣 area of the mountains, describes it as a stone span about seven meters long that joins two peaks halfway up the mountain. At its narrowest point it is barely a half-foot wide, and here a cataract (the Fei pu 飛瀑) plunges 1,000 feet into a ravine below.

L. 39: In his "Rhapsody on Mountain Dwelling," Xie Lingyun also refers to the moss-covered stones of the Stone Bridge; see *Song shu* 67.1758.

L. 40: According to Li Shan (11.6b), the Azure Screen (Cui ping 翠屏) is a stone wall located on the Stone Bridge. Kong Lingfu (cited by Li Shan 11.6b) says that its was a boulder that blocked one end of a stone bridge on Scarlet Wall Mountain. It had a path to the side that barely allowed several persons to pass.

LL. 41–42: According to the commentary to Gu Kaizhi's *Qimeng ji*, "to cross Stone Bridge, one clings to the cliff wall, grasps the stalks of creeping fig and grape vines" (cited by Li Shan 11.6b).

20   By unfolding their dual wonders they show their auspice:
Scarlet Wall, rising like rosy clouds, stands as a guidepost;
The Cascade, spraying and flowing, delimits the way.

IV

Seeing these numinous signs, I resolve to go on;
Suddenly I begin to move.
25   I meet plumed men on Cinnabar Hill,
Search for the blessed chambers of immortality.
As long as the Terrace range can be scaled,
Why yearn for the Storied City?
Released from the constant cravings of the "realm-within,"
30   Cheered by the exalted feeling of transcendency,
I don wooly homespun, all furry and fleecy,
Wield a metal staff, jingling and jangling.
I push through a murky mass of wild thickets,
Scale the soaring steepness of scarps and cliffs,
35   Ford You Stream and straightway advance,
Cross the Five Boundaries and swiftly push on.
Straddling the vaulted Hanging Ledge,
I look down into absolute darkness, a myriad fathoms below
I tread slippery stones covered with moss,
40   Cling to Azure Screen that wall-like stands,
Grasp the long fig creepers on bending trees,
Snatch flying stalks of trailing grape.

L. 43: The *locus classicus* for the expression *chui tang* 垂堂, which literally means "to brink the hall," is the *Shï ji* biography of Yuan Ang (101.2740; *Records*, 1:521): Yuan Ang said to Emperor Wen, "Your servant has heard that the son of a thousand gold-piece estate in sitting does not brink the hall."

L. 55: According to Gu Zuyu (see *Dushi fangyu jiyao* (92.3885), the Numinous Stream (Ling xi 靈溪) was located twenty *li* east of Tiantai prefecture. Near the sea, it joined You Stream.

L. 57: The residual dust is the "six dusts" (*liu chen*) or *gunas* (senses): *se* 色 (sight, *rūpa*), *sheng* 聲 (sound, *śabda*), *xiang* 香 (smell, *gandha*), *wei* 味 (taste, *rasa*), *chu* 觸 (touch, *sparśa*), and *fa* 法 (thought, *manas*).

L. 58: The Five Hindrances (*Wu gai* 五蓋) or *Nīvarana* are: *tan yin* 貪淫 (desire and licentiousness, *kāmacchanda*); *chen hui* 瞋恚 (rage and anger, *vyāpāda*); *chenhun shuimian* 沈惛睡眠 (dullness and drowsiness; *styānamiddha*); *tiaoxi* 調戲 (frivolity, *auddahatyakautrya*); *yi* 疑 (doubt, vicikitsā). See Erich Zürcher, *The Buddhist Conquest of China*, 2:375, n. 43.

L. 59: Xi is Fu Xi; Nong is Shennong.

L. 60: The Two Laos are Laozi and Lao Laizi 老萊子, who was sometimes confused with Laozi.

L. 62: According to the *Hainei shizhou ji* 海內十州記 (Record of the Ten Continents within the Seas), attributed to Dongfang Shuo, the City of the Immortals (Xian du 僊都) was a purple stone palace on the Blue Sea Isle (Cang hai dao 滄海島) located in the Northern Sea. See *Baoyan tang miji* 寶顏堂秘笈 edition, p. 3b.

LL. 63–66: According to the commentary to Gu Kaizhi's *Qimeng ji* (cited by Li Shan 11.8a), the "Tiantai Mountains had twin gateways in the midst of the blue empyrean. Above them are carnelian towers, agate groves, sweet springs, and articles of immortals, all complete." As Sun Chuo depicts them, these gateways, terraces, and halls are all imaginary. However, later gazetteers specify their exact location. Zhu Jian (12.3a) speculates that people of a later time derived the names from Sun Chuo's rhapsody.

L. 69: Eight Cinnamon (Ba gui 八桂) is the name of a legendary grove that the *Shanhai jing* (10.1b) locates east of Panyu 番隅 (near modern Guangzhou). According to Guo Pu, the eight trees were so large, they formed a grove. Zhu Jian (12.3a) notes that the *Dushi fangyu jiyao* (89.3735) mentions a group of five peaks in the Tiantai Mountains, one of which is called Eight Cinnamon. I suspect that this name is quite late, and in fact may be derived from Sun Chuo's *fu*.

L. 70: The *Mao jun neizhuan* 茅君內傳 (Esoteric Biography of Lord Mao), attributed to Li Zun 李遵 (n.d.), cited in *Hou Han shu* 28B.1000, n. 4), says that on Gouqu 句曲 Mountain (= Mao shan 茅山 of modern Jurong *xian*, Jiangsu), the Five Polypores grow. "The first is called Dragon Transcendent Polypore. It resembles kraken and dragon carrying one another (?). If one ingests it, he will become Transcendent Chancellor of the Grand Culmen. The second is called Triply-created Polypore Its scarlet hues are lustrous. Its branches and leaves have sounds like bells and chimes. Break it and reconnect it, and it immediately returns to its former state. Ingest it and one becomes Grandee of the Great Culmen. The third is called Swallow Embryo Polypore. Its color is purple, and it is shaped like mallow. On its leaves there is the form of a swallow. Its lustrous radiance is penetrating. Ingest one stalk and one will be appointed Dragon-and-Tiger Transcendent Lord of Grand Purity. The fourth is called Night-glower Polypore. Its color is blue, and its fruit is pure white like a plum. Viewed at night, its fruit resembles the moon, its light illumining a whole room. Ingest one stalk and one will become a Transcendent Officer in Grand Purity. The fifth is called Jade Polypore. Cut one open and eat it, and one will be appointed Honorable Notary Proper and True of the Three Officers."

L. 73: The Standing Tree (Jian mu 建木) is a fabulous tree mentioned in several early texts. The *Huainanzi* (4.3a–b) and *Lüshi chunqiu* (13.3b) describe it as the tree upon which the gods ascend and descend. "At midday it casts no shadow, and when one calls, there is no echo.

248

Though once imperiled at the brink,
I shall exist forever in eternal life.
45 As long as I steadfastly plight my faith to the Hidden Darkness,
I can tread the layered steepness and find it smooth.

V

Once I successfully scale the nine switchbacks,
I find the road straight and smooth, long and clear.
I indulge in the vast clarity of mind and eye,
50 Give free rein to the relaxed ease of slowly pacing.
Spreading tender grasses, lush and luxuriant,
Shaded by tall pines, stalwart and stately,
I view the graceful gliding of soaring simurghs,
Hear the concordant chorusing of singing phoenixes.
55 Once I cross the Numinous Stream and wash myself,
I purge vexatious thoughts from mind and breast,
Cleanse the residual dust in its whirling flow,
Expel the haunting gloom of the Five Hindrances.
I pursue the vanished tracks of Xi and Nong,
60 Tread the dark trail of the Two Laos.

VI

I climb up and down for one night, two nights,
Until I reach the City of Immortals.
Twin gateways, thrusting into the clouds, flank the road,
Carnelian terraces, mid-sky, hang overhead,
65 Vermilion pavilions stand lucent and lustrous through the woods,
Jade halls dimly shine from high nooks.
Rose clouds, streaked and striped, glide into lattices;
The dazzling sun fulgently flares through silken filigree.
Eight Cinnamon, thick and tall, brave the frost;
70 Five Polypores, laden with blooms, unfold at dawn.
Gentle breezes store fragrance in sunny groves,
Sweet springs bubble and burble from shady moats,
The Standing Tree erases shadows for a thousand *xun*,

This probably is because it is in the center of Heaven and Earth." See also *Shanhai jing* 10.4a and 18.3b–4a for other descriptions of it.

L. 74: The word *qi* in this line possibly is short for *yuqi* 玗琪, a tree that the *Shanhai jing* (11.4b) claims grew on the slopes of the Kunlun Mountains. Guo Pu identifies *yuqi* as a type of scarlet jade. Lacking a precise identification, I have simply called it the "gem tree."

L. 75: On the immortal Wang Qiao, see "Western Capital Rhapsody," L. 305.

L. 76: The correspondents-to-truth are the *luohan* 羅漢 or Buddhist arhats who resided at the summit of the Tiantai peaks. See Mather, "Mystical Ascent," p. 241, n. 100.

L. 78: This line seems derived from a saying of Laozi, as recorded in *Huainanzi* 1.10b (cf. *Laozi* 43): "The softest thing in the world rides over the hardest things in the world. It emerges from where there is nothing, and enters into where there are no gaps."

L. 81: Cf. *Zhuangzi* 8.14a, where the Yellow Lord asks a young horse herder how to govern the empire. The boy answered, "Governing the empire, how is it different from herding horses? All you need do is get rid of what harms the horses." "That which harms the horses." (*hai ma* 害馬) is excessive activity.

LL. 83–84: Sun Chuo alludes to the famous *Zhuangzi* (1.1b–2b) parable of Butcher Ding, who used a mystical approach to butchering an ox: "When I began cutting up an ox, what I saw was nothing but an ox, but after three years, I no longer saw a whole ox. Now I encounter things with my spirit, and I do not look with my eyes." Thus, in his carving he never meets with any obstacles.

L. 87: Xihe is charioteer of the sun.

L. 89: Dharma drums (*fa gu* 法鼓) summon the monks to assembly.

L. 91: Li Shan (11.9a) identifies the Celestially-venerated (Tian zong 天宗) as Lao jun 老君 or the deified Laozi. However, as Zhu Jian (12.3b) points out, the term Celestially-venerated appears in the "Yue ling" (see *Li ji zhushu* 17.14a) as the name of the heavenly bodies (sun, moon, and stars) worshiped by the Son of Heaven in the tenth month. Zhu argues that it is only fitting from the mountain heights, which are near the luminous heavenly bodies, to pay one's respects to the celestial gods.

L. 93: Jade oil (*yu gao* 玉膏) is a liquid form of jade, which when drunk, confers immortality. The *Shanhai jing* (2.14a) mentions a mountain that produces a jade that has a white oil. "Its springs froth and foam, gurgle and burble. The Yellow Lord on this dines and feasts. This produces black jade, from which comes a jade oil that is used to water cinnabar trees."

L. 94: The Floriate Pond (Hua chi 華池) is a legendary lake in the Kunlun Mountains. See *Lun heng jijie* 11.218, citing "The Basic Annals of Yu" in the *Shi ji*. Cf. *Shi ji* 123.3179, which reads "Jasper Pond" for "Floriate Pond."

L. 95: The doctrine of "beyond images" (*xiang wai* 象外) is the Tao, which cannot be verbalized or even represented in images. The term apparently was current in Sun Chuo's time. It appears in a debate recorded in Pei Songzhi's *Sanguo zhi* commentary (10.319–20). For a translation, see Mather, "Mystical Ascent," p. 244, n. 108.

L. 96: The texts of "non-origination" (*wu sheng* 無生) are Buddhist texts. For a brief explication of the concept of non-origination in early Chinese Buddhism, see Mather, "Mystical Ascent," p. 244, n. 109.

LL. 97–98: Existence (*you*) here means the profane realm of illusion and desire. In the Taoist thought of this period, Non-existence (*wu*) was considered the source of Existence. The goal of both Buddhist and Taoist adepts was to obtain communion with the ultimate reality, which was beyond form.

L. 99: The Mayahana Buddhists taught the doctrine that *se* 色 (form, matter, *rūpa*) is empty (void and illusory). Sun Chuo's line is an elaboration on this theory. If one understands that form is emptiness, then he can obliterate even the distinction between form and emptiness.

Gem trees, glittering and gleaming, hang with pearls.
75 Wang Qiao, driving a crane, pierces the sky;
"Correspondents-to-truth," their staves flying, tread the void.
Galloping with the swift speed of spiritual transformation,
Suddenly they emerge from Existence and enter Non-existence.

VII

And then
When my sightseeing completes its circuit,
80 My body is calm, my heart is at ease.
What "harms the horses" has been expelled,
Worldly affairs all are rejected.
Wherever I cast my blade it is always hollow;
I eye the ox but not as a whole.
85 I focus my thoughts on secluded cliffs,
Clearly chant by long streams.
Then,
When Xihe reaches the meridian,
The coursing vapors are lifted high.
Dharma drums, booming, spread their sounds;
90 Various incenses fragrantly waft their fumes.
Now we shall pay our respects to the Celestially-venerated,
And assemble the immortal hosts.
I ladle the black jade oil,
Rinse my mouth in Floriate Pond springs.
95 Inspired by the doctrine of "beyond images,"
Illumined by the texts on "non-origination,"
I become aware that I have not completely dismissed Existence,
And realize that there are interruptions in the passage to Non-
    existence.
I destroy Form and Emptiness, blending them into one;

251

L. 100: This line is ambiguous. Professor Mather ("Mystical Ascent," p. 244) translates differently: "Oblivious of Actuality-itself, I gain the Mystery." The question is how to construe *ji you* 郎有 (Mather's "Actuality-itself"). Li Shan (11.9b) takes *ji* as verb meaning "to go to." He cites Wang Bi's theory of *wu* (Non-existence) as the source of *you* (Existence). "Although Wang considered Non-existence as the root, Non-existence used Existence to do its work. If one wishes to understand Non-existence, one must base himself on Existence. Thus, one 'proceeds to Existence' and attains the Mystery." Mystery (*xuan* 玄) is another name for the ulimate reality (*wu*). Wang Bi (see *Laozi*, A.1b) defines it as "dark, silent, and non-existent."

L. 101: The two names are "that having name" (*you ming* 有名) and "the nameless" (*wu ming* 無名), epithets for Existence and Non-existence respectively in *Laozi* 1: "The nameless is the beginning of Heaven and Earth, and the named is the mother of the myriad things.... These two come from a common source but differ in name."

L. 102: According to Li Shan (11.9b–10a) the Three Banners (*San fan* 三幡) are form (*se*), emptiness (*kong*), and contemplation (*guan*). Li bases his explanation on a letter from the Buddhist layman Xi Chao 郗超 (336–377), part of which he cites: "The various people of recent times who discuss the Three Banners are still full of desire. Having contemplated form and emptiness, they proceed separately to contemplate consciousness. Although they all reside in a single existence, they are subject to two contemplations. This explanation is the most reasonable." Li Shan concludes: "In Xi Chao's view, form, emptiness, and contemplation are the Three Banners; consciousness, emptiness, and contemplation are also the Three Banners." Sun Chuo rejects any distinction between form, emptiness, and contemplation, and reduces them to Non-existence, which is single and indivisible.

LL. 103–4: Sun Chuo stresses the complementary relationship that exists between speech and silence as both manifestations of the Tao. Li Shan (11.10a) explains: "Words are generated from the Tao, and the Tao is expounded by words. The Tao relies on words, but their basic ordering principle reverts to the empty unity." The language of the line is similar to *Zhuangzi* 9.7a: "If one utters non-words, he may speak his entire life and never say anything. Yet, if one does not speak his entire life, he will never cease speaking."

L. 1: The area north, south, and east of Yangzhou is plain. Only to the west are there hills. See L. 5n below.

L. 2: Green Kola is my fanciful invention for Cangwu, which here refers to the commandery in extreme south China. See "Rhapsody on the Imperial Park," L. 28n. Swollen Sea (Zhang hai 漲海) is another name for the Southern Sea. See *Erya yishu* C4.7b.

L. 3: Purple Pass (Zi sai 紫塞) is another name for the Great Wall built by the Qin. According to the *Gujin zhu* (A.7a), the soil used to built the Qin wall was purple, and hence the name Purple Pass. Goose Gate (Yan men 鴈門) was a commandery located northwest of modern Dai *xian*, Shanxi.

L. 4: The Transport Canal (Cao qu 漕渠) is the Han Canal 邗溝, originally built in 486 B.C. by the state of Wu to connect the Yangzi with the Huai River; see *Zuozhuan*, *Ai* 9; Legge, 5:819; Chen Dazuo and Zhu Jiang, "Hancheng yizhi," pp. 45–47. It later became part of the Grand Canal that extends from Yangzhou to Huaian 淮安, The image Bao Zhao intended to convey here is ambiguous. Depending on how one construes *duo* 柂, which can mean "to pull" or "rudder" (on the problems of the correct reading see Liang Zhangju 13.6a), the line could be portraying Guangling towing the canal, or Guangling as a boat with the canal as its rudder (see *Wei Jin Nanbei chao wenxueshi cankao ziliao*, p. 516, n. 4).

L. 5: Kun Ridge is Kunlun Ridge 崑崙崗, also known as Guangling Ridge and Hillock Ridge (Fu gang 阜崗). These are other names for the modern Shu Ridge 蜀崗, a long low ridge of hills that stretches west from Liuhe 六合 to Wantou 灣頭 (formerly called Zhuyu wan 茱萸灣) northwest of Yangzhou. The city of Guangling was built on top of it. See *Taiping huanyu ji* 123 4a–b; *Dushi fangyu jiyao* 23.1063; Akedanga 阿克當阿 and Yao Wentian 姚文田

100   Suddenly I proceed to Existence where I attain the Mystery.
      I release the two names that come from a common source,
      Dissolve the Three Banners to a single Non-existence.
      All day long giving oneself to conversation's delights,
      Is the same as the still silence of not speaking.
105   I merge the myriad phenomena in mystic contemplation,
      Unconciously join my body with the Naturally-so.

Rhapsody on the Ruined City

BAO MINGYUAN

I

Smooth and gently sloping, a level plain:
Southward gallops to Green Kola and Swollen Sea,
Northward races to Purple Pass and Goose Gate.
With the Transport Canal in tow,

5   And Kun Ridge as its axle,
It is a nook of doubling rivers and enfolding passes,
A hub where four highways converge, where five intersect.

IN THIS RHAPSODY Bao Zhao (*zi* Mingyuan) describes the ruined city of Guangling 廣陵. Chinese archaeologists have located the site of ancient Guangling on Shu gang 蜀崗, two kilometers northwest of modern Yangzhou. See Ji Zhongqing 紀仲慶, "Yangzhou gucheng zhi bianqian chutan" 揚州古城址變遷初探, *Wenwu* (1979:9):pp. 43–56. The city goes back at least to 486 B.C., when King Fuchai of Wu built the fortified city of Han 邗城. See Chen Dazuo 陳達祚 and Zhu Jiang 朱江, "Hancheng yizhi yu Hangou liujing quyu wenhua yicun de faxian" 邗城遺址與邗溝流經區域文化遺存的發現, *Wenwu* (1973:12):pp. 44–54. In the early Han dynasty, King Liu Pi of Wu established Guangling as one of the grandest cities in the empire. Guangling reputedly had a circumference of fourteen and a half *li* (approximately seven kilometers; see *Hou Han shu*, "Zhi," 21.3461, n 1; Ji Zhongqing, "Yangzhou gucheng," pp. 48–49). In 154 B.C. Liu Pi even dared to instigate what turned out to be an unsuccessful revolt of seven kingdoms against Emperor Jing. See *Shi ji* 106.2823–36; *Records*, 1:466–85. Because of its location on the north bank of the Yangzi across from the capital, Guangling was a strategic city throughout the Six Dynasties. In the winter of A.D 225, the Wei emperor Cao Pi led his army to the "old city of Guangling" hoping to cross the Yangzi and engage Sun Quan of Wu in battle. When he could not sail his boats across the frozen waters, he exclaimed, "Truly it is Heaven that separates north and south!" (see *Sanguo zhi* 2.85; 47.1132, n. 3).
       In 443, Emperor Wen enfeoffed his sixth son, Liu Dan 劉誕 (433–459), as king of Guangling (see *Song shu* 79.2025; *Nan shi* 14.396). In 447, Liu Dan's father-in-law Xu Zhanzhi 徐湛之 came to Guangling as governor of Southern Yanzhou 南兗州 (modern Yangzhou).

(1758–1827), comps. *Yangzhou fu zhi* 揚州府志 (Gazetteer of Yangzhou Prefecture) (Taibei: Chengwen chubanshe, 1974), 8.500–502; Gu Zuyu, *Dushi fangyu jiyao* 23.1063; Ji Zhongqing, "Yangzhou gucheng," pp. 44–47. According to the *Hetu kuodi xiang* (cited by Li Shan 11.10b), Kun Slope passed through Guangling as an "earthen axle." The idea is that Kun Slope steadied the city like a chariot axle.

LL. 14–15: This clearly is a reference to the activities of King Liu Pi of Wu, who recruited fugitives from all over the empire to mine the copper in the hills and boil sea water to make salt. See *Shi ji* 106.2822; *Records*, 1:466; *Han shu* 35.1904. According to the *Taiping huanyu ji* (123.4a), the mountains from which the Liu Pi obtained copper were the Datong 大銅 (Great Copper) Mountains, located seventy-two *li* west of Yangzhou. Wei Zhao locates them in Guzhang 故鄣 (northwest of modern Anji 安吉, Zhejiang). See *Han shu* 35.1904, n. 1.

LL. 17–18: Cf. "Western Metropolis Rhapsody," LL. 92–93. The laws and institutes must be the sumptuary regulations that stipulated the maximum size of a building. Anything beyond the stipulated limit was deemed "extravagant."

L. 22: The phrase *banzhu* 板築 (literally "planks and rammer") refers to the method of building ancient Chinese walls. The space between facing boards was filled with earth and then tamped down in layers until solid. According to Qu Shuiyuan (p. 180, n. 20), here *benzhu* is metonymy for walls.

II

In the past
During its age of consummate splendor,
Chariots rubbed axle-hub to axle-hub,
10   Men bumped shoulder to shoulder,
Settlements and ward gates covered the land,
Singing and piping pierced the sky.
It multiplied wealth with its salt fields,
Dug profits from the copper hills.
15   In talent and man power it was strong and rich;
Warriors and steeds were well-trained and well-fitted.

Thus, it was able
To exceed the laws of Qin,
Surpass the institutes of Zhou,
And carve lofty fortresses,
20   Dredge deep moats,
Planning for long reigns and a propitious mandate.

Thus,
Rammed earth walls and parapets, grandly constructed,

He must have found the city in bad condition, for he began the repair of old wall towers, restocked the ponds north of the city with plants and fish, and built new breeze pavilions, moon viewing towers, flute terraces, and zither chambers. "Fruit and bamboo were lush and luxuriant, flowers and herbs were planted in rows" (see *Song shu* 71.1847). However, these repairs apparently were not sufficient, for in 449, because of Guangling's 'withered and decrepit" condition, the emperor transferred Liu Dan's fief to Sui 隨 (modern Suizhou 隨州, Hubei).

In January 451, an army of the Northern Wei invaded the Guangling area and advanced as far as Guabu 瓜步 (southeast of modern Liuhe 六合 *xian*, Jiangsu), directly across the Yangzi from the capital. Within a month, the Song army repelled the invaders, but not before the area around Guangling had been reduced to "barren land with nothing remaining" (see *Nan shi* 2.52). Liu Dan returned to Guangling in 457 and ordered the repair of the damage inflicted by the Wei invaders (see *Song shu* 79.2027; *Nan shi* 14.397). Suspicious of Liu Dan's increasing independence, Emperor Xiaowu 孝武 (reg. 454–464) had him charged with plotting rebellion. In 459 an army led by Shen Qingzhi 沈慶之 stormed Guangling and killed Liu Dan. Shen had all adult males in the city put to death, and women were given as "rewards to the army" (see *Song shu* 6.123; 79.2036).

Li Zhouhan (11.13a) claims that Bao Zhao accompanied Liu Zixu 劉子頊 (wrongly cited as Liu Zizhen 劉子瑱), Prince of Linhai 臨海 (457–466), to Guangling where he rebelled. According to Li, when Bao Zhao saw Guangling in ruins, he was reminded of King Liu Pi of Wu, who had failed in his attempted revolt during the Former Han. "Equating the deeds of Zixu with those of Pi, Bao Zhao was roused to write this *fu* as a means of criticizing Zixu."

L. 23: The well-curb refers to the series of well-curb shaped trusses that formed that tower. See "Western Capital Rhapsody," L. 276n.

L. 24: On the Five Peaks, see "Eastern Capital Rhapsody," L. 319n.

L. 25: Many commentators have been baffled by the term *San fen* 三墳, which commonly designates a set of three ancient scriptures (see *Wen xuan*, volume one, p. 507, n 190). I have followed the suggestion of Hong Liangji 洪亮吉 (1746–1809), who cites one of the enigmas from the "Celestial Questions" (see *Chuci buzhu* 3.5b) in which *fen* is used in the sense of "to divide": "The nine grades of territory, how was Yu able to divide (*fen*) them?" See *Xiao dushu zhai zalu* 曉讀書齋雜錄 (Miscellaneous Notes from the Morning Reading Studio), in *Hong Beijang xiansheng quanji* 洪北江先生全集 (The Complete Works of Hong Liangji), Shou jing tang 授經堂, 1877–79, *ce* 25, B.16b. For other interpretations, see Zhu Jian 12.4a; Hu Shaoying 13.6b–7a; Liang Zhangju 13.7a.

L. 30: The *locus classicus* for the phrase *gu huo* 固護 is the *Record of Rites* (see *Li ji zhushu* 2 21b), where it means "tenacious and rapacious." Bao Zhao has extended it to the sense of "solidity and defense."

L. 32: The three dynasties are the Han, Wei, and Jin.

L. 35: Li Shan (11.11b), citing Wang Yi's *Chuci* commentary, seems to equate *ze kui* 澤葵 with *shui kui* 水葵, which is the name for two different plants: *xing cai* 莕菜 (fringed water lily) or *chun cai* 純菜 (water shield). Zhu Jian (12.4b) notes that both are water plants that would not grow on the side of wells. Fang Yizhi (see *Tong ya* 42.4a) claims the *ze kui* is a type of moss that clings to the ground like small pine leaves. The slightly larger ones are called *chang song* 長松. Zhu adds that although Fang's description fits the well-side habitat, there is no clear evidence for the identification. Zhu apparently was unaware of the *Shu yi ji* passage (A.9b) that gives *ze kui* as one of several names for moss. I have thus invented the name "marsh moss" for it.

L. 37: The *hui* 虺 specifically is the bamboo snake. See Read, *Dragon and Snake Drugs*, p. 50, #121 The *yu* 蜮, also called *duan hu* 短狐, is the bombardier-beetle. See Read, *Insect Drugs*, pp. 178–80, #92.

L. 38: The *jun* 麕 is the river deer. See Read, *Animal Drugs*, #368. *Wu* is short for *wushu* 鼯鼠, flying squirrel.

Well-curb lookouts and beacon towers, meticulously crafted,
In measure higher than the Five Peaks,
25   In breadth wider than the Three Divisions,
Jutted up like sheer cliffs,
Abruptly rose like long clouds.
They built lodestones to resist assault,
Daubed carmine loam to make soaring designs.
30   Beholding the solidity and defense of its foundation walls,
Couldn't a single lord's house hold them for ten thousand years?
Yet, as three dynasties have entered and exited,
And over five hundred years have passed,
It has been carved like a melon, split like beans.

III

35   Marsh moss clings to the wells,
Wild kudzu vines tangle the paths;
The halls are filled with snakes and beetles,
By stairs contend deer and flying squirrels.
Wood sprites and mountain demons,
40   Field rats, wall foxes,

However, Liang Zhangju (13.6b) points out that Liu Zixu was just eleven years old at the time of his rebellion, which actually was instigated by another prince and his adviser. Thus, the analogy with Liu Pi is not apposite. Qian Zhonglian 錢仲聯 further observes that while Bao Zhao served on Liu Zixu's staff, Liu was governor of Jingzhou (in modern Hubei), and that he never accompanied Liu to Guangling. Following He Zhuo (*Yimen dushu ji* 45.25a), Qian surmises that Bao wrote "Rhapsody on the Ruined City" around 459–460 to depict the destruction the city suffered during Liu Dan's revolt. See *Bao Canjun jizhu* 鮑參軍集注 (1957; rev. Shanghai: Guji kanxingshe, 1980), 1.14–15.

Although Qian's interpretation is widely accepted, I think it is possible that the ruin Bao Zhao describes is not his contemporary Guangling, but the old Han ruin of Guangling. Under the title "Rhapsody on the Ruined City," Li Shan (11.10a) cites the *Collected Works* (presmably Bao Zhao's collected works), which says: "written upon climbing the old city of Guangling" (for the correct reading see Hu Kejia, *Wen xuan kaoyi* 2.23b). The *Taiping huanyu ji* (123.4a) under the entry Wu cheng 蕪城 (Ruined City) has the following intriguing statement: "It is the prefectural capital. In ancient times it was Hangou cheng 邗溝城 (= Hancheng). After the Han it was ruined and destroyed. This is the place about which the Song literatus Bao Mingyuan wrote a fu." Similarly, the *Jiaqing chongxiu da Qing yitong zhi* 嘉慶重修大清一統志 (Comprehensive Gazetteer of the Qing, Revised during the Jiaqing Period) (*Sbck*, 97.1a) considers Wucheng as the old Han ruin: "In the sixth year of Huangchu, Emperor Wen visited the old city of Guangling. This is the Ruined City about which Bao Zhao wrote a fu." The identification of Bao's Ruined City with the Han ruin of Guangling makes sense in terms of the poem itself, for in the *fu*, Bao makes repeated references to Liu Pi, the Wu king who rebuilt

L. 45: Lɪ Shan (11.2a) says that *bao* 虣 is an ancient script form for *bao* 暴 (violent), which makes no sense in this context. Li also notes that that some texts read *han* 虤 for *bao*. The *Erya* (C6.3b) defines *han* as a white tiger. This seems to be the same creature listed in the *Shuowen* (5A.2109a–2110a) as *mi* 虤. See Liang Zhangju 13.7b, who insists that the *Wen xuan* text should be emended to *mi*.

Howling in the wind, shrieking in the rain,
Appear at night, take flight at dawn.
Hungry hawks sharpen their beaks,
Cold kites hoot at young birds.
45　Crouching felines, lurking tigers,
Suckle blood, sup on flesh.

Fallen thickets blocking the road
Grow dense and dark on the ancient highway.
White poplars early shed their leaves;
50　Wall grasses prematurely wither.
Bitter and biting is the frosty air;
Roaring and raging, the wind's might.
A lone tumbleweed bestirs itself;
Startled sand flies without cause.
55　Brushy scrub darkly stretches without end;
Clustered copses wildly intertwine.
The surrounding moat had already been leveled;
The lofty turrets too have fallen.
Looking straight ahead for a thousand miles and beyond,
60　One only sees rising yellow dust.

Guangling in the early Han. Further, Bao portrays the site as a long-existing ruin. The "moat had already been leveled," the corner wall towers had collapsed, rats, foxes, deer, squirrels, snakes, and beetles inhabit the chambers and halls. Such description hardly befits a city that had only recently been ravaged. In fact, there is no evidence to indicate that Guangling was ruined or abandoned as a consequence of the 459 siege. See Cao Daoheng 曹道衡, "Bao Zhao jipian shi wen de xiezuo shijian" 鮑照幾篇詩文的寫作時間, Wen shi 16 (1982): 199. Bao is more likely to have visited Guangling in 451, when he accompanied his patron Liu Jun 劉濬 (429–453), who led a force to the Guangling area to refortify Guabu after the Northern Wei invasion. Bao very well may have found the old city of Guangling in ruins.

For other commentaries to the fu, I have consulted Qian Zhonglian, ed., Bao Canjun jizhu 1.13–24; Rao Zongyi, "Wucheng fu fawei" 蕪城賦發微, Dongfang zazhi 41.4 (1945): 58–61; Qu Shuiyuan, Han Wei Liuchao fu xuan, pp. 178–82; Wei Jin Nanbei chao wenxueshi cankao ziliao, pp. 515–24; Feng Dalun 馮大綸, in Gujin wenxuan 4–1505–8; Lin Junrong 林俊榮, Wei Jin Nanbei chao wenxue zuopin xuan 魏晉南北朝文學作品選 (Jilin: Jilin renmin wenxue chubanshe, 1980), pp. 141–46; Pei Jinnan, et al., Han Wei Liuchao fu xuan zhu, pp. 144–49. Previous translations include: von Zach, in Deutsche Wacht 15 (1929) and rpt. in Die Chinesische Anthologie, 1:162–64; Georges Margouliès and W. R. Trask, "Great Chinese Prose," Asia 34 (1934): 303; Margouliès, Anthologie raisonnée, pp. 140–42; Jerome Chen and Michael Bullock, Poems of Solitude (London: Aberlard-Schumann, Ltd., 1960), pp. 39–42 and rpt. in Cyril Birch and Donald Keene, eds. Anthology of Chinese Literature. From Early Times to the Fourteenth Century (New York: Grove Press, 1965), pp. 190–93; Itō Masafumi and Ikkai Tomoyoshi, Kan Gi Rikuchō Tō Sō sambun sen, pp. 201–2; Obi Kōichi, Monzen, 2:76–81; Watson, Chinese Rhyme-Prose, pp. 92–95.

L. 67: Wu corresponds to modern Jiangsu; Cai, to eastern Henan; Qi, to Shandong; and Qin to Shaanxi

L. 68: See "Western Metropolis Rhapsody," L. 714n and L. 717n

L. 71: The Eastern Capital is Luoyang.

L. 73: The fragrant plant *hui* 蕙 (sweet basil; melilotus) represents female beauty and goodness.

L. 78· The term *li gong* 離宮 literally means "detached palace." However, because of its use in Sima Xiagru's "Tall Gate Palace Rhapsody," which tells of an empress living alone in a detached palace, the term has acquired the sense of "sequestered palace." See David R. Knechtges, "Ssu-ma Hsiang-ju's 'Tall Gate Palace Rhapsody,'" *HJAS* 41.1 (1981), 47–64.

L. 85: The wells probably imply "well fields."

Focus one's thoughts, quietly listen:
The heart is pained and broken.

IV

As for
Carved gates, embroidered curtains,
Sites of singing halls and dance pavilions;
65　Carnelian pools, prase trees,
Lodges of fowling groves and fishing isles;
The music of Wu, Cai, Qi, and Qin,
Amusements of the dragon-fish, ostrich, and horse:

All have vanished in smoke, have been reduced to ashes,
70　Their brilliance engulfed, their sounds silenced.
Exquisite consorts from the Eastern Capital,
Beauties from southern states,
With hearts of melilot, complexions of white silk,
Jade features, scarlet lips:
75　There is none whose soul rests unburied in somber stones,
Whose bones lie unscattered in bleak dust.
Can you recall the joyful pleasures of sharing the carriage,
Or the painful misery of the sequestered palace?

Heaven's way, how is it
80　That so many swallow grief?
I grasp my zither and name a tune;
I play "The Song of the Ruined City."
The song goes:
Border winds are fierce,
Above the wall it is cold.
85　Wells and paths have vanished,
Hillocks and mounds are destroyed.
A thousand years, ten thousand ages,
Everyone is gone—what can one say?

Hall of Numinous Brilliance in Lu

1 Vermillion Gateways	4 The Speedway
2 Tall Portals	5 Sunlit Pavilion
3 The Grand Stairway	6 Watersoaked Terrace

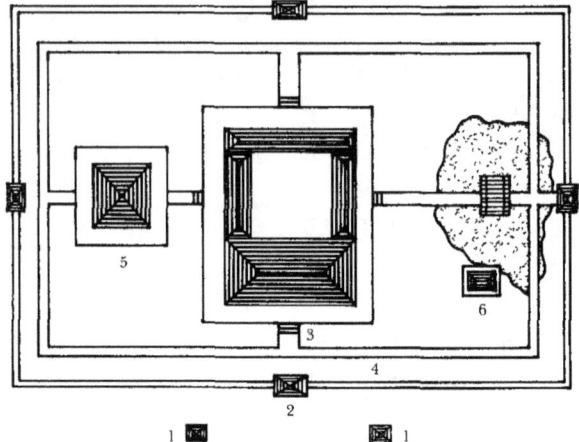

[1] For his dates, see *Shi ji* 17.841–58, which gives 26 years as the length of his rule in Lu. *Han shu* 14.410 says his rule lasted 28 years. *Han shu* 6.170 places his death in 128 B.C.

[2] Cf. *Shi ji* 59.2095; *Records*, 1.452; *Han shu* 53.2413.

[3] Duke Xi 僖 of Lu (reg. 659–627 B.C.) sent the ducal son Xi Si 奚斯 to restore the temple of Jiang Yuan (the mother of Hou Ji, the founder of the Zhou house), and build the temple of Duke Min 閔 (reg. 661–660 B C), Duke Xi's father. (I follow Zhu Jian's emendation of Duke Min for Duke Wen of Zhang Zai's commentary) See *Mao shi zhushu* 20.2.15b, Zheng Xuan's commentary.

[4] These were the two main Former Han palaces in Chang'an. They are described extensively in the "Western Capital Rhapsody" and "Western Metropolis Rhapsody."

[5] See LL. 78–79 below.

[6] Wang was from Yicheng, which was located in Nan 南 (South) Commandery.

[7] On this poem, see "Western Capital Rhapsody," n. 15.

Rhapsody on the Hall of Numinous Brilliance in Lu

WANG WENKAO   Commentary by Zhang Zai

The Hall of Numinous Brillance in Lu was built by Liu Yu, King Gong, who was the son of Lady Cheng, concubine of Emperor Jing.[1] Originally, when King Gong first established a capital in his lesser state, he was fond of palaces and halls.[2] Thus, based on the old foundation erected by Duke Xi of Lu, he built this hall.[3] When the Han began to weaken in the middle of the dynasty, bandits and brigands raced and rampaged, and all the halls, including the Everlasting and Jianzhang palaces,[4] were ruined and destroyed. Yet, Numinous Brilliance alone survived intact. Upon reflection, I wonder if this could be because a divine intelligence rested here and supported it to preserve the Han house. Yet, that its design and dimensions correspond to the stars and constellations above is further reason for its prolonged stability.[5] I have traveled from the southern frontier to peruse the classics in Lu.[6] Upon seeing this I was astounded. I said, "Alas! The inspiration of a poet arises from his reaction to things. Thus, when Xi Si lauded Duke Xi, and sang of the Grand Chamber, the duke's feats and accomplishments were preserved in the lyrics, and his virtuous renown was displayed in the music.[7] Objects are glorified in rhapsodies, and deeds are

THIS RHAPSODY by Wang Yanshou (*zi* Wenkao) describes the Hall of Numinous Brilliance (Ling guan dian 靈光殿), which was constructed by the Han king, Liu Yu 劉餘, King Gong 恭 of Lu 魯 (reg. 154–129/128 B.C.). The palace continued to be used by Lu kings in the Later Han. See *Hou Han shu* 42.1424. The southern gateway of the hall was five hundred paces (693 m) southeast of the Confucian Temple in Qufu 曲阜, Shandong. The foundation, which was still standing in the sixth century, was 24 *zhang* (55.44 m) from east to west, 12 *zhang* (27.72 m) from north to south, and over 1 *zhang* (2.31 m) high. Behind the main hall were east and west wings, each 4 *zhang* (9.24 m) wide and 16 *zhang* (37.5 m) long. North of the two wings were the residential halls (called *bie she* 別舍). In the eastern section, there was a bathing pond some 40 paces (55.6 m) square. See Li Daoyuan 4.25.94; Ye Dasong, *Zhongguo jianzhu shi*, p. 425.

LL 1–2: The opening lines of the *fu* are subject to two different readings. The phrasing is derived from the opening line in the "Canon of Yao" (in *Shang shu zhushu* 2.6a) which is variously understood as (A) "obedient and observant of antiquity, Emperor Yao" or (B) "if we examine antiquity, (we find) Emperor Yao ..." (for a summary of the variant interpretations, see Karlgren, "Glosses on the Book of Documents," pp. 44–45, #1207). If one follows interpretation B, as do von Zach (*Die Chinesische Anthologie*, 1:165) and Obi Kōichi (*Monzen*, 2:84), one must break the lines into three instead of two, and render them as follows: "Ah, if we examine antiquity, / We find our ancestors the imperial Han, / Were profound and wise, reverent and bright." Although this interpretation accords with the prevailing modern understanding of the "Canon of Yao" passage, I have rejected it on the following grounds: (1) The prosodic pattern clearly requires two six-syllable lines The six lines following the opening lines are all six-syllable lines with the same rhyme in even-numbered lines. Dividing the first two lines into three violates this pattern. (2) Interpretation A of the "Canon of Yao" was the preferred one in Wang Yanshou's time. It is the interpretation given in the pseudo-Kong Anguo commentary (see *Shang shu zhushu* 2.6a–b), which Zhang Zai paraphrases (11.14a) in his commentary to Wang's *fu*.

L. 3: Cf. *Mao shi* 293: "Thus, its great grandeur." The Five Eras are the reigns of Yao, Shun, and the dynasties of Xia, Yin, and Zhou.

L. 4: Tang is Yao, the reputed ancestor of Liu Bang, the Han founder. See "Eastern Capital Rhapsody," L. 60n. The Han ruled by virtue of fire.

L. 5: Cf. *Zhou yi zhushu* 3.27a (Hexagram 26, "Commentary on the Images"): "Upholding the way of Heaven. Success."

L. 7: See "Wei Capital Rhapsody," L. 39n.

L. 8: Cf. *Zhou yi zhushu* 3 9a (Hexagram 20, "Commentary on the Decision"): "The sage uses the divine way to establish instruction, and the empire submits to him."

L. 9: Cf. "Canon of Yao" (*Shang shu zhushu* 2.8a; Legge 3:17): "When the hundred clans became clearly distinguished, he harmonized the myriad states."

L. 10: Cf. "Counsels of Gaoyao" (*Shang shu zhushu* 4.16b; Legge 3:69): "He generously orders the (relationships among) the nine kindred." On the various interpretations of the nine kindred, see Karlgren, "Glosses on the Book of Documents," p. 47, #1211.

L. 11: The filial grandson is Liu Yu, King Gong of Lu.

L. 12: Cf. *Mao shi* 300/2: "The King said, 'Uncle, / I enfeoff your eldest son, / Make him lord in Lu '"

L. 13: According to Zhang Zai (11.14b), the *jie gui* 介圭 (large jade tablet) was 1 foot, 2 inches long.

L. 14: Cf. *Mao shi* 300/3: "He bestowed him hills and streams, / Land, fields, and dependent states."

L. 15: There may be an implied comparison between the Hall of Numinous Brilliance and the Bi gong 閟宮 (Closed Temple), the famous Lu temple celebrated in *Mao shi* 300 and reputedly built by Xi Si. Zhang Zai (11.15a) cites the name of the temple as Mi gong 秘宮, the Sacred Temple, which possibly means one version of the *Shi* read *mi* instead of *bi*.

L. 16: On Purple Tenuity (i.e., the Purple Palace), which here represents the imperial palace, see "Western Capital Rhapsody," L. 143n.

L. 17: Lesser Yang is east. Wang Yanshou probably is referring here to the Luminous Hall constructed by Emperor Wu in 110/109 B.C. See *Shi ji* 28.1401; *Han shu* 1243; *Records*, 2:64. It was located four *li* southwest of Fenggao 奉高 (east of modern Taian 泰安) near Mount Tai in the Lu area. See *Han shu* 28A.1581.

L. 18: The Lu area was under the protection of the constellations Kui 奎 (Straddler) and Lou 婁 (Harvester). See *Han shu* 28A.1662.

acclaimed in eulogies. Without rhapsodies, without eulogies, how can one relate anything about such things?" Thus, I have composed the following rhapsody:

I

Ah, obedient and observant of antiquity, our emperors Han,
Ancestors profound and wise, reverent and bright.
More splendrous than the Five Eras' great grandeur,
They were heir to Tang's fiery essence.
5   Upholding the way of Heaven with good success,
They expanded the cosmos and built a capital,
Set forth an August Pivot on which to found their enterprise,
And harmonizing with the divine way, they achieved great
          tranquility.

And then,
When the hundred clans were clearly distinguished,
10 And the nine kindred were generously ordered,
They enfeoffed a filial grandson,
Made him lord in Lu.
They bestowed on him a large jade tablet as a propitious emblem,
Lodged him in a dependent state where he opened his domain.
15 Then, he erected the sacred Hall of Numinous Brilliance,
Matched as adjunct to Purple Tenuity.
It succeeds the Luminous Hall in the Lesser Yang sector,
Is lustrously arrayed in Straddler's field.

II

Viewing the form of that Numinous Brilliance:
20 Jaggedly jutting, tall and towering,

Wang Yanshou visited the hall while in his early twenties with his father, the famous *Chuci* commentator Wang Yi. They had left their home in Yicheng 宜城 (south of modern Yicheng, Hubei) *to read the classics in Lu and study computation with a venerable master who resided* on Mount Tai. See *Hou Han shu* 80A.2618; *Bowu zhi* 4 2b. This *fu* is a masterpiece of description and provides the most detailed literary record of a Han palace's construction and architectural features. There are two previous translations: von Zach, "Das Lu-ling-kwang-tien-fu des Wang Wen-k'ao," *AM* 3 (1926), 467–76 and rpt. in *Die Chinesische Anthologie*, 1:164–69; and Obi Kōichi, in *Monzen* 2:82–98.

L. 21: The rhyming binome *leikui* 嶵峞 (**lwei-khwei*) possibly is an inversion of *weilei* 峞嶵 (**·jwei-lwei*), which occurs in *Zhuangzi* (8.1a) as the name of a mountain. I suspect the signific is *lei*, which means "piled"; hence, my "piled and peaked."

L. 31: Although Zhang Zai (11.15b) seems to treat *long jue* 隆崛 as a combination, in this context *jue* clearly is part of the rhyming binome *juewu* 崛㟅 (**gjwet-ngjwet*), "spiring and soaring." See Hu Shaoying 13.9a.

L. 33: The basic meaning of the rhyming binome *zengling* 繒綾 (**dzjieng-ljeng*) is "tiered" or "layered." The signific probably is conveyed by *zeng* (layered). For information on related expressions, see Hu Shaoying 13.9b.

L. 36: Piled Boulders (Jishi 積石) was a mountain range located southwest of the Han prefecture of Heguan 河關 (west of modern Daohe 導河 *xian*, Gansu). It is a source of the Yellow River. See *Han shu* 28A.1532, 28B.1611.

L. 40: On the Changhe Gate, see "Western Metropolis Rhapsody," L. 97n.

Preciptously poised, piled and peaked.
How terrifying,
How daunting it is!
High and haughty, unusual, unique,
25 Luxuriantly beautiful, broad and spacious!

Intricately conjoined and connected,
It stretches without bound!
By far the rarest thing in the world, it stands alone;
Ah, what a magnificent wonder, what a massive maze!
30 Sublimely it stands, mountainlike, twisting and twining,
Loftily spiring and soaring into the cerulean clouds.
Limitless, boundless, it rises tier upon tier,
Steep, layered and laminated like dragon scales.
Pure, clear and candid, gleaming and glistening,
35 Fulgent, bright and brilliant, it illumines the earth.
Its form is like the lofty heights of Piled Boulders mount,
And further resembles the awesome divinity of God's chamber.

Lofty ramparts are linked like ridges, joined like peaks;
Vermilion gateways, steep and stately, stand in pairs.
40 Its tall portals emulate the Changhe Gate;
Two chariots running abreast enter together.

III

Then, we cross the grand stairway,
To reach the main hall.
Looking up and down, gazing back and forth,
45 East and west, we ramble and roam.
These ornaments of scarlet hues,
What are they all for?

Gayly glistening, lustrously glinting,
Flowing and flooding, they splendently spread.
50 White walls, brilliantly gleaming, shine like the moon;
Vermeil columns, rubescently glaring, flare like lightning.

Streaked like rosy sunrise, luxuriant as clouds,
Now dark, now bright,
They flash and flame, flicker and flutter,
55 Grandly aglow, gloriously ablaze.

L. 57: Hu Shaoying (13 10a) notes that *hong* 霂 is an unknown graph. He suggests that it is a corrupt form of *hong* 泓. The *Shuowen* (11A.4987) glosses it as "descriptive of sinking downward"; hence, my "plunges."

L. 64: On *langgan* (ruby), see "Southern Capital Rhapsody," L. 158n.

L. 67: The *Six Comm.* text reads *xiao* 宵 (night) for You Mao's *xiao* 霄 (clouds). Hu Shaoying (13.10a–b) shows that the two graphs are interchangeable in the sense of "night."

L. 68: *Xuan shi* 旋室 could be Jade Chamber (see "Sweet Springs Palace Rhapsody" L. 108n). However, in this context *xuan* in the sense of winding probably is intended. See *Huainanzi* 4.26, commentary.

L. 69. These may be the women's chambers.

L. 70: Commentators have variously explained the puzzling use of *zhichu* 跙蹰 (to walk to and fro). Zhang Zhai (11.16b) explains it as a small room beside joined galleries. He also notes that there is a variant *yi* 移 for *zhi*. Li Shan (11.16b) simply treats *zhizhu* as a binominal descriptive, and glosses it as "joined together." Zhang Xian (11.22a) takes *zhichu* in its usual meaning, and paraphrases the line to say: "Slowly we walk in the western wing." Citing the *Erya* (B1.5b), which glosses *yi* as "to join," the *Wen xuan kaoyi* of Hu Kejia (2.24b) presents a convincing arguments for following the variant reading *yichu*. I suspect that *yizhu* (*drjai-drjua* ?) is an alliterative binomial descriptive, with *yi* (to join) as its signific. I have thus translated it as "continuously conjoined."

L. 73: The alliterative binome *yayi* 黶翳 (**'jap-'jei*) does not occur elsewhere. I suspect that it is a synonym compound composed of two elements, "black" and "veiled"; hence, my "sombrously shrouded." The rhyming binome *yipi* 懿濞 (**'jiei-phjwei*) offers no clue to its meaning. I supply "drifting into infinity" simply to make sense of the line. I do not know what the word means.

L. 76· "Ridgepole and roof" are metonymy for "building."

L. 79: Zhu Jian (12.5b) observes that in order to conform to the rhyme, the usual Juzi 娵觜 has been inverted to Ziju. The *Erya* (B4.11b) identifies Juzi with the lunar mansions Yingshi 營室 (House Builder) and Dong bi 東壁 (Eastern Wall), stars in Pegasus and Andromenda. The association with construction is obvious. Commentators have variously explained Juzi; see Hao Yixing's commentary in *Erya* B4.12a and Schlegel, *Uranographie*, 1 : 304. I have followed Schafer (see *Pacing the Void*, p. 76) in rendering it Loggerhead Turtle.

LL. 82–83: Both the eastern and western wings had three four-sided compartments. The compartments must have been divided into nine subcompartments. The eight sectors refer to the subcompartments: the north, south, east, and west subcompartments, plus those on the four corners. The nine corners (*jiu yu* 九隅) include the eight sectors plus the center subcompartment.

L. 86: The floating posts (*fu zhu* 浮柱) are king posts. They were called *zhuru zhu* 侏儒柱 (dwarf posts) in Song times See Li Jie 李誡 (1035–1108 or ca. 1065–1110), *Yingzao fashi* 營造法式 (Modes of Construction) (Tabei: Lianjing, 1974), 1.11a. They were described as floating because they had no secure bases (Zhang Zai 11.17a). Cf. "Sweet Springs Palace Rhapsody," L. 98.

L. 89: Zhu Jian (12.6a) equates *ququ* 蘧蘧 with *ququ* 渠渠 (great and grand) of *Mao shi* 135/1.

We creep into the northern edifice and dwell within:
Down it plunges, so chasmally gaping, sheer and steep,
Massive, broad and bright, spaciously spread,
Hissing through it, soughing and sighing, the wind is chilly and cold
60 The drip, drip from the eaves creates a sound,
As startling as the echoes of pealing thunder.
The ears, dinned and deafened, lose their power of hearing;
The eyes, dazed and dazzled, lose their power of sight.
In balanced array are fine-ground stones and rubies;
65 Symmetrically arranged are nephrite finials and floresence of jade.

Then, we open the gilded door and enter north:
Black night, dim and dusky, darkly descends.
Winding rooms, twisting and twining, lie secluded and sequestered;
Cavernous chambers, removed and remote, are dark and deep.
70 The western wing, continuously conjoined, is quiet and still;
The eastern wing, in its layered depths, is murky and mysterious:
Up it soars in blinding blur, dimly descried,
Minutely seen, sombrously shaded, drifting into infinity.
The soul, quivering and quavering, takes alarm;
75 The heart, frightened and fearful, is struck with terror.

IV

And then
We carefully examine ridgepole and roof,
View its manner of construction.
The design corresponds to the heavens,
Above, is modeled on the Loggerhead.
80 Deceptive and deceiving, it rises like clouds,
Peaked and pointed, laced and latticed.
In three compartments, four exteriors,
Eight sectors, and nine corners,
A myriad pillars, leaning in clusters,
85 Ruggedly rising, provide mutual support.

Floating posts, sublimely soaring, suspended like stars,
Are perilously poised on high, cleaving and clinging.
Flying rafters, arched and arced, pointing like rainbows,
Raised aloft, great and grand, soar en masse.

L. 90: The *lu* 櫨 is a confusing term, primarily because the *Shuowen* text (see 6A.2499a–2501a) that explains it is corrupt. The *Yingzao fashi* (1 9a) equates it with the Song term *dou* 枓 (bearing block). See also Glahn, "Some Chou and Han Architectural Terms," pp. 105, 107.

L. 91: The term *ji* (also read *jian*) 枅 is the Han equivalent for the Song term *gong* 栱 (bracket arm). See *Yingzao fashi* 1.8a. The *ji* could be square or curved as in this case. Another name for the curved *ji* was *luan* 欒. See *Shuowen* 6A.2501a–b, especially Duan's commentary; Glahn, "Some Chou and Han Architectural Terms," pp 107–8.

L. 92: The *Shuowen* (6A.2502a–2503a) explains the *er* 栭 as the uppermost member on top of a bracket arm (*ji*). It was probably a type of cap block or capital. See Glahn, "Some Chou and Han Architectural Terms," p. 108.

L. 93: The term *cheng* 㭼 is a variant form of *tang* 樘, which the *Shuowen* glosses (6A.2496a–b) as "diagonal post." According to Zhang Zai (11.17b) it was three feet long and rested on top of the rafters. I have called it a strut.

L. 103 The sky window (*tian chuang* 天窓) is not a skylight, but a name for the cupola. See Sickman and Soper, *The Art and Architecture of China*, p. 383. It must have been painted with intricate filigree patterns (Zhang Xian 11.24a).

L. 104: The square well (*fang jing* 方井) is a caisson formed by beams that cross in the shape of the character for well 井. This one must have been painted as a lotus pool. See *Yingzao fashi* 2.7b; Paul Demiéville, Review of *Che-yin Song Li Ming-tchong Ying tsao fa che*, in *BEFEO* 25 (1925):240.

LL. 105–9: Cf. "Western Metropolis Rhapsody," LL. 102–3.

L. 109: The alliterative binome *zhuozha* 宎咤 (**trjwet-trag*) probably has for its signific *zhuo*, which is a descriptive for things protruding from a cave. See *Shuowen* 7B.3291b, especially Duan's commentary. In this context, *zhuozha* describes the lotus pods "bulging and bloating."

L. 110: The *Shuowen* (6A.2498a–2499a) explains *jie* 棨 (also written 梮 or 節) as *bolu* 欂櫨, bracket construction. However, the *Erya* (B1.4b) says that *jie* is another name for *er*, capital or cap block (see L. 92n above). Guo Pu (*Erya* B1.4b) confuses the matter by glossing *jie* as *lu*, bearing block. Hao Yixing (*Erya* B1.4b) shows that *jie* refers to the uppermost portion of a bracket construction. Glahn ("Some Chou and Han Architectural Terms," p. 109) argues that there were two different types of bearing blocks, one on the top of a column (the *jie*), and the other on top of a bracket arm. Thus, I have rendered *jie* as cap block. Zhang Zai (11.18a) says cloud patterns were painted on the cap blocks.

The *zhuo* 梲 is another name for king post. See *Erya* B1.4b; *Yingzao fashi* 1.11a. Zhang Zai (11.18a) says the king posts were painted with pondweed designs.

L. 111: The *Shuowen* (6A.2503b–2504a) explains *jue* 桷 as square-shaped rafters. Duan Yucai (cited in *Shuowen* 6A.2504b) suggests that *jue* has the meaning of *lengjue* 棱角 (angular). Elsewhere the *Shuowen* (6A.2504b–2506a) mentions that *jue* is the Qi and Lu area word for rafter. Dragon figures were painted on the rafters (Zhang Zai 11.18a).

L. 112: Arthur Waley has translated LL. 112–65 in *The Temple*, pp. 95–96.

L. 115: Hu Shaoying (13.14a) claims that the rhyming binome *fenxin* 奮舋 (**pjwen-hjen*) is equivalent to *fenxing* 憤興 (**phjen-hjeng*), "furiously aroused." The signific must be *fen* (roused, furious). My "in a furious frenzy" is an attempt to find an alliterative equivalent.

L. 117: Li Shan (11.18b) glosses *han* 頷 as "shaking the head." Hu Shaoying (13.14a–b) shows that it means jaws. Zhu Jian (12.6b) observes that if the sense of "shaking the head" is intended, the graph should be written 頷.

L. 118: The Vermilion Bird is the legendary avian creature that ruled over the south.

L. 119: I follow Zhu Jian (12.6b) who takes *teng she* 騰蛇 as the Leaping Serpent, a type of dragon that reputedly was capable of causing clouds and mist to rise. See *Erya* C4.10a.

L. 120: Li Shan (11.18b) glosses the rhyming binome *jieye* 孑蜺 (**kjiat-ngiet*) as "extending the head"; hence, my "heaves its head."

270

90 Layered bearing blocks are preciptously piled, precariously
             positioned;
    Curved bracket arms, bent and bowed, concatentate like chains.
    Mushroom-shaped capitals are thickly arrayed, closely clustered.
    Bracing struts, like bifurcating branches, lean at angles;
    Laterally twisting and turning, they jut sidewards,
95 Conjoined and connected, braced and trussed together.
    Below, lush and luxuriant, they are splendently adorned;
    Above, steeply spiring, they are joined layer upon layer.
    Intricately imbricating, they mass like fishscales;
    Diverging and dividing, they splay and spread,
100 Hither and thither, continuously connected,
    Each in its own direction.

    V

    And then,
    Suspended purlins tied to the sloping roof,
    Sky windows with figured filigree:
    In a round pool on the square well,
105 Invertly planted are lotus,
    Bursting with floresence, erupting in bloom,
    Their blossoms spread and open,
    Their green pods and purple fruit,
    Bulging and bloated like dangling pearls.
110 Cloud cap blocks, pondweed king posts,
    And dragon rafters are carved and incised.

    Flying birds and running beasts,
    Are given form by the wood.
    Prowling tigers, clawing and clasping in vicious clenches,
115 Raise their heads in a furious frenzy, manes bristling.
    Curly dragons leap and soar, twist and twine,
    Their jowls seeming to move as they limp and lumber along.
    The Vermilion Bird, with outspread wings, perches on the cross-
             beams;
    The Leaping Serpent, coiling and curling, winds round the rafters,
120 The White Deer heaves its head among the brackets,
    A coiling wivern, writhing and wriggling, clings to the lintels,

L. 122: Citing the *Shuowen* (see 2B.876a–b), Li Shan (11.18b) explains *quan* 跧 as "to kick." Hu Shaoying (13.14b) shows that here it means "to crouch."

Li Zhouhan (11.25a) explains the *fu* 柎 as a cross-timber on top of a bearing block. Glahn ("Some Chou and Han Architectural Terms," p. 109), who calls this a cushion timber, says that it "supports a purlin inside a building and is placed on a bracket construction."

L. 127: Zhang Zai (11.18b) explains *yiyi* 狋狋 (**ngjiei-ngjiei*) as "descriptive of looking." Zhu Jian (12.7a) shows that *yi* has the meaning of "angry." Cf. *Shuowen* (10A.4393a–b), where *yi* is glossed as "descriptive of a dog in anger." Hu Shaoying (13.15a) thinks *yi* should be written *shi* 眎, which is an old form of *shi* 視 (to look). Since the sense of angry seems appropriate in this context, I have rendered *yiyi* as "glaring and glowering."

L. 128: These are painted figures of foreigners from the north. According to Zhang Zai (11.19a), they are placed in the highest position because men are more honorable than animals. According to the *Ruan Fu biezhuan* 阮孚別傳 (The Separate Biography of Ruan Fu), cited in the *Shishuo xinyu* commentary (6.180; chapter 23/15), Ruan Xian 阮咸 (234–305) in a letter to his aunt said, "The Hunnish slave girl has given birth to a Hunnish son." His aunt wrote back citing this line from Wang Yanshou's *fu*, advising him to name the child "Distantly Huddled." See Mather, *Shih-shuo Hsin-yu*, p. 377. Hu Shaoying (13.15b) cites this reference to show that Wang's *fu* must have been extremely popular if a woman could recite from it.

L. 129: Li Shan (11.19a) reads *yanya* 儼雅 (solemn and serious) as a binome meaning "descriptive of kneeling." Liang Zhangju (13.11b) argues that *ya* (proper, solemn) should be read with *ji* 跽 (to kneel). I think that *yanya* is a synonym compound modififying *ji*.

L. 130: Li Shan (11.19a) explains the rhyming binome *qisi* 欺猥 (**gjeh-sjeh*) as "large-headed." Li Zhouhan (11.25b) glosses it as "narrow of face." Hu Shaoying (13.15b–16a) speculates the word is composed of *qi* (**gjeh*) 頄, glossed in *Shuowen* (9A.3955b–56a) as "ugly" and *si* (**sjeh*) 顋 (cheeks); hence, my "horrid-headed."

Li Shan (11.19a) explains *diao xue* 鵰眈 (**tiehw-hjwet*) as "to look at like eagles." Li reads *jue* as *jue* 矞 (to look nervously.) Hu Shaoying argues that this word should be an alliterative compound. Thus, he reads *diao* as *zhou* (**tiehw*) 睊 (looking from deep, sunken eyes). However, even in the reading *zhouxue*, this is not an alliterative compound. Following Li Shan, I translate "gaping like eagles."

L. 131: *Six Comm.* reads (A) *yao* 顤 for You Mao (B) *yao* 鸋. Zhu Jian (12.7a–b) shows that A does not exist in dictionaries, and that B has the sense of concave head; hence, my "hollow skulls"

The rhyming binome *yaoliao* 顤顟 (**ngiehw-liehw*) is descriptive of a high, uneven head. Cf. *Shuowen* (9A 3926b–27b), *yao* 顤 (large-headed) I have approximated this with "beetled brows."

L. 135: On the Jade Girl, see "Sweet Springs Palace Rhapsody," L 160n.

L. 143: Vermeil and blue are metonymy for painting.

L. 149: This phrase is from the "Celestial Questions" (see *Chuci buzhu* 3.1b).

L. 150: The Five Dragons are five brothers named Huangbo 皇伯, Huangzhong 皇仲, Huangshu 皇叔, Huangji 皇季, and Huangshao 皇少. Their clan name was Long 龍 (Dragon). They were successors to the Sovereigns of Man (see L. 151n), and rode through the skies on dragons. See Li Shan (11.19b), citing an apocryphon to the *Chunqiu*, and *Mh*, 1 : 19.

L. 151: The Nine Sovereigns of Man are legendary rulers of remote antiquity. They were all brothers, and each lived three hundred years. They are described as riding chariots of clouds drawn by six plumed birds, and are credited with dividing the land into nine provinces, with each brother ruling over a single province. See *Yiwen leiju* 11.207; *Mh*, 1 : 19.

LL. 152–53: Fuxi usually is represented in Later Han times as having a serpent body and human head. Nugua 女媧, variously identified as Fuxi's sister or wife, is depicted as a creature similar to Fuxi. See Loewe, *Ways to Paradise*, pp. 57–58.

The wily hare creeps and crouches beside the cap blocks,
Gibbons and monkeys climb and clamber in mutual pursuit.
Black bears, tongues protruding, fangs bared,
125 Draw back, hunching and hunkering from their heavy loads.
With leveled heads they gaze and glance,
Gaping and goggling, glaring and glowering.

Hunnish figures distantly huddle on the upper columns,
Solemn and serious they kneel face to face;
130 Brave, horrid-headed, gaping like eagles,
With hollow skulls, beetled brows, bulging eyes;
Their visages as if saddened by this perilous place
Are painfully wrinkled, laden with grief.
Divine immortals straightly stand amongst the purlins,
135 The Jade Girl, peeping from a window, looks below.
Suddenly all is a bleary blur, vaguely visualized,
As the shadowy likeness of ghosts and spirits.

Here they have painted Heaven and Earth,
Multiform beings of every type and kind:
140 Various creatures wondrous and strange,
Mountain demons, sea spirits.
They have sketched and preserved their forms,
Conferring them to vermeil and blue.
A thousand changes, ten thousand transformations,
145 Each thing distinctly described.
Following set colors to image each kind,
They perfectly capture their essence.

Above, they record the Opening of Chaos,
The beginnings of remote antiquity.
150 The Five Dragons flying wing to wing,
The Nine Sovereigns of Men,
Fuxi's scaly body,
Nügua's serpent torso;
Vast Chaos simple and crude,
155 Its form dimly descried;

L. 157: Tang is Yao; Yu is Shun.

LL. 158–59: Cf. *Shang shu* 3.9b ("Canon of Shun"), referring to Shun's granting of rewards to meritorious lords: "They were clearly tested by their feats. They were given chariots and robes for their service." (Translation derived from Karlgren, "Book of Documents," p. 5.

L. 160: Commentators do not agree on the identity of the Three *Hou* 后 (literally "Sovereigns"). Zhang Zai (11.19b) says they are the rulers of the Xia, Yin, and Zhou. Liu Liang (11.26b–27a) identifies them as Jie of Xia, Zhou of Shang, and You of Zhou, all of whom lost their empires because of their oppressive rule and infatuation with female favorites. Since the next line mentions "depraved consorts," I have followed Liu.

L. 161: The depraved consorts are Mei Xi 妹嬉, Da Ji 妲己, and Bao Si, favorites of Jie, Zhou, and You respectively. See *Guo yu* 7.2a–b.

L. 168: The following lines described the covered elevated passageways that connected various parts of the palace complex.

L. 169: The speedway was part of the covered passageway reserved for the use of the king, who was the only person allowed to gallop a horse on it.

L. 170: I am not certain whether *yang xie* 陳榭 is a proper noun or simply is the name for a type of building. Zhu Jian (12.7b) explains the *xie* as a tall room built on top of a terrace from which one could gaze out. Ye Dasong (see *Zhongguo jianzhu shi*, p. 425 and figure 8–13) treats *yang xie* as the name of a large terrace west of the main hall. I have simply called it a pavilion.

L. 174: Liang Zhangju (13.12a–b) argues that *jian tai* 漸臺 need not be the tower's name, but simply a general name for a tower built in the water. I have called it watersoaked terrace.

L. 178: The Floriate Canopy here is the constellation corresponding to seven stars in Cassiopea. See Schlegel, *Uranographie*, 1:533.

L. 181: Li Shan (11.20b) says the tower was so high, one could sit within it and "ride" (*cheng* 乘) the sunbeams. Hu Shaoying (13.17a) thus proposes to read *cheng* (ride) for *chui* 垂 (to fall).

L. 186: Cf. "Rhapsody on the Imperial Park," L. 178n.

Bright and brilliant, clearly seen,
The Yellow Lord, Tang, and Yu.
Chariots and caps they gave for service,
Jackets and skirts, as marks of distinction.

160 Last come the Three Tyrants,
Depraved consorts, misguided rulers,
Loyal statesmen, filial sons,
Heroic knights, chaste women,
Worthies and fools, the failed and accomplished,
165 None have gone unattested.
The wicked are warnings to the world,
The good are examples for posterity.

V

And then:
Connecting corridors joining the palace,
The speedway circling and surrounding,
170 Sunlit pavilions outwardly gazing,
High towers and soaring belvederes,
Long passageways ascending and descending,
Bannisters and balustrades spreading and sprawling
A watersoaked terrace overlooking a pond,
175 Spiring tier after tier, nine stories high,
Stalwartly stands, conspicuous and alone,
Distinct in its uncommon form.
It soars so high it crosses the Floriate Canopy;
Above, one can see the celestial courtyard.
180 Its soaring staircase, tall and towering,
Climbing the clouds, journeys aloft.
Sitting within, one can ride the sunbeams;
Below, one can see shooting stars.

A thousand gates, all alike,
185 Ten thousand doors, seemingly as one,
Jut forth from crags and crannies,
Twining and twisting, winding and weaving:
One can travel for several miles,
Look up and never see the sun.

L. 194: "Terrestrial numina" is *Kun* numina, on which see "Western Capital Rhapsody," L. 142n.

L. 195: Zhang Zai (11.20b) explains *chun yin* 純殷 as "grand centrality." For *yin* in the sense of center, see *Shang shu shuzheng* 6.14a ("Tribute of Yu"), pseudo-Kong commentary. For another interpretation of *yin*, see Karlgren, "Glosses on the Book of Documents," p. 151, # 1367. "Azure vastness" is metonymy for Heaven.

LL. 198–201: These are all auspicious symbols.

L. 208: The Most Exalted is the emperor.

L. 209: Cf. *Mao shi* 5/2: "It is fitting that your sons and grandsons multiply."

190 What fine delicacy in such grand beauty!
    What a wondrous feat of human effort!
    Except for a great genius in tune with the gods,
    Who could accomplish this great achievement?
    It rests on a precious configuration of terrestrial numina,
195 Inherits "grand centrality" from the azure vastness,
    Embraces the changes and transformations of the yin and yang,
    Absorbs the ethereal fumes of Primal Breath.
    Dark nectar froths and foams in shaded fosses,
    Sweet dew, covering roofs, reaches below,
200 Red osmanthus burgeons and blooms south and north,
    Thoroughwort and polypores wave lithe and lissome east and west.
    Propitious winds, blowing and blustering, sough and sigh,
    Wafting sweet scents, ever fragrant.
    Gods and spirits brace ridgepole and roof;
205 After a millenium they are stronger than ever.
    Long shall it enjoy peace and tranquility, felicity and fortune;
    As long as the great Han, it shall endure.
    This truly is the domicile of the Most Exalted,
    Suitable for extending life, fit for sons and grandsons.
210 If it can be prized to this extent,
    Who would say it is not to be praised?
    The Envoi says:
    Red, red the numinous hall,
    Sublimely soars, arching aloft,
    Splendent, massive and huge.
215 It is precipitously poised, peaked and pinnacled,
    Jaggedly jutting, crinkled and crankled,
    Like towering tors standing together.

    Sinuously snaking, tortuously turning,
    Winding and weaving, bending and bowing,
220 Sidewards it slants and slopes.
    Dim and dusky, sombrously shaded,
    As if covered in a murky mass of clouds,
    Cavernously it gapes, dark and gloomy.

    Its verdant virescence, purpureal splendor,
225 Grand and glorious as giant pearls,
    Are enveloped in dazzling sunlight.

277

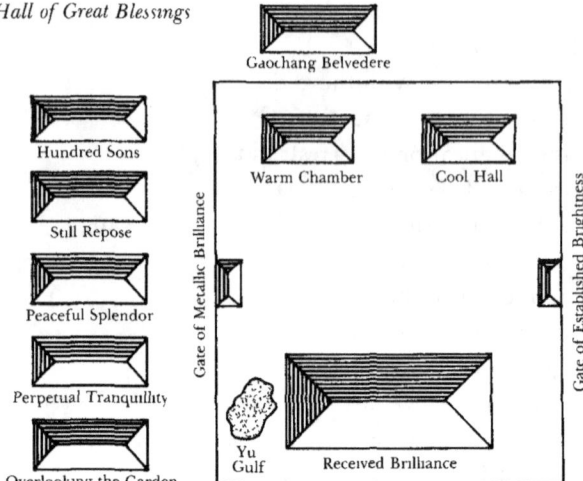

Hall of Great Blessings

Gaochang Belvedere

Hundred Sons

Still Repose

Peaceful Splendor

Perpetual Tranquillity

Overlooking the Garden

Gate of Metallic Brilliance

Warm Chamber

Cool Hall

Gate of Established Brightness

Yu Gulf

Received Brilliance

L. 2: Cf. *Mao shi* 243/1: "Era after era it has had wise kings."

L. 3: Wu is Cao Cao, known posthumously as Emperor Wu of Wei.

L. 4: Wen is Cao Pi, Emperor Wen of Wei. Cf. the "Taijia" chapter of the *Classic of Documents* (*Shangshu zhushu* 8.18a; Legge 3:199), referring to Tang, the founder of the Shang: "Heaven reflected upon his virtue, and thereupon settled the great mandate upon him."

L. 5: Cf. "Eastern Capital Rhapsody," LL. 58–59.

L. 6: "Following the seasons" refers to observing the seasonal ritual regulations as stipulated by the "Yue ling."

L. 7: Emperor Augustus is Cao Rui, Emperor Ming of the Wei.

L. 8: Cf. "Eastern Capital Rhapsody," L. 102.

278

The ultimate wonder, the consummate spectacle,
Since the invention of ridgepole and roof,
Its like has never been seen.

230 It was spirits who built her,
To bless our house of Han,
That it never decay.

Rhapsody on the Hall of Great Blessings

HE PINGSHU

I

Grand indeed is the Wei!
Era after era it has had kings sage and wise.
Wu established the primal foundation;
Wen had the great mandate settled upon him.

5   Both embodied Heaven in creating institutions,
Followed the seasons in establishing government.
Next came Emperor Augustus:
Then redoubled is our luster, increased is our splendor!
Afar, His standard is the natural process of yin and yang,

THIS RHAPSODY by He Yan (*zi* Pingshu) celebrates the construction of the Hall of Great Blessings (Jingfu dian 景福殿), which was built sometime after A.D. 232 in the Wei city of Xuchang 許昌 (the old Wei city of Xuchang is located in Gucheng 古城 Village in Xuchang *xian*, Henan). This hall stood in the southeast corner of the city (see *Yuanhe junxian tu zhi* 8.225), and was built at a cost of over eight million cash (see *Shuijing zhu* 4.22.37). After the completion of the palace, Emperor Ming ordered his court officials to compose *fu* commemorating the event (see the *Dian lue* 典略 cited by Li Shan 11.22a). Other *fu* probably written for this occasion include: Bian Lan 卞蘭 (fl. ca. A.D. 230), "Rhapsody on the Xuchang Palace" (in *Yiwen leiju* 62.1113–14; Wei Dan 韋誕 (fl. ca. 200–230), "Rhapsody on the Hall of Great Blessings" (in *Yiwen leiju* 62.1124; Xiahou Hui 夏侯惠 (fl. ca. 230), "Rhapsody on the Hall of Great Blessings."

He Yan's *fu* contains a detailed description of the hall and, like Wang Yanshou's piece on the Hall of Numinous Brilliance, is rich in architectural detail. Previous translations include: von Zach, "Aus dem Wen-hsuan ---Ho Yen's poetische Beschreibung des Ching-fu-Palastes (in Hsu-ch'ang)," *MS* 4 (1939–40):441–50 and rpt. in *Die Chinesische Anthologie*, 1:170–79; Obi Kōichi, *Monzen*, 2:99–122.

L. 10: Cf. *Han shu* 49.2293, Chao Cuo's "Response to an Edict": "In plotting peace for the empire, all base themselves on the feelings of men."

L. 13: Cf. the "Yi and Ji" chapter of the *Classic of Documents* (*Shang shu zhushu* 5.12a–b; Legge 3:89): "When the head is intelligent, and the limbs are good, all affairs will be settled."

L. 14: Cf. "Counsels of Gaoyao" (*Shangshu zhushu* 4.22a; Legge 3:73): "Within the Celestial Order there are social rules."

L. 15: This should be the sixth year of Emperor Ming's reign.

L. 17: On *guiyou* of the third month of Taihe 6 (April 14, 232), Emperor Ming made his inspection tour in the east. See *Sanguo zhi* 3.99. The *Five Comm.*'s edition omits *shou* 狩 (to hunt). Hu Shaoying (13.18a) adduces good evidence to show that this is an interpolation from the commentary.

LL. 19–21: According to the ancient rites (see *Li ji zhushu* 11.29a–30a, "Wang zhi"), as part of the eastern inspection tour, the ruler performed sacrifices to hills and streams, visited centenarians, "examined the seasons and months, and stipulated the days."

L. 23: This would be the sixteenth day of the sixth lunar month (= July 21, 232).

L. 24: The Sylvan Bell (Linzhong 林鍾) pitchpipe corresponds to the sixth month. See *Li ji zhushu* 16.8a.

L. 25: The Great Fire Star is Antares.

L. 27: This is a phrase from the "Yue ling" under the sixth month. See *Li ji zhushu* 16.11b.

L. 28: Cf. "Wei Capital Rhapsody," L. 369n. The Nine Officers are the Nine Chancellors.

L. 30: According to the "Yue ling" (see *Li ji zhushu* 16.11b), in the sixth month the land was humid and hot.

L. 34: Cf. "Yi and Ji" (*Shangshu zhushu* 5.1a; Legge 3:76): "The emperor said, 'Come Yu, you must also speak your fine words.'"

L. 35: Lord Xiao is Xiao He, the Former Han minister who helped plan the building of the Everlasting Palace. See "Western Capital Rhapsody," L.37n and "Eastern Capital Rhapsody," L. 16n.

L. 36: Sun Qing is Xunzi, the Zhou philosopher. It is not clear why he is mentioned here.

L. 38: This is a phrase from *Zuozhuan*, *Wen* 18 (Legge 5:282).

LL. 39–40: When Emperor Gaozu of the Former Han saw the "grandeur and elegance" of the newly constructed Everlasting Palace, he complained to Xiao He, who replied: "The empire has not yet been pacified, and thus we should take this opportunity to complete the palaces and halls. Moreover, the Son of Heaven deems the area within the four seas as His household. Without grandeur and elegance, He shall have nothing with which to affirm His majesty. Moreover, it will ensure that later ages will have no way to expand on it." See *Shi ji* 8.385–86; *Han shu* 1B.64; *Records*, 1:110–11; *HFHD*, 1:118.

10 Near, His base is the true feelings of creatures and men.
　Above, He reverently examines the vast Way of antiquity,
　Below sets forth principles of goodness that shall endure through
　　　　　　the ages.
　The numerous affairs having been settled,
　The Celestial Order is exceedingly clear.
15 Thus, after two plus three years,
　The state has become rich and the punishments fair.

　In the third month of the year He tours the east,
　And arrives in Xuchang.
　He performs the gazing sacrifice to hill and stream,
20 Examines the seasons, judges the terrain,
　Consoles men of exalted age,
　Leads the people in plowing and sericulture.
　In the sixth month, when the moon turns full,
　And the Sylvan Bell is recorded among the pipes,
25 And the Great Fire Star is overhead at dusk,
　Mulberry and catalpa thickly flourish,
　Heavy rains seasonally fall:

　The Three Directors and Nine Officers,
　Grand scholars, great masters,
30 Moved by the stifling stagnation of humidity and heat,
　Ponder the vagaries of life:
　Thinking upon Min and Yue who remain unpacified,
　They realize there can be no respite from military campaigns.

　Then do they speak these fine words:
35 "Of old there was Lord Xiao,
　And Sun Qing as well,
　Both prescient and learned,
　Intelligent and true, generous and sincere.
　They both unfailingly claimed:
　　　　If a palace is not grand, not elegant,
40 　　　It cannot serve to unite the people or affirm numinous might;
　　　　If it is not ornate, not adorned,
　　　　It cannot serve to teach posterity or perpetuate achievement.
　Thus, contemporaries of the age reap its success and benefits;
　Later ages shall rely on its heroic fame.

281

L. 45: Xuchang originally was named Xu prefecture. Cao Cao established it as the capital for the last Han emperor, Emperor Xian. After Cao Pi received Emperor Xian's abdication here, he renamed it Xuchang. In A.D. 220, after Cao Pi had declared himself emperor of the Wei, an apocryphon appeared that said, "Han by Xu flourishing (Xu *chang* 許昌) will lose the empire." Li Yun 李雲, prefect of Baima 白馬, then submitted a memorial that cited the appearance of a "flourishing aura" (*chang qi* 昌氣) at Xu to justify Wei's replacement of the Han. See Dull, "Historical Introduction," pp. 307–8 (with some errors in translation); Carl Leban, "Managing Heaven's Mandate: Coded Communications in the Accession of Ts'ao P'ei, A.D. 220," in *Ancient China: Studies in Early Civilization*, p. 328.

LL. 50–51: According to the "Yue ling" (see *Li ji zhushu* 17.9b, 17.11b), in the first month of winter, the Son of Heaven rode the dark chariot and donned furs for the first time. Thus, we know that Emperor Ming ordered construction of the Xuchang palaces to begin in the ninth month.

L. 56: Cf. *Mao shi* 242/1.

L. 58: Li Shan (11.24a) thinks this line must refer to the victory of the Wei general Tian Yu 田豫 over the Wu envoy Zhou He 周賀 at Chengshan 成山 (on the extreme tip of the Shandong peninsula). This event occurred either in the ninth or tenth month of 232, just when the Xuchang halls were being constructed. See *Sanguo zhi* 3.99, 47.1136.

L. 59: The bribes and gifts possibly refer to those presented by Wu to Wei's ally, Gongsun Yuan 公孫淵 In 228, Emperor Ming appointed him governor of Liaodong. Soon thereafter, Gongsun Yuan began to initiate contacts with Sun Quan of Wu, and "frequently exchanged gifts with him" (*Sanguo zhi* 8.252). In the ninth month of the Taihe reign, Emperor Ming sent Tian Yu on an expedition against him. Although he failed to defeat Gongsun Yuan, he did rout a group of rebels under the command of Zhou He at Chengshan (see L. 58n), and "took all of their soldiers prisoner." See *Sanguo zhi* 26.728; Sun Zhizu, *Wen xuan Li zhu buzheng* 1.34a. The curse of the sea refers to Wu, or possibly Gongsun Yuan.

L. 60: Cf. "Rhapsody on the Hall of Numinous Brilliance in Lu," L. 15n.

L 62. Hu Shaoying (2.8a) shows that *dandan* 耽耽 (*tem-tem) is a variant of *tantan* 淡淡 (*dem-dem), "deep and cavernous." Cf. *Shi ji* 48.1961, n. 3 and "Western Metropolis Rhapsody," L. 140.

L. 69: Li Shan (11.24b) explains *linlang* 琳琅 as a type of gem. Liang Zhangju (13.14a) and Hu Shaoying (13 18b) present convincing arguments to show that it is descriptive of the sound made by the ringed-jade and the pearl ornaments.

L. 70: Orion's Banner (Shen qi 參旗) is a group of nine stars in Orion. Nine Streamers (Jiu liu 九旒 or 九斿) is constellation of nine bow-shaped stars in Eridanus and Lepus. See Schlegel, 1:384–85. The banners in the palace are compared to constellations.

45 Moreover, Xuchang:
Is a place upon which great fortune has settled,
A named signalled in charts and prophesies.
If its virtues and propriety are such as this,
Why cannot palaces and halls be built?"

The emperor then says, "Let it be so!"
50 His dark chaise having been harnessed,
And His light furs donned,
Then does He command the attendants:
Rites and cermonials, let them be prepared!
He carefully measures days and toil,
55 Exactly reckons expenditure and labor,
Assembles common people for planning and building,
But only when they have time to spare from their farming work.
Using the spoils presented by the Eastern Hosts,
Gifts and bribes from the curse of the sea,
60 He erects the sacred Hall of Great Blessings,
Replete with the design and dimensions of an imperial dwelling.

II

And then they,
Erect on a lavish scale the tiered cope, deep and cavernous,
Build a high foundation, large and lofty;
Range in rows figured columns, glinting and glistening,
65 Sternly stand a staircase, tall and towering.
Flying eaves, winglike, rise and soar;
Upturned roofs, borne aloft, sail on high.
Streaming behind are plumes and fur, lush and luxuriant;
Dangling down are ringed-jade and pearls, jingling and jangling.
70 Orion's Banner and Nine Streamers,
Flap and flutter in the wind.
Shiny and clear, splendent and bright,
Vermeil hues glitter and glow.

Thus, its florid exterior:
Flares and flashes, blazes and blares,
75 Resplendent, lustrously shining,
As the sun and moon clinging to the skies.

L. 78: Li Shan (11.24b) vaguely explains *tuigai* 退槪 as "dark and deep, unclear." With no great confidence that I have rendered its correct meaning, I have translated the constituent parts as "fading forms"

L. 80: Cf. *Mao shi* 291/6: "They are closely arrayed, like the teeth of a comb."

L. 81: Li Shan (11.24b–25a) admits he does not know the meaning of *lian* 㻲. He then cites an anonymous commentator who explains it as describing a mass of trees joined together. Li Zhouhan (11.33b) gives the fanciful gloss of "beautiful." None of the Qing commentators ventures to explain the word. Based on the parallel with *teeth of a comb* in the preceding line, I have rendered it as "giant chain."

L. 91: Cf. *Mao shi* 230/1: "Dainty and delicate are the yellow birds."

L. 97: Li Zhu 離朱 is another name for Li Lou, a man known for his sharp eyesight. Cf. "Rhapsody on the Tall Poplars Palace," L. 208n.

L. 100: On the bellframe, see "Western Metropolis Rhapsody," LL. 122–25n. Li Shan (11.25b) vaguely explains the rhyming binome *lunbin* 輪囷 (**ljwen-pjien*) as "descriptive of shape." Hu Shaoying (13.19b) claims that it is a variant of *lunjun* (**ljwen-gjwen*) 輪菌 (in L. 106), used to avoid redundancy. In both lines, Hu thinks the binomes mean "tall and large." However, the usual meaning of *lunjun* is "bent and twisted." Perhaps *lunbin* means something like "sinuously spiring."

L. 101: Cf. "Eastern Capital Rhapsody," L. 145.

L. 102: The fierce beasts are the posts of the bell frames. Cf. "Western Metropolis Rhapsody," LL. 122–25n.

L. 103: "Temper" in this line is used in the sense of firmness.

Its inner recesses:
Shrouded and veiled, dark and dim,
Vague visions, fading forms,
Are like night stars continuously conjoined.

80 Like teeth of a comb, rooms are closely clustered,
Yet form a giant chain, lavish and vast,
All-embracing, widely meandering,
Never the same form.

Viewed from afar:
    It is like spreading vermilion clouds casting bright patterns in
        the sky;
85 Examined close up:
    It is like gazing upon lofty mountains crowned with drooping
        clouds.
Ah, what a magnificent wonder, how grand and elegant!
So intricately patterned, it is hard to describe!
Such are its general features.

As for:
High purlins perilously poised,
90 Soaring roofs touching rainbows:
Delicate and dainty, dark and dusky,
They swing and sway with the clouds,
Stretch like birds, spire like mountains,
As if soaring, as if still.
95 Stately they stand, jaggedly jutting,
There is no seeing where they reach.
Even a man of Li Zhu's keen powers of vision
Would be dazed and dazzled, unable to distinguish clearly.

III

And then,
They erect a main southern gate, gaping wide,
100 Install bellframes, sinuously spiring.
Engraved bells, raised aloft, hang on high;
Savage beasts boldly stand, arrayed in pairs.
Embodying fierce fortitude in their vast temper,
Their sound clangs and clangors like thunder.

L 105: The long-limbed Tartars are statues.

L. 109: *Yun* is *yun xiang* 芸香, *Murraya exotica*, the honey bush. See Read, *Medicinal Plants*, p. 105, #352

L. 115: What I have translated as "shrill" is *shang* 商, the note of the musical scale to which autumn corresponds.

L. 121: Li Shan (11.26a) explains *qian* 褰 as "to open." Based on the *Shuowen* (8A.3711b), which glosses *qian* as *ku* 絝 (*khwah*), Hu Shaoying (13.20a) explains it as *kua* (*khwah*) 跨 (straddle). Thus, Li Shan's paraphrase: "The long rafters straddle (*kua*) the distance."

L. 128: Cf. *Lun yu* 8/7.

L. 132: Cf. "Rhapsody on the Imperial Park," L. 199n.

L. 134: Li Shan (11.26b) explains *pian* 楄 as "a short beam attached to the *yangma* (the beam supporting the corner of the eaves). See L. 136n below.

L. 136: The *Yingzao fashi* (1.10b–11a and 5.5a) equates *yangma* 陽馬 with the Song term *jue liang* 角梁, corner beam. Its function was to support the corner of the eaves. Cf. Ma Rong's "Rhapsody on the Western Residence of General Liang" (cited by Li Shan 11.26b): "They (the beams?) soar so far they receive the eaves, / Where the *yangma* touches the sloping roof."

105 Then long-limbed Tartars,
    Their silver torsos gnarled and knotted,
    Sit in the hall beside the tall gate,
    To manifest the mighty spirit of our sage ruler.
    Honey bush and pollia fill the courtyards,
110 Sophora and storax cover the roofs.
    They are joined by thousand-year trees,
    Mingled with purple hazels.
    Some received favor for their auspicious names;
    Others were prized for their good timber.
115 Bearing fruit in shrill autumn,
    Unfolding blossoms in verdant spring,
    They grow dense and dark, lush and luxuriant,
    Sweet and fragrant.

IV

    Now for its construction:
120 Long beams, colorfully designed,
    Straddle openings below, rest wondrously poised above.
    Purlins and struts, manifoldly layered,
    Their strength engaged, their forms disjoined,
    Scarlet as arching rainbows,
125 Red as dashing wiverns,
    South reach the sunlit eaves,
    North extend to the darkest limits.
    Though their load is heavy, and their course long,
    Their service is exeedingly great.

V

130 And then,
    Placed row to row are figured rafters painted scarlet,
    Hung with patterned finials made of round and pointed jade
    They arch like divine dragons ascending and descending,
    Glisten like the streaming radiance of the sun and moon.
    Then there are the short laths,
135 Splayed like ribs, spread like wings,
    Received by the corner beams,

L. 140: The *Yingzao fashi* (1.8b) equates *fei (y)ang* 飛抑 with the Song term *fei ang* 飛昂, flying lever. This is "a long slanting arm running out through the wall plane to help brace the weight of the eaves" (Sickman and Soper, *Art and Architecture*, p. 384). See also Glahn, "Some Chou and Han Architectural Terms," p. 111.

L. 141: The *yuan* 輨 must be a shaft similar to the chariot shaft. Cf. Bian Lan's "Rhapsody on the Xuchang Palace" (in *Yiwen leiju* 62.1113): "Twin shafts (*yuan*) uphold the purlins."

L. 144: Li Shan (11.27a) explains the white aperture (*bai jian* 白間) as white paint applied to the edge of the blue door engraving. However, Hu Shaoying (13.21a–b) convincingly shows that He Yan is describing white windows with small coin-shaped perforations.

L. 146: I have followed the You Mao text here, which has *chen* 晨 (morning) for *Six Comm.*'s *huang* 晃 (blazing).

L. 148: According to the *Guangya* (9A.10a), the Hook Star (Gou xing 鉤星) is another name for the Time Star (Chen xing 辰星) or Mercury. See "Western Metropolis Rhapsody," LL. 72–74 under Chronographic Star.

L. 150–51: These lines describe the dome ceiling that has a whorled design like that of a snail shell.

LL. 152–53: Cf. "Western Metropolis Rhapsody," L. 102 and "Rhapsody on the Hall of Numinous Brilliance in Lu," LL. 105–9.

L. 154: The pondweed well is the caisson of the ceiling. Cf. "Western Metropolis Rhapsody," L. 102n, where I translated the same term "figured ceiling."

L. 162: On the *er* (cap block), see "Rhapsody on the Hall of Numinous Brilliance in Lu," L. 92n.

L. 163: Yan Shigu (*Han shu* 65.2844, n. 4) explains *jushu* 寠數 as a round cushion used to carry pots on the head. Li Shan (11.27b) says the cap blocks were intricately joined like a *jushu*. However, Zhu Jian (12.10a) cites the *Shi ming* (3.40), which treats *jushu* as a descriptive binome meaning "cramped and constricted."

L. 164: The *Yingzao fashi* (1.8b) classifies the *jian* 橵 as a type of flying lever (see L. 140n above). The *Shuowen* (6A.2518b–2519a) laconically explains *jian* as a "wedge," probably to refer to its function in reinforcing timber. Glahn ("Some Chou and Han Architectural Terms," p. 111) suggests that the *jian* "originally was the horizontal pole on which the bracket constructions carrying the eaves were placed, and which functioned as a lever arm."

On the *lu* (bearing block), see "Rhapsody on the Hall of Numinous Brilliance in Lu," L. 90n

Hu Shaoying (13.23a) ingeniously explains *geluo* 各落 (*grak-glak*) as a rhyming binome similar to *cuoluo* 錯落 (*sjiak-glak*), "randomly ranged."

L. 165: On the *luan* (curved bracket), see "Wu Capital Rhapsody," L. 345n.

L. 168: Cf. "Western Metropolis Rhapsody," L. 111.

Joined to the round and square.
Between mottled cracks they daub white;
Thick or thin, each has a pattern.

140 Flying levers flitting like birds,
Paired shafts as their support,
Rush the narrows, pierce the void,
Conjoined and connected, one upon another.

Bright, bright, white apertures,
145 Are neatly arrayed like rows of coins;
Morning sunlight shines within,
Streaming reflections are cast without,
Fiery as the Hook Star in the Sky River,
Dazzling as bridges of clouds touching the heavens.

150 A giant snail inching along, in multiple convolutions,
Twists, suspended above, to form a protective dome.
Roots and stems planted upside down,
Lotuses bursting and spreading into bloom,
Encircle the pondweed well,
155 Are woven into the intricate filigree.
Their red corollas compactly commingle,
Crisscrossing like vermeil silk;
Their blossoms, rubescently glittering,
Rampantly spread like fine brocade.
160 Such elaborate ornament, intricate craft,
Cannot be completely described.

VI

And then,
Magnolia cap blocks in crowded layers,
Cramped and constricted, are positioned by the carpenter's square.
Levers and bearing blocks, randomly ranged, join one to another;
165 Curved brackets, bent and bowed, intertwine.
Gilded columns are evenly spaced,
Jade plinths upholding their bases.
Blue door-engraving and silver knockers,
These adorn portals and gates.

LL. 170–71: The architectural terminology is confusing here. According to Li Shan (11.27b), the inner purlins (mei 枚) extended outside to the eaves, where they joined the eave purlins (fu 抨).

L. 172: Pi 榐 and lu 栌 seem to be synonyms for eaves. See Fang yan shuzheng 13.18b; Shuowen 6A.2506b–2507a. I suspect they are dialect words. See Shuowen 6A.2504b–2506a, which says lu is a Chu word for eave.

LL 176–77: Bian Lan in his "Rhapsody on the Xuchang Palace" locates the Warm Chamber (Wen fang 溫房) and Cool Hall (Liang shi 涼室) in the north part of the Xuchang Palace complex.

LL. 178–79: Established Brightness (Jian yang 建陽) is the eastern gate; Metallic Brilliance (Jin guang 金光), the western gate.

LL. 186: The Rites of Zhou (see Zhou li zhushu 16.17b), under the office Managers of Clams, mentions "white splendor" (bai cheng 白盛), a mixture of powdered clam shells that was used to whitewash walls.

L. 188: See "Western Capital Rhapsody," L. 194n.

L. 192: The phrase yun se 允塞, as probably understood in He Yan's time, literally means "truly fills (the empire)." It comes from the a line in the "Canon of Shun" (see Shang shu zhushu 3.1b; Legge 3:29) praising the virtues of Shun: "His profound wisdom, cultivated intelligence, and genial reverence truly fill (the empire)." In order to make sense of the phrase in English, I have freely rendered it as "abundant virtues."

L. 193: Chonghua is Shun. See "Wei Capital Rhapsody," L. 624n.

L. 194: The office of Master of Works (Gong gong 共工) reputedly existed in the time of Shun. See "Shun dian" (Shangshu zhushu 3.24b; Legge 3:45). Here He Yan uses it as an elegant term for the imperial painters.

L. 195: Cf. "Yi and Ji" (Shang shu zhushu 5.5a; Legge 3:80–81): "With the five pigments clearly applied to the five colors, make the robes. You ensure that it is done."

L. 198: The pepper rooms are the women's compartments. Cf. "Western Capital Rhapsody," L. 178n.

LL. 200–201: Lady Yu (Yu ji 虞姬), also known as Juanzhi 捐之, was a wife of King Wei 威 of Qi (reg. 378–343 B.C.). At the beginning of his reign. he entrusted the rule of his state to a sycophant, Zhou Pohu 周破胡, who allowed other states to encroach upon Qi territory. Zhou, who was jealous of able and virtuous officials, conspired with the Grandee of E 阿 to slander the able official, the Grandee of Jimo 即墨. After Lady Yu made an eloquent speech exposing the slander, King Wei granted the Grandee of Jimo a fief of ten thousand households and ordered the Grandee of E and Zhou Pohu boiled to death. Subsequently, he recovered the lost territory, and Qi was well governed from then on. See Lienü zhuan 6.17a–18b; O'Hara, Position of Woman, pp. 169–71.

The Five Comm.'s text reads si 俟 (await, need) for Six Comm.'s and You Mao ning 佞 (fawning). Li Zhouhan (11.39a) thus interprets the line differently: "They know that a well-governed state needs a virtuous minister."

LL. 202–3: Queen Jiang (Jiang hou 姜后) was the wife of King Xuan of Zhou King Xuan was in the habit of rising late, and thus Queen Jiang refused to leave her chamber. Removing her hairpins and earrings, she ordered her governess to report to the king that it was her own licentiousness that caused him to lose propriety and come late to court. After hearing these words, King Xuan diligently attended to court affairs. See Lienu zhuan 2.1b; O'Hara, Position of Woman, p. 49.

170 The twin inner purlins are so long,
Even the double eave-purlins are ornamented.
The eaves follow the edges,
Circumscribe the four directions,
Like the ranks of captain and commandant,
175 On duty in the frontier zones.

Warm Chamber adjoins its eastern wing;
Cool Hall dwells at its western side.
Open Established Brightness and scarlet flames fulgently flare;
Part Metallic Brilliance and cool breezes arrive.
180 Thus, in winter it is not chilly or cold,
In summer, there is no sweltering heat.
It is so perfectly balanced, so fitted to the mean,
Here one can prolong his years.

The marble bases of ramparts and walls,
185 Their brilliance lustrously shines.
The Zhou practice was "white splendor";
Now it is light blue.
Golden discs studding the wall sashes,
Are here in double layers.
190 Luminous pearls and kingfisher plumes,
Are everywhere to be seen.

VII

Revering the abundant virtues of former kings,
Admiring the non-action of Chonghua,
Our sovereign commands the Masters of Works to have paintings
          made,
195 And ensure that the five pigments are clearly applied.
They paint forms from the ancient past,
To serve as warning and monition.
For ladies of the pepper rooms,
These are examples, these are models.

200 By viewing the comportment of Lady Yu,
They understand how a fawning minister governs a state.
After seeing how Queen Jiang removed her girdle pendants,
They realize what was honored in ages past.

291

L. 204: Zhongli Chun 鍾離春 was a girl from the town of Wuyan 無鹽 in Qi. She was extremely ugly and had not been able to find a husband. She then requested an audience with King Xuan 宣 of Qi (reg. 342–324 B.C.), who received her. She then warned him of four dangers threatening his state. Impressed with her sage advice, King Xuan appointed her his queen. See *Lienü zhuan* 6.19b–21a; O'Hara, *Position of Woman*, pp. 171–74.

L. 205: Lady Fan (Fan ji 樊姬) was the wife of King Zhuang 莊 of Chu (reg. 613–591 B.C.). Citing her own example of yielding to younger and more beautiful concubines, she convinced the king to dismiss the minister Yu Qiuzi 虞邱子, who had served in office for more than ten years without advancing able men or dismissing the incompetent. He then appointed the able Sunshu Ao 孫叔敖 to take Yu Qiuzi's place. See *Lienü zhuan* 2.8a–9a; O'Hara, *Position of Woman*, pp. 56–58.

L. 206: Once when Emperor Cheng was roaming the rear courtyard (the women's compartments), he invited the Favored Beauty Ban to share his cart. Lady Ban declined saying that in the paintings of ancient times, sage rulers were always accompanied by able ministers. Only the depraved last rulers of the Three Dynasties had female favorites at their sides. See *Han shu* 97B.3983–84; Watson, *Courtier and Commoner*, pp. 260–61.

L. 207: Mother Meng (Meng mu 孟母) was the mother of Mencius. When Mencius was small, they lived near a graveyard, where he imitated the gravediggers. Thinking this not a fitting activity, she moved beside a market. When the young Mencius began to imitate the merchants and and their customers, she moved beside a school. Here, Mencius sent our ritual utensils, imitated the yielding and bowing of the scholars, and began to study the six classics. See *Lienü zhuan* 1.15b; O'Hara, *The Position of Woman*, p. 39.

L. 213: Cf. *Zuozhuan*, *Zhao* 7 (Legge 5:617).

LL. 214–15: Cf. *Zhong yong* 20/10 (Legge 1:407): "Being devoted to study, one approaches knowledge. Through hard practice one approaches benevolence."

L. 218: Li Shan (11.30a) says this refers to viewing the paintings.

L. 219: After hearing Confucius iterate a series of wise maxims, Zizhang "wrote them on his sash" so that he would be reminded of them always. See *Lun yu* 15/5. Li Shan (11.30a) interprets this line to say: "How can viewing paintings from dawn to dusk be as good as the act of writing maxims on one's sash?" Lu Yanji (11.40b) interprets its in the opposite sense: "Why bother writing on one's sash, for these paintings provide a sufficient warning." Li Zhouhan derives his interpretation from a questionable gloss on *yu* 與 (together with, compared with) as *yong* 用 (use). Li Shan's interpretation betters fits with L. 217, which essentially says it is better to practice what you preach.

L. 221: Cf. "Western Metropolis Rhapsody," L. 269 and "Rhapsody on the Hall of Numinous Brilliance in Lu," LL. 180–81.

L. 224: See "Wu Capital Rhapsody," L. 334n and "Wei Capital Rhapsody," L. 194n.

L. 225: The *xi* 梏 is the large bar that joins the two holes of a cangue. Here, it must be the bars of the balustrade. The bars were decorated with carnelian.

L. 230: On the *zouyu*, see "Eastern Capital Rhapsody," L. 138n.

L. 234: Tenebrous (*yin* 陰) signifies north.

LL. 236–37: The right side chamber is on the west side. Still Repose (Qing yan 清晏) is the name of detached hall. Cf. Wei Dan's "Rhapsody on the Hall of Great Blessings" (in *Yiwen leiju* 62.1124):

Detached halls and separate lodges,
Glisten like serried stars:
Peaceful Splendor, Enduring Goodness,
Peaceful Repose, Perpetual Tranquility.

They deem worthy the forthright words of Zhongli,
205 Admire the self-abnegation of Lady Fan,
Extol Lady Ban for declining the cart,
Praise Mother Meng's choice of neighborhood.
Thus, if one would broaden his wisdom,
He first must listen much.
210 But listening much increases the babble,
And the increased babble confounds the truth.
Not being confounded—wherein lies that?
Its lies in selecting good men.
Thus, if one would establish virtue,
215 He first must approach benevolence.
If one wishes no flaws in this principle of comportment,
He must fully emulate ancient men who practiced the Way
Day viewing, night perusing,
How compare they with "writing on the sash."

VIII

220 And now
Steps and stairs, continuously stretching,
High and far, journey into the clouds.
Latticed railings, grandly placed,
Are set by compass, formed by square.
Balustrades like leaping serpents,
225 Their bars resembling carnelian blossoms,
Are like wiverns coiling,
Are like curly dragons at rest.
Black balconies rise one after another,
Their lustrous designs bright and brilliant.
230 The *zouyu* upholding the decking,
Their plain background revealing a benevolent exterior,
Show the propitious manifestation of a celestial omen,
Bespeaks of distant barbarians coming to court.

A tenebrous hall faces north,
235 With nine gates and balconies side by side.
The right side chamber, Still Repose,
Aligned west to east,

LL. 238–39: Wei Dan mentions Perpetual Tranquility (Yong ning 永寧) and Peaceful Splendor (Anchang 安昌) in his "Rhapsody on the Hall of Great Blessings." In his "Rhapsody on the Xuchang Palace" (see *Yiwen leiju* 62.1114) Bian Lan refers to the emperor's "visiting the towering tors of Peaceful Splendor," where he viewed a variety show of dancing, singing, and acrobatics. Nothing is known about the Hall Overlooking the Garden (Lin pu 臨圃).

LL. 240–41: Wei Dan mentions the Hall of the Hundred Sons (Baizi 百子): "We admire Hundred Sons, that singular dwelling, / Extol its good and auspicious name" (in *Yiwen leiju* 62.1124)

L. 243: This line is cited verbatim from *Mao shi* 1/1.

L. 244: Cf. *Mao shi* 240/1, which praises Tairen, the mother of King Wen of Zhou, and his wife, Taisi: "Reverent and respectful was Tairen" and "Taisi inherited their fair name."

L. 245: Cf. *Mao shi* 299/4: "There is none he does not honor; / He himself prays for their blessing."

L. 247: Cf. "Rhapsody on the Hall of Numinous Brilliance in Lu," L. 209.

L. 248: This line is identical to a line in Cai Yong's "Temple Inscription for the Late Grand Commandant Lord Qiao" (see *Cai Zhonglang ji* 1.1a).

L. 250: This line is verbatim from *Mao shi* 299/3.

L. 252: In his "Rhapsody on the Xuchang Palace" (see *Yiwen leiju* 62.1114), Bian Lan mentions the Hall of Received Brilliance, where the emperor discourses on the ancients, reforms customs, "retires the empty and false," treasures worthy men, and disdains trinkets and jewels.

L. 260: Cf. "Western Capital Rhapsody," L. 154n.

L. 262: He Yan here refers to what must have been a type of Chinese football. According to Liu Xiang's *Bie lu* (see *Quan Han wen* 38.8a), there was a tradition that the game was invented by the Yellow Lord. He then reports others (perhaps more credibly?) claim that it began in the Warring States period. Football was not simply a game, but was intended to test the martial skills of soldiers. According to Li Shan (11.31a), there were two sides of six men each. He also mentions something called the *ju shi* 鞠室 (literally "ball house"), which I take to be the goal. There is an inscription about the game by Li You (see *Quan Hou Han wen* 50.5a), which also mentions the two sides of six. Bian Lan's "Rhapsody on the Xuchang Palace" (cited by Li Shan 11.31a) describes the same game:

They install the imperial throne at the football field,
To watch the sparkling spectacle of wondrous talent.
Two sides of six face off and practice their skills;
Their bodies, nimble and quick, seem to fly."

L. 266: Or following Lu Yanji (11.42b), "After deciding the victor, they disperse and return home."

L. 267: The idea is that football has so many rules, a football match was like an adjudication. Note that the word *ju* (*kjok*) 鞠 (ball) is homophonous with *ju* (*kjok*) 鞫 (judicial investigation).

L. 271: The Terrace of Perpetual Beginning (Yong shi 永始) must have been devoted to agriculture. Wei Dan's "Rhapsody on the Hall of Great Blessings" (cited by Liu Liang 11.42b–43a) mentions the emperor's visiting this terrace and "Learning of the hardships of sowing and planting, / Admiring the diligence of the farmers."

Joins to Perpetual Tranquility,
Peaceful Splendor, Overlooking the Garden,
240 And reaches to Hundred Sons,
That place where the harem dwells.
Who then dwells here?
Pure maidens, coy and comely.
Reverent and respectful of fair name,
245 All pray for many blessings.
What blessings are these?
"May your sons and grandsons,
Be bright, be wise,
Be intelligent, be clever.
250 May they long be granted a rare old age,
So the multitudes may rely on them."

IX

To the south there is:
The front hall of Received Brilliance,
The chamber where the emperor proclaims His rule
Here he receives worthies, employs the able,
255 Inquires of methods, seeks rectitude,
Regulates the entire world,
Molds and fashions the mores of the state.
Clouds move, rain spreads,
Permeating all the assorted things.

260 West there are:
Left a staircase, right a ramp,
And an exercise field.
Two sides of six in opposing squads,
Stand face to face like wings of a hall.
Nimble and quick, they seize every chance;
265 They are almost like armies at war.
The inspection over, they all return home;
One may compare it to government and law.
They use it for practicing commands;
How is it for amusement alone?

270 For a buttress there is a tall terrace;
This is Eternal Beginning.

L. 278: The plates were used to catch dew. Cf. "Western Capital Rhapsody," L. 299n.

L. 279: Cf. Wei Dan, "Rhapsody on the Hall of Great Blessings" (cited by Li Shan 11.31b): "In Yu Gulf, that sacred pond, / Limpid waters swell and surge."

L. 288: I assume this dragon is a waterspout in the shape of a dragon.

L. 291: He Yan here refers to the so-called "double-boat," a type of catamaran usually described as two boats lashed together.

L. 292: On the great fowl, see "Western Metropolis Rhapsody," L. 216n.

L. 298: The All-Encompassing Pond (Xian chi 咸池) is a group of three stars in Auriga. See Schlegel, 1:389; Ho Peng-yoke, p. 91. It was the stellar fish-pond and the pool in which the sun bathed. Li Shan (11.32a) cites several Han dynasty apocrphya that identify it as a five-star constellation in charge of gathering and nourishing the five grains; hence, the association with abundance.

LL. 300–301: Wei Dan's "Rhapsody on the Hall of Great Blessings" (cited by Li Shan 11.32b) mentions both the Gaochang 高昌 (named for Karakhojo?) and Jiancheng 建城 (Erect Wall) towers: "Looking north we see Gaochang, / Glancing sideways we spy Jiancheng." The *Five Comm.* reads *jie* 揭 (upthrust) for *Six Comm.* and You Mao *jie* 碣 (to mark off).

Tiered corridors, double gates,
Are waiting for rampageous rebels.
There are stores in hilly stacks;
275   There is nothing they do not contain.
As precautions against the unforseen,
They are here provided.

X

And then,
They erect the towering Cloud Piercing plates,
Dredge the Yu Gulf, that sacred pond.
280   Pure dew is heavy and thick,
Limpid waters swell and surge.
They plant it with auspicious trees,
Seed it with fragrant grasses.
Dark fish, frisking and frolicking,
285   White birds, albescently glistening,
Dive and drift, soar and swoop,
Rejoicing in our Sovereign's Way.

And now,
From a curly dragon water spouts and pours,
Canals and fosses crisscross flow.
290   On land are placed halls and lodges,
On water, light skiffs lashed together.
In bamboo groves nest great fowl and herons;
In these ripples play culter and hemiculter.
Abundance equal to the Huai and the Sea,
295   Wealth richer than mountains and hills,
Copiously collected, vastly gathered,
How can one count it all?
Even the grand spectacle of the All-Encompassing Pond,
How is it worthy of compare?

XI

300   And then,
Erected as landmark, the lofty Gaochang belevedere,
Marking the way, the spiring chalets of Jiancheng:

297

LL. 304–5: These are elevated passageways between buildings.

L. 306: The nine wastes simply refer to the limits of the world.

L. 307: The vast plan could be the pattern of the rivers and hills, or as Li Zhouhan (11.44a) says, the "long-range plans for the state."

L. 308: On the Three Markets, see "Wei Capital Rhapsody," L. 399n.

LL. 311–13: "No Luxurious Ease" ("Wu yi" 無逸) is a chapter in the *Classic of Documents*. In it the Duke of Zhou is reported as saying, "The Gentleman sets himself on having no luxurious ease. If he first understands the hardship and toil of sowing and reaping (= farming), and then takes his ease, he will understand the suffering of the lesser folk." He then goes on to enumerate the number of years ruled by various Shang and Zhou sovereigns. Those who cared for the suffering of their people enjoyed long reigns, while those who pursued a life of luxurious ease had short reigns. See *Shang shu zhushu* 16.9a–17a; Legge 3:464–73. The word *nian* 年 can be understood either as "harvest" or "years" (referring to the years ruled by the various ancient rulers mentioned in the "No Luxurious Ease" chapter). An alternative rendering for L. 312 is: "As we ponder the plenty or lack enjoyed by the harvest."

LL. 320–21: Duke Jing of Yan asked Yanzi if by living near a market he could discern the dear from cheap. Yanzi replied, "Toeless shoes are dear while straw sandals are cheap." This was a sutble hint that Duke Jing's punishments, which involved amputation of the toes, were too harsh. Duke Jing then reduced his punishments. See *Yanzi chunqiu* 6.6a–8b.

L. 337: Cf. *Liezi* 5.62: King Mu sighed and said, "Can human skill equal the feats of the Transmuter of things?" The Transmuter of things is nature.

Tall and towering, like monticules they stand;
Perilously poised, like peaks they rest.
Soaring corridors invade the clouds,
305 Floating stairways hang in the air.
Afar we glimpse the nine wastes,
Distantly regard a vast plan.
Below we see the Three Markets,
What they have, what they have not.

310 By observing the farmers' weeding and hoeing,
We truly understand the hardship and toil of sowing and reaping
Pondering how long rulers have enjoyed their years,
We recall the lamentation of "No Luxurious Ease."

Moved by the abundance of things, we become deep in thought;
315 For dwelling on high, we worry about danger.
We know that Heaven's blessing is not easy to hold;
But we fear that the profane world finds this hard to understand.
By observing the quality of the tools and implements,
We perceive honesty or falsity in popular custom.
320 By regarding what is dear and cheap,
We realize the inequity or severity of punishments.
Thus, these towers are a means of examining customs and aiding
    instruction;
How are they only for revelrous pleasures or honoring wasteful
    dissipation?

The garrison quarters, ranged in bureaus,
325 Thirty-two in number,
Are positioned like stars, arrayed like constellations,
Interwoven like silk, imbricating like fishscales.
With A and B, C and D,
They name their ranks.
330 Every room and chamber is the same,
All courtyards and halls seem as one.
One exits here, enters there,
Wishes to return, but forgets the way.

Consider the carpenters' multiple skills:
335 Truly, ten thousand transformations could not exhaust them all!
There is nothing too difficult for them to know;
Indeed, they match in eminence the Transmuter of things.

299

L. 338: The foundation is round above like Heaven and square below like Earth (Zhang Xian 11.45b).

LL. 340–41: According to the *Zhou li* (see *Zhou li zhushu* 41.23a; Biot, 2:553–54), a carpenter used a water-level suspended from cords and a gnomen (*nie* 臬) that measured the length of the shadow at sunrise and sunset. In L. 341 the *bu* 不 should be excised. See Liang Zhangju 13.18b.

L. 350: On Gongshu Ban, see "Western Metropolis Rhapsody," L. 186n.

L. 351: The Stonemason Shi was so skillful, he could chop a speck of mud off a man's nose without doing the slightest injury. See *Zhuangzi* 8.16a.

L. 362: The palace of the Yellow Lord reputedly was located on the Kunlun Mountains.

L. 364: "Compass and square" are metonymy for design.

L. 365: Li Zhouhan (11.47a) notes that this line refers to locating rooms such as the Warm Chamber on the east side, and the Cool Hall on the west (see LL. 176–77 above) presumably to conform to geomantic considerations.

In accord with Heaven and Earth, they lay the foundation;
Following the constellations, they build and construct.
340 In construction, there is nothing so fine it does not accord with the
          shadow's measurement;
In building, there is nothing so minute it fails to follow the water-
          level or gnomen.

Thus,
Its rising tiers seem piled one upon another,
With standing timbers like those of a forest,
Joined into sections, cut off into regions,
345 Matted like leaves, splayed liked branches.

Now diverging and dividing, each in different directions,
Now closely clustered, attached together,
Hither and thither they stretch past one another,
Each with its own destination.
350 Even Gongshu would abandon his compass and square;
Stonemason Shi would not know where to chop.

XII

Having exhausted their craft in design and planning,
How could colorful decoration be left undone?
And thus,
They adorn it with vermilion and green,
355 Embellish it with prase and cinnabar,
Dot it with gold and silver,
Spangle it with rubies.
A lustrous brilliance dazes and dazzles,
Patterned hues glitter and glisten.
360 Cool breezes gather and create melodious sounds,
The morning sun, brightly shining, adds luster.
Even the divine palace of the Kunlun peaks,
How could it surpass in splendor?

XIII

Since its compass and square conform to Heaven and Earth,
365 And its disposition follows the four seasons;

301

L. 367: Cf. *Mao shi* 303/2: "And then it commanded the Lord, / Everywhere hold ye the nine possessions." Nine possessions is simply another name for the nine provinces.

L. 369: He Yan alludes to a song attributed to the sage minister Gaoyao in the "Yi Ji" chapter of the *Classic of Documents* (see *Shang shu zhushu* 5.17a–b; Legge 3:90):

Oh, the great head is bright indeed!

Oh, the legs and arms are good indeed!

All things are pleasant indeed!

L. 375: "Standing on tiptoe" implies imminence. Cf. *Shi ji* 8.392: "Their destruction can be awaited standing on tiptoe."

L. 380: Cf. LL. 311–13n above.

L. 381: See L. 369n. The line may also refer to the "Counsels of Gaoyao" chapter in the *Classic of Documents*.

L. 384: This line must be an allusion to *Huainanzi* 8.8b–10a, which in a rhapsodic manner describes five types of "aimless abandon": (1) abandon in wood (large, expensive palaces and halls); (2) abandon in water (artificial moats and ponds, boating); (3) abandon in earth (erecting high walls, huge parks, tall gateways); (4) abandon in metal (bells, cauldrons, and other expensive vessels); (5) abandon in fire (burning forests for hunting, smelting metal for vessels).

L. 388: This line possibly refers to the appearance in February 233 of a dragon in a well at Mopo 摩陂 in Jia 郟 prefecture (modern Jia *xian*, Henan). See *Sanguo zhi* 3.99. Emperor Ming personally went to see the dragon and then changed his reign title to Blue Dragon.

L. 389: On the tortoise writing, see "Eastern Metropolis Rhapsody," L. 130n.

L. 393: "Great and splendrous land" is another name for China.

Thus,
The six directions enjoy great success,
The nine possessions, tranquility and ease,
Each household embraces the custom of yielding,
And each person sings the song "Pleasant Indeed!"
370 All are calm and comfortable, self-content,
And thus they are placid and serene, without a care.
If we examine history's rulers and rate their achievements,
None had the supreme rule that we now enjoy.
The destruction of those states of Wu and Shu,
375 We can eagerly await, standing on tiptoe.

Yet, our sage highness, still assiduous and alert, never erring,
Seeking from his realm a means of self-enlightenment,
Summons loyal and upright scholars,
To open the road of fairness and honesty.
380 He recalls the Duke of Zhou's warning from the past,
Admires Gaoyao's classical counsel,
Removes useless officials,
Reduces reasons for creating incidents,
Abolishes elaborate rites that lead to aimless abandon.
385 Returns popular taste to Grand Simplicity.

Thus, He can
Cause the singing phoenixes of Mt. Qi to soar here,
Receive the white ring of Lord Yu.
A green dragon has been seen in a pond,
A tortoise-writing has appeared at the source of the He,
390 Sweetwater springs bubble in pools and gardens,
The divine polypore grows in hills and parks.
He has garnered blessings bestowed by gods and spirits,
Gathered supreme felicity for this great and splendrous land.
He is added as a fourth to the Three August Ones, a sixth to the Five
          Emperors;
How are the Zhou and Xia worth mentioning?

303

L. 1: Emperor Gui 媯 is Shun. After he married the two daughters of Yao, he took up residence at the bend (*rui* 汭) of the Gui River (south of modern Yongji 永濟 *xian*, Shanxi). His descendants later assumed Gui as a surname. See *Shi ji* 35.1575; *Mh*, 4:169. The "Canon of Yao" (see *Shang shu zhushu* 2.24b; Legge 3:27) refers to Yao's dwelling as Gui-Rui 媯汭, which is variously interpreted as (confluence of the)Gui and Rui rivers, or "bend of the Gui." See Karlgren, "Glosses on the Ta Ya and Sung Odes," pp. 81–82, #910; "Glosses on the Book of Documents," pp. 70–71, #1246.

L. 2: Tang here refers to the sage emperor Yao. Before Shun became emperor, he served under Yao.

L. 3: According to Li Shan (12.1b), water covered such a vast expanse, it served as "Heaven's guiderope." Mu Hua alludes to the great deluge that began in the time of Yao and eventually was tamed by the Great Yu. Cf. Huan Tan's *Xin lun* (cited by Li Shan 12.1b; see also Pokora, *Hsin-lun*, p. 183, G1): "During the time of Xia Yu, a great flood frothed and foamed."

L. 9: According to *Mencius* 3A/4, during the time of Yao the waters flowed out of their channels and inundated the entire earth. Concerned about this, Yao appointed Shun to office to control the raging waters. Yu dredged the Nine Streams and cleared the courses of the Ji 濟 and Ta 漯 rivers to carry the water into the Sea. He also dredgred the Ru 汝 and Han rivers and opened channels for the Huai and Si 泗 rivers so that they poured into the Yangzi.

L. 10: Hu Kejia (2.27b) says 泼 should be emended to *wo* (**ok 沃 (to pour, to water) to rhyme with *zuo* (*dzhak) 鑿 in the following couplet. See also Hu Shaoying 14.1a–b.

L. 11· Dragon Gate (Long men 龍門), also known as Yu men 禹門 (Yu's Gate), is located about thirty kilometers north of modern Hancheng, Shanxi. According to tradition, Yu chiselled an opening in the mountain here to allow passage for the Yellow River The banks on both sides of the river form a gateway for the water. See *Shang shu zhushu* 6.21a–b; Legge 3:127; *Shuijing zhu* 1.4.57.

304

12

RIVERS AND SEAS

Rhapsody on the Sea

MU XUANXU

I

Of old, under Emperor Gui,
In the era of the great Tang,
Heaven's guiderope began to froth and foam,
Causing blight, bringing on disease.

5   Giant breakers spread and sprawled
A myriad miles, without bound;
Long swells rolled and tossed,
Streaming and stretching into the eight marches.

And then Yu
Pared mounds and hills overlooking the banks,

10   Breached dikes and ponds allowing the water to drain,
Opened Dragon Gate, jaggedly jutting,
Broke open hills and peaks, chiseling and boring through.

THIS RHAPSODY by Mu Hua (*zi* Xuanxu) is one of many early *fu* written about the sea. Extracts from other early sea rhapsodies (the earliest by Ban Biao of the Later Han) are preserved in the *Yiwen leiju* (8.152–54). Because it was preserved in the *Wen xuan*, Mu Hua's piece is the only complete *fu* on the subject to survive. The Jin dynasty critic Li Chong gave Mu Hua's *fu* a mixed review: "Master Mu's 'Rhapsody on the Sea' is powerful indeed! But its head and tail are disjoined. Although it has the appearance of a polished piece, yet it seems incomplete" (*Han lin lun*, cited by Li Shan 12 8b). What Li Chong perhaps criticizes is the lack of an introduction and epilogue, which most *fu* have. Mu's *fu* begins abruptly with an allusion to the myth of the Great Yu who tamed a giant deluge by channeling all the waters into the sea. Most of the remainder of the *fu* describes the sea's waters, particularly its waves (Mu uses at least a half dozen different words for wave), replete with all manner of binomial descriptives. Mu's *fu* is notable for its reference to luminous marine organisms and possibly icebergs (see LL. 165–66) as well as a long passage on a giant whale (LL. 171–84).

    The *fu* previously has been translated by von Zach, in *De Chineesche Revue* 3 (1929), and rpt. in *Die Chinesische Anthologie*, 1 : 180–83; Watson, *Chinese Rhyme-Prose*, pp. 72–79; Obi Kōichi, *Monzen*, 2 : 123–37.

L. 13: For an analogous use of *lue* 略 (to demarcate), see *Shang shu zhushu* ("Tribute of Yu") 6.9a; Legge 3:102. See also Karlgren, "Glosses on the Book of Documents," p. 145, #1355.

L. 16: *Six Comm.* read *qing* 傾 (to topple) for You Mao *po* 波 (waves).

L. 17: Cf. *Shang shu zhushu* ("Tribute of Yu") 6.25a–26b (Legge 3:134, 137): "(Yu) channeled the He from Piled Boulders as far as Dragon Gate.... From the Min Mountains he channeled the Jiang."

L. 36: Li Zhouhan (12.3a) says this line refers to the tidal bore. "When the bore rises the hundred rivers reverse their flow, as if the sea were blowing them. When the tide falls, it is as if the sea were gathering them."

L. 37: The Han River does not flow into the sea. Han probably is used only for rhyme. See Liang Zhangju 13.20a.

L. 38: Mu Hua borrows the phrase *xiang ling* 襄陵 (overtop the hills) from the "Canon of Yao" in the *Classic of Documents* (see *Shang shu zhushu* 2.19b; Legge 3:77). However, Li Zhouhan (12.3a) probably is correct in glossing *ling* here as "to overcome." I thus have rendered *xiang ling* as "engulf." Li Shan (12.2b) notes that *xi* (*tshiak) 舄 is interchangeable with *chi* (*thjak) 斥 (salt flat) Cf. *Shang shu zhushu* ("Tribute of Yu") 6.9b (Legge 3:102); *Lüshi chunqiu* 16.12a; *Han shu* 29.1677.

L 40: The Grand Luminary (Da ming 大明) should refer to the sun, but here it must be the moon. Thus, one scholar has suggested emending reading *ye* 夜 (night) for *da*. See Zhu Jian 12.10b. The moon is correlated with metal (hence the Metallic Pivot) and sets in a grotto. Li Shan (12.2b) cites Fu Tao's 伏滔 (ca. 317–396) "Rhapsody on Gazing at the Breakers," which describes the moon in similar terms: "The Metallic Pivot steadies its reins, / The albescent moon announces its fullness." Cf. *Yiwen leiju* 9.165 for a slightly different reading for the first line

L. 41: Soaring Brightness (Xiang yang 翔陽) is the sun. On Fusang, see "Western Metropolis Rhapsody," L. 438n.

Once the massing mountains had been demarcated,
And the hundred streams were dispersed underground,
15 Broad and boundless, calm and clear,
The leaping waves sped off with the current.

When the Jiang and the He had been channeled,
Though a myriad crevices all the waters began to flow,
Leaving the Five Peaks pushing and poking upward,
20 The Nine Continents drained and dried.

Dribbling droplets, soaking waters,
Dense and dark as clouds and fog;
Burbling streams trickling and trilling,
None failed to come pouring in.
25 Oh, this vast numinous sea,
Long has it received and transported!
Such breadth,
Such wonderment,
All befit its greatness!

II

30 And such is its form:
Flooding and flowing, tossing and tumbling,
It floats the sky, shoreless,
Surging and swelling, profoundly plunging,
Remotely ranging, distantly distended;
Waves like serried mountains,
35 Now joined, now scattered;
Inhaling and exhaling the hundred rivers,
Cleaning and clearing the Huai and Han;
Engulfing broad salt flats,
Mingling and merging far and wide.

40 Now when
The Grand Luminary turns its reins toward the Metallic Pivot
    grotto,
And Soaring Brightness swiftly speeds from Fusang's ford,
Tossing sand and swashing against rocks
The wind rages and roars on island beaches.

L. 59: Li Shan (12.3b) explains the rhyming binome *dake* 眔匑 (**dep-kep*) as "layer upon layer." The meaning perhaps derives from *ke*, which is phonetically and semantically related to *he* 合 (**gep*); hence, my "merging and melding." See *Shuowen* 9A.4047b, Duan Yucai's commentary and Zhu Jian 12.10b–11a.

L. 63: Li Shan (12.3b) explains *shishi* 濕濕 as descriptive of opening and closing. However, *shishi* also can describe shaking and rocking movement. Cf. *Mao shi* 190/1; hence, my "shaking and shuddering."

L. 64: On *pahua* 葩華 (spreading and scattering), see "Western Metropolis Rhapsody," L. 214n and Zhu Qifeng, *Ci tong*, p. 0771.

According to Li Shan (12.3b), the rhyming binome *cunu* 踧汹 (**tsjok-njok*) has the basic meaning of "cramped and gathered together." *Guanyun* (p. 437) glosses it as "descriptive of the patterns of the water." I suspect that the signific is *cu*, which basically means "cramped." Mu Hua is describing in this line how the waters first scatter (*pahua*, my "spreading and sprawling"), then gather (*cunu*, my "crowded and cramped"). See Zhu Jian 12.11a

And then roused to fury,
45 Welling waves heave and foam,
Clashing and colliding with one another,
Scattering spray, lifting breakers.

Their form is like the wheels of Heaven,
Revolving and rotating, furiously turning;
50 Or like the axles of earth,
Thrusting, pushing, vehemently spinning.
Their ridges and crests soar on high, then falter and fall,
Like the Five Peaks swaying and swirling, pounding one upon
                another.
Wildly they surge and sink, piled and packed together;
55 Swollen, they dash and dart, crest and collapse.
Whirling and twirling, they form raging troughs;
Combing and rolling, they jet into pointed peaks.
Swiftly, riffles and ripples popple on the sides,
While the giants, merging and melding, clash with one another.
60 Startled waves thunderously race,
Stampeding waters scatter and gather again:
They open and close, dissolve and merge,
Spurting and spouting, shaking and shuddering,
Spreading and sprawling, crowded and cramped,
65 Frothing and foaming, pitching and plunging.

III

Then when
Dust clouds and dark skies recede and dissolve,
Nothing moves, nothing stirs,
And the lightest dust does not fly,
Or the tenderest vines do not quiver,
70 Still gaping and gulping,
Remnant waves continue their solitary heaving,
Swelling and surging, steep and tall,
Jaggedly jutting like mounts and hills.

Further, branches and forks, spuming and seething,
75 Turbulent and tempestuous, form tributaries.
They divide us from the Man, separate us from the Yi,
And wind one after another for ten thousand miles.

L. 83: The "hundred-foot" is the main mast.

L. 84: Li Shan (12.4a) explains *shao* 綃 as the long piece of wood from which sails were hung. The early Tang name for it was *fan gang* 帆綱, which means "yard" or "boom." See Kariya Ekisai 狩谷棭齋 (1775–1835), ed. and comm., *Senchū Wamyō ruiju shō* 箋注倭名類聚抄 (Encylopedia of Japanese, Annotated) (Tokyo: Insatsukyoku, 1883), 3.62a–b.

L. 94: Cf. "Wu Capital Rhapsody," L. 158.

L. 95: Li Shan (12.4b) cites the "Painting of the Rhapsody on the Sea" by Lu Sui 陸綏 (5th century), which describes the horse-swallower (*maxian* 馬銜) as a beast with the head of a horse, one horn, and a dragon's body.

L. 96: On Tianwu, see "Wu Capital Rhapsody," L. 670n.

L. 97: On Wangxiang, see "Eastern Metropolis Rhapsody," L. 571n.

L. 108: Li Shan (12.5a) glosses the alliterative binome *hexu* 呵欨 (*ha-hjwet*) as "descriptive of not being clear." However, Liu Liang (12.6a) explains it as describing the speed of the spouting light and color. The signific element possibly is *he* (to spout); hence, my "spewing and spouting."

If then
Border wastes must see swift report,
Or royal command must be quickly proclaimed,
80 They gallop fleet steeds, ply their sweeps,
To cross the sea or scale mountains.

And then,
They await a strong wind,
Hoist the hundred-foot,
Secure long yards,
85 Hang sails and sheets.

Watching the waves, they depart for afar,
Glistening brightly, gliding like a soaring bird,
Swift as a startled duck lost from its mate,
Sudden as if drawn by six dragons.
90 At once they cover three thousand miles,
Before morning's end they reach their destination.

IV

But if a man
Approaches the deep laden with sin,
Swearing empty oaths, uttering false prayers,
Then sea elves block his way,
95 Horse-swallowers impede his path,
Tianwu suddenly appears, dimly descried,
Wangxiang briefly shows himself, a fleeting specter.
A host of demons meets and confronts him,
Glaring and glowering, beguiling and bewitching.

100 Tearing the sails, splitting the mast,
Fierce winds begin their dreadful destruction.
All is opened wide, as if transformed by spirits,
Then turns dark and dim, like sombrous dusk.
Their breath, like heavenly vapors,
105 Misty and murky, spreads like clouds.
Fleeting and flashing, like streaking lightning,
A hundred hues weirdly appear,
Spewing and spuming, pale and pallid,
Flickering and fluttering without measure.

311

L. 114: Li Shan (12.5a) explains the alliterative binome *chenchuo* 趻踔 (**thjem-thok*) as "descriptive of the forward and backward motion of the waves." However, Hu Shaoying (14.4a) points out that the basic sense is a "moving in an abnormal manner" (cf. *Shuowen* 2B.905b–906a), as in the *Zhuangzi* (17 261) description of the hobbling gait of the monopod Kui: "On this one leg I wamble and wobble (*chenzhuo*) along."

L. 116: Although Li Shan (12 5a) explains the alliterative binomes *huohui* 濩洅 (**huak-hjwed*) and *huowei* 濩湏 (**guak-gjued*) as "the sound of waves," Zhu Jian (12.11a) shows that they both are descriptive of the rolling and pitching motion of the waves. I have roughly translated them as "pitching and plunging" and "rolling and tossing."

L. 122: Hu Shaoying (14.4a–b) shows that *cheche yui* 掣掣洩洩 is a reduplication of *cheyi* 掣曳 (variant 瘛), which basically means "to pull." Cf. *Erya* A3.13b–14a.

L. 123: The land of the Black Teeth (Hei chi 黑齒) was located above Dawn Valley. Its people had black teeth, ate rice and snakes. See *Huainanzi* 4.8b–9a.

L. 129: On the Vermeil Shore, see "Eastern Capital Rhapsody," L. 209n.

L. 130: The Heavenly Barrens (Tian xu 天墟) is a lunar mansion (β Aquarii, α Equulei) located in the north part of the heavens. See *Erya* B4.11a; Zhu Jian 12.11b; Schlegel, *Uranographie*, 1:214–25.

L. 131: Split Wood (Xi mu 析木) is the name of the Jupiter station corresponding to the northeast areas of Yan and You (northern Hebei). It also stands for the ford of the Sky River. See *Erya* B4.10b; *Zuozhuan*, *Zhao* 8 (Legge 5:623); Schlegel, *Uranographie*, 1:156.

L. 132: Qing 青 and Xu 徐 are areas along the Shandong coast.

L 137: The *kun* 鯤 is a legendary giant fish of the Northern Sea. It is so large, no one knows how many miles long it is. See *Zhuangzi* 1.1.

L. 139: Taidian 太顛 was one of the assistants to King Wen of Zhou. According to the *Qin cao* 琴操 (Zither Tunes) attributed to Cai Yong (cited by Li Shan 12.5b), King Zhou of Yin imprisoned King Wen at Qiangli and had chosen a day to kill him. Thereupon, Taidian and other loyal vassals of King Wen obtained a large cowry shell from the water and presented it as ransom for their lord.

L. 140· On Lord Sui's pearl, see "Western Capital Rhapsody," L. 192n.

110 Surging billows grind together,
    Their turbulent forces colliding,
    Like crumbling clouds, spattering rain,
    Swashing and splashing,
    Wambling and wobbling, advancing and retreating,
115 Sputtering and spouting, flowing and flooding,
    Pitching and plunging, rolling and tossing,
    Sweeping the clouds, dousing the sun.

V

    And then
    Sailors and fishermen
    Travel south and to the extreme east.
120 Some are smashed and drowned in caverns of turtles and alligators,
    Some are hung and caught on jagged reefs,
    Some are hauled and dragged to the realm of naked men,
    Some drift and float to the land of Black Teeth men,
    Some glide like duckweed, scudding and whirling along,
125 Some following the homing winds, return on their own.
    They only know how frightful were the wonders they saw,
    And are oblivious of whether the places they passed were near or far.

    But these are the general limits:
    South it soaks the Vermeil Shore,
130 North waters the Heavenly Barrens,
    East extends to Split Wood,
    West pushes upon Qing and Xu.
    The area it spans, dim and distant,
    Stretches ten-ten-thousand leagues and more.
135 It spouts clouds and rainbows,
    Enfolds dragons and fish,
    Hides the scaly *kun*,
    Conceals spirit dwellings.
    How does it only collect
    Tai Dian's precious cowry,
140 Or Lord Sui's luminous pearl?
    Could it be that one frequently hears of things collected by the world,
    While those unnamed seem nonexistent?

313

L. 149: Mu Hua probably is referring to the fifteen legendary giant turtles that supported the islands of the Eastern Sea on their backs. See *Liezi* 5.52–53.

L. 152: Grand Clarity (Tai qing 太清) is a place in the heavens located forty *li* from the earth. See *Baopuzi* 15.7b.

LL. 155–56: The Balmy Breeze (Kai feng 凱風) is the southern wind. Broad Blast (Guang mo 廣莫) is the northern wind. See *Erya* B4.6b; *Lushi chunqiu* 13.2b–3a; *Huainanzi* 3.4a–4b; Major, "Nomenclature of Winds," pp. 67–68.

L. 158: On the mermen (literally "shark people"), see "Wu Capital Rhapsody," LL. 288–90.

L. 161–62: According to Zhang Xian (12.8b), the cloud brocade is the morning rose clouds. Cf. Cao Zhi, "Song of the Qi Zither" (fragment cited by Li Shan 12.6b): "Mussels and oysters blanket shores and banks, / Their brilliant colors like brocade red."

L. 165: The sunlit ice (*yang bing* 陽冰) perhaps describes icebergs. The term first occurs in the *Yanzi chunqiu* (5.7a and for corrected text see "Jiaokan" B.5a–b), which makes the general statement that "*yin* ice is frozen while *yang* ice is five inches thick." Wang Niansun (see *Dushu zazhi* (6/2.4b–5a) explains that *yang* ice is ice exposed to the sun. "The Rhapsody on *Yang bing*" by Lin Zi 林滋 (*jinshi* 843) seems to be describing an iceberg. See *Wenyuan yinghua* 39.9a–b.

L. 166: The "shadowy fire" (*yin huo* 陰火) probably is some sort of marine bioluminescence. The fourth century scholar Wang Jia 王嘉 (ob. 390) describes the *yin huo* of Floating Jade Mountain (Fu yu shan 浮玉山), located west of the Western Sea: "Beneath the mountain there is a huge cavern, and within the cavern there is water with a color like fire. In daylight it is translucent and luminous, but at night it casts its brilliance outside the cavern. Even if waves and breakers pour and pound upon it, its light is not extinguished." See Wang Jia, *Shi yi ji* 拾遺記 (Record of Neglected Matters) (Beijing: Zhonghua shuju, 1981), 1.23. On the *yin* fire, see also Schafer, *Vermilion Bird*, p. 139.

L. 167: This line may refer to the self-kindling fire of Xiaoqiu 蕭邱, a mountain located in the Southern Sea. See *Baopuzi*, "Wai pian," 1.3b.

L. 168: The Nine Springs are in the underworld.

Moreover, for things rarely heard of in this world,
How can one discern their names?
145 Thus, one can only vaguely visualize their features,
Dimly depict their forms.

VI

Now,
Within their watery respository,
And the courts of their unplumbed depths,
There are lofty islands borne by giant turtles,
150 Tall and towering, standing alone,
Cleaving the giant waves,
Pointing to Grand Clarity,
Thrusting mighty boulders,
Roosts for a hundred numina.
155 When the Balmy Breeze rises, southward they travel;
When the Broad Blast arrives, northward they journey.
Within their shores there are:
Natural jewels, aquatic wonders,
Houses of the mermen,
The eery shimmer of scarlet stones,
160 The strange essence of scale and shell.

And now,
A cloudy brocade spreads a pattern along sandy shores,
A gauzy gossamer casts luster over the seams of mussels and snails,
Manifold colors brandish their splendor,
A myriad hues conceal their brilliance:
165 Sunlit ice that does not melt,
Shadowy fires burning underwater;
Glowing coals that rekindle themselves,
Casting their fulgor into the Nine Springs;
Vermilion flames, green smoke,
170 Dark and dense, curling and swirling upward.

VII

Of fish
There is the sea-spanning whale,

315

L. 193: The *Five Comm.* text reads *wu* 騖 (to race) for You Mao and *Six Comm. wu* 霧 (fog).

L. 194: Hu Shaoying (14.6a) shows that *yiyi* 洩洩 (*djad-djad) is interchangeable with *yiyi* 裔裔 (*djad-djad). The word means "gracefully gliding." Cf. "Shu Capital Rhapsody," LL. 305–6n.

L. 199: The three luminaries are the sun, moon, and stars.

L. 201: Cf. "Southern Capital Rhapsody," L. 226n.

L. 202: The *Baopuzi* (15.7a) explains *cheng qiao* 乘蹻 (riding on the heels) as a technique for flying in the air without being hindered by mountains or rivers.

Looming lordly, swimming alone,
Leveling cragged peaks,
Toppling tall breakers,
175 Devouring the scaled and shelled,
Swallowing dragon boats.
He sucks in waves and giant rollers mass and merge;
He blows out billows and the hundred streams backward flow
If perchance he flounces and flounders in spent waves,
180 And beached dies on salty flats,
His giant scales shall pierce the clouds,
His dorsal fins shall prick the sky,
The bones of his skull will form peaks,
And his oozing oil will become ponds.

VIII

185 Now,
In bights of cragged isles,
Shelves of sand and stone,
The winged and feathered engender their chicks,
Breaking the eggs to bring young birds to life.
Ducklings, fluffy and flossy,
190 Baby cranes, sleek and silky,
Flying in flocks, bathing in pairs,
Play in the openings, float on the deeps.
Like hovering fog they soar aloft,
Gliding gracefully in a steady stream.
195 Their fluttering motion creates thunder,
Their thrumming wings become a grove.
Back and forth they screech and squawk,
Wondrously hued, unique in voice.

IX

And then,
When the three luminaries shine clear,
200 Heaven and Earth glow and gleam,
Without drifting on Lord Yang's billows,
One may ride his arches and break away,

L. 203: Master Anqi 安期 was a native of Fuxiang 阜鄉 in Langye. He sold medicines on the shore of the Eastern Sea. After he became renowned as the Thousand-Year-Old Man, the First Qin Emperor sought him out and conversed with him for three days and three nights. After the emperor left, Anqi disappeared, leaving only a pair of sandals behind. In a letter he announced, "Some years hence seek me on Penglai Mountain." The emperor dispatched two envoys to find him, but they had to turn back when they encountered a storm at sea. See *Liexian zhuan* A.25.

L. 204: The Yellow Lord's tumulus was on Mount Qiao 橋, which the *Han shu* (28B.1617) locates south of Yangzhou 陽州 (modern northern Shaanxi). The modern tomb is located about a kilometer northwest of Huangling 黃陵, Shaanxi. According to legend, it was here that the Yellow Lord ascended to Heaven and became an immortal. See *Shi ji* 12.463, 28.1396.

L. 210: The barren murk is the Northern Sea.

LL. 214–15: The Donator (Qian 乾) and Receptor (Kun 坤) trigrams represent Heaven and Earth respectively.

L. 222: The Abysmal (Kan 坎) trigram represents water.

L. 223: Cf. *Zhou yi zhushu* 2 32a (Hexagram 15, "Commentary on the Images"): "Modest, modest is the Gentleman. In lowness he nurtures himself."

To view Anqi on Penglai,
See the Lord's image on Mount Qiao.

205 A host of immortals, distantly descried,
Feast on jade by pristine shores,
Walk in sandals left at Fuxiang,
Dress in plumes and pinions, dangling and drooping.

They soar to the pond of Heaven,
210 Play in the barren murk.
Though revealing their forms, they have no desires;
Forever and ever, eternally they live.

X

Further, as for the sea's capacities:
It embraces Donator's mysteries,
215 Enfolds Receptor's realm.
The gods here reside,
Also spirits here dwell.
What wonder does it not have?
What marvel does it not store?
220 Broad and boundless, this accumulation of streams!
Though receiving their forms, empty within it remains.
Vast indeed the Abysmal's power!
In lowness it makes its abode.
Enlarging what goes forth, accepting what comes in,
225 It is the grand eminence, the metropolis.
Of the assorted things and living species,
What does it have, what does it not?

L. 1: The five substances are metal, wood, water, fire, and earth. Cf. *Zhozhuan, Xiang* 27 (Legge 5:534): "Heaven produces the five substances, and the people equally use them."

L. 2: Cf. *Huainanzi* 1.10a–b: "Of the things of the world, nothing is weaker than water. But it is so large it cannot be spanned, so deep it cannot be fathomed.... Thus, we call it the supreme virtue."

LL. 3–4: The traditional belief was that the Yangzi had its source in the Min Mountains of Sichuan. See *Shang shu zhushu* 2.28b (cf. Legge 3:137): "From the Min Mountains he channeled the Yangzi." Cf. *Xunzi* 20.7b: "Of old, the Yangzi issued from the Min Mountains. When it first issued forth, its source could overflow a goblet;" and *Kongzi jiayu* 2.16a: "The Yangzi begins in the Min Mountains Its source could overflow a goblet."

L. 5: This is the Luo 洛 River of Sichuan. It had its source in the Zhang 漳 Mountains, flowed south and entered the Jian 湔 River east of the Han prefecture of Xindu 新都 (modern Xindu, Sichuan). See *Han shu* 28A.1597; *Shuijing zhu* 33.6.8.

Mei 沫 is another name for the Dadu 大渡 River of southwestern Sichuan. It entered the Qingyi 青衣 River, which flowed into the Yangzi at the Han prefecture of Nan'an 南安 (modern Leshan 樂山).

L. 6: Li Shan (2.9a) explains Ba 巴 as Ba commandery, and Liang as Liangzhou 梁州, the ancient name for the southwestern area of China. Liu Liang (12.12a) identifies Ba and Liang as two mountains. The Ba Mountains most likely would be the Daba 大巴 chain that extends southwest of Xixiang 西鄉 in Shaanxi west to the area of Nanjiang 南江 in Sichuan. The Liang Mountains presumably are the Gaoliang 高梁 Mountains located north of modern Liang shan 梁山 *xian*, Sichuan.

L. 7: Shaman Gorge (Wu xia 巫峽), located in western Hubei, is one of the great gorges through which the Yangzi passes.

L. 8: River Ford (Jiang jin 江津) here refers to a location on Meihui 枚回 Isle, north of Jiangling This seventy-*li* island divided the Yangzi into a north and south section. According to Li Daoyuan, the Yangzi increased in size here. See *Shuijing zhu* 6.34.26.

L. 10: Cf. *Shang shu zhushu* 2.19b ("Canon of Yao"): "Oh, you Four Peaks: rolling and reeling, flood waters everywhere injurious, enfold mountains, overtop hills, vast and wide, swelling to the skies."

LL 11–12: Guo Pu probably is following *Mengzi* 3A/4 (Legge 3:251), which says the Great Yu "dredged the Ru and Han, and regulated the Huai and Si, so that they flowed into the Yangzi." Cf. "Rhapsody on the Sea," L. 9n. However, the only one of these rivers that actually flows directly into the Yangzi is the Han. The Ru and Si enter the Huai, which flows to the sea. Some scholars have sought to explain this ostensible lapse in *Mengzi* and by Guo Pu by arguing that the Yangzi and Huai rivers were connected by the Han Canal. See Zhang Yun'ao 7.9b–11b; Zhu Jian 12.13a–b.

L. 13: The Yuan 沅 and Li 澧 rivers enter the Yangzi at Lake Dongting.

L. 14: On the Ju and Zhang rivers see "Rhapsody on Climbing the Tower." LL. 5–6.

L. 15: Ju 崏 possibly is another name for the Meng 蒙 Mountains in western Sichuan. Lai is the Qionglai 邛崍 Mountains, located southwest of modern Xingjing 滎經, western Sichuan. The *Shanhai jing* 5.28b–29a mentions them both as sources of the Yangzi. In his commentary to this passage, Guo Pu says that Mount Lai was the source of the Southern Jiang (= Qiong River), and Mount Ju was the source of the Southern Jiang (perhaps the Qingyi River). See also Zhu Jian 12.14a–b.

L. 16: Guo Pu here is referring to the Nine Rivers (Jiu jiang 九江), the names and location of which have been debated in Chinese scholarship. The expression first appears in the "Tribute of Yu" (see *Shang shu zhushu* 6.14a; Legge 3:113). According to the pseudo-Kong Anguo commentary to this "Tribute of Yu" passage, the Yangzi divided into nine tributaries in Jingzhou (the Hubei-Hunan area). Guo Pu apparently follows the tradition that Lake Pengli

Rhapsody on the Yangzi river

GUO JINGCHUN

I

Ah! The five substances are of equal use,
But water's virtue is the most efficacious of all.
The Yangzi that courses from the Min Mountains,
Issuing its source from an overflowing cup,
5 Passes first the Luo and Mei,
Gathers a myriad streams from Ba and Liang,
Collides with Shaman Gorge, swiftly rushing,
Ascends River Ford, rising and distending,
And reaching a size most large, churns like the sea,
10 Its form swelling to the skies, broad and boundless.
It encloses the Han and Si,
Embraces the Huai and Xiang,
Engorges the Yuan and Li,
Inhales the Ju and Zhang.
15 It divides its source at Ju and Lai,
Branches into nine tributaries at Xunyang,

THIS RHAPSODY by Guo Pu (*zi* Jingchun) is a poetic description of the largest Chinese
river, the Yangzi (Yangtze). In high epideictic style Guo Pu presents the Yangzi as the River
(Jiang) *par excellence*, issuing from the Min Mountains of Sichuan, raging through the Three
Gorges of Western Hubei, and engorging the rivers of Central China as it courses eastward to
the sea. Guo Pu was one of the most learned men in Chinese history, and his *fu* is full of recondite
lore and language. Li Shan (12.8b) cites the *Jin zhongxing shu* 晉中興書 (History of the Jin
Restoration), compiled by He Fasheng 何法盛 (fifth century), which says that "because the
King of the Restoration (i.e., Sima Rui, who in 318 established the Eastern Jin "Restoration")
took up residence south of the Yangzi," Guo Pu wrote this *fu* "to relate the beauty of streams and
waterways."

    Previous translations of the *fu* include von Zach in *De Chineesche Revue* 3 (1929) and rpt.
in *Die Chinesische Anthologie*, 1:184–92 and Obi Kōichi, *Monzen*, 2:138–59.

(modern Poyang Lake) in the Xunyang area was formed by nine rivers. The lost geographical treatise, the *Xunyang di ji* 潯陽地記 (Records of Xunyang Area), compiled by Zhang Sengjian 張僧監 (n.d.), cited in *Shang shu zhushu* 6.14a–b, gives a list of what presumably were the nine Xunyang tributaries. Many later scholars argue that the Nine Rivers of the "Tribute of Yu" refer to Lake Dongting See Zhang Yun'ao 7.12a–13b.

L. 17: Li Shan (12.9b) cites an unnamed scholar who locates Scarlet Shore (Chi an 赤岸) in *Yu* 輿 (for this reading see Hu Kejia, *Kaoyi*, 2.30a) prefecture of Guangling, the location of the Yangzi River bore. Cf. Mei Sheng's "Seven Stimuli," *Wen xuan* 34.12a. Hu Shaoying 14.7b cites the *Nan Yanzhou ji* 南兖州記 (Records of Southern Yanzhou), a gazetteer of Yangzhou attributed to Ruan Xuzhi 阮敍之 (n.d.), which identifies Scarlet Shore as a mountain located five *li* east of Guabu 瓜步 Mountain in the Yangzhou area.

L. 18: Chaisang 柴桑 was a prefecture south of modern Jiujiang, Jiangxi.

L. 21: Jiangdu 江都 (southwest of modern Yangzhou) was a prefecture of Guangling. To its east there was a Yangzi River Shrine. See *Han shu* 28B.1638; *Hou Han shu*, "Zhi," 21.3461; *Jin shu* 15.452.

L. 22: The word *zong* 宗 (to reverence, to pay homage to) comes from a phrase in the "Tribute of Yu" (see *Shang shu zhushu* 6.14a; Legge 3:113): "The Jiang and Han pay court and reverence to the sea."

L. 23: The Five Lakes (Wu hu 五湖) are variously identified. The *Wu lu* 吳錄 (Register of Wu), compiled by Zhang Bo 張勃 (4th century?), cited by Li Shan (12.10a), says Five Lakes is another name for Lake Tai. Wei Zhao (cited in *Guo yu* 21.1b and *Shi ji* 29.1407, n. 2) explains that the name refers to the five bays of Lake Tai's eastern shore, each called a "lake": Ling 菱 (east of Moli Mountain 莫釐), Mo 莫 (northwest of Moli Mountain), Xu 胥 (west of Xu 胥 Mountain), You 游 (east of Chang 長 Mountain), and Gong 貢 (west of Chang Mountain). See *Shi ji* 2.59, n. 4. Li Daoyuan (see *Shuijing zhu* 5.29.52) names them as Lake Tai and four lakes near Lake Tai: Changdang 長蕩, She 射, Gui 貴, and Ge 滆. Sima Zhen (see *Shi ji* 29.1407, n. 2) says that the lakes include the five large lakes Guo Pu mentions in LL. 225–26 below: Juqu 具區 (Lake Tai), Yao-Ge 洮滆, Pengli, Qingcao 青草, and Dongting. Zhang Yun'ao (7.13b–16a) argues that since the Yangzi River does not connect with Lake Tai, the Five Lakes cannot include it. He concludes that the Five Lakes consist of all of the lakes mentioned by Sima Zhen except Lake Tai.

L. 24: The expression "Three Rivers" (*San jiang* 三江), which first appears in the "Tribute of Yu" (see *Shangshu zhushu* 6.12a; Legge, 3:108), has been the subject of endless controversy in traditional Chinese scholarship. According to one view, the Jiang consisted of three large sections, the Northern Jiang (Bei jiang 北江), the Southern Jiang (Nan jiang 南江), and the Central Jiang 中江. Thus, Zheng Xuan (cited in *Chuxue ji* 6.123) explains that the Han River formed the Northern Jiang, Lake Pengli (modern Poyang) formed the Southern Jiang, and the main portion of the Yangzi from the Min River was the Central Jiang. Other commentators identify the Three Rivers as waterways in the Lake Tai area: the Wu 吳 (= Wusong 吳松), Qiantang 錢唐, and Puyang 浦陽 (Wei Zhao, *Guo yu* 20.1b); Song (= Wusong), Lou 婁, and Dong 東. See *Shang shu zhushu* 6.11a, citing the *Wu di ji* 吳地記 (Records of the Wu Area) of Zhang Bo (same as *Wu lu* cited in L. 23n above?). Li Daoyuan (see *Shuijing zhu* 5.29.56) cites Guo Pu as specifying them as the Min, the Song (= Wusong), and the Zhe 浙 (in modern Zhejiang). However, Zhang Yun'ao (7.16b–17b) argues that none of these explanations properly accounts for the word *guan* 灌 (to water), and he concludes that Guo Pu intends them to refer to the three sources of the Yangzi: the Great Jiang (Da jiang 大江), which has its source in the Min Mountains; the Southern Jiang, which has its source in the Qionglai Mountains; and the Northern Jiang, which has its source in the Ju Mountains. See L. 15n above.

L. 25: The Six Provinces are Yi 益 (Sichuan), Liang 梁 (eastern Sichuan, western Shaanxi), Jing 荊 (Hubei, Hunan), Jiang 江 (Jiangxi), Yang 揚 (Jiangsu and Zhejiang), and Xu 徐 (parts of Jiangsu, Shandong, and Anhui).

Drums its giant bore on Scarlet Shore,
Sinking the receding waves at Chaisang.

II

Enmeshing the teeming flow,
20   Presiding over brook and canal,
It reveals its wondrous conflux at Jiangdu,
Where merging streams pay homage and eastward converge.
Pouring into Five Lakes, spreading vast and far,
Watered by Three Rivers, surging and swelling,
25   It douses and drenches the realm of the Six Provinces,

L. 26: The "land of flaming brilliance" is the south.

L. 28: Cf. *Zhou yi zhushu* 3.33b–34a (Hexagram 29, "Commentary on the Images"): "Heaven's perils cannot be climbed; Earth's perils are mountains and rivers, mounds and barrows."

L. 35: On Emei, see "Shu Capital Rhapsody," L. 16n. Li Shan (12.10b) says Quanyang is an inversion for Yangquan 陽泉, which is a prefecture located north of modern Mianzhu 緜竹, Sichuan. Since Yangquan is located far from Mount Emei, I follow Zhang Xian (12.13b), who takes Yangquan as referring to the Yangzi (its source?). I have loosely rendered it as Southern Springs.

L. 36: On Yulei, see "Shu Capital Rhapsody," L. 14n. Li Daoyuan (see *Shuijing zhu* 6.33.2), who cites Guo Pu's line, says that at Yulei Mountain the Tuo 沱 River "branches eastward."

L. 37: Mount Heng 衡, located north of modern Hengshan 衡山, Hunan, was the Southern Buttress of Jingzhou. See *Zhou li zhushu* 32 11a. Mount Huo 霍, also known as Tianzhu 天柱, located in modern Qianshan 潛山, Anhui, in some texts is designated as the sacred peak (buttress, marchmount) of the south. See *Erya* B7.5b–6a.

L. 38: Mount Wu 巫, east of modern Wushan 巫山 in Sichuan, overlooks the Yangzi. Mount Lu 廬 is south of modern Jiujiang, Jiangxi.

L. 43: Xinyang 信陽 means "south of Xinling" 信陵, which was the name of a Jin dynasty prefecture located in Jianping 建平 commandery. See *Jin shu* 15.456. According to Li Daoyuan (see *Shuijing zhu* 6.34 20), the Yangzi passed eastward to the south of Xinling. It probably was located near modern Zigui 秭歸, Hubei. See Zhu Jian 12.17b.

L. 44: I follow Wang Niansun (see *Dushu zazhi*, "Zhiyu," B.31a–b) and Hu Shaoying (14.7b–8a) in understanding *cong* 淙 as "to drain into."

The Grand Gulf (Da huo 大壑) is the large bottomless ravine millions of miles east of Bohai. All of the waters of the world, including the Sky River, flow into it. See *Liezi* 5.52. Li Shan (12.10b–11a) cites an unknown work, the *Xuanzhong ji* 玄中記 (Records from the Dark), which identifies Wojiao 沃焦 (my Exsiccator of Waters) as a mountain located 30,000 *li* from the southern quarter of the Eastern Sea. Waters ceaselessly flow into it. Another name for it is Weilu 尾閭 (Final Conflux), which Sima Biao (cited by Li Shan 53.5a–b) identifies as a rock 40,000 li square and 40,000 *li* thick. All of the water of the world collects here and evaporates.

L. 45: East of Ba refers to the location of the Three Gorges of the Yangzi.

L. 46: The Lord of Xia is Yu, who opened a course for the Yangzi.

LL. 49–50: Tiger Fangs (Hu ya 虎牙) and Thorn Portal (Jing men 荊門) are two mountains on the northern and southern banks of the Yangzi respectively. They are located northwest of modern Yidu 宜都, Hubei. According to Sheng Hongzhi's *Jingzhou ji* (cited by Li Shan 12.11a), Thorn Portal was closed at the top and open at the bottom in the shape of a gate. Tiger Fangs was a red stone cliff with white streaks that resembled tiger teeth. See also *Shuijing zhu* 6.34.22 for a similar description.

L. 51: Guo Pu here describes the deep pools of the gorges. They are so deep, they have nine vortexes extending downward.

Criss-crosses the land of flaming brilliance,
As a means
To set a boundary between China and outland,
To strengthen the perilous impasses of Heaven and Earth.

III

      Huffing and puffing for a myriad miles,
30   It inhales and exhales a numinous tide,
      Spontaneously ebbing and flowing,
      Now evening, now morning;
      Rousing its swift power, ahead it drives,
      And then, pulsing with anger, forms a bore.
35   Emei serves as guide-stone for the Southern Springs,
      Yulei acts as marker for the Eastern Branch;
      Heng and Huo, precipitously piled, form an interlocking buttress,
      Wu and Lu, peaked and pinnacled, vie in steepness.
      It blends the numina, purges the air,
40   Beating and battering, molds things together,
      Sets aflow the wind, belches thunder,
      Arches rainbows, scatters rosy clouds.
      Departing Xinyang, long it journeys,
      To drain into Grand Gulf and Exsiccator of Waters.

IV

45   As for
      The gorges east of Ba,
      Dredged and bored by the Lord of Xia:
      Sheer banks, one hundred thousand feet high,
      Wall-like stand, streaked like rosy clouds;
      Tiger Fangs boldly juts, steeply spiring;
50   Thorn Portal towers like a gateway, broad and boundless,
      Vortical pools in swirls of nine, plunge and surge,
      Their spurting flow roaring like thunder, shooting like lightning.
      Startled billows suddenly scatter,
      Frightened waves soar and pound;
55   Swift eddies gyring in layers,
      Raging rapids leaping in folds,

L. 58: The binomes *penghuo* 澎濦 (*phwang-hak*) and *xuezhuo* 潎瀄 (*ghok-dzhok*) probably are onomatopoeic expressions. My "thrashing and lashing" and "raging and roaring" are approximations.

L. 59: The alliterative binome *pingbei* 漂渼 (*bhjueng-bhuad*) is a variant of *pengpai* (surging and swelling). See "Rhapsody on the Imperial Park," L. 51n.

The alliterative binome *hongkuai* 灇潎 (*hueng-huad*) is a variant of *hangkai* (troublous and turbulent). See "Rhapsody on the Imperial Park," L. 56n.

L. 60: The alliterative binome *kuihuo* 潰濩 (*guet-guak*) is a synonym compound meaning "spreading and sprawling."

The elements of the alliterative binome *xuehuo* 泬瀄 (*huat-huak*) provide no clear clue to its exact meaning. I have followed Li Shan (12.11b), who sees in the word the sense of water colliding and rushing together; hence, my "crashing and colliding."

L. 61: Li Shan (12.11b) explains the alliterative binomes *yuhuang* 潏皇 (*gjiuet-guang*) and *huyang* 滶泱 (*'uet-'ang*) as descriptive of the rapid movement of the waters. Hu Shaoying (14.9a) compares *yuhuang* with *lihuang* 聿皇 (*ljuet-guang*), which occurs in Yang Xiong's "Plume Hunt Rhapsody" (L. 180) in the sense of "swiftly moving." The significic in *huyang* obviously is *hu* (swift). My "dashing and darting" and "scurrying and scudding" are attempts to convey the swiftness of the waves' motion.

L. 62: This line contains alliterative binomes that have the same initial: *shushan* 潚潝 (*sjok-sjam*) and *shenshuo* 潣瀄 (*sem-sjok*). Li Shan (12.11b) explains both as descriptive of the water's speed. I suspect that *shushan* is a synonym compound (*shu* 'sudden' + *shan* 'flashing'). Perhaps in *shenshuo* the significic is *shen*; cf. *chen* 闖 (*threjm*) 'to rush out' (*Shuowen* 20B.5341a).

L. 64: The rhyming binome *weilei* 渨溾 (*'juei-ljuei*) perhaps has for its significic *lei* (piled); hence, my "peaked and piled."

L. 65: The rhyming binomes *zeyu* 溭淢 (*dzrjek-hjiuek*) and *jinyun* 澵湏 (*dzrejn-ghjuen*) are not otherwise attested Li Shan (12.11b) glosses both as "irregularly follow one upon another." However, *zeyu* clearly is related to *ceyu* 惻淢 (*tshrjek-hjiuek*), which describes a state of agitation (see *Wen xuan*, 18.23b). The *Shuowen* (11A.4951a) glosses the element *yu* as "rapidly flowing." To combine the senses of agitated and swiftness I have rendered it as "raging and racing." I suspect that the significic in *jinyun* is *yun*, which is homophonous with *yun* 磒 (to fall); hence, my "pitching and plunging."

L. 68: Although Li Shan (12.11b) explains the rhyming binome *liwu* 硉矹 (*luet-nguet*) as descriptive of the rocks tossed by the waves, the basic meaning of the word is "to project," "to jut." See *Citong*, p. 2399. I suspect the significic is *wu* 兀 (to project upward). See *Shuowen* 8B.3822b-23a.

L. 69: I follow Hu Shaoying (14.9a) in reading *yan* 演 as *yin* 潱 (to flow submerged).

L. 73: For *le* 泐 in the sense of "split," see *Zhou li zhushu* 39.7a. I have freely rendered it here as "crannied."

L. 74: Note the euphony of the two rhyming binomes in this line: *leku* 礐硞 (*lek-khek*) and *luoque* 磥礭 (*luk-kuk*). None of the elements provides any good clue to their meaning. I have derived my "scraped and scored, pitted and pocked" from Li Shan (12.12a), who says the words describe the rugged, uneven appearance of the rocks beaten by the water.

L. 77: The rhyming binome *wangguang* 汪洸 (*'uang-kuang*) is not otherwise attested. Li Shan (12.12a) explains it as describing the broad and deep expanse of the water, which is the sense assigned to the element *wang* in the *Shuowen* (11A.4953a-b). Although I am not certain that the element *guang* actually contributes to the sense of the word, I have attempted to incorporate it into my "spaciously sparkling" (cf. *Shuowen* 11A.499a-b for *guang*, "the bubbling brightness of water").

L. 80: I suspect that the rhyming binome *yunlin* 涒鄰 (*gjuen-ljien*) may be related to the inverted form *linjun* 轔囷 (*ljien-gjuen*), which has the sense of "twisting"; hence, my "twisting

Batter the cliffs, astir and aroused,
Thrashing and lashing, raging and roaring,
Surging and swelling, troublous and turbulent,
60 Spreading and sprawling, crashing and colliding,
Dashing and darting, scurrying and scudding,
Swiftly streaking, rapidly rushing,
Whirling and swirling, twining and twisting,
Peaked and piled, spurting and spouting,
65 Raging and racing, pitching and plunging,
Laced and linked like dragon scales.
Prase-colored sand tosses and tumbles to and fro,
Giant rocks, jaggedly jutting, advance and retreat;
Wherever the submerged flow gushes and spouts,
70 Or where the hastening current grinds and grates,
Banks and bluffs become crannied scarps,
Twisting shores and mountain ridges become creviced cliffs,
Piled boulders in secluded streams,
Become scraped and scored, pitted and pocked.

V

75 And now
Reservoirs of plunging abysses,
Pools of haunted lakes:
Crystal clear, spaciously sparkling,
Flowing and flooding, deep and diluvian,
Broad and boundless, rolling and reeling,
80 Twisting and twirling, turning and churning;
Bubbling bright, limpid and lucent,
Streaming with luster, casting off radiance,
Wasteful and wide, distantly distended,
Boundlessly spread, vast and far.
85 Examine them, and they are without form;
Explore them, and they are without end.

and twirling." The following rhyming binome *wanlin* 圓潾 (*ʾjuen-ljien*; for this reading see Hu Shaoying 14.10a), my "turning and churning," may be a related word.

L. 90: The Grand Culmen (Tai ji 太極) is the source of the yin and yang, which by their complementary action generate all things.

L. 91: Li Shan (12.12b) explains the rhyming binome *xiadie* 浹渫 (*ʾtsiap-diap*) as descriptive of the vast expanse of the waves. Both elements have the meaning of "pervasive"; hence, my "spaciously spread."

L. 95: Lord Yang is god of the waves See "Southern Capital Rhapsody," L. 226n.

Li Shan (12.12b) explains the alliterative binome *ee* 硪硪 (*ngep-nga*) as descriptive of shaking movement. However, Hu Shaoying (14.10a) certainly is right in arguing that it describes the height of the waves; hence, my "tall and towering." Cf. *ji'e* 岌峩 (*ngjep-nga*), "tall and towering."

L. 96: I have interpreted the rhyming binome *wanyan* 涴演 (*ʾjuan-ran*) as consisting of two elements: *wan* (winding = sinuous) and *yan* (stretching).

L. 97: Li Shan (12.12b) glosses the rhyming binome *yinlun* 浺瀹 (*ngjien-gljuen*) as descriptive of swirling. I suspect that *yin* may be a variant of *yun* 沄 (*gjuen*), which the *Shuowen* (11A.4956b–57a) glosses as "swirling flow"; hence, my "twirling and swirling."

Li Shan (12.12b) explains the alliterative binome *wawai* 溾瀤 (ʾuah-ʾuei) as descriptive of "unevenness." I have taken the first element in the sense of *wa* 窊 (to sink); hence, my "pitching and plunging."

L. 105: The river pig (*jiang tun* 江豚) is the Yangzi River porpoise. The sea swine (*hai xi* 海狶) is the marine dolphin. See Read, *Fish Drugs*, p. 83, #176; Schafer, *Vermilion Bird*, p. 313, n. 272.

L. 106: According to Guo Pu (see his commentary to *Erya* C4.3b), a small paddlefish is called a *shuwei* 叔鮪. The *wang wei* 王鮪 is a large sturgeon.

L. 107: The *gu* 鯌 (also read *hua*) is a legendary flying fish mentioned in the *Shanhai jing* (4.9a). Guo Pu says it has wings like a bird, and a call like a mandarin duck. I have invented the name bonefish for it (not to be confused with *Albula vulpes* (bonefish, ladyfish).

Li Shan (12.13a) cites an "old explanation" that says the *lian* 鰊 resembles a rope (*sheng* 繩). Zhu Jian (13.1a) points out that *Guangyun* (see p. 387) says the *lian* resembles the *sheng* 䰶, which is a word for roe (see *Erya* C4.3b). Since the identification of this fish is uncertain, I have invented the name ropefish for it

The *teng* 鰧 also appears in the *Shanhai jing* (5.20b), which describes it as resembling the *gui* 鱖 (mandarin fish), having blue markings, a red tail, and dwelling in holes of rocks. Read (*Fish Drugs*, p. 46, #151) calls it rockfish

The *chou* 鮋 is the hemiculter. See "Western Metropolis Rhapsody," L. 648n.

L. 108: The *ling* must be *lingli* 鯪鯉, the pangolin. See *Chuci buzhu* 3.9b, Wang Yi's commentary.

The *lun* 鯩 appears in the *Shanhai jing* (5.20a–b), which describes it as black and resembling the *fu* 鮒 (golden carp). Hu Shaoying (14.11b) equates *lun* with *guan* 鯶, which is the false salmon (*Elopichthys bambusa*). See Read, *Fish Drugs*, pp. 22–23, #138.

The *lian* 鰱 is the silver carp, also called whitefish. See Read, *Fish Drugs*, p. 10, #129.

LL. 109–10: The deer's antlers perhaps belong to the *lu yu* 鹿魚 (deer fish). Li Shan (12.13a) cites the lost *Linhai [shui tu] yiwu zhi* 臨海水土異物志 (Memoir on Strange Land and Water Creatures of Linhai), compiled by Shen Ying 沈瑩 (3rd century A D.), which describes the deer fish as over two feet long, with horns, and feet beneath its belly. I am unable to identify the other fish mentioned here

Vapors, spuming and fuming, thick as fog,
At times dark and dense as smoke,
Simulate primal chaos before matter congealed,
90 Resemble the Grand Culmen that forms the sky.

VI

Long swells spaciously spread,
Steep rapids precipitously piled,
Whirling eddies twisting like winding ravines,
Racing waves tumbling like collapsing hills;
95 Lord Yang, towering tall, rising like a bluff,
Giant billows, sinuously stretching, rolling like clouds,
Twirling and swirling, pitching and plunging,
Now sunken, now cresting;
Agape as if Earth had split,
100 Widemouthed, as if Heaven had opened;
Batter meandering banks, wind and weave,
Panic collapsing waves, smashing one another,
Drum against caves and caverns, roaring and rumbling,
Then spouting and spurting, mount the banks.

VI

105 Among the fish:
River pig, sea swine,
Paddlefish, sturgeon,
Bonefish, ropefish, rockfish, hemiculter,
Pangolin, striped carp, false salmon, whitefish,
Some with deer antlers or elephant's trunk,
110 Others with tiger features or dragon face,
Scales and armor intricately imbricating,
Light and lustrous, colorful as brocade;
Raise their dorsal fins, fan their tails,
Spout waves, spray foam,
115 Push against the current, gasping and gulping,
Frolic and frisk with the waves;
Some shooting forth colors and dazzling the deep,
Others puffing their gills amidst the reefs.

329

L. 120: The *Zilin* (cited by Li Shan 12.13a) says the *zong* 鯮 is a fish of the Southern Sea. Because it has a stone (otolith) in its head, it is called *shishou* 石首 (stonehead). Read identifies *shishou* as the croaker, which is found both in the sea and rivers. However, Read rejects the identification of *zong* with *shishou*. See *Fish Drugs*, pp. 22–26. The *Guangya* (10B.14b) also equates the *zong* with the *shishou*. Wang Niansun in his *Guangya* commentary explains that there were two varieties, the foot-long type called *huanghua yu* 黃花魚, and the larger two-to-three-foot size, called *tongluo yu* 同羅魚. Thus, I have retained the English name croaker.

In his commentary to the *Shanhai jing* (1.6b), Guo Pu describes the *ji* 鮆 as a thin, narrow fish with a long head. The largest ones are over a foot long, and there are many of them in Lake Tai. Another name for it is *dao yu* 刀魚 (knife fish). Read (see *Fish Drugs*, pp. 30–31, #142) identifies it as the anchovy. See also *Erya* C4.4a–b; *Shuowen* 11B.5230b–31a. The croaker and anchovy both are migratory fish; hence, the phrase "in accord with the seasons."

L. 122: The diving swan may be a cormorant.

The *Shanhai jing* (1.2b–3a) describes the fish-ox (*yu niu* 魚牛) as an oxshaped fish that dwells on dry land, has a snake's tail, wings, and feathers beneath its ribs. Its name is *lu* 鮱. Zhu Jian (13 1b) points out that since Guo Pu mentions the *lu* in L 199, the fish-ox may be the *yongyong* mentioned in Sima Xiangru's "Rhapsody on the Imperial Park" (see L. 82n).

L. 123. The *Shanhai jing* (1.9b) describes the tiger-kraken (*hu jiao* 虎蛟) as having a fish's body and serpent's tail. Hao Yixing (*Shanhai jing* 1.9b) equates it with the shark referred to in the *Bowu zhi* (3.4a) as *jiao cuo* 蛟錯. However, Zhu Jian (13.1b–2a), noting that Guo Pu in his *Shanhai jing* commentary says that the *hu jiao* is a type of dragon, argues that it cannot be a fish. I have thus called it tiger-kraken.

In his *Shanhai jing* commentary (5.29a), Guo Pu refers to the *gou she* 鉤蛇 (hook-snake) of Yongchang. It was so named because it lay in the water and hooked men, oxen, and horses from the bank.

L. 124: The *Shuowen* (13A.6002b–3a) says the *lun* 蜦 (also read *li*) is a type of black snake that hides in sacred pools and is capable of producing wind and rain. The *Shuowen* commentators show that this *lun* is the same as the *li* 蜧, a black serpent mentioned in Xu Shen's *Huainanzi* commentary (cited by Li Shan 12.14b). However, Zhu Jian (13.2a) notes that Guo Pu mentions the *li* in L. 147, and thus argues that this *lun* must be the bullfrog of the *Bencao gangmu* (see Read, *Insect Drugs*, p. 162, #84).

The *tuan* 鱄 possibly is a variant of *tuan* 鱒 (also read *zhuan*), a fish similar to the *fu* (golden carp) mentioned in the *Shanhai jing* (1.10a). The *tuan* of Dongting was particularly famous. See *Lushi chunqiu* 14.5b, where *pu* 鱒 probably is a mistake for *tuan* (see *Shuowen* 10B.5221a). In the pronunciation *zhuan*, there is a modern fish identified as the *Trachurus japonicus*, a type of scad. See *Cihai*, p. 3909). Being unsure of the identification, I have used scad.

The *Guang zhi* 廣志 (Gazetteer of Guang), cited by Li Shan (12.13b), says the *hou* 鱟 resembles the folding fan. The female always carries the male on its back. If it loses the female, the male cannot survive. Read (see *Turtle and Shellfish Drugs*, pp. 37–38, #215) identifies it as the horseshoe or king crab. Cf. "Wu Capital Rhapsody," L. 626n; Zhu Jian 13.2b; Schafer, *Vermilion Bird*, p. 209.

The *Linhai shui tu yiwu zhi* (cited by Li Shan 12.13b) describes the *mei* 媚 as resembling a shrimp. Eating it will enhance a person's looks; hence, the name *mei* (beautifier). The *mei* also is the name of the parasite that lives inside the tortoise shell. See Read, *Turtle and Shellfish Drugs*, pp. 78–79, #241 It probably is a type of hermit crab

L. 125: The *Linhai shui tu yiwu zhi* (cited by Li Shan 12.13b) describes the *fen* 鱝 as a fish resembling a round plate, with a mouth below its belly, and poison in the tip of its tail. Read (see *Fish Drugs*, pp. 97–99, #183) says it is the stingray.

The *Linhai shui tu yiwu zhi* (cited by Li Shan 12.13b) describes the *yang* 蟥 as a tortoise with a thin body, with a mouth resembling the webs of a goose. Another name for it is *xia she*

Giant whales riding the swells, exit and enter;
120 Croakers and anchovies in accord with the season go forth and
        return.

VII

And then
Water creatures in wondrous array:
There are
Diving swans, fish-oxen,
Tiger-krakens, hook-snakes,
Bullfrogs, scads, king and hermit crabs,
125 Stingrays, duck-tortoises, leathery turtles,

guı 呷蛇龜 (snake-swallowing tortoise). Read (see *Turtle and Shellfish Drugs*, p. 21, #206) calls it duck tortoise.

The *Linhaı shui tu yıwu zhı* (cited by Li Shan 12.13b) says the *mı-ma* 龜鼊 is similar to the *jupı* 龜鼊 (loggerhead turtle). It is as large as a mat and gives birth to its young in white sand on the seashore. Read (see *Turtle and Shellfish Drugs*, p. 16, #201A) identifies it as the leathery turtle.

L. 126: *Wang yao* 王珧 probably is a mistake for *yuyao* 玉珧, also known as *jıangyao* 江珧, which Guo Pu (see *Shanhai jing* 4.4a) explains as a type of small mussel. The *Lınhaı shuı tu yıwu zhı* (cited in *Taıping yulan* 943.4189–90) describes it as two inches long, five inches wide, large on top and small on the bottom. Its adduct (*zhu* 柱) was considered especially tasty. See *Erya* C4.8a; *Shuowen* 1A.192b–93a; Tu Benjun 屠本畯 (fl. 1596), *Mınzhong haıcuo shu* 閩中海錯疏 (Notes on the Marine Varieties of Fujian), *Congshu jicheng*, C.27; Read, *Turtle and Shellfish Drugs*, p. 79, #242.

The *Lınhaı shuı tu yıwu zhi* (cited by Li Shan 12.13b) describes the *haı yue* 海月 (sea-moon) as a white shell as large as a mirror. Its central muscle is as large as a hairpin and is edible. Read (see *Turtle and Shellfish Drugs*, p. 79, #242) identifies both *yuyao* and *haıyue* as the window shell (window oyster, *Placuna placenta*). *Cıhaı* (p. 1671) identifies *jiangyao* as *Pınua (Atrina) pectınata* or pen shell, and the *haı yue* (p. 1774) as window shell.

L. 127: The *Lınhaı shuı tu yıwu zhi* (cited by Li Shan 12.13b) describes the *tu rou* 土肉 (earth-meat) as a black five-inch-long mouthless and eyeless sea creature with thirty legs.

The *shı hua* 石華 (stone-flower) is a shellfish that attaches itself to rocks. Its meat is like that of the oyster. See Tu Benjun, *Minzhong haicuo shu*, C.28.

L. 128: The *Linhaı shuı tu yıwu zhı* (cited by Li Shan 12.14a) describes the *san zong* 三䗋 as resembling a large oyster; hence, my "giant oysters."

Li Shan (12.14a) cites an "old explanation" that says the *fou jiang* 蚯江 is a small crablike creature with twelve legs.

L. 129: The *Nanzhou yıwu zhı* 南州異物志 (Memoir of Strange Creatures of Nanzhou), compiled by Wan Zhen 萬震 (third century A.D.), cited by Li Shan 12.14a, describes the parrot snail (*yingwu luo* 鸚鵡螺) as shaped like an inverted cup with a bird-shaped head. Viewed toward its belly, it resembles a parrot. Read (see *Turtle and Shellfish Drugs*, p. 73, #236) identifies it as the pearly nautilus. See also Schafer, *Vermılıon Bırd*, p. 208.

L. 130: The *Nanyue zhı* 南越志 (Gazetteer of Southern Yue), compiled by Shen Huaiyuan 沈懷遠 (fl. ca. 465), cited by Li Shan (12.14a) describes the *suojıe* 璅蛣 as a shellfish between one inch and three inches long. Inside its stomach is a baby crab shaped like an elm pod. Read (see *Turtle and Shellfish Drugs*, pp. 79–80, #242) thinks this might be the scallop. See also Qu Dajun 屈大均 (1630–1696), *Guangdong xinyu* 廣東新語 (New Words from Guangdong) (Hongkong: Zhonghua shuju, 1974), 23.580.

L. 131: According to the *Nanyue zhı* (cited by Li Shan 12.14a), the *shui mu* 水母 (water-mother) is a creature found on the seacoast. In the Eastern Sea it is called *zha* 蛇. It is pure white and covered with foamlike droplets, has no ears or eyes, and thus does not know enough to avoid men. A shrimp parasite attached to it warns of danger. Read (see *Fish Drugs*, p. 109, #187) says *shu mu* is the Cantonese name for jelly fish. See also Schafer, *Vermılıon Bird*, p. 207.

L. 132: The *Erya* (C4.9a) explains *hang* 魧 as a large cowry. The *Shangshu dazhuan* (cited by Li Shan 12.14a) says that when King Wen of Zhou was imprisoned at Qıanglı, Sanyi Sheng 散宜生 went to the banks of the Yangzi and Huai rivers and obtained cowries as large as wheel rings. He presented them to King Zhou of Shang as ransom for King Wen.

L. 133: In his *Erya* commentary (C4 6a), Guo Pu identifies the *han* with the *kuılu* 魁陸 or ark shell (*wa longzı* 瓦壟子). The *Linhaı shuı tu yıwu zhı* (cited by Li Shan 12.14a) says it has a diameter of four feet (inches?), and its back resembles a tiled furrow. See Read, *Turtle and Shellfish Drugs*, pp. 61–63, #229.

Pen shells, window shells,
Earth-meats, stone-flowers,
Giant oysters, twelve-legged crabs,
Parrot snails, whorled whelks;
130 Scallops with crabs in their maws,
Jelly fish with shrimp for eyes,
Puple cowries like wheel rims,
Giant ark shells that fill a cart,

L. 134: The *Yiwu zhi* (cited by Li Shan 12.14a) says the *bang* 蚌 (fresh water mussel, clam) resembles the giant clam. It is pure white like jade.

L. 135: The *shi jie* 石砝 (or *jie* 砎) is the sea anemone. See Read, *Turtle and Shellfish Drugs*, pp. 70–71, #234. In his preface to his "Rhapsody on the Sea Anemone" Jiang Yan says another name for it is *zi xiao* 紫蕭 (purple angelica). It has feet and flowers in the spring (or "after spring rains"). See *Yiwen leiju* 97.1677 and *Jiang Wentong ji* 1.23a. The *Nanyue zhi* (cited by Li Shan 12.14a) says that it blossoms after spring rains.

L. 136: The *Nanyue zhi* (cited by Li Shan 12.14b) says the *juzhu* 鋸䱜 has a single head and branching tail, is two to three feet long, has feet on the left and right, and is shaped like a silkworm Zach (*Die Chinesische Antholgie*, 1 : 187) translates it as "Tintenfisch" (cuttle fish). The description also fits that of the squid or octopus. I have arbitrarily called it a squid.

L. 137: The rhyming binome *kuilei* 磈磥 (*khuei-luei*) and its variants (see Zhu Qifeng, *Ci tong*, p. 1344) usually describe the jagged, uneven contours of mountains. Guo Pu here uses it to describe the rugged surface of oyster beds, sometimes referred to as oyster mountains (*hao shan* 蠔山). The *Lingbiao lu yi* 嶺表錄異 (Register of Strange Things beyond the Ranges), compiled by Liu Xun 劉恂 (10th century), *Congshu jicheng*, C.21, describes such beds as ten to twenty feet high, "steep and sheer as mountains." See also Tu Benjun, *Minzhong haicuo shu* C.27 and Read, *Turtle and Shellfish Drugs*, p. 40, #216.

L. 140: For the *longli* 龍鯉 (dragon-carp), Li Shan refers to the *longyu* 龍魚 (dragon-fish) of the *Shanhai jing* (7.4a–b). This creature lives on hillocks and has the appearance of a carp (emending the text as suggested by Hao Yixing). The divine sages ride it to travel the nine wastes. The same creature (written *bang yu* 㾊魚) appears in the *Huainanzi* (4.9a). Yuan Ke 袁珂 proposes that it is the same as the *lingli* 陵鯉 (literally "hill-carp"), which is the pangolin (see L. 108n above). This creature traditionally was represented as a carp that burrowed into the tops of hills. See Yuan Ke, ed. and comm., *Shanhai jing jiaozhu* 校注 (*Classic of Mountains and Seas* Collated and Annotated) (Shanghai: Guji chubanshe, 1980), 2.224 and Read, *Dragon and Snake Drugs*, p. 23, #106. Whether or not this is the pangolin (see Zhu Jian 13.3b–4a, who rejects the identification), clearly Guo Pu has in mind the carp that transforms into a dragon. See "Eastern Metropolis Rhapsody," L. 125n.

L. 141: Hao Yixing thinks that this nine-headed bird (the *qicang* 奇鶬) is the same as the *jiu feng* 九鳳 (nine-headed phoenix). See *Shanhai jing* 17.3b. This legendary avian had a human face and bird body. However, as Zhu Jian (13.4a) and Hu Shaoying (14.14a–b) point out, *qicang* is another name for the bird variously known as *gui ju* 鬼車 (phantom wheel) and *jiutou wu* 九頭烏 (nine-headed crane). According to legend, it originally had ten heads, but lost one when a dog bit it off. Read (see *Avian Drugs*, pp. 91–92, #320) says it is the goatsucker.

L. 142: On the three-footed turtle, see *Shanhai jing* 5.37b, where Guo Pu says its name is *neng* 能 (or *nai*). See also *Erya* C4.7a, where Guo Pu says that a pool of the Jun 君 Mountains of Wuxing commandery (modern Yixing 宜興, Jiangsu) produces three-footed turtles.

L. 143: Zhang Yun'ao (7.17b) notes that the "Memoir on Auspicious Omens" of the *Nan Qi shu* (18.356) mentions the capture of a six-eyed tortoise that had inscribed on its belly the words "myriad joys." Zhang Shinan 張世南 (ob. post 1230) mentions a so-called six-eyed tortoise discovered in what is now modern Vietnam. It actually had two normal eyes, and the four extra eyes were eyelike patterns on the shell. See *Youhuan jiwen* 游宦紀聞 (The Recorded Knowledge of a Traveling Official), *Zhibuzu zhai congshu*, 2.8a–b.

L. 144: Li Shan (12.14b) equates the *zhen bie* 顮鼈 (ruddy turtle) with the *zhubie* 珠鼈 (pearl turtle) of the *Shanhai jing* (4.4a), which it describes as shaped like a lung, with eyes and six feet, and producing pearls. Another name for the creature is vermilion (*zhu* 朱) turtle (see *Lushi chunqiu* 14.5b); hence, the adjective "ruddy." For a full discussion of the name, see Zhu Jian 13 4a–b and Read, *Turtle and Shellfish Drugs*, pp. 29–30, #211–12.

L. 145: Li Shan (12.14b) cites the *Shanhai jing*, which says the *wen pi* 文鮁 is shaped like

Jadelike mussels gleaming and glittering with sparkling pearls,
135 Sea anemones flaunting their blossoms in response to the season,
Squid, limp and loose, dangling their tentacles,
Black oysters, gnarled and knurled, spined and spiked.
Some toss and tumble in the tide and waves,
Others swirl and sink in the mud and sand.

VIII

140 And then
One-horned dragon-carps,
Nine-headed goatsuckers,
Three-legged turtles,
Six-eyed tortoises;
Ruddy turtles, lung-shaped, spring forth spitting pearls,
145 Striped mollusks, resounding like lithophones, produce fine jade;

an inverted *diao* 銚 (a long-handled pan), with a bird's head and fish's tail. It was used for making lithophones and produced pearls. Although the modern text of *Shanhai jing* (2.28b) reads *ru* 絮 for *wen*, Hao Yixing argues that the ancient text read *wen*. Duan Yucai equates it with the *pin* 玭, a type of Huai River mollusk that produced a musical pearl. The word is equivalent to *pin* 蠙 (mollusk). I have rendered *wen pi* as "striped mollusk." The fine jade is *qiu* 璆 (also written 球), which was used to make lithophones. See *Shuowen* 1A.133a–34a.

L. 146: The *Shanhai jing* (4.2b) describes the *tiaoyong* 儵鱅 as shaped like a yellow snake with fish fins. When entering and leaving water, it gives off light. I have called it the luminous snake.

L. 147: On the *li* (my sacred serpent), see L. 124n above.

L. 148: The *Shanhai jing* (3.9b) describes the *boma* 駁馬 as having an ox's tail, white body, and a single horn. Its cry is like a human shout. Yu Yue thinks it may be another name for the foreign animal called the *fuba* 符拔 (*bjuah-bhwat), which is described as similar to a *qilin* (the Chinese "unicorn"), but without horns. See *Yulou zazuan* 俞樓雜纂 (Miscellaneous Notes from Yu's Studio), 1879 edition, 23.6b–7a. The word *fuba* obviously is a transcription of a foreign word. Chavannes accepts the equation with Greek *boubalis* (antelope), a highly tenuous identification. See "Trois Généraux chinois de la dynastie des Han orientaux," *TP* 7 (1906), 232 In Guo Pu's line, the *boma* clearly is a mythical creature. I have simply called it a chimera.

L. 149: The *Nanyue zhi* (cited by Li Shan 12.15a) describes the water rhino (*shui si* 水兕) as an oxlike animal that inhabited the waters from east of Xigong 西鞏 prefecture to the sea. Lord Yang here is metonymy for waves.

LL. 150–51: Cf. "Wu Capital Rhapsody," LL. 288–90n.

L. 152: "Spare provisions" refers to Yu's spare provisions (*Yu yuliang* 禹餘糧), a name for brown hematite. See Read and Pak, *Mineral Drugs*, p. 48, #7a.

L. 153: Li Shan (12.15a) cites an "old explanation" that describes sandy mirror (*sha jing* 沙鏡) as resembling mica.

LL. 154–55: In his *Erya* commentary (C1.36a), Guo Pu compares the seaweeds *guan* 綸 (sweet tangle) and *zu* 組 (algae) to the twisted seal cords worn by officials. Cf. "Wu Capital Rhapsody," L. 173n.

L. 156: Purple laver (see "Wu Capital Rhapsody," L. 173n) is another algal sea plant.

L. 158: On stone sail, see "Wu Capital Rhapsody," L 175n.

L. 159: On duckweed fruit, see "Wu Capital Rhapsody," L. 637n.

L. 161: The *Yiwu zhi* (cited by Li Shan 12 15b) says *yunjing* 雲精 (essence of cloud) is a variant name for *yunmu* 雲母 (mica). See also Read and Pak, *Mineral Drugs*, p. 24, #39.

Candescent silver (*zhu yin* 燭銀) is one of the precious objects mentioned in the *Mu Tianzi zhuan* (1.3b) as possessed by the Son of Heaven. In his *Mu Tianzi zhuan* commentary, Guo Pu says this is silver with a pure light like that of a candle.

L. 162: The *Shuowen* (1A.191a–92b) explains *li* 蛤 as a type of giant clam used to decorate objects.

The *Shuowen* (1A.197a–198a) explains *liu* as *biliu* 璧琉, a luminous stone from the Western Barbarians. It is a transcription of Sanskrit *vaidurya*, beryl. See "Plume Hunt Rhapsody," L. 242n.

In his *Shanhai jing* commentary (16.3b), Guo Pu explains *xuangui* 璿瑰 (variant *xuan* 璇) as a type of jade. See also *Shanhai jing* 17.1a and *Mu Tianzi zhuan* 4.1b. *Xuan* by itself is a type of fine jade. See *Shuowen* 1A.131a–33a.

L. 163: In his *Shanhai jing* commentary (4.4b), Guo Pu explains *shui bi* 水碧 (water prase) as *shui yu* 水玉 (rock crystal). See Read and Pak, *Minerals and Stones*, p. 23, #37. Li Shan (12.15b) says *qian min* 潜珉 also is a type of *shui yu*. However, by itself *min* is a variant of *min* 珉 (agate); hence, my "submerged agate."

L. 164: In his *Shanhai jing* commentary (5.15b), Guo Pu says that in the first year of

Luminous snakes, thrashing their wings, cast off light,
Divine serpents, twisting and twining, dive and frolic;
Chimeras leap the waves, bellowing and frisking about,
Water rhinos roar like thunder to Lord Yang.
150 Guests from the deep build houses at bottoms of cliffs;
Mermen construct lodges in the cascading flow.
Spreading like hail, spare provisions;
Scattered like stars, sandy mirror.
Green seaweed vies in tanglement,
155 Elegant algae compete in brilliance;
Purple laver, bright and brilliant, blankets in clusters,
Green moss is tousled and matted on slippery rocks;
Stone sail, dense and dark, covers the isles,
Duckweed fruit timely appears, drifting and floating.

IX

160 Beneath the waters
Gold ore, cinnabar granules,
Mica, candescent silver,
Giant clams, beryl, fine jade,
Water prase, submerged agate,
Singing stones arrayed on sunlit isles,

Yongkang (A D. 300), Xiangyang commandery presented singing stones. When struck, these jadelike blue rocks could be heard for seven or eight *li*. Guo further mentions that a district of Quanling 泉陵 prefecture in Lingling commandery (north of modern Lingling in Hunan) had two sites that produced singing stones. One, shaped like a drum, was called a stone drum.

L. 165: The "Tribute of Yu" (see *Shang shu zhushu* 6.11a; Legge 3: 107) mentions floating lithophones in the Si River. Lithophones were often made of stone taken from rivers.

L. 167: Hu Shaoying (14.15b) notes that *lin* 郴 is a miswriting for *lin* 獜. In the doublet form, *linlin* is a descriptive that Karlgren interprets as meaning "fretted." See "Glosses on the Kuo Feng Odes," p. 204, #294. However, that sense is not relevant here, and I have followed Lü Xiang (12.20b) in construing *lin* as shore.

LL. 168–69: Cf. *Xunzi* 1 4a: "When jade is in a mountain, the plants and trees will be moist; when a pool produces pearls, the banks are never dry."

L. 171: In his *Shanhai jing* commentary (2.15a), Guo Pu says the *chen gu* 晨鵠 (morning swan) is a type of osprey. The *Erya* (C5.4a) and *Shuowen* (4A.1489b–92b) equate the *tianji* 天雞 (sky fowl) with the *han* 翰, a bird with red feathers. This possibly is the golden pheasant. See Read, *Avian Drugs*, p. 41, #271.

L. 172: The *Shanhai jing* (5.7a) describes the *yao* 鴢 as shaped like a duck with a blue body, vermilion legs, and scarlet tail. The *Erya* (C5.10b) equates it with the *touyao* 頭鴢, which probably is the *jiaolu* 鵁鸕, or squacco heron (see Hao Yixing's *Erya* commentary).

The *Shanhai jing* (16.5a) simply lists a yellow *ao* 鷔, which probably is the same as the *dan* 鷤 bird of *Shanhai jing* 7.2b. See Hao Yixing's commentary to these passages in the *Shanhai jing*. Guo Pu (see *Shanhai jing* 7.2b) says they are inauspicious birds like the owl. Thus, I have rendered *ao* as owl.

The *Shanhai jing* (5.11a) mentions the *di* 狄 (**died/diad?*) as shaped like an owl (or following Li Shan 12.6a, "duck"). It has ears, three eyes, and makes a sound like a deer. Xu Kai's 徐鍇 (920–974) *Shuowen jiezi xizhuan* 說文解字繫傳 (Appended Commentary to the *Shuowen jiezi*, cited in *Shuowen* 4A.1626b) cites this line writing *bo* 䴯 (**puat*) for *di*. The *bo* is a bird similar to a duck. Liang Zhangju (14.11b) argues that *bo* rhymes better with *yue* 月 (**ngjuat*) and *gua* 眣 (**kuat*) below. Following Liang, I render *bo* as duck.

L. 173: The sun birds (*yang niao* 陽鳥) are birds such as geese that migrate with the shifting of the sun. The "Tribute of Yu" mentions them as dwelling in Lake Pengli. See *Shang shu zhushu* 6.11b; Legge 3: 108.

L. 174: The darkest month (*xuan yue* 玄月) is the ninth month, when all things wither and turn black. See *Erya* B4.6a–b.

L. 183: Gathered Plumes (Ji yu 積羽) is a desolate thousand-*li* expanse located in the remote north. See *Zhushu jinian*, Legge 3: 151

L. 184: Bo is Bohai, and Jie is Jieshi 碣石 (north of modern Changli 昌黎, Hebei), the mountain that overlooks Bohai See *Han shu* 28B 1657.

L. 185: Zhu Jian (13.5b) cites the *Bencao shiyi* 本草拾遺 (Omissions from the Basic *Pharmacopoeia*) of Chen Cangqi 陳藏器 (fl. ca. 725) (see *Bencao gangmu* 35.2050), which describes the *lin* 橉 as a large tree with white flowers It grows in the mountains of south China, and its wood is extremely hard. Smith-Stuart (p. 358) mentions the uncertain identification of *Prunus spinulosa*. Another name for the tree is *tan* 檀, which commonly is a name for several types of rosewood (*Dalbergia, Pterocarpus*).

L. 186: Zhu Jian (13.5b) cites the *Yu pian*, which says the *li* 梬 has a fruit similar to the loquat. He comments that this description could fit the *lizhi* 荔枝 (litchee) except for the fact that the *lizhi* does not grow on the banks of the Yangzi. Nothing is known about the *han* 楟, except that it probably is similar to the *li* (see *Guangyun*, p. 354, which says the *li* is a small *han*). Being uncertain of the identifications, I have arbitrarily rendered *li* and *han* litchee and loquat respectively.

165   Floating lithophones displayed on shaded banks:
      Some cast bright colors amongst light ripples,
      Others glow and glitter on banks and shores.
      There is not a forest that is not wet,
      Nor a single bank that is not wet.

X

170   Among the feathered species there are:
      Morning swans, sky fowl,
      Herons, owls, ducks, and gulls.
      Sun birds here do soar,
      Arriving in the darkest month.
175   A thousand kinds, ten thousand voices,
      Screech and squawk to one another,
      Their sleek quills preened in the wind,
      Their thrumming wings flapping and fluttering.
      They paddle and play, scattering pearly drops,
180   Splash and plash, spraying foam.
      Gathering like spreading alpenglow,
      Scattering like parting clouds,
      They brood and molt at Gathered Plumes,
      Come and go at Bo and Jie.

XI

185   Rosewood and purple willow thickly throng on banks and shores,
      Litchee and loquat forest the ridges and array the peaks.

L. 187: On peach branch bamboo, see "Southern Capital Rhapsody," L. 70n. On the *yundang* bamboo, see "Wu Capital Rhapsody," L. 233n. Schafer (*Vermilion Bird*, p. 293, n 57) says it probably is *Dendrocalamus latiflorus* (tree bamboo).

L. 189: On *jia* (marshgrass) and *pu* (cattail), see "Southern Capital Rhapsody," L. 99n.

L. 190: The *Erya* (C1.19b) equates the *hong* 紅 with the *longgu* 蘢古, also commonly known as *hong cao* 葒草, which is *Polygonum orientale* (prince's feather), an annual, large-leaved plant that grows as high as three feet. In the autumn it hangs with clusters of light-red flowers. See Lu Wenyu, p. 55, #62; Smith-Stuart, pp. 343–44.

LL. 191–92: Hu Shaoying (14.17a–b) suggests that the white ears are the hairy panicles of the marshgrass, and the purple floss must be that of the cattail. Cf. Xie Lingyun, "Going from South Mount to North Mount, Passing through the Lake and Gazing," *Wen xuan* 22.14b: "Now cattails are laden with purple floss."

L. 195: The *li* is *jiangli* (selinum), on which see "Rhapsody of Sir Vacuous," L. 70n.

L. 199: The *ling* is *lingli* or pangolin. See L. 108n above. On the fish-ox, see L. 122n. above. *Six Comm.* writes *qiqu* 崎嶇 for You Mao *kuiju* 跻跔. The former reading is an obvious attempt to simplify the text. Li Shan (12.16b) cites the *Bicang*, which glosses *kui* as "to leap," and the *Sheng lei*, which glosses *ju* as "to raise a foot." I have construed the word as a binome and rendered it as "hop and hobble."

L. 200: Although the *Wen xuan* text reads *ta* 獺 (otter), Li Shan (12.16b–17a) cites a *Shanhai jing* passage that in the received version (5.9b) reads *xie* 猲 for *ta*. Thus, the *Wen xuan* text originally may have read *xie*. The *Shanhai jing* describes the *xie* as a scaly, doglike creature with fur resembling pig bristles. In another passage (5.37a), the *Shanhai jing* mentions a water creature called *jie* 頡, which Guo Pu says was like a black dog. This possibly may be another word for *ta* (otter). See Liang Zhangju 14.12b; Zhu Jian 13.6b; Hu Shaoying 14.17b–18a.

LL. 201–2: On the *wei* (proboscis monkey), see "Western Capital Rhapsody," L. 357n. On the *jue* (hoolock), see "Southern Capital Rhapsody," L. 67n. Cf. "Rhapsody on the Imperial Park," L. 248.

L. 203: In his *Shanhai jing* commentary (5.28b), Guo Pu says the *kui niu* 夒牛 is a large ox found in Shu. Read (*Animal Drugs*, #356) lists it under Tibetan yak. The evening sun here is metonymy for western mountains.

L. 204: On the *yuanchu* (phoenix), see "Southern Capital Rhapsody," L. 68n.

L. 208: The phrase *qubie* 區別 appears in *Lun yu* 19/12 in the sense of "divided into classes." Guo Pu uses it here to mean "branch into tributaries."

L. 210: On the Final Conflux, see L. 44n above.

L. 212: On *gu* 菰 (water bamboo), see Smith-Stuart, p. 210.

L. 213: The bearded plants are rice and wheat.

L. 214: Fine herbage refers to rice and water bamboo. See *Li ji zhushu* 5.19b–20a.

Peach branch and tree bamboo
Truly abundant, grow in groves.
Marshgrass and cattails spread like clouds,
190 Colored by thoroughwort and prince's feather.
Flaunting white ears,
Bristling purple floss,
They shade pools and bights,
Blanket the long river.
195 Fragrant selinum, rife and thick,
Water pine dark and dense,
Cluster on the shore lush and luxuriant,
Burgeon beneath the surface, green and verdant.
Pangolins and fish-oxen hop and hobble on margin and bank,
200 Beavers and otters peep and peer from clefts and holes.
Swift monkeys, poised on the void, display their skills,
A solitary hoolock climbs a precipice, relaxed and at ease;
Yak calves spring and bound in the evening sun,
Phoenix chicks try their wings east of the hills.

XII

205 It follows bights and creates sandspits,
Meets brooks and opens channels,
Scours ravines and engenders bays,
Branches into tributaries and forms lakes.
Swelling it are freshets and washes,
210 Draining it is the Final Conflux,
Marking its course is halcyon-hued greenery,
Floating on its waters is drifting water bamboo.
Rife are bearded plants unsown by human hand,
Sprouting tall is fine herbage growing naturally.
215 Water chestnuts and lotus, distended like scales,
Water fruits, spreading in clusters:
Uplifting their stalks, drenching their petals,
Cleansing their spikes, scattering their berries,
They flap and flutter with the wind,
220 Toss and tumble with the waves,
Their streaming brilliance glistening beneath the surface,
Their radiant luster flaming like scarlet fire.

341

L. 223: On Yunmeng, see Sima Xiangru's "Rhapsody of Sir Vacuous," LL. 47–48.

Thunder Lake (Lei chi 雷池) is located ten kilometers east of modern Wangjiang 望江 xian, Anhui. It was formed by the waters of the old Thunder River that gathered southeast of Wangjiang. See Taiping huanyu ji 125.10a–b; Zhu Jian 13.7b–8a.

L. 224: On Pengli, see L. 16n above. Green Grass (Qing cao 青草) Lake, also known as Baqiu 巴邱, was located south of Dongting Lake. In high water, it joined with Dongting. See Zhu Jian 13.8a–b.

L. 225: Juqu is another name for Lake Tai. See "Wu Capital Rhapsody," L. 65n.

Yao 洮, also known as Changdang 長蕩, is a lake located near modern Liyang 溧陽 and Jintan 金壇, Jiangsu. See Taiping huanyu ji 92.10b.

Ge 滆, also known as Xige 西滆 and Shazi 沙子, is a lake located southwest of modern Changzhou. Its mid portion touches on Yixing, east it extends to Lake Tai, and westward connects with Wupugang 蕪蒲港. See Taiping huanyu ji 92.5a. Although Yu and Ge are separate lakes, it is possible Guo Pu conceived of them as one. See Shi ji 29.1407, n. 2, Sima Zhen's commentary.

L. 226: Li Shan (12.18a) cites the Shuijing zhu, which locates Zhu 朱 Lake in Liyang. This passage is not in the received text of the Shuijing zhu. Zhu Jian (13.8b) thinks that it is the lake commonly known as Zhu gou 朱溝, located some thirty li from Liyang.

Chan 涳 is a lake located east of the confluence of the Mian 沔 (modern Han) and Xia 夏 rivers. According to the Shuijing zhu (5.28.48), the Mian River joined the Chan and other lakes to form a vast body of water three hundred li in circumference. "Vast as the Azure Sea, its great depths and giant swells entwined with the Jiang and Mian. Thus, Guo Pu's rhapsody says, 'To its sides there are . . . the Zhu, Chan, Dan, and Chao.'"

Lake Dan 丹 probably is short for Danyang 丹陽, a lake located near Liyang prefecture. See Zhu Jian 13.8b.

Lake Chao 漅 is modern Lake Chao 巢, located west of Chao xian, Anhui.

LL. 229–32: In his Shanhai jing commentary (13.3b), Guo Pu says that Dongting is the name of an underground cavern located in Baling 巴陵 (modern Yueyang 岳陽, Hunan). This Dongting thus refers to Dongting Lake of modern Hunan. Guo then adds that Mount Bao of Lake Tai has an underwater cavern called Dongting. See "Wu Capital Rhapsody," L. 671n. The Shuijing zhu (5.29.53), which cites these lines from Guo Pu's fu, has a confusing passage about Mount Bao and its subterranean passage that "southward communicates with Dongting" (which Dongting?). Zhu Jian (13.9a–b) cites Yang Xiong's "Plume Hunt Rhapsody" (LL. 233–34), which described an underground cavern (possibly the Dongting Cavern) ending at Cangwu, which is roughly in the Hunan Lake Dongting area. It is possible that Guo Pu thought Dongting of Baling and Dongting of Lake Tai were joined by an underground cavern For example, the Taiping huanyu ji (91.7b) cites a Junguo zhi 郡國志 (Monograph on Administrative Geography), which says that the underground cavern of Mount Bao reaches westward as far as Mount Emei.

L. 236: The Sunshi ruiying tu 孫氏瑞應圖 (Master Sun's Chart of Auspicious Responses), cited by Li Shan (12.18b), says peaked clouds (xiao yun 梢雲) are auspicious clouds that appear during the reign of a virtuous ruler. "Like a tree they are peaked and pointed."

L. 238: Qin Gao 琴高 was a skilled zither player who served King Kang of Song (reg. 317–285 B C.). After practicing the arts of the immortals for over two hundred years, he entered the Zhuo 涿 River (one text reads Tang 碭 River), where he captured a young dragon. The next time he appeared, he emerged from the river riding a red carp. See Liexian zhuan A.22.

L. 239: On Bingyi, see "Western Metropolis Rhapsody," L. 643n.

L. 240: On the Jiang Consorts, see "Southern Capital Rhapsody," L. 29n and "Wu Capital Rhapsody," L. 157n.

L. 244: These winds are the winds of the eight directions.

XIII

To its sides there are
Yunmeng, Thunder Lake,
Pengli, Green Grass,
225 Juqu, Yao, Ge,
Zhu, Chan, Dan, and Chao,
As far as the eyes can see for several hundred miles,
Wasty and wide, candid and clear.
And then there are
Mount Bao and Dongting,
230 The tunnel of Baling,
Their subterranean roads everywhere communicating,
Their dark caverns sombrous and secluded.
Germ of gold and petals of jade fill them within,
Carnelian pearls and wondrous stones coruscate without,
235 Black dragons coil around their bases,
Peaked clouds crown their summits.
This is where sea elves roam and play,
Where Qin Gao divinely soared.
Bingyi, reclining on the waves, casting haughty glances,
240 The Jiang consorts, brows knitted, gazing and gaping:
Slapping the surging swells, cavort like ducks,
Sipping the halcyon-hued auroral mists, flex and bend.

XIV

If then
The firmament is clear and calm,
And the eight winds cease to soar:

LL. 247–48: On the boat Flying Cloud, see "Wu Capital Rhapsody," L. 594n. On Yuhuang, see "Wu Capital Rhapsody," L. 599n and *Shuowen* 8B.3816a.

L. 249: Cf. "Wu Capital Rhapsody," LL. 592–93n. The combination *zhulu* 舳艫 literally means "stern and bow." The *Shuowen* (8B.3806a–b) says that according to the Han Code, *zhulu* also is a measure of boat length. Following Duan Yucai's emendation of the *Shuowen* text, each square *zhang* (ten feet) is one *zhulu* In Guo Pu's line, I think *zhulu* is metonymy for boats in a fleet. Cf. *Han shu* 6.196: "The emperor sailed the Yangzi ..., stern and bow stretching a thousand *li*." Li Fei 李斐 (3rd century A.D.) comments that *zhulu* refers to the great number of boats that were linked stern to bow in an unbroken line for a thousand *li*. See *Han shu* 6.197, n. 5 and *HFHD*, 2:95, n. 29.3.

L. 253: On Jiao and Yi, see "Wei Capital Rhapsody," L. 4n.

L. 254: You is the geographical region roughly corresponding to modern northern Hebei and Liaoning. Lang is short for Lelang; see "Eastern Metropolis Rhapsody," L 622n.

L. 255· The Southern Limits is the southernmost extremity of the world. Cf. *Huainanzi* 4.2a.

L. 256· The Eastern Wastes (Dong huang 東荒) is the region described in chapter 14 of the *Shanghai jing* Most of the places of this imaginary land lay beyond the Eastern Sea.

L. 258: The wind sock, called *wu liang* 五兩 ("five-ounce"), was a fifty-foot banner plaited with five ounces of chicken feathers. See *Huainanzi* 11.12b; Needham, Volume 3, p. 478. Note that the *Bing shu* 兵書 (Book on Weaponry) cited by Li Shan (12.19a) says the feathers weighed eight ounces.

L 266: Cf. *Zhuangzi* 1.1: "In the Northern Murk there is a fish.... It transformed into a bird ... whose wings are like clouds that span the sky."

L. 271: On Feilian, see "Western Capital Rhapsody," L. 330n.

L. 272: Quhuang 渠黃 is one of the legendary fleet steeds of King Mu of Zhou. See *Mu Tianzi zhuan* 1 4b.

245 Boatmen then grip their oars,
    Ferrymen then edge their craft to the shore,
    To drift away on Flying Cloud,
    To sail off on Yuhuang,
    Stern and bow linked together,
250 A myriad leagues of continuous masts.
    Against the whirling eddies, or with the current,
    Either fishing or trading,
    They steer for Jiao and Yi,
    Set their course for You and Lang,
255 Reaching as far as the Southern Limits,
    Extending into the Eastern Wastes.

XV

And then
They scan vapors and miasmas in the clear morning glow,
Watch the movements of the wind sock.
When a distant wind begins to rage, pulsing repeatedly,
260 Or a great norther with its powerful blast purges the air,
    Blowing slow but not sluggish,
    Swift but not cruel,
    They hoist sail and quickly make passage,
    Skimming the swells, plowing the deep.
265 Charging the waves, they release the rudder,
    And like streaking lightning disappear in the distant murk
    Scudding like morning alpenglow in solitary travel,
    Distantly viewed as cloudlike wings cleaving a peak,
    In a twinkling they have gone several hundred leagues,
270 Or in an instant they have coursed a thousand.
    Feilian would have no way to descry their course,
    And Quhuang would be unable to catch their shadows.

XVI

And then
Reed-gatherers and fishermen,
Cast down from rivers and mountains,
275 Whose clothes are of feathers and homespun,

L. 277: In his *Erya* commentary (2B.2b), Guo Pu explains that the fish garth (*jian* 槮) was made by damming the stream with pieces of wood. The fish entered the garth to escape the cold, and they were caught.

L. 279: Li Shan (12.20a) says that *tong* 筩 and *sa* 灑 are names of hooks (reading *gou* 鉤 for *diao* 釣 after Hu Shaoying 14.19b). Hu Shaoying suggests that *sa* may be used in the sense of *fansa* 汎灑 (scattered), referring to the great numbers of hooks in the water.

L. 284: The "Caltrop Gatherer" song is mentioned in *Huainanzi* 18.17b.

L. 286: Cf. *Chuci buzhu* 16.14a ("Yuan shi" of "Jiu tan"): "Following wind and waves, I journey south and north."

L. 295: The "hidden and vanished" (*yin lun* 隱淪) was one of five types of divine persons listed in Huan Tan's *Xin lun*. See *Quan Hou Han wen* 15.6a; Pokora, *Hsin-lun*, p. 150.

LL. 297–98: Daizong is Mount Tai. Cf *Gongyang zhuan*, *Xi* 31 (*Gongyang zhuan zhushu* 13 20b–21a): "Why sacrifice to Mount Tai, the Yellow River, and the Sea ? For mountains and rivers to be able to water the hundred *li* with their nourishing moisture, the Son of Heaven must perform sequential sacrifices to them. Striking the rocks, (clouds) come forth, and (land) the breadth of a finger or hand is covered. What spreads rain over the empire in less than a morning—it can only be Mount Tai."

LL. 303–4: Li Shan (12.21a) says that Guo Pu uses the analogy of weaving (for the correct reading of the text see Hu Kejia, *Wen xuan kaoyi* 2 32a). The talismans and omens provide guidelines for understanding Heaven and Earth, interlacing and interweaving with the affairs of Man.

Whose foods are vegetables and minnows:
Dam the sloughs to make fish-garths,
Block river inlets with strings of fish-traps.
Hooks and jigs hang barb to barb,
280 Nets and seines are cast from interlocking boats.
Some wind their reels from overhanging banks,
Some in mid-rapids sideways turn their boats.
Oblivious of dusk, only at nightfall do they return,
Singing the "Caltrop Gatherer" and beating time on the wales.
285 Proud and satisfied with a single tune,
Following wind and waves they end their years.

XVII

And then
Bounded by winding cliffs,
Hollowed by cavernous ravines,
Dredged by tributaries and forks,
290 Battered by morning and evening tides,
It is the place where all rivers and streams gather and return,
Where clouds and fog fume and steam,
Where precious wonders are transformed and produced,
Where great marvels are encaved and lodged.
295 It receives perfected men hidden and vanished from the world,
Issues extraordinary men from its divine soul,
Spreads numinous moisture over a thousand leagues,
Surpassing the rock-striking clouds emanating from Daizong.
As for its strange transformations so swift and sudden,
300 Talismans and omens of numerous kinds:
Their actions and reactions follow no pattern,
But responding to events they appear,
Acting as guides and standards for Heaven and Earth,
Intertwining the affairs of Man.
305 Such wonders cannot be fully conveyed in speech,
Such matters cannot be completely conveyed in writing.

XVIII

Now then:

L. 307: On the spiritual essence of the Min Mountains ascending to become the Eastern Well constellation, see "Shu Capital Rhapsody," LL. 388–89n.

L. 308: Lord Yang is god of the waves. See "Southern Capital Rhapsody," L. 226n.

L. 309: Qixiang 奇相 is the goddess of the Yangzi. According to the *Jiang ji* 江記 (Records of the Yangzi) by Yu Zhongyong 庾仲雍 (n.d.), she was a daughter of the Lord of Heaven who died and became goddess of the Yangzi. There were shrines dedicated to her both near the source and mouth of the Yangzi. See *Shi ji* 28.1373, n. 11; *Guangya* 9A.6a; Zhu Jian 13.11a; Hu Shaoying 14.20a.

L. 310: On the Xiang Beauties, see "Western Metropolis Rhapsody," L. 644n.

LL. 311–12: According to legend, the Great Yu once was crossing the Yangzi when a yellow dragon started to carry the boat away on its back. Everyone in the boat was frightened except for Yu, who looked up to Heaven and sighed, "I have received my fate from Heaven, and I have used all my effort to nurture the people. . . . Death has to do with fate. Why should I fear a dragon?" The dragon then lowered its ears and tail and disappeared. See *Lushi chunqiu* 20.6a.

LL. 313–14: Jing Fei is Jing Cifei 荆次非, a man of Chu who obtained a precious sword at Gansui 干遂 in Wu (northwest of modern Wu *xian*, Jiangsu). Upon his return, he was crossing the Yangzi when two krakens surrounded his boat. Cifei jumped into the river and killed them with his sword. Upon his return to Chu, his king rewarded him with a jade tablet. See *Lushi chunqiu* 20.5b. Taie 太阿 is one of the three swords made by the famous Wu swordmakers Ou Yezi 歐冶子 and Ganjiang. See *Yue jue shu* 11.2a.

LL. 315–16: Yaoli 要離 volunteered to assassinate the powerful Prince Qingji 慶忌 for King Helu of Wu. (Helü had killed Qingji's father.) In order to provide a means of approaching Qingji, Yaoli had Helü accuse him of a crime and burn his wife and children to death. Yaoli then fled to Wei, where he told Qingji of Helu's brutality. Qingji then agreed to return to Wu and assist Yaoli in killing Helu. While crossing the Yangzi, Yaoli pulled out his sword and stabbed Qingji, who then pushed Yaoli into the water. Three times he pushed him beneath the surface, and each time Yaoli floated up. Although Qingji's attendants wished to put Yaoli to death, Qingji stopped them. Just before dying of his wounds, Qingji ordered that Yaoli be allowed to return to Wu. In Wu, Yaoli committed suicide. See *Lushi chunqiu* 11.5b; *Wu Yue chunqiu* 4.4b–5a. Li Zhouhan (12.28a) points out that Guo Pu uses *ge* 戈 (halberd) instead of sword for purposes of rhyme.

LL. 317–18: Lingyun 靈均 is one of Qu Yuan's sobriquets. According to legend, Qu Yuan committed suicide by clasping a heavy stone and throwing himself into the river. The fisherman was a recluse whom Qu Yuan met while strolling the banks of a river. After scolding Qu Yuan for his uncompromising integrity, the fisherman paddled away singing a song. See *Chuci buzhu* 7.2b; Hawkes, *Ch'u Tz'u*, pp. 90–91.

LL. 319–20: According to the *Zhushu jinian* (B.6a; Legge 3 : 151), King Mu of Zhou led his army to Jiujiang 九江 where he crossed the Yangzi on a bridge formed by turtles and alligators. For the names of King Mu's eight steeds, see *Liezi* 3.32–33 and *Mu Tianzi zhuan* 1.4a–b.

L. 321: On Jiaofu, see "Southern Capital Rhapsody," L. 29n.

L. 322: Lord Yuan of Song dreamed he saw a man with disheveled hair peering at him through the side gate of his palace. The man said to him, "I come from the Zailu Pool. I was sent by the Clear Yangzi as an emissary to the Lord of the Yellow River, but the fisherman Yuju caught me." When he awoke, Lord Yuan ordered his attendants to divine the dream's meaning. They said that the man with disheveled hair actually was a divine turtle. Lord Yuan then ordered Yuju brought to court and present the turtle. The turtle was killed and used for divination. See *Zhuangzi* 7.178

L. 323: The Great Clod (Da kuai 大塊) is a name for *Tao*. See H. G. Creel, "The Great Clod: A Taoist Conception of the Universe," in Chow Tsetsung, ed. *Wen-lin*, pp. 257–68.

L. 324: Cf *Mengzi* 4B/18: "Water from a spring gurgles and gushes, never ceasing day or night. It fills all the hollows before advancing and then casts itself into the sea."

The spiritual essence of the Min Mountains cast its luster into the
  Eastern Well,
Lord Yang concealed his form in the great waves;
Qixiang obtained the Way and lodged her spirit here,
310 To match her numinous clarity with the Xiang Beauties.
The frightful yellow dragon that lifted the boat
Understood Lord Yu's sighs to Heaven.
Bold was Jing Fei who captured the krakens!
He generated his power from the Taie sword.
315 Fearsome was Yaoli who schemed against Qingji!
In midstream he thrust his halberd.
I lament Lingyun who clasped a stone,
Sigh for the fisherman's rowing song;
Recall when Mu of Zhou forded his army,
320 And drove his eight steeds over tortoises and alligators;
Sorrow for Jiaofu who lost his girdle pendant;
Grieve for the divine emissary caught in a net.
Magnificent the forms that flow from the Great Clod,
Which blends the myriad things, returning them all to a single
  hollow.

L. 327: You Mao writes *er* 而 for *zhi* 之 of *Six Comm*. I have followed *Six Comm*. See Liang Zhangju 14.17a.

L. 328: Cf. Ban Gu's "Appraisal" to the *Han shu* "Monograph on Waterways" (29.1698): "The rivers and springs of the Middle Kingdom number in the hundreds, but none is more illustrious than the Four Waterways, and (of these), the Yellow River is the most revered." Apparently Guo Pu praises the Yangzi as the equal of the Yellow River (the He).

325 To ensure that its water is never depleted and ever constant,
It receives a great pneuma from numinous concord.
If we examine the most wondrous sights among rivers and
waterways,
Truly none is more illustrious than the Jiang and the He.

Biographical Sketches

BAN BIAO 班彪 (A.D. 3–54), *zi* Shupi 叔皮, native of Anling (northeast of modern Xianyang, Shaanxi).

Ban Biao, the father of Ban Gu and Cao Daogu, is best known as a historian. Information on his life is contained in *Han shu* 100 (written by his son Ban Gu), and *juan* forty of the *Hou Han shu*.

Ban Biao came from a family of scholar-officials who held high positions during the last part of the Former Han. His uncle Ban You 班斿 was on Liu Xiang's editorial staff and was frequently summoned to read books for the emperor, who gave him duplicate books from the imperial collection. His aunt was Favorite Beauty Ban, Emperor Cheng's concubine and a distinguished poetess. His father, Ban Zhi 班穉, lost his position in the Wang Mang era (A.D. 9–22) for failing to submit a poem praising Wang Mang's administration.

Around 25, Ban Biao joined the staff of Wei Ao 隗囂 (ob. 33), a military leader who established an independent regime at Tianshui 天水 (modern eastern Gansu). At Anding 安定, about 350 *li* west of Chang'an, Ban composed "Rhapsody on a Northern Journey," which is contained in *Wen xuan* chapter 9. This poem recounts Ban's travels from Chang'an through the eastern Gansu area. Ban remained in Wei Ao's service about four years. After failing to convince Wei that the house of Liu should be restored to rule, he wrote "Discourse on the Mandate of Kings" (*Wen xuan* 52), an essay that attempts to justify the legitimacy of the Liu ruling house. After Wei rebelled in A.D. 30, Ban joined the satrap Dou Rong 竇融 (16 B.C.–A.D. 62), a Guangwu loyalist who held sway in western Gansu. Ban accompanied Dou to the capital around 36, and Emperor Guangwu, who was impressed with the memorials Ban wrote on behalf of Dou, named him an "Abundant Talent" and appointed him prefect of Xu 徐 (south of modern Sihong 泗洪, Jiangsu), a position he resigned on grounds of illness. He eventually accepted several brief appointments in the imperial chancellory.

Ban Biao's principal interest was scholarship, particularly history. Dissatisifed with other scholars' efforts to write a sequel to Sima Qian's *Shi ji*, he wrote "several tens of *juan*" of a history that may have served as the basis for Ban Gu's *Han shu*. Sometime between 47 and 51, he served on the staff of grand minister over the masses, Su Kuang 王況 (ob. 51). During his tenure the emperor accepted Ban's proposal to reinstitute the Former Han practice of appointing a grand tutor for the heir-apparent. Ban Biao died in 54 while serving as as chief of Wangdu 望都 (modern Wangdu *xian*, Hebei).

353

References
Van der Sprenkel. *Pan Piao, Pan Ku, and the Han History.*
Lo Tchen-ying. *Les Formes et les méthodes historiques en Chine.*

BAO ZHAO 鮑照 (ca. 414–466), *zi* Mingyuan 明遠. Sources do not agree on his native place. The ancestral home of the Bao clan probably was Shangdang 上黨 (modern Changzi 長子, Shanxi). Later, one branch may have moved to Donghai 東海 of Xuzhou (modern Yancheng 郯城, Shandong). Thus, he is variously known as a Shangdang or Donghai man.

Bao Zhao was a skilled writer of poetry, rhapsodies and parallel prose. What little information there is about his life is found in short notices inserted in the *Song shu* (51.1477–80) and *Nan shi* (13.36) biographies of his patron Liu Yiqing 劉義慶 (403–444). Another valuable source is the preface to Bao's collected works by Yu Yan 虞炎 (fl. 483–493).

Bao spent much of his official career on the staffs of Song princes. From ca. 439 to 444, he served as attendant gentleman to Liu Yiqing, Prince of Linchuan 臨川, whose entourage included such literary luminaries as Yuan Shu 袁淑 (408–453) and He Zhangyu 何長瑜 (ob. 443). During Liu Yiqing's tenure as governor of Jiangzhou 江州 (roughly corresponding to modern Jiangxi and Fujian), Bao trekked the area around Jiujiang and wrote several poems about Mount Lu. In 440, he accompanied Liu Yiqing to Guangling 廣陵 (modern Yangzhou), where Liu assumed his new post as governor of Southern Yanzhou 南兗州. Bao probably wrote his poem "Composed on the Road While Returning to the Capital" (in *Wen xuan*, chapter 27) during the trip from Jiangzhou to Guangling. After Liu Yiqing died in 444, Bao resigned his position as attendant gentleman and returned home, possibly near the capital, Jiankang.

In 445, Bao joined the staff of Liu Yiji 劉義季 (415–447), Prince of Hengyang 衡陽, who served as overseer of Liang 梁 commandery (modern Dangshan 碭山, Anhui) and governor of Xuzhou 徐州 (roughly modern southern Shandong and northern Jiangsu). After Liu Yiji's death in 447, Emperor Wen's second son, Liu Jun 劉濬 (429–453), Prince of Shixing 始興, who was serving as governor of Yangzhou 揚州 (modern Nanjing), appointed Bao as attendant gentleman. In 449, Bao accompanied Liu Jun to Jingkou 京口 (modern Zhenjiang, Jiangsu), where Bao's family possibly once lived. In January 451, the armies of the Northern Wei invaded the south and reached as far as Guabu 瓜步, on the north bank of the Yangzi across from Jiankang. After the Song army quickly repelled the invaders, Liu Jun led a force to refortify Guabu, and Bao probably accompanied him. It is not known whether Bao was still in Liu Jun's service in 453, when Liu and his brother instigated a rebellion against Emperor Wu. It is more probable he took up a post in 452 as prefect of Yongan 永安 (modern Sui 隨 *xian*, Hubei), followed by a position as prefect of Haiyu 海虞 (east of modern Changshou 常熟, Jiangsu) around 454.

Ca. 456, after serving briefly in the capital as erudite in the Imperial Academy and chamberlain in the secretariat, Bao took up another local government post as prefect of Moling 秣陵, on the southern outskirts of Jiankang. Attributed to this period is "Admiring the Moon in My Office by the West City Gate" (in *Wen xuan*, chapter 30), a poem reflecting on his separation from a loved one as the moon becomes full.

Little is known of Bao's activities from 454 to 464, when he joined the staff of Liu Zixu 劉子頊 (457–466), Prince of Linhai 臨海. Yu Yan's claim that he served as prefect of Yongjia is doubtful, for Yongjia was not a prefecture in the Song period. Claims by some scholars that Bao visited Guangling after Liu Dan's abortive rebellion in 460 are difficult to support (see introduction to "Rhapsody on the Ruined City").

In 462, the five-year-old Liu Zixu held the post of governor of Jingzhou 荊州 (roughly modern Hubei). The actual administration of Jingzhou must have been in the hands of senior officials such as Bao Zhao, who served first as acting adjutant and later as legal adjutant in the forward army. In February 466, Liu Zixun 劉子勛 (457–466), Prince of Jin'an 晉安, encouraged by his adviser Deng Wan 鄧琬 (407–466), rebelled and declared himself emperor at Xunyang. Liu Zixu soon joined the rebellion, and thus Bao Zhao had no choice but to serve the rebel regime. By September 466, imperial forces routed the rebel army and Liu Zixu was ordered to commit suicide. Soliders under the command of local Jingzhou commanders entered Jiangling and killed Liu Zixu's staff members, including Bao Zhao.

Bao's best known poem is "Rhapsody on the Ruined City" (in *Wen xuan*, chapter 11), a moving description of the desolate and wasted city of Guangling. Another of Bao's *fu* included in the *Wen xuan* (chapter 14) is "Rhapsody on Dancing Cranes," which describes a troupe of performing cranes.

As a *shi* poet, Bao is most distinguished for his *yuefu*. The *Wen xuan* (chapter 28) contains eight of his *yuefu*, including "Leaving from the North Gate of Ji" and "Song of Dongwu," both of which are "border poems" about military service beyond the northern frontier. Bao Zhao also wrote numerous imitation poems. His three "Imitating Ancient Style" poems and "Imitating the Style of Liu Gonggan" (in *Wen xuan*, chapter 31) all express a common Bao Zhao theme, the frustrations of an embittered scholar-official who has failed to achieve high position and meritorious service.

References

Miao Yue. "Bao Mingyuan nianpu" 鮑明遠年譜. *Wenxue yuekan* 3.1 (1932):5–18.

Wu Peiji 吳丕績. *Bao Zhao nianpu* 鮑照年譜. Changsha: Shangwu yinshuguan, 1940.

Wu Defeng 吳德風. "Bao Zhao nianpu buzheng" 鮑照年譜補證. *Youshi xuezhi* 5.1 (1956):1–27.

Chen Yixin 陳貽焮. "Bao Zhao he tade zuopin" 鮑照和他的作品. *Wenxue yichan* 1957:pp. 182–90.

Itō Masafumi 伊藤正文. "Hō Chō den ronkō" 鮑照伝論稿. *Kobe daigaku bungakukai kenkyū* 14 (1957):18–55.

Qian Zhonglian. "Bao Zhao nianbiao" 鮑照年表. In *Bao Canjun ji zhu*, pp. 431–42.

Kotzenberg, Heike. *Der Dichter Pao Chao* (+466). *Untersuchungen zu Leben und Werk*. Ph. D. Dissertation, Rheinische Friedrich-Wilhelms-Universitat zu Bonn. Bonn: Rheinsiche Friederich-Wilhelms-Universitat, 1971.

Zhang Zhiyue 張志岳. "Bao Zhao ji qi shi xintan" 鮑照及其詩新探. *Wenxue pinglun* (1979:1):pp. 58–65.

Cao Daoheng 曹道衡. "Guanyu Bao Zhao de jiashi he jiguan" 關于鮑照的家世和

籍貫. *Wen shi* 7 (1979) : 191–97.

———. "Bao Zhao jipian shi wen de xiezuo shijian" 鮑照幾篇詩文的寫作時間. *Wen shi* 16 (1982) : 189–202.

Ding Fulin 丁福林. "Yu Yan Bao Zhao ji xu de yichu chuanxie cuowu" 虞炎鮑照集序的一處傳寫錯誤. *Wen shi* 15 (1982) : 124.

———. "Guanyu Bao Zhao de jiguan" 關于鮑照的籍貫. *Wen shi* 20 (1983): 253–58.

———. "Bao Zhao ren qianjun canjun de shijian" 鮑照任前軍參軍的時間. *Wen shi* 22 (1984) : 190.

CAO DAGU 曹大家, married name of Ban Zhao 班昭 (ca. 49–ca. 120), *zi* Huiban 惠班, native of Anling 安陵 (northwest of modern Xianyang, Shaanxi).

Ban Zhao, the daughter of Ban Biao and the younger sister of Ban Gu, was the foremost female scholar and poet of the Han dynasty. The main source of information on her life is a short account in the *Hou Han shu* (84.2784–92).

Nothing is known of Ban Zhao's early life. Around A.D. 63, at the age of fourteen, she married Cao Shou 曹壽 (zi Shishu 世叔) by whom she had a son named Cao Cheng (see introduction to "Rhapsody on an Eastward Journey"). When Ban Gu died in A.D. 92, he had not finished compiling the *Han shu*, and Emperor He 和 (reg. 89–105) summoned Ban Zhao to finish it. The distinguished scholar Ma Rong received instruction in reading the work from her. The emperor also assigned her the duty of tutoring the empress and palace ladies. At this time she received the honorific Dagu 大家, which possibly means something like "Great Aunt." Ban Zhao was on particularly close terms with Empress Dowager Deng 鄧太后. During her regency (106–121), she consulted Ban Zhao on government affairs.

Ban Zhao was the most talented poet of her time, and the emperor often called upon her to compose *fu* on exotic tribute objects. Her "Rhapsody on the Great Bird" (in *Yiwen leiju* 92.1596) describes a Parthian ostrich her elder brother Ban Chao sent from Central Asia. In 95, she composed "Rhapsody on an Eastward Journey" (in *Wen xuan*, chapter 9), which recounts her travels through central Henan as she accompanied her son Cao Cheng to his first post as chief of Changyuan 長垣 (modern Changyuan *xian*, Henan).

Ban Zhao is best known for her "Nü jie" 女誡 or "Instructions for Daughters," probably written around 108. It contains a set of seven detailed instructions for female behavior and probably was intended for her daughters, or girls of her family. She also wrote a commentary to Ban Gu's "Rhapsody on Communicating with the Hidden" (cited in *Wen xuan*, chapter 14).

When Ban Zhao died around 120, Empress Deng mourned for her and assigned a special official to attend to her funeral.

References
Swann, Nancy Lee. *Pan Chao: Foremost Woman Poet of China.*

GUO PU 郭璞 (276–324), *zi* Jingchun 景純, native of Wenxi 聞喜 (modern Wenxi, Shanxi), Hedong 河東 commandery.

Guo Pu was a learned scholar and poet of the Eastern Jin. The best source of information on his life is his biography in the *Jin shu* (72.1899–1910). He also is the subject of several anecdotes in the *Shishuo xinyu*.

Guo Pu came from a family of minor officials. His father, Guo Yuan 郭瑗, served on the staff of the grand secretary Du Yu 杜預 (222–284). As a young man Guo studied the occult arts with an Elder Guo, who lived in the Hedong area. Around 310, when the Xiongnu Liu Cong 劉聰 declared himself emperor of a new Han dynasty in the north, Guo Pu fled to the south where he first joined the staff of Yin You 殷祐, governor of Xuancheng 宣城 (modern Xuancheng, Anhui) as military adviser. Guo's main function was to perform divinations concerning Yin's military operations. In 311, Guo accompanied Yin to the capital, where he attracted the notice of the chancellor Wang Dao 王導 (276–339), who frequently commissioned Guo to explain the meaning of various portents. In 320, Guo was appointed gentleman-compiler, and in 321 he was promoted to gentleman in the secretariat. That same year, he became an associate of the military strongman Wang Dun 王敦 (266–324), who held sway in the Hunan-Hubei area. When Wang Dun revolted in early 322, Guo had taken leave to mourn for his mother, who died in Jiyang 暨陽 (modern Jiangyin 江陰, Jiangsu), not too far from the capital. In 324, Wang Dun had Guo beheaded for failing to produce a divination favorable to his planned usurpation of the throne.

Guo Pu was the most learned man of the Six Dynasties period. He wrote commentaries to the *Chuci*, *Shanhai jing*, *Erya*, *Mu Tianzi zhuan*, *Fang yan*, and Sima Xiangru's "Rhapsody of Master Vacuous" and "Rhapsody on the Imperial Park." He was a prolific *fu* writer. His "Rhapsody on the Yangzi River" (in *Wen xuan*, chapter 12), is one of the most learned poems of world literature. Guo also wrote a series of "Poems on Roaming in Transcendency," seven of which are in the *Wen xuan* (chapter 21).

References

Kōzen Hiroshi. "Shijin to shite no Kaku Haku" 詩人として郭璞. *Chūgoku bungaku hō* 19 (1963): 17–67.

Funazu (Funatsu) Tomihiko 船津富彥. "Kaku Haku no yūsenshi no tokushitsu ni tsuite" 郭璞の遊仙詩の特質について. *Tōkyō Shinagaku hō* 10 (1964): 53–70.

Pease, Jonathan Otis. "Kuo Pu's Life and Five-Colored Rhymes (An 'Immortal' Chin Dynasty Writer and Diviner, 276–324)." M.A. Thesis, University of Washington, 1980.

HE YAN 何晏 (ob. 249), *zi* Pingshu 平叔, native of Wan prefecture, Nanyang commandery (modern Nanyang, Henan).

He Yan is best known for his advocacy of the Mysterious Learning (*Xuanxue* 玄學), a philosophy rooted in Taoist metaphysics, and his commentary to the *Lun yu*. He Yan's biography was omitted from the *Sanguo zhi*. He has only a short notice in Cao Shuang's biography (9.292). The information cited in Pei Songzhi's commentary (*Sanguo zhi* 9.292–93) is all from hostile sources. He also figures prominently in many *Shishuo xinyu* anecdotes.

He Yan was the grandson of the Han dynasty general He Jin 何進 (ob. A.D. 189). His father died when he was a young child. Shortly after becoming minister of works in 196, Cao Cao selected He's mother, née Yin 尹, as a concubine, and thus He was reared in the palace with Cao Cao's other sons, including Cao Pi, who detested He Yan for his dissolute ways. According to one source, Cao Pi never referred to He Yan by his proper name, but always called him "bastard." He Yan married the Princess Jinxiang 金鄉, whom some sources identify as his half-sister. Emperor Wen (Cao Pi, reg. 220–227) refused to appoint him to office, and Emperor Ming (reg. 227–239) gave him only sinecure appointments. During the Zhengshi 正始 era (240–248), He was a leading member of the group of "pure conversationalists" who belonged to the coterie of the regent Cao Shuang 曹爽 (ob. 249). Cao appointed him regular cavalier attendant, palace attendant, and master of writing, in which capacity he was in charge of recommending men for office. He was executed in 249 when Sima Yi 司馬懿 (179–251) seized power from Cao Shuang.

He Yan was a skilled poet. His only extant *fu*, "Rhapsody on the Hall of Great Blessings," which he wrote to celebrate the construction of a great palace in Xuchang, is contained in *Wen xuan*, chapter 11. He also wrote commentaries to the *Lun yu* and the *Zhou yi*, as well as a treatise on Taoism, the "Dao de lun" 道德論 (Discourse on the Way and Power). Only his *Lun yu* commentary, the *Lun yu jijie* 論語集解 (Collected Explanations of the *Lun yu*), in ten *juan*, is extant.

References

K. C. Hsiao. Frederick W. Mote, trans. *A History of Chinese Political Thought.* Volume 1: From Beginnings to the Sixth Century A.D. (Princeton: Princeton University Press, 1979), pp. 607–12.

Lü Kai 呂凱. *Wei Jin xuanxue xiping* 魏晉玄學析評 (Taibei: Shiji shuju, 1980), pp. 127–32.

Mather, *Shih-shuo Hsin-yü*, pp. 523–24.

MU HUA 木華 (fl. ca. 290), *zi* Xuanxu 玄虛, native of Guangchuan 廣川 (modern Zaoqiang 棗强, Hebei).

Virtually nothing is known about Mu Hua's life. According to the *Mu Hua ji* 木華集 (Collected Works of Mu Hua) cited by Li Shan (12.1a), he served as master of records under Yang Jun 楊駿 (ob. 291). His only extant piece is "Rhapsody on the Sea" contained in *Wen xuan*, chapter 12.

PAN YUE 潘岳 (247–300), *zi* Anren 安仁, native of Zhongmou 中牟 prefecture (modern Zhongmou *xian*, Henan), Xingyang commandery

The most important source of information on his life is found in the *Jin shu* (55.1500–7), which seems based in part on Pan's preface to his "Rhapsody on Living in Idleness" (contained in *Wen xuan*, chapter 16). He also is the subject of many anecdotes in the *Shishuo xinyu*. Both he and his nephew Pan Ni 潘尼 (ca. 250–310) were leading poets of the late third century.

Pan Yue was born into a family of prominent officials. His father Pan Pi 潘芘

(ob. ca. 280) served as capital clerk of Langye (in modern Shandong), which in this period was the equivalent of a governor (*taishou*). From an early age Pan displayed keen talent in his studies and was known in his home village as "the wonder child." One of his earliest compositions must have been "Rhapsody on Pheasant Shooting" (in *Wen xuan*, chapter 9), written around 266 while Pan was living with his father in Langye. Another of his early compositions is "Rhapsody on the Widow" (in *Wen xuan*, chapter 16), which laments the death of Ren Hu 任護, the husband of his wife's sister.

Pan's first appointment was in late 266, when he served as assistant to the minister of works. While in Luoyang, he became good friends with Xiahou Zhan 夏侯湛 (243–291). When Xiahou Zhan died in 291, Pan wrote a moving tribute to him, "Dirge for Regular Attendant Xiahou" (contained in *Wen xuan*, chapter 57). In 268, Pan composed on behalf of Emperor Wu of the Jin (reg. 265–290) "Rhapsody on the Sacred Field" (in *Wen xuan*, chapter 7), a *fu* celebrating the ceremonial plowing of the imperial plot. Beginning in the late 270's, he served on the staff of the grand marshal, Jia Chong 賈充 (217–282). At this time he composed the "Autumn Inspirations Rhapsody," in which he expressed his disillusionment with official life. For unknown reasons, around 279 Pan left the capital to serve in local administration, first as prefect of Heyang 河陽 (west of modern Meng 孟 xian, Henan, on the north bank of the Yellow River across from Luoyang). Later, around 282, he was transfered to Huai 懷 prefecture (modern Wuzhi 武陟 xian, Henan). His poems "Written in Heyang Prefecture" and "Written in Huai Prefecture" (both in *Wen xuan*, chapter 26) describe his dissatisfaction with official service away from the capital and his home.

Around 285, Pan returned to the capital, where he served as gentleman in the secretariat of finance and adjudicator under the commandant of justice. Immediately upon his return, he visited the graves of his father-in-law Yang Zhao 楊肇 (ob. 275) and his brothers-in-law (Yang Zhao's sons), Yang Tan 楊潭 and Yang Shao 楊韶 near Mount Song, south of Luoyang. His "Rhapsody on Cherishing the Old" (in *Wen xuan*, chapter 16) is a lamentation over their death. In early 290, Pan was dismissed from office for committing some unspecified offence, but returned to court later that same year to join the staff of Yang Jun 楊駿 (ob. 291), father of Empress Yang, who had served as regent for the ailing Emperor Wu and grand tutor to his successor, the imbecile Emperor Hui (reg. 290–306). In 291 Yang Jun was assassinated in a palace coup instigated by Empress Jia, but Pan Yue's life was spared through the intercession of a friend who happened to be in charge of executions. The following year, he traveled from Luoyang to the old Han capital of Chang'an, where he assumed the post of prefect. His journey took him through many historical sites, which he described in a long *fu* titled "Rhapsody on a Westward Journey" (in *Wen xuan*, chapter 10).

Around 293, Pan returned to the capital where he was a member of the entourage of Jia Mi 賈謐 (ob. 300), the Empress' nephew. After serving briefly as erudite, he resigned because of his mother's illness. For the next few years (ca. 296–297), Pan lived in retirement in Luoyang. His "Rhapsody on Living in Idleness" (in *Wen xuan*, chapter 16), written during these years, contrasts his life as an official with his seemingly contented existence as a retired gentleman. He spent part of his leisure time at the Golden Valley estate of Shi Chong 石崇 (249–300), where many literary figures congregated to drink and feast, listen to music, and write verse. Pan's poem "A Poem Written at a Golden Valley Gathering" (in *Wen xuan*, chapter 20) comes from this period.

In late 297, Pan returned to office as gentleman composer and regular cavalier attendant. In the same year he composed "Dirge for Ma, Overseer of Qian" (in *Wen xuan*, chapter 57), a lament for Ma Dun 馬敦 who died in prison that year. In 298, Pan Yue's wife died. His three poems, "Lamenting the Deceased" (in *Wen xuan*, chapter 23) and his prose piece "Lamenting the Eternally Departed" (in *Wen xuan*, chapter 57) express his deep sense of loss. The poems are the earliest known examples in Chinese literature of a poet's lament for his deceased wife.

In 300, Pan Yue's patron Jia Mi was assassinated in a coup led by Sima Lun 司馬倫 (ob. 301). Pan was arrested after Sun Xiu 孫秀 (ob. 301), who long had harbored a grudge against Pan, falsely accused him of plotting rebellion with Sima Jiong 司馬冏 (ob. 302), prince of Qi, and Sima Yun 司馬允 (ob. 301), prince of Huainan. Pan and his entire family, including his aged mother, were executed.

In addition to his fame as a poet, Pan is known as one of the most handsome men in Chinese history. An often-repeated anecdote mentions that whenever he traveled the streets of Luoyang, women joined hands in a circle around him and threw fruit at him. He always returned home with his cart fully laden.

References

Li Changzhi 李長之. "Xi Jin shiren Pan Yue de shengping ji qi chuangzuo" 西晉詩人潘岳的生平及其創作. *Guowen yuekan* 68 (June 1968):25–32.

Takahashi Kazumi 高橋和巳. "Han Gaku ron" 潘岳論. *Chūgoku bungaku hō* 7 (1957): 14–91.

Kōzen Hiroshi. *Han Gaku Riku Ki*.

Fu Xuancong 傅璇琮. "Pan Yue xinian kaozheng" 潘岳系年考證. *Wen shi* 14 (1982):237–57.

SIMA XIANGRU 司馬相如 (179–117 B.C.), *zi* Zhangqing 長卿, native of Cheng-du, Shu commandery (modern Chengdu, Sichuan).

Sima Xiangru is the best known *fu* writer of the Former Han dynasty. The most important sources of information about his life are his *Shi ji* (*juan* 117) and *Han shu* (*juan* 57) biographies.

Nothing is known about Sima Xiangru's ancestors. He may have been distantly related to the Qin general Sima Cuo, who led an invasion of Shu in the late fourth century B.C. Around 150 B.C., at about the age of twenty-five, Sima Xiangru traveled to Chang'an, the capital, where he was able to purchase a court appointment as gentleman. A few years later he accepted an invitation to join the literary salon at the court of Liu Wu 劉武, King of Liang 梁 (reg. 168–144 B.C.), whose entourage included such accomplished writers as Mei Sheng and Zou Yang. At Liang, he found the leisure to develop his literary skills, particularly in the newly emerging *fu* genre. His best known work from this period is "Rhapsody of Sir Vacuous" (in *Wen xuan*, chapter 7), a long, effusive description of the huge Yunmeng hunting preserve in the old kingdom of Chu.

After the death of Liu Wu in 144 B.C., Sima Xiangru returned to Shu, where by virtue of his poetic talent, he became the protégé of a prominent Shu official. In 142 B.C., he scandalized Shu society by eloping with Zhuo Wenjun 卓文君, the daughter of a wealthy iron manufacturer. To support themselves, he and his wife ran a wine shop until Wenjun's father was shamed into recognizing their marriage. Around 137 B.C., Sima Xiangru returned to the capital at the invitation of the young Emperor Wu (reg. 140–87 B.C.), who wished to meet the author of "Rhapsody of Sir Vacuous." Upon his arrival in the capital, he presented to the emperor the "Rhapsody on the Imperial Park" (in *Wen xuan*, chapter 8), which so pleased the emperor that he appointed him to the post of palace gentleman. Sima's primary duty was to compose occasional poems for the entertainment of court officers and guests.

Around 131 B.C., he served as Emperor Wu's special emissary in the southwest, where he mediated a dispute between a general sent to pacify the area and the local people. To convince them of the emperor's good intentions, Sima Xiangru composed "Proclamation Addressed to Ba and Shu" (contained in *Wen xuan* 44). Sima Xiangru returned again to Shu in the following year, this time to open new roads and to establish Han control over the area. In the middle of his mission, Sima encountered much opposition to his plans to establish regular contacts with the southwestern tribes, particularly from prominent men of Shu. He then wrote a dispatch, "Objecting to the Elders of Shu" (in *Wen xuan*, chapter 44), a dialogue between the Shu elders, who plead against opening communication with the tribes, and the imperial envoy, who wins them over with words about imperial beneficence. Reputedly Sima Xiangru's true views were conveyed in the speech of the elders.

Sima Xiangru spent his later years in semi-retirement, occasionally accompanying the emperor on outings and hunts. After a visit to the tomb of the last Qin emperor, he composed "Rhapsody Lamenting the Second Qin Emperor," which may have been intended as a subtle warning to Emperor Wu that his ostentation and extravgance might have the same dire consequences for the Han as they did for the Qin. Around 120 B.C. he wrote another admonitory *fu*, "Rhapsody on the Great Man," which in one section pokes fun at Emperor Wu's obsession with alchemists and magicians who promised to discover for him the secret of immortality. The following year he retired to the mausoleum town of Maoling, where he died in 117 B.C. Just before his death he wrote "Essay on the *Feng* and *Shan* Sacrifices" (in *Wen xuan*, chapter 48), a memorial addressed to Emperor Wu urging him to perform sacrifices on Mount Tai. Also attributed to Sima Xiangru is "Rhapsody on Tall Gate Palace" (*Wen xuan*, chapter 16), reputedly written out of sympathy for Empress Chen, who had fallen out of favor with Emperor Wu.

References
Hervouet. *Un Poète de cour sous les Han: Sseu-ma Siang-jou.*
———. *Le Chapitre 117 du Che-ki.*
Jian Zongwu. *Sima Xiangru Yang Xiong ji qi fu zhi yanjiu*, pp. 9–174.

SUN CHUO 孫綽 (314–371), *zi* Xinggong 興公, native of Zhongdu 中都 (northwest of modern Pingyao 平遙, Shanxi), Taiyuan commandery.

Sun Chuo was a prominent poet and philosopher of the Eastern Jin. The most important source of information on his life is his biography in the *Jin shu* (56.1544–47). He also is the subject of numerous anecdotes in the *Shishuo xinyu*.

Sun Chuo was the grandson of Sun Chu 孫楚 (ca. 218–293), a prominent mystical verse writer who served as governor of Pingyi 馮翊 (modern Dali 大荔 *xian*, Shaanxi) during the early 290's. Around 309, his father Sun Zuan 孫纂 left his home in Shanxi and took up residence in Guiji 會稽 (modern central Zhejiang). Thus, Sun Chuo must have been born in the south. For over ten years, Sun Chuo lived as a semi-recluse, trekking the hills and rivers of the Guiji area. In a *fu* entitled "Rhapsody on Fulfilling My Original Resolve," he declared his contentment with life close to nature. However, later in life he accepted numerous government appointments including military adviser to the military strongman Yu Liang 庾亮 (289–340); chief clerk for Yin Hao 殷浩 (305–356), governor of Yangzhou; chief clerk under Wang Xizhi while Wang served as governor of Guiji; and regular cavalier attendant and gentleman compiler under the dictator Huan Wen 桓溫 (312–373). His highest post was that of minister of justice, the title that frequently is attached to his name.

Sun Chuo's most famous piece is "Rhapsody on Roaming the Celestial Terrace Mountains" (in *Wen xuan*, chapter 11), a long *fu* that recounts Sun's physical and mystical ascent of the Tiantai peaks of Zhejiang. When Sun showed the piece to his contemporary Fan Qi 范啓 (fl. mid-fourth century), Fan reputedly said, "Try throwing it on the ground; it will surely resound like metal bells and stone chimes" (trans. Mather, *Shih-shuo Hsin-yü*, p. 137, IV/86). Sun also wrote numerous dirges and grave inscriptions for powerful men, notably Huan Wen and Yu Liang.

References
Mather, Richard B. "The Mystical Ascent of the T'ien-t'ai Mountains."
Cao Daoheng 曹道衡. "Jindai zuojia liukao" 晉代作家六考, *Wen shi* 20 (1983): 187–88.

WANG CAN 王粲 (177–217), *zi* Zhongxuan 仲宣, native of Gaoping 高平 (southwest of modern Zou 鄒 *xian*, Shandong), Shanyang commandery.

Wang Can was the most distinguished of the Seven Masters of the Jian'an (196–219) period. The primary source of information on his life is his biography in the *Sanguo zhi* (21.597–99).

Wang Can came from a prominent official family of the Late Han. His grandfather Wang Chang 王暢 (ob. 169) served as Minister of Works. His father Wang Qian 王謙 served as chief clerk to the powerful general He Jin 何進 (ob. 189), who unsuccessfully tried to arrange a marriage between his and Wang's families. Around 190, Wang Can moved from Luoyang to Chang'an, where the satrap Dong Zhuo 董卓 (ob. 192) had transferred the puppet emperor Xian 獻 (reg. 190–220) and his court. Here he met the venerable scholar Cai Yong 蔡邕 (132–192), who was so excited to meet the thirteen-year-old son of this distinguished family, he put his sandals on backwards. Cai was so impressed with Wang's intelligence, he promised to present him with his book collection.

In 193, at the age of sixteen, Wang was appointed attendant gentleman of the yellow gate, but because Chang'an still was in turmoil after the assassination of Dong

Zhuo in 192, he resigned his post and left for the south, where he joined Liu Biao 劉表 (144–208), governor of Jingzhou 荊州 (roughly modern Hubei and Hunan). Liu was from Wang Can's native place of Gaoping and had studied under Wang's grandfather. On his way to Xiangyang, where Liu Biao had his headquarters, Wang wrote the first of two "Seven Laments" (in *Wen xuan*, chapter 23), in which he graphically depicts the anarchy and carnage that inflicted the Western Capital.

Liu Biao was not impressed with Wang Can. He found his features "too sickly" and his manner too rude and casual. Thus, Liu did not appoint him to his inner circle of advisers, but employed Wang primarily as a secretary to compose official correspondence. During the fifteen years he spent in Jingzhou, Wang composed many poems, some of which are contained in the *Wen xuan*. The poems include the second of his "Seven Laments" (in *Wen xuan*, chapter 23), in which Wang expresses his longing to return to his home in the north, three poems presented to other members of Liu Biao's entourage (also in *Wen xuan*, chapter 23), and his "Rhapsody on Climbing a Tower" (in *Wen xuan*, chapter 11).

After Liu Biao's death in 208, Wang Can ingratiated himself with Cao Cao by urging Liu Biao's successor, Liu Cong 劉琮 to pledge allegiance to Cao Cao. Under Cao Cao, Wang received high office and rank. Cao first appointed him aide to the chancellor and Marquis of Guannei. Sometime between 208–213, he served in the ceremonial post of military councilor and libationer. When Cao Cao established the Wei kingdom in 213, he appointed Wang as one of his four palace attendants, and thus he became a member of Cao's inner circle. In the same year, Cao assigned Wang the task of composing ritual songs to celebrate the construction of the Wei ancestral temples. While accompanying Cao Cao on military campaigns, Wang composed both *fu* and *shi*. Between 215 and 216, he wrote five "Poems on Following the Army" (in *Wen xuan*, chapter 27), that praise the martial exploits of his patron. Wang wrote other occasional poems, including "The Lord's Feast" (in *Wen xuan*, chapter 20), written at a banquet presumably hosted by Cao Cao. Probably also from the period of his service to Cao Cao is "Recitation on History" (in *Wen xuan*, chapter 21), a poem lamenting the death of the three worthies who were put to death so as to serve their lord Duke Mu of Qin (ob. 630 B.C.) in the afterlife.

In 216, Wang Can accompanied Cao Cao on an expedition against Sun Quan of Wu. He became ill and died on February 17, 217. Cao Zhi composed a dirge for him, which is contained in *Wen xuan* 56.

References

Miao Yue. "Wang Can xingnian kao" 王粲行年考. *Zeshan banyuekan* 責善半月刊 2.21 (1942):7–13; rpt. in Miao Yue. *Du shi cun gao* 讀史存稿 (Beijing: Sanlian, 1963):pp. 116–26.

Itō Masafumi 伊藤正文. "Ō San den ron" 王粲伝論. *Kanbun kyōshitsu* 1.66 (1964): 1–10; 2.67 (1964):19–30.

———. "Ō San shi ronkō" 王粲詩論考. *Chūgoku bungaku hō* 20 (1965):28–67.

Miao, Ronald C. "A Critical Study of the Life and Poetry of Wang Chung-hsüan." Ph.D. Dissertation, University of California, Berkeley, 1969.

Shimasada Masahiro 下定雅弘. "Ō San shi ni tsuite" 王粲詩について. *Chūgoku bungaku hō* 29 (1978):46–81.

Miao, Ronald C. *Early Medieval Chinese Poetry; The Life and Verse of Wang Ts'an* (A.D. 177–217). Wiesbaden: Franz Steiner Verlag, 1982.

WANG YANSHOU 王延壽 (fl. 163), *zi* Wenkao 文考 and Zishan 子山, native of Yicheng 宜城 (modern Yicheng *xian*, Hubei), Nan commandery.

Wang Yanshou was the son of the *Chuci* commentator Wang Yi. What little is known about his life is contained in a note appended to his father's biography in the *Hou Han shu* (80A.2618).

Wang Yanshou was a gifted *fu* writer. As a young man he accompanied his father to Lu (modern Shandong) where they studied the classics and computation with one Bao Zizhen 鮑子眞 of Mount Tai. While in the area, they visited Qufu 曲阜 where Wang Yanshou composed the "Rhapsody on the Hall of Numinous Brilliance" (in *Wen xuan*, chapter 11), which describes a famous palace located southeast of the Confucian temple in Qufu. The most famous piece attributed to Wang is "Rhapsody on a Dream" (in *Guwen yuan* 3.1a–2a), written at the age of twenty to exorcise demons who had appeared to him in a frightful nightmare. He also wrote a humorous *fu* on a monkey ("Rhapsody on the Monkey," in *Guwen yuan* 3.2b–3b). On his return to Yicheng from Lu, Wang drowned crossing the Xiang River. He was just over twenty years old at the time.

YANG XIONG 揚雄 (53 B.C.–A.D. 18), *zi* Ziyun 子雲, native of Chengdu, Shu commandery (modern Chengdu, Sichuan).

Yang Xiong was a leading scholar, poet, and philosopher of the Han dynasty. The most important source of information on his life is his biography in the *Han shu* (*juan* 87), much of which is copied from Yang Xiong's own "Autobiography."

Yang Xiong claimed descent from a northern aristocratic family that fled south during the internecine war that afflicted the state of Jin in the sixth century B.C. Around 115 B.C. Yang's immediate ancestors had fled to the small prefecture of Pi 郫 (modern Pi *xian*, Sichuan), located on the southern slopes of the Min Mountains in Shu. Here they had a small plot of land, on which they made a living from farming and sericulture. Yang was a studious lad, and earned a considerable reputation as a skilled writer of rhapsodies in the style of Sima Xiangru. Sometime between 24 and 21 B.C., Yang composed "Rebutting Sorrow," an intricate poetic refutation of Qu Yuan's "Encountering Sorrow."

Around 20 B.C. Yang left Shu for Chang'an, the capital, where by virtue of his poetic skill he obtained appointment as gentleman. His principal duty at court was to write rhapsodies and other compositions for the emperor. His best known occasional pieces, all composed around 11 B.C., include "Rhapsody on the Sweet Springs Palace" (in *Wen xuan* 7), describing an imperial sacrifice at the Sweet Springs Palace north of Chang'an; the "Plume Hunt Rhapsody" (in *Wen xuan*, chapter 8) and "Rhapsody on the Tall Poplars Lodge" (in *Wen xuan*, chapter 9), both of which concern an imperial hunt in the Shanglin Park. According to Yang Xiong's own introductions to these rhapsodies, his primary purpose lay in moral suasion (*feng* 風),

and thus the poems contain subtle criticisms of activities Yang found repugnant, notably imperial ostentation. Around 9 B.C., the emperor commissioned Yang to compose a panegyric for the portrait of the great general Zhao Chongguo 趙充國, who earned acclaim for his victory over the Western Qiang (Tibetans) in 61 B.C. (see "Eulogy for Zhao Chongguo" in *Wen xuan*, chapter 47.)

The emperor and the court apparently were oblivious of the reprimands Yang inserted in his *fu*, and instead praised his works for their elegant, lofty literary style. Thus, Yang began to doubt the efficacy of the rhapsody as a means of suasion, and he vowed to cease writing them, turning instead to scholarship and philosophy. Around 2 B.C., Yang completed a long philosophical treatise titled *Taixuan* 太玄 (Great Mystery). (The modern title is *Taixuan jing* 太玄經 or *Canon of Great Mystery*.) Modeled on the *Classic of Changes*, the *Taixuan* combines a Taoist-like quietism with a Confucian concern for order and morality.

Although Yang repudiated the *fu*, he did not cease writing poetry. The *Taixuan* itself can be read as a long philosophical poem that uses frequent rhyme and numerous artfully conceived poetic images. Yang also wrote several poetic works that are indistinguishable from the *fu*, notably "Justification against Ridicule" (contained in *Wen xuan*, chapter 45), an apologia defending Yang's lack of political ambition.

Yang Xiong further elucidated his ideas on literature in the *Fa yan* 法言 (Exemplary Sayings), a collection of aphorisms written in the style of the *Lun yu*. Although Yang probably completed the *Fa yan* around A.D. 10, it purports to include his responses to questions put to him by his associates over a period of time. A central theme of the work is the neglect of orthodox Confucian values, which Yang believed had become distorted by many Han and pre-Han thinkers. The second chapter of the book contains Yang Xiong's famous denunciation of the *fu*, which he characterized as the "worm-carving and seal-cutting" of a young boy.

During Wang Mang's Xin dynasty (A.D. 9–22), Yang continued to hold office, and in the view of some later scholars, his service to Wang Mang was tantamount to treason. His most controversial work is "Denigrating Qin and Praising Xin" (contained in *Wen xuan*, chapter 48), a long memorial that contrasts the great accomplishments achieved by Wang Mang with the tyranny of the Qin. In A.D. 10, after being mistakenly implicated in an anti-Wang Mang plot, Yang barely escaped death after attempting to commit suicide by jumping from the Tianlu Gallery. He spent his final years in the post of palace attendant grandee. Before his death in A.D. 18, Yang completed the *Fang yan* 方言 (Regional Words), which glosses various dialect and unusual words he had collected over a twenty-seven-year period.

References

Dong Zuobin 董作賓. "Fangyan xuejia Yang Xiong nianpu" 方言學家揚雄年譜, *Guoli Zhongshan daxue yuyan lishi yanjiusuo zhoukan* 8 (1928):82–88.

Knechtges, David R. "Yang Shyong, the *Fuh*, and Hann Rhetoric." Ph.D. Dissertation, University of Washington, 1968.

Doeringer. "Yang Hsiung and His Formulation of a Classicism."

Ding Jiemin 丁介民. *Yang Xiong nianpu* 揚雄年譜. Taibei: Jinghua chubanshe, 1975.

Xu Fuguan 徐復觀. "Yang Xiong lunjiu" 揚雄論究. *Dalu zazhi* 50.3 (1975), 103–45; rpt. in *Liang Han sixiang shi*, pp. 303–409.

Knechtges. *The Han Rhapsody.*

Jian Zongwu. *Sima Xiangru Yang Xiong ji qi fu zhi yanjiu*, pp. 175–339.

Knechtges, David R, trans. *The Han shu Biography of Yang Xiong.*

Bibliography

ABBREVIATIONS

AM	*Asia Major*
BEFEO	*Bulletin de l'École Française de l'Extrême Orient*
BIHP	*Bulletin of the Institute of History and Philology, Academia Sinica (Guoli zhong-yang yanjiuyuan lishı yuyan yanjiusuo jikan* 國立中央研究院歷史語言研究所集刊
BMFEA	*Bulletin of the Museum of Far Eastern Antiquities*
BSOAS	*Bulletin of the School of Oriental and African Studies*
CLEAR	*Chinese Literature Essays Articles and Reviews*
HFHD	*History of the Former Han Dynasty*
HJAS	*Harvard Journal of Asiatic Studies*
JAOS	*Journal of the American Oriental Society*
Mh	*Mémoires historiques*
MS	*Monumenta Serica*
MTB	*Memoirs of the Research Department of the Toyo Bunko*
Records	*Records of the Grand Historian*
Sbby	*Sibu beiyao*
Sbck	*Sibu congkan*
TP	*T'oung Pao*

Akendanga 阿克當阿 and Yao Wentian 姚文田 (1758–1827), comps. *Yangzhou fu zhi* 揚州府志 (Gazetteer of Yangzhou Prefecture). Taibei: Chengwen chubanshe, 1974.

Aoki Masaru 青木正兒. "Shakuyaku no wa" 芍藥之和 (The Blended Sauce), in *Aoki Masaru zenshū* 青木正兒全集 (Complete Works of Aoki Masaru). 10 volumes. Tokyo: Shunju sha, 1969–75. 8:64–76.

Bielenstein, Hans. *The Bureaucracy of Han Times.* Cambridge: Cambridge University Press, 1980.

Biot, Edouard, trans. *Tcheou-Li, Rites des Tcheou.* 3 vols. 1851; rpt. Taipei: Ch'eng Wen Publishing Co., 1969.

Birch, Cyril and Donald Keene, eds. *Anthology of Chinese Literature.* From Early Times to the Fourteenth Century. New York: Grove Press, 1965.

Bodde, Derk. *Statesman, Patriot, and General in Ancient China.* New Haven: American Oriental Society, 1940.

Boltz, William G. "*Chuang Tzu*: Two Notes on *Hsiao Yao Yu*," *BSOAS* 43.3 (1980): 532–43.

————. "Kung kung and the Flood: Reverse Euhemerism in the *Yao tien*," *TP* 67 (1981): 141–53.

Boodberg, Peter A. "Cedules from a Berkeley Workshop in Asiatic Philology," *Tsing Hua Journal of Chinese Studies* 7.2 (1969): 1–39.

Cao Daoheng 曹道衡. "Guanyu Bao Zhao de jiashi he jiguan" 關于鮑照的家世和籍貫 (Concerning Bao Zhao's Ancestry and Native Place), *Wen shi* 7 (1979): 191–97.

————. "Bao Zhao jipian shi wen de xiezuo shijian" 鮑照幾篇詩文的寫作時間 (The Dates of Several Poems and Essays by Bao Zhao), *Wen shi* 16 (1982): 189–202.

————. "Jindai zuojia liukao" 晉代作家六考 (Six Studies of Jin Writers), *Wen shi* 20 (1983): 185–94.

Chalmers, J. "The Foo on Pheasant Shooting," *Chinese Review, Notes and Inquiries* 1 (1872–73): 322–24.

Chavannes, Edouard. "Trois Généraux chinois de la dynastie des Han orientaux," *TP* 7 (1906): 210–69.

Chen Dazuo 陳達祚 and Zhu Jiang 朱江. "Hancheng yizhi yu Han 'gou liujing quyu wen hua yicun de faxian" 邗城遺址與邗溝流經區域文化遺存的發現 (Cultural Remains Discovered at the Ruins of Hancheng and the Area through Which Flowed the Han Canal," *Wenwu* (1973: 12), pp. 44–54.

Chen, Jerome and Michael Bullock. *Poems of Solitude*. London: Aberlard-Schumann, Ltd., 1960.

Chen Yixin 陳貽焮. "Bao Zhao he tade zuopin" 鮑照和他的作品 (Bao Zhao and His Writings), *Wenxue yichan* 1957: 182–90.

Chen Zuolong 陳祚龍. "Dunhuang xieben 'Deng lou fu' jiaozheng" 敦煌寫本登樓賦斠證 (Collation of the Dunhuang Manuscript of 'Rhapsody on Climbing the Tower,'" *Dalu zazhi* 21.5 (1960): 173–78.

Cheung Siu-cheong (Zhuang Zhaoxiang 莊兆祥) and Li Ninghon (Li Ninghan 李甯漢), eds. *Chinese Medicinal Herbs of Hong Kong*. Vol. 1. Hong Kong: Commercial Press, 1978.

Chmielewski, Janus. "Yi putao yi ci wei li lun gudai Hanyu de jieci wenti" 以葡萄一詞爲例論古代漢語的借詞問題 (Using the Example of Grape to Discuss the Question of Loan Words in Ancient Chinese), *Beijing daxue xuebao* (1957: 1): pp. 71–81.

————. "The Problem of Early Loan-words in Chinese as illustrated by the Word 'p'u-t'ao,'" *Rocznik Orientalistyczny* 22.2 (1958): 7–45.

————. "Two Early Loan-Words in Chinese," *Rocznik Orientalistyzny* 24.2 (1961): 65–85.

Coblin, W. South. *A Handbook of Eastern Han Sound Glosses*. Hong Kong: The Chinese University Press, 1983.

Creel, H. G. "The Great Clod: A Taoist Conception of the Universe," in *Wen-lin*, edited by Chow Tse-tsung, pp. 257–68.

Dai Zhen 戴震 (1724–1777), comm. *Fangyan shuzheng* 方言疏證 (Exegetical Evidence for the *Fangyan*). Sbby.

Demiéville, Paul. Review of *Che-yin Ming-tcheng Ying tsao fa che*, in *BEFEO* 25 (1925): 213–64.

Dien, Albert E., trans. "Excavation of the Ch'in Dynasty Pit Containing Pottery Figures of Warriors and Horses at Ling-t'ung, Shensi Province," *Chinese Studies in Archeology* 1.1 (1979): 8–55.

Ding Fulin 丁福林. "Yu Yan Bao Zhao ji xu de yichu chuanxie cuowu" 虞炎鮑照集序的一處傳寫錯誤 (A Transcriptional Error in Yu Yan's Preface to Bao Zhao's Collected Works), *Wen shi* 15 (1982): 124.

———. "Guanyu Bao Zhao de jiguan" 關于鮑照的籍貫 (Concerning Bao Zhao's Native Place), *Wen shi* 20 (1983): 253–58.

———. "Bao Zhao ren qianjun canjun de shijian" 鮑照任前軍參軍的時間 (When Bao Zhao Served as Adjutant to the Forward Army), *Wen shi* 22 (1984): 190.

Ding Jiemin 丁介民. *Yang Xiong nianpu* 揚雄年譜 (Chronological Biography of Yang Xiong). Taibei: Jinghua chubanshe, 1975.

Doeringer, Franklin M. "Yang Hsiung and His Formulation of a Classicism." Unpublished Ph.D. Dissertation, Columbia University, 1971.

Dong Zuobin 董作賓. "Fangyan xuejia Yang Xiong nianpu" 方言學家揚雄年譜 (Chronological Biography of Dialectologist Yang Xiong)," *Guoli Zhongshan daxue yuyan lishi yanjiusuo zhoukan* 8 (1928): 82–88.

Duan Gonglu 段公路 (fl. ca. 869). *Bei hu lu* 北戶錄 (Register of North-facing Doors). *Congshu jicheng.*

Duan Yucai 段玉裁 (1735–1815). *Shi jing xiaoxue* 詩經小學 (Philological Studies of the *Classic of Songs*). *Huang Qing jingjie.*

Dubs, Homer H. "The 'Golden Man' of Former Han Times," *TP* 33 (1937): 1–14, 191–92.

———. "An Ancient Chinese Mystery Cult," *Harvard Theological Review* 35 (1942): 221–240.

Duyvendak, J. J. L. *The Book of Lord Shang.* 1928; rpt. Chicago: University of Chicago Press, 1963.

Egami Namio 江上波夫. "Kyōdo no kichiku ni tsukite" 匈奴の奇獣に就きて (The Strange Animals of the Xiongnu), in *Yūrashia kodai hoppō bunka: Kyōdo bunka ronkō* ユーラシア古代北方文化：匈奴文化論考 (Ancient Northern Culture of Eurasia: Studies of Xiongnu Culture). 1948; rpt. Tokyo: Yamakawa, 1950.

———. "The K'uai-t'i, the T'ao-yu and the Tan-hsi, the Strange Donestic (sic) Animals of the Hsiung-nu," *MTB* 13 (1951): 87–123.

Fayun 法雲 (Song). *Fanyi mingyi* 翻譯名義 (The Meaning of Translated Buddhist Terms). *Sbck.*

Feng Dalun 馮大綸, comm. "Wu cheng fu" 蕪城賦 (Rhapsody on the Ruined City), *Gujin wenxuan* 4: 1505–8.

Feng Yan 封演 (*jinshi* 756). *Fengshi wenjian ji jiaozheng* 封氏聞見記校證 (Master Feng's Record of Knowledge Collated and Verified). Peiping: Harvard-Yenching Institute, 1933.

Fu Xuancong 傅璇琮. "Pan Yue xinian kaozheng" 潘岳系年考證 (Investigation of Pan Yue's Chronology), *Wen shi* 14 (1982): 237–57.

Fujiwara Takashi 藤原尚. "'Seisei fu' ni okeru ningenkan" 西征賦における人間観 (The World View of "Rhapsody on a Westward Journey"), *Nihon Chūgoku gakkai hō* 21 (1968):210–33.

Funazu (Funatsu) Tomihiko 船津富彦. "Kaku Haku no yūsenshi no tokushitsu ni tsuite" 郭璞の遊仙詩の特質について (On the Special Qualities of Guo Pu's Roaming in Transcendency Poems), *Tōkyō Shinagaku hō* 10 (1964):53–70.

Gan Bao 干寶 (fl. 317–322). *Sou shen ji* 搜神記 (Notes on Exploring the Supernatural). Beijing: Zhonghua shuju, 1979.

Gan Daxin 甘大昕. "Shuangsheng dieyun lianmian zi yanjiu" 雙聲叠韻聯綿字研究 (Study of Alliterative and Rhyming Compounds), *Guowen yuekan* 50 (December 1946):1–11.

Gu Zuyu 顧祖禹 (1631–1692). *Dushi fangyu jiyao* 讀史方輿紀要 (Essentials of Geography for Reading History). Beijing: Zhonghua shuju, 1955.

Hainei shizhou ji 海內十州記 (Record of the Ten Continents within the Seas). Attributed to Dongfang Shuo 東方朔 (ca. 154–93 B.C.). *Baoyan tang miji* 寶顏堂秘笈.

Hao Yixing 郝懿行 (1757–1825). *Jin Song shu gu* 晉宋書故 (Notes on Jin and Song Histories). *Yueya tang congshu* 粵雅堂叢書.

Hayashi Minao 林巳奈夫. *Chūgoku In-Shu jidai no buki* 中国殷周時代の武器 (Chinese Weapons of the Yin and Zhou Periods). Kyoto: Jimbun kagaku kenkyujo, 1972.

He Changqun 賀昌羣. "Feng sui kao" 烽燧考 (Study of Beacons), *Guoli Beijing daxue sishi zhounian jinian lunwen ji* 2.1 (1940):77–102.

He Peixiong 何沛雄. "Shanglin fu zuo yu Jianyuan chunian kao" 上林賦作於建元初年考 (Investigating the Composition of "Rhapsody on the Imperial Park" in the First Year of Jianyuan), *Dalu zazhi* 36.2 (1968):52–56.

Ho Peng-yoke (He Bingyu 何炳郁). *The Astronomical Chapters of the Chin shu*. Paris and The Hague: Mouton, 1961.

Hong Liangji 洪亮吉 (1746–1809). *Xiao dushu zhai zalu* 曉讀書齋雜錄 (Miscellaneous Notes from the Morning Reading Studio). *Hong Beijiang xiansheng quanji* 洪北江先生全集 (The Complete Works of Hong Liangji). Shoujing tang 授經堂, ed.

Hsiao, K. C. Frederick W. Mote, trans. *A History of Chinese Political Thought*. Volume 1: From Beginnings to the Sixth Century A.D. Princeton: Princeton University Press, 1979.

Hulsewé, A. F. P. "Again the Crossbow Trigger Mechanism," *TP* 64 (1978):253.

Itō Masafumi 伊藤正文. "Hō Chō den ronkō" 鮑照伝論稿 (Study of Bao Zhao's Biography), *Kobe daigaku bungakukai kenkyū* 14 (1957):18–55.

———. "Ō San den ron" 正粲伝論 (Study of Wang Can's Biography), *Kanbun kyōshitsu* 1.66 (1964):1–10; 2.67 (1964):19–30.

———. "Ō San shi ronkō" 王粲詩論考 (Study of Wang Can's Poetry), *Chūgoku bungaku hō* 20 (1965):28–67.

Ji Zhongqing 紀仲慶. "Yangzhou gucheng zhi bianqian chutan" 揚州古城址變遷初探 (Preliminary Investigation into the Changes in the Site of the Ancient City of Yangzhou), *Wenwu* (1979:9):43–56.

Jian Zongwu 簡宗梧. "Shanglin fu zhuzuo niandai zhi shangque" 上林賦著作年代之商榷 (Consideration of the Date of Composition of "Rhapsody on the Imperial Park"), *Dalu zazhi* 48.6 (1974):260–62.

———. *Han fu yuanliu yu jiazhi zhi shangque* 漢賦源流與價值之商榷 (Consideration of the Origins of the Han Rhapsody and Its Worth). Taibei: Wen shi zhe chubanshe, 1980.

Jiang Liangfu 姜亮夫. *Qu Yuan fu jiaozhu* 屈原賦校注 (Qu Yuan's Rhapsodies Collated and Annotated). Hong Kong: Shangwu yinshuguan, 1964.

Jiaqing chongxiu da Qing yitong zhi 嘉慶重修大清一統志. Comprehensive Gazetteer of the Qing, Revised during the Jiaqing Period). *Sbck*, Second Series.

Kariya Ekisai 狩谷棭齋 (1775–1835), ed. and comm. *Senchū Wamyō ruiju shō* 箋注倭名類聚抄 (Encyclopedia of Japanese, Annotated). Tokyo: Insatsukyoku, 1883.

Karlgren, Bernhard. *Grammata Serica Recensa*. 1957; rpt. Kungsback: Elanders Boktryckeri Aktiebolag, 1972.

Knechtges, David R. "Yang Shyong, the *Fuh* and Hann Rhetoric." Unpublished Ph.D. Dissertation, University of Washington, 1968.

———. "The Liu Hsin/Yang Hsiung Correspondence on the *Fang* yen," *MS* 33 (1977):309–25.

———. Review of Yves Hervouet, *Le Chapitre 117 du Che-ki*, *CLEAR* 1.1 (1979): 104–6.

———. "Ssu-ma Hsiang-ju's 'Tall Gate Palace Rhapsody,'" *HJAS* 41.1 (1981): 47–63.

———, trans. *The Han shu Biography of Yang Xiong (53 B.C.–A.D. 18)*. Occasional Paper No. 14, Center for Asian Studies, Arizona State University. Tempe: Center for Asian Studies, 1982.

———, trans. *Wen xuan or Selections of Refined Literature*. Volume One: Rhapsodies on Metropolises and Capitals. Princeton: Princeton University Press, 1982.

Kominami Ichirō 小南一郎. "Seiōbo to shichi seki denshō" 西王母と七夕伝承 (Queen Mother of the West and the Seventh Night Legend), *Tōhōgaku hō* 46 (1974):33–81.

Kopetsky, Elma E. "Two *Fu* on sacrifices by Yang Hsiung," *Journal of Oriental Studies* 10 (1972):85–118.

Kotzenberg, Heike. *Der Dichter Pao Chao (+466). Untersuchungen zu Leben und Werk*. Ph.D. Dissertation, Rheinische Friederich-Wilhelms-Universitat zu Bonn. Bonn: Rheinische Friederich-Wilhelms-Universitat, 1971.

Kōzen Hiroshi 興膳宏. "Shijin to shite no Kaku Haku" 詩人として郭璞 (The Poet Guo Pu), *Chūgoku bungaku hō* 19 (1963):17–67.

Leban, Carl. "Managing Heaven's Mandate: Coded Communications in the Accession of Ts'ao P'ei, A.D. 220," in *Ancient China: Studies in Early Civilization*, edited by David T. Roy and Tsuen-Hsuin Tsien, pp. 315–41.

Lei pian 類篇 (The Categorized Thesaurus). *Siku quanshu zhenben*, Series 6. Taibei: Shangwu yinshuguan, 1975.

Lévy-Bruhl, Lucien. *Les Fonctions mentales dans les sociétes inferieures*. Paris: Alcan, 1912.

Li Changzhi 李長之. "Xi Jin shiren Pan Yu de shengping ji qi chuangzuo" 西晉詩人潘岳的生平及其創作 (The Life and Creations of the Western Jin Poet Pan Yue), *Guowen yuekan* 68 (June 1948):25–32.

Li Chi, trans. *The Travel Diaries of Hsü Hsia-k'o*. Hong Kong: The Chinese University Press of Hong Kong, 1974.

Li Fang-kuei (Li Fanggui 李方桂). "Shanggu yin yanjiu" 上古音研究 (Studies on Archaic Chinese), *Tsing Hua Journal of Chinese Studies* 9.1 (1971):1–60; English trans. by Gilbert Mattos, "Studies on Archaic Chinese," *MS* 31 (1974–75): 219–87.

Li Jie 李誡 (1035–1108 or ca. 1065–1110). *Yingzao fashi* 營造法式 (Modes of Construction). Taibei: Lianjing, 1974.

Li T'ien-yi, ed. *Selected Works of George A. Kennedy.* New Haven: Far Eastern Publications, 1964.

Li Xueqin 李學勤. *The Wonder of Chinese Bronzes.* Beijing: Foreign Languages Press, 1980.

Lin Junrong 林俊榮. *Wei Jin Nanbei chao wenxue zuopin xuan* 魏晉南北朝文學作品選 (Literary Selections from the Wei, Jin, and North-South Dynasties). Jilin: Jilin renmin wenxue chubanshe, 1980.

Ling Chunsheng 凌純聲. "Zhongguo jiu de qiyuan" 中國酒的起源 (The Origins of Chinese Wine), *BIHP* 29 (1958): 883–907.

Liu Xun 劉恂 (10th century). *Lingbiao lu yi* 嶺表錄異 (Register of Strange Things Beyond the Ranges). *Congshu jicheng.*

Loewe, Michael. *Records of Han Administration.* 2 vols. Cambridge: Cambridge University Press, 1967.

———. "The Case of Witchcraft in 91 B.C.," *AM*, n.s. 15 (1970): 159–96; rpt. in *Crisis and Conflict*, pp. 37–90.

——— . "K'uang Heng and the Reform of Religious Practices (31 B.C.)," *AM*, n.s. 17.1 (1971): 1–27; rpt. in *Crisis and Conflict*, pp. 154–92.

———. *Crisis and Conflict in Han China 104 B.C. to A.D. 9.* London: George Allen and Unwin, 1974.

———. *Ways to Paradise: The Chinese Quest for Immortality.* London: George Allen and Unwin, 1979.

———. "The Han View of Comets," *BMFEA* 52 (1980): 1–31.

Luo Changpei 羅常培 and Zhou Zumo 周祖謨. *Han Wei Jin Nanbei chao yunbu yanbian yanjiu* 漢魏晉南北朝韻部演變研究 (Study of the Rhyme Group Changes in the Han, Wei, Jin, and North-South Dynasties). Beijing: Kexue chubanshe, 1958.

Lü Kai 呂凱. *Wei Jin xuanxue xiping* 魏晉玄學析評 (Critical Analysis of the Mysterious Learning of the Wei and Jin). Taibei: Shiji shuju, 1980.

Margouliès, Georges and W. R. Trask, trans. "Great Chinese Prose," *Asia* 34 (1934): 148–51, 300–303, 408–11, 568–74.

Mather, Richard. "The Mystical Ascent of the T'ien-t'ai Mountains," *MS* 20 (1961): 226–45.

Matsumoto Nobuhiro 松本信廣. "Kanho meigi kō" 甘蔗名義考 (Study of the Term Sugar), in *Gogaku ronsō* 語學論叢 (Collected Essays on Linguistics), pp. 72–81. Tokyo: Keiō gijuku gaigaku gogaku kenkyūjo, 1948.

Mayer, K. P. "On Variations in the Shapes of the Components of the Chinese *Nu-chi* (Crossbow Latch)," *TP* 52 (1965–66): 1–7.

Miao, Ronald C. "A Critical Study of the Life and Poetry of Wang Chung-hsuan." Unpublished Ph.D. Dissertation, University of California, Berkeley, 1969.

——— . *Early Medieval Chinese Poetry: The Life and Verse of Wang Ts'an (A.D. 177–217).* Wiesbaden: Franz Steiner, 1982.

Miao Yue 繆鉞. "Bao Mingyuan nianpu" 鮑明遠年譜 (Chronological Biography of Bao Zhao), *Wenxue yuekan* 3.1 (1932): 5–18.

————. "Wang Can xingnian kao" 王粲行年考 (Study of Wang Can's Career and Dates), *Zeshan banyuekan* 責善半月刊 2.21 (1942):7–13.

————. *Du shi cun gao* 讀史存稿 (Writings on History). Beijing: Sanlian, 1963.

Ōba Osamu 大庭脩. "Kanno setsu ni tsuite—shōsei kasetsu no zentei" 漢の節について—将軍仮節の前提 (The Han Token of Credence—The Premise of the General's Taking a Token of Credence), *Tōzai gakujutsu kenkyūjo kiyō* 東西学術研究所紀要 2 (1969):23–58.

Pease, Jonathan Otis. "Kuo P'u's Life and Five-Colored Rhymes (An 'Immortal' Chin Dynasty Writer and Diviner, 276–324)." Unpublished M.A. Thesis, University of Washington, 1980.

Pei Jinnan 裴晉南 *et al.*, eds. and comm. *Han Wei Liuchao fu xuan zhu* 漢魏六朝賦選注 (Rhapsodies of the Han, Wei, and Six Dynasties Selected and Annotated). Shanghai: Guji chubanshe, 1983.

Pelliot, Paul. Review of Berthold Laufer, *Jade*. *TP* 13 (1912):433–46.

Peterson, Willard J. "Making Connections: 'Commentary on the Attached Verbalizations' of the *Book of Changes*," *HJAS* 42.1 (1982):67–116.

Pulleyblank, E. G. "Consonantal System of Old Chinese: Part II," *AM*, n.s. 9 (1962):206–65.

Qian Daxin 錢大昕 (1728–1804). *Nianer shi kaoyi* 廿二史考異 (Variorum on the Twenty-two Histories). *Qianyan tang congshu*.

Qian Zhonglian 錢仲聯, ed. and comm. *Bao Canjun ji zhu* 鮑照年表 (Collected Commentaries to the Complete Works of Bao Zhao). 1957; rev. Shanghai: Guji kanxingshe, 1980.

Qu Dajun 屈大均 (1630–1696). *Guangdong xinyu* 廣東新語 (New Words from Guangdong). Hong Kong: Zhonghua shuju, 1974.

Quan Zuwang 全祖望 (1705–1755). *Jiqi ting ji* 鮚崎亭集 (Collection from the Mussel Bank Pavilion). *Sbck*.

Rao Zongyi 饒宗頤. *Chuci dili kao* 楚辭地理考 (Study of the Geography in the *Chuci*). Shanghai: Shangwu yinshuguan, 1946.

————. "Dunhuang xieben 'Deng lou fu' chongyan" 敦煌寫本登樓賦重研 (Further Study of the Dunhuang Manuscript of "Rhapsody on Climbing the Tower"), *Dalu zazhi* 24.6 (1962):167–69.

Schafer, Edward H. "Orpiment and Realgar in Chinese Technology and Tradition," *JAOS* 75.2 (1955):73–78.

————. "Cultural History of the Elaphure," *Sinologica* 4 (1956):250–74.

Scott, John. *Love and Protest, Chinese Poems from the Sixth Century B.C. to the Seventeenth Century A.D.* New York: Harper & Row, 1972.

Serruys, Paul L-M. "Remarks on the Nature, Functions and Meaning of the Grammatical Particle in Literary Chinese," *JAOS* 96.4 (1976):543–69.

Shang shu da zhuan 尚書大傳 (Grand Commentary on the *Shang shu*). *Sbck*.

Shen Qinhan 沈欽韓 (1775–1831). *Han shu shuzheng* 漢書疏證 (Exegetical Evidence for the *Han shu*). Zhejiang shuju, 1894 ed.

Shen yi jing 神異經 (Classic of Supernatural Wonders). *Han Wei congshu*.

Shi Zhimian 施之勉. "*Shiji* Sima Xiangru liezhuan jiaozhu" 史記司馬相如列傳校注 (Sima Xiangru's *Shi ji* Biography Collated and Annotated), Part 1, *Dalu zazhi* 56.1 (1978):6–25; Part 2, *Dalu zazhi* 56.2 (1978):82–97; Part 3, *Dalu zazhi*

56.3–4 (1978) : 196–200; Part 4, *Dalu zazhi* 56.5 (1978) : 247–50; Part 5, *Dalu zazhi* 57.1 (1978) : 42–50; Part 6, *Dalu zazhi* 57.2 (1978) : 91–100; Part 7, *Dalu zazhi* 57.3 (1978) : 139–48; Part 8 (1978) : 192–96; Part 9, *Dalu zazhi* 57.5 (1978) : 238–43; Part 10, *Dalu zazhi* 57.6 (1978) : 287–92.

Shimasada Masahiro 下定雅弘. "Ō San shi ni tsuite" 王粲詩について (On Wang Can's Poetry), *Chugoku bungaku ho* 29 (1978) : 46–81.

Shiratori Kurakichi. "On the Territory of the Hsiung-nu Prince Hsiu-t'u Wang and His Metal Statues for Heaven Worship," *MTB* 5 (1930) : 1–77.

Swann, Nancy Lee. *Pan Chao: Foremost Woman Scholar of China*. New York: The Century Company, 1932.

Takahashi Kazumi 高橋和己. "Han Gaku ron" 潘岳論 (Study of Pan Yue), *Chūgoku bungaku hō* 7 (1957) : 14–91.

Tan Qixiang 譚其驤, chief ed. *Zhongguo lishi ditu ji* 中國歷史地圖集 (The Historical Atlas of China). 8 vols. Shanghai: Ditu chubanshe, 1982.

Thun, Nils. *Reduplicative Words in English*, A Study of Formations of the Types *Tick-tick, Hurly-burly*, and *Shilly-shally*. Upsala: Carl Bloms Boktrycheri, 1963.

Ting Pang-hsin 丁邦新. *Chinese Phonology of the Wei-Chin Period: Reconstruction of the Finals as Reflected in Poetry*. Institute of History and Philology, Academia Sinica, Special Publication No. 65. Taipei: Academia Sinica, 1975.

Tjan Tjoe Som (Zeng Zhusen 曾珠森), trans. *Po Hu T'ung* 白虎通, *The Comprehensive Discussions in the White Tiger Hall*. 2 vols. Leiden: Brill, 1949, 1952.

Tu Benjun 屠本畯 (fl. 1596). *Minzhong haicuo shu* 閩中海錯疏 (Notes on the Marine Varieties of Fujian). *Congshu jicheng*.

Wang Jia 王嘉 (ob. 390). *Shi yi ji* 拾遺記 (Record of Neglected Matters). Beijing: Zhonghua shuju, 1981.

Ware, James R. "Once More the 'Golden Man,'" *TP* 34 (1938) : 174–78.

Watson, Burton. *Early Chinese Literature*. New York: Columbia University Press, 1962.

Wen Yiduo 聞一多. *Chuci jiaobu* 楚辭校補 (Collations to the *Chuci* Supplemented). 1942; rpt. in *Wen Yiduo Chuci yanjiu lunzhu shizhong* 聞一多楚辭研究論著十種 (Ten Studies of the *Chuci* by Wen Yiduo). Hong Kong: Weiya shuwu, n.d.

Wu Defeng 吳德風. "Bao Zhao nianpu buzheng" 鮑照年譜補證 (Supplement to the Chronological Biography of Bao Zhao), *Youshi xuezhi* 5.1 (1956) : 1–27.

Wu Peiji 吳丕績. *Bao Zhao nianpu* 鮑照年譜 (Chronological Biography of Bao Zhao). Changsha: Shangwu yinshuguan, 1940.

Wu Renjie 吳仁傑 (ob. ca. 1200). *Liang Han kanwu buyi* 兩漢刊誤補遺 (Supplement to Errata in the Two Han Histories). *Wuyingdian juzhenban shu* ed.

Wu Yun 吳雲 and Tang Shaozhong 唐紹忠, eds. and comm. *Wang Can ji zhu* 王粲集注 (Commentary to the Complete Works of Wang Can). Xinyang, Henan: Zhongshou shuhuashe, 1984.

Xu Fuguan 徐復觀. "Yang Xiong lunjiu" 揚雄研究 (Study of Yang Xiong), *Dalu zazhi* 50.3 (1975) : 103–45; rpt. in Xu Fuguan, *Liang Han sixiang shi*, pp. 303–409.

Xu Shiying 許世英, comm. "Deng lou fu" 登樓賦 (Rhapsody on Climbing the Tower), in *Gujin wenxuan* 2 : 513–16.

Yen Chun-chiang. "The Chuch-tuan as Word, Art Motif and Legend," *JAOS* 89.3 (1969) : 578–99.

Yu pian 玉篇 (Jade Thesaurus). *Sbck*.

Yu Shaochu 俞紹初, ed. *Wang Can ji* 王粲集 (Collected Works of Wang Can). Beijing: Zhonghua shuju, 1980.

Yu Yue 俞樾 (1821–1907). *Yulou zazuan* 俞樓雜纂 (Miscellaneous Notes from Yu's Studio). 1879 ed.

Yuan Ke 袁珂, ed. and comm. *Shanhai jing jiaozhu* 山海經校注 (*Classic of Mountains and Seas* Collated and Annotated). Shanghai: Guji chubanshe, 1980.

Zach, Erwin von, trans. "Das Lu-ling-kwang-tien-fu des Wang Wen-k'ao," *AM* 3 (1926):467–76.

———. "Yang Hsiung's Poetische Beschreibung des Himmelsopfers im Lustschloss (Kanchuan fu)," *Sinica* 2 (1927):190–93.

———. *Aus dem Wen-hsüan. Die Reise nach den Westen (Hsi-cheng-fu,* W.H.C. 10) von P'an Yo, gestorben 300 n. Chr. Frankfurt-am-Main: China Institut, 1930.

———. "Aus dem Wen-hsuan—Ho Yen's poetische Beschreibung des Ching-fu-Palastes (in Hsu-ch'ang)," *MS* 4 (1939–40):441–50.

Zhang Shinan 張世南 (ob. post 1230). *Youhuan jiwen* 游宦紀聞 (The Recorded Knowledge of a Traveling Official). *Zhibuzu zhai congshu.*

Zhang You 張有 (1054–post 1124). *Fugu bian* 復古編 (Compilation of Restored Graphs). *Sbck.*

Zhang Zhiyue 張志岳. "Bao Zhao ji qi shi xintan" 鮑照及其詩新探 (New Exploration of Bao Zhao and His Poetry). *Wenxue pinglun* (1979:1):pp. 58–65.

Zhongguo mingsheng cidian 中國名勝詞典 (Dictionary of China's Famous Sites). Shanghai: Shanghai cishu chubanshe, 1981.

Zhou Chu 周處 (4th cent. A.D.). *Yangxian feng tu ji* 陽羨風土記 (Record of Customs and Geography of Yangxian). *Suxiang shi conghsu* 粟香室叢書.

Index

David R. Knechtges is Professor of Chinese
at the University of Washington

Library of Congress Cataloging-in-Publication Data
(Revised for volume 2)

Wen hsuan. English.
Wen xuan, or, Selections of refined literature.

(Princeton library of Asian translations)
Translation of: Wen hsüan.
Includes bibliographies and indexes.
Contents: v. 1. Rhapsodies on metropolises and capitals—v. 2. Rhapsodies on
sacrifices, hunting, travel, sightseeing, palaces and halls, rivers and seas.
1. Chinese literature—To 221 B.C.—Translations into English.
2. Chinese literature—Ch'in and Han dynasties, 221 B.C.–220 A.D.—
Translations into English.   3. Chinese literature—220–589—Translations
into English.   4. English literature—Translations from Chinese.   I. Hsiao,
T'ung, 501–531.   II. Knechtges, David R.   III. Title: Wen xuan.
IV. Series.

PL2490.W4613 1982   895.1'08'002   81-47930
ISBN 0-691-05346-4 (set)